I0874586

Fiscal State Aid Schemes

Series on International Taxation

VOLUME 90

Series Editors

Prof. Ruth Mason, University of Virginia School of Law
Prof. Dr Ekkehart Reimer, University of Heidelberg

Introduction & Contents

The Series on International Taxation deals with a wide variety of topics in the global tax arena. The authors include many of the field's leading experts as well as talented newcomers. Their expert views and incisive commentary have proven highly useful to practitioners and academics alike.

Objective

The volumes published in this series are aimed at offering high-quality analytical information and practical solutions to international tax practitioners.

Readership

Practitioners, academics and policy makers in international tax law.

Frequency of Publication

2-3 new volumes published each year.

The titles published in this series are listed at the end of this volume.

Fiscal State Aid Schemes

Selectivity and Limits to Enforcement

Sophia Piotrowski

Wolters Kluwer

Published by:
Kluwer Law International B.V.
PO Box 316
2400 AH Alphen aan den Rijn
The Netherlands
E-mail: lrs-sales@wolterskluwer.com
Website: www.wolterskluwer.com/en/solutions/kluwerlawinternational

Sold and distributed by:
Wolters Kluwer Legal & Regulatory U.S.
920 Links Avenue
Landisville, PA 17538
United States of America
E-mail: customer.service@wolterskluwer.com

ISBN 978-94-035-0389-9

e-Book: ISBN 978-94-035-0399-8
web-PDF: ISBN 978-94-035-0409-4

© 2025 Sophia Piotrowski

All rights are reserved, including those for text and data mining, AI training, and similar technologies. No part of this publication may be reproduced, stored in a retrieval system, or transmitted in any form or by any means, electronic, mechanical, photocopying, recording, or otherwise, without written permission from the publisher. Permission to use this content must be obtained from the copyright owner.

Table of Contents

List of Abbreviations

AFMP	Agreement on the Free Movement of Persons
AG	Advocate General
AöR	Archiv des öffentlichen Rechts
ATT	Irish Air Travel Tax
BB	Betriebsberater
BFHE	Entscheidungen des Bundesfinanzhofs
BIT	Bulletin for International Taxation
BPOT	Business Property Occupation Tax
BStBL	Bundessteuerblatt
BTR	British Tax Review
BVerfG	Bundesverfassungsgericht (Federal Constitutional Court of Germany)
BVerfGE	Entscheidungen des Bundesverfassungsgerichts
Camb. Yearb. Eur. Leg. Stud.	Cambridge Yearbook of European Legal Studies
CFC	Controlled Foreign Corporation
ChFR	Charter of Fundamental Rights
CJEU	Court of Justice of the European Union
CLJ	Cambridge Law Journal
CMLR	Common Market Law Review
DRD	Dispute Resolution Directive
DStR	Deutsches Steuerrecht
DTC	Double Taxation Convention
EC	European Community
ECLR	European Competition Law Review

ECSC	European Coal and Steel Community
EJLS	European Journal of Legal Studies
EStAL	European State Aid Law Quarterly
EU	European Union
EuZW	Europäische Zeitschrift für Wirtschaftsrecht
FR	Finanz-Rundschau
GAAR	General Anti-Abuse Rule
GBER	General Block Exemption Regulation
GC	General Court
HFSt	Heidelberger Beiträge zum Finanz- und Steuerrecht
IFA	International Fiscal Association
Intertax	International Tax Review
IRET	Institute for Research on the Economics of Taxation
ISR	Internationale Steuer-Rundschau
IStR	Internationales Steuerrecht
ITPJ	International Transfer Pricing Journal
JECLAP	Journal of European Competition Law & Practice
KStG	Körperschaftsteuergesetz, German Corporate Income Tax Act
MNE	Multinational Enterprise
NTJ	National Tax Journal
OECD	Organisation for Economic Co-operation and Development
R&D	Research and development
Rev.	Review
TEU	Treaty on European Union
TFEU	Treaty on the Functioning of the European Union
TIOPA	Taxation (International and Other Provisions) Act
TNI	Tax Notes International
VAT	Value Added Tax
W. Comp.	World Competition
WTJ	World Tax Journal
YEL	Yearbook of European Law

Preface

This book explores the application of European State aid law to Member States' tax measures. It focuses on aid that derives directly from the law or other types of abstract provisions, i.e., fiscal aid schemes as opposed to individual aid. It aims to contribute to an overall understanding of the architecture of fiscal State aid law by considering the particularities of taxation both on the level of the existence of aid under Article 107(1) Treaty on the Functioning of the European Union (TFEU) and the legal consequences of infringements of State aid law. The author addresses the two main objections that have frequently been raised against the case law of the European courts on fiscal aid schemes, namely (i) an allegedly overly broad reading of Article 107(1) TFEU and (ii) the supposedly unjust consequences of infringements of State aid law. These objections do have some merit but they can be or have already been addressed without putting the increased application of State aid law to Member States' tax laws in recent years as such into question. Member States' fiscal sovereignty as well as taxpayer rights limit any excessive application of fiscal State aid law. The book is structured in two parts. Part I deals with the existence of aid under Article 107(1) TFEU, and in particular the criterion of 'selective advantage' as the only relevant criterion of State aid in practice. It also examines the impact of Member States' fiscal sovereignty on the interpretation of selectivity. Part II addresses the legal consequences of infringements of State aid law and potential general or case-by-case limits to recovery motivated by taxpayer rights as well as selected procedural law solutions to tackle legal uncertainty.

This book is based on a thesis approved as a dissertation at Friedrich-Alexander-Universität Erlangen-Nürnberg under the title 'Fiscal State Aid Schemes, Member State Sovereignty, and Taxpayer Rights – An Exploration of the Notion of Material Selectivity and Limits to Enforcement'. It was reviewed by Prof. Roland Ismer and Prof. Philip Baker KC, OBE. Prof. Bernhard Wegener was the third member of the examination board. Date of the thesis defence: 7 March 2024.

Acknowledgements

First and foremost, I would like to express my deepest gratitude to my supervisor Prof. Roland Ismer for the opportunities, the discussions, the feedback, the advice, the patience, and the freedom I was given for the past years. I am extremely thankful for the constant support and encouragement that has enabled me to continue on my path in academia.

I am also immensely grateful to Prof. Philip Baker KC, OBE for agreeing to be the second supervisor of my thesis and for his extremely valuable comments on my thesis.

I will always be thankful to the late Prof. Klaus Meßerschmidt for offering me the chance to work for him and for being the first to encourage me to go into academia.

During the course of my PhD I was fortunate to be able to undertake research stays at the University of Oxford and at Universidad de Complutense de Madrid as well as work at the Court of Justice of the European Union (CJEU) for three months. Thank you very much to Prof. Mike Devereux, Prof. John Vella, Prof. José Almudí Cid, Prof. Dr Dres. h.c. Juliane Kokott, and Prof. David Hummel for giving me this opportunity and for the extremely valuable discussions and insights during my time abroad.

Thank you very much to series editors Prof. Ruth Mason and Prof. Ekkehart Reimer for accepting my book for publication in the Series on International Taxation.

I also gratefully acknowledge the generous support of the German Academic Scholarship Foundation (Studienstiftung des deutschen Volkes).

Moreover, I would like to thank my friends and colleagues from the Chair for Tax Law and Public Law at Friedrich-Alexander-University Erlangen-Nuremberg Dr Stefanie Baur-Rückert; Dr Manuel W. Haußner, Dr Christian von Hesler, Dr Katharina Artinger, Dr Daniela Endres-Reich, Dr Elena Fuchs, Dr Christoph Gradl, Stefanie Güllich, Quirin Jackl, Ronja Reinwald, Brigitte Schüller, Dr Magdalena Schwarz, and Prof. Sabrina Wagner as well as my friends Prof. Bernardo Olivares Olivares and Prof. Alice Pirlot.

Finally, and most importantly, I am eternally grateful to my family and to my partner Cláudio for their unwavering support.

Acknowledgments

CHAPTER 1

Introduction

As far back as the year 1961, Member States' taxes were subjected to State aid control. In *De Gezamenlijke Steenkolenmijnen in Limburg*,[1] the Court clarified that the concept of aid under the European Coal and Steel Community (ECSC) Treaty[2] does not only comprise positive subsidies but also interventions through which charges that would normally be included in an undertaking's budget are mitigated.[3] This ground-breaking statement was the first acknowledgement that tax benefits can constitute forbidden State aid under what is now Article 107 TFEU (Treaty on the Functioning of the European Union).[4] Nevertheless, in the following decades, State aid law was only rarely applied in the area of taxation. It was therefore often overlooked by Member States' legislators, tax administrations and taxpayers alike.

This finding stands in stark contrast to the fundamental freedoms. The freedoms have radically transformed Member States' tax systems by ensuring equal tax treatment of cross-border and domestic constellations in both inbound and outbound cases. However, they have always had one blind spot: They do not cover cases of reverse discrimination. Therefore, they could not prevent Member States from implementing special tax regimes to attract investment. More than that, the fundamental freedoms even promoted tax competition in the sense that they ensured that undertakings were able to move freely within the internal market and thus make use of these tax benefits.[5]

As the awareness of the downsides of tax competition increased, first attempts were made to resort to fiscal State aid law to reign it in. The Commission can tackle 'selective advantages' under Article 107(1) TFEU regardless of whether they are

1. Case 30/59 *De Gezamenlijke Steenkolenmijnen in Limburg v. High Authority of the European Coal and Steel Community* EU:C:1961:2.
2. Treaty establishing the European Coal and Steel Community, ECSC Treaty [1951].
3. Case 30/59 *De Gezamenlijke Steenkolenmijnen*, p. 19.
4. Consolidated versions of the Treaty on European Union and the Treaty on the Functioning of the European, TEU and TFEU [2016] C 202/1.
5. According to Francesco de Cecco, *State Aid and the European Economic Constitution*, 131f. (2013), European integration has exacerbated tax competition among Member States.

awarded to foreign or domestic undertakings. Accordingly, the 1997 Code of Conduct for Business Taxation explicitly pointed out that some of the tax measures targeted by the Code could potentially be covered by the State aid provision.[6] From an enforcement perspective, the advantage of relying on State aid control as opposed to the Code of Conduct is that the former is a powerful deterrent due to the threat of recovery and the far-reaching executive powers of the Commission.[7] Starting with the 1998 Commission Notice on business taxation, the Commission started to actively promote the applicability of State aid law in the area of taxation.[8] While the Notice was certainly drafted in the context of efforts to reign in harmful tax competition between Member States, its scope went much further. These developments were followed by a first wave of landmark judgments on fiscal State aid.[9] These judgments laid the groundwork for what was to come.

At this point, clearly, neither Member States nor taxpayers were fully aware of the hidden potential of State aid law to fundamentally transform tax systems. The issues surrounding harmful tax competition within the European Union (EU) and the ensuing possibilities for tax planning continued to exist and were even exacerbated by a growing digitalization of business models.

Yet in the wake of the financial crisis, but also following data leaks, such as the Luxembourg Leaks, which provoked major public outcries, urgent solutions for the perceived under-taxation of multinational enterprises (MNEs) appeared necessary.[10] Theoretically, the issue could have been addressed through positive integration, but the unanimity requirement made this notoriously difficult to achieve.[11] The Commission thus again (re)discovered State aid law as a highly efficient tool to tackle certain forms of tax competition, but also covert subsidizations of national champions through tax measures.[12]

---

6. Resolution of the Council and the Representatives of the Governments of the Member States, meeting within the Council of 1 December 1997 on a code of conduct for business taxation [1998] OJ 2/2, J.
7. Carlo Pinto, *Tax Competition and EU Law*, 192 (2003). *See* Mario Monti, *How State Aid Affects Tax Competition* 8 EC Tax Rev. 208ff. (1999) https://doi.org/10.54648/ecta1999053 for an explanation of the origins of the Commission's agenda on harmful tax competition. By contrast, the fundamental freedoms are not equipped to tackle the most common forms of tax competition as they do not prohibit reverse discrimination, Wolfgang Schön, *Taxation and State Aid Law in the European Union* 36 CMLR 911, 918f. (1999) https://doi.org/10.54648/239680.
8. Commission Notice on the application of the State aid rules to measures relating to direct business taxation [1998] OJ C 384/3.
9. *See, e.g.*, Case C-143/99 *Adria-Wien Pipeline and Wietersdorfer & Peggauer Zementwerke* EU:C:2001:598; Case C-88/03 *Portugal v. Commission* EU:C:2006:511; Joined Cases C-182 and 217/03 *Belgium and Forum 187 v. Commission* EU:C:2006:416; Case C-148/04 *Unicredito Italiano* EU:C:2005:774. Ruth Mason, *Tax Competition and State Aid* 43 YEL 1, 5 (2023) https://doi.org/10.1093/yel/yead001 points out that the first wave concerned aid schemes, whereas the second wave particularly targets individual aid.
10. On the dangers of law-making based on data leaks Shu-Yi Oei & Diane Ring, *Leak-Driven Law* 65 UCLA L. Rev. 532ff. (2018) https://doi.org/10.2139/ssrn.2918550.
11. *See* on this Georg Kofler, *EU Power to Tax: Competences in the Area of Direct Taxation*, in Panayi et al. (eds), Research Handbook on European Union Taxation Law, 11, 16ff. (2020).
12. *See* for an overview of the two waves and the link with the Code of Conduct: Dimitrios Kyriazis, *Fiscal State Aid Law as a Tool Against Harmful Tax Competition in the EU: déjà vu?* 42 YEL 1, 23ff. (2022) https://doi.org/10.1093/yel/yeac007.

The past decade has thus brought a flurry of activity in the field of State aid law and taxation, with the Commission trying to reign in tax competition, whereas the taxpayers concerned, often with the help of Member States' governments, and increasingly also the General Court and the Court of Justice of the European Union (CJEU), have in turn tried to reign in the Commission. The Commission has tackled several tax rulings under the State aid regime.[13] Simultaneously, a number of landmark judgments on aid schemes have been published.[14] Even more recently, the case law has branched out, addressing new types of taxes, such as turnover-based taxes.[15] In light of all this, European State aid law as applied to taxation has now become one of the most controversial areas of EU law.

The topic of State aid law would of course be much too wide even for an extensive monograph, at least when it purports to develop new ideas. We will therefore limit our analysis in two respects: First, we will focus on fiscal aid. Second, we limit ourselves to fiscal aid schemes.

§1.01 FOCUS ON THE PARTICULARITIES OF FISCAL AID

To grasp the particularities of fiscal aid, a closer look at the two-tier structure of Article 107 TFEU is warranted: First, Article 107(1) TFEU lays down the criteria for the *existence* of aid. Where a measure amounts to aid under Article 107(1) TFEU, the Member State must notify the proposed measure to the European Commission under Article 108(3), (1) TFEU. Second, Article 107(2), (3) TFEU specifies the requirements for the *compatibility* of aid. State aid *is* compatible with the internal market when the legal requirements of Article 107(2) TFEU are met. By contrast, the Commission enjoys 'wide discretion'[16] in its decision on whether it considers aid under Article 107(3) TFEU compatible with the internal market. Under Article 108(3), (3) TFEU, the Member State may not implement aid until the Commission has decided on the compatibility of the proposed measure. Where a Member State - knowingly or unknowingly - infringes upon this stand-still provision, the aid is generally recovered for 10 years if it is subsequently found to be incompatible with the internal market. There is no recovery

13. *See* only Joined Cases T-760/15 and 636/16 *Netherlands v. Commission* EU:T:2019:669; Joined Cases T-778 and 892/16 *Ireland v. Commission* EU:T:2020:338.
14. *See* only Joined Cases C-20 and 21/15 P *Commission v. World Duty Free Group* EU:C:2016:981; Case C-203/16 P *Andres (faillite Heitkamp BauHolding) v. Commission* EU:C:2018:505.
15. Case C-75/18 *Vodafone Magyarország* EU:C:2020:139; Case C-323/18 *Tesco-Global Áruházak* EU:C:2020:140.
16. Case C-225/91 *Matra v. Commission* EU:C:1993:239, para. 24; Case 310/85 *Deufil v. Commission* EU:C:1987:96, para. 18. Critical as to the use of this discretion, e.g., Markus Ludwigs, *Demokratieferne Gestaltung der europäischen Beihilfeaufsicht* 28 EuZW 41ff. (2017). Pointing to the soft law that limits discretion: Johannes Laitenberger & Thomas Lieflaender, *Beihilfeaufsicht: die Versöhnung von unabhängiger Rechtsdurchsetzung mit direkter Wirkung und demokratiegesteuerter Ermessensausübung* 38 EuZW 281f. (2017).

if this would lead to an infringement of a general principle of EU law, such as the principle of protection of legitimate expectation.[17]

The existence of aid under Article 107(1) TFEU requires that four cumulative criteria be met. The CJEU phrases the four criteria as follows:

> classification of a national measure as 'State aid', within the meaning of Article 107(1) TFEU, requires all the following conditions to be fulfilled. *First*, there must be an intervention by the State or through State resources. *Second*, the intervention must be liable to affect trade between the Member States. *Third*, it must confer a selective advantage on the recipient. *Fourth*, it must distort or threaten to distort competition.[18]

According to long-standing case law, 'measures which, in various forms, mitigate the burdens normally included in the budget of an undertaking and which, accordingly, without being subsidies in the strict meaning of the word, are similar in character and have the same effect are considered to constitute aid'.[19] Consequently, the first criterion is usually straightforward in tax matters. The second and the fourth criteria are often not clearly separated. Yet in any case – while somewhat unsatisfactory – the threshold for meeting these criteria is generally very low.[20] Moreover, fiscal aid will often be operating aid (as opposed to so-called investment aid).[21] On this, the CJEU has stated the following: 'In principle, operating aid, that is to say aid which [...] is intended to release an undertaking from costs *which it would normally have had to bear in its day-to-day management or normal activities*, distorts the conditions of competition [...].'[22]

The existence of fiscal aid under Article 107(1) TFEU thus hinges almost exclusively on the third criterion, and in particular on selectivity. While the Court of Justice (CJEU) might conceivably afford greater importance to the criteria of Article

17. *See* Art. 16(1) of Council Regulation (EU) 2015/1589 of 13 July 2015 laying down detailed rules for the application of Art. 108 of the Treaty on the Functioning of the European Union [2015] L 248/9ff.
18. *See* only Case C-280/00 *Altmark Trans and Regierungspräsidium Magdeburg* EU:C:2003:415, para. 75; Joined Cases C-341 and 342/06 P *Chronopost and La Poste v. UFEX and Others* EU:C:2008:375, paras 121f.; Case C-140/09 *Fallimento Traghetti del Mediterraneo* EU:C:2010:335, para. 31; Case C-39/14 *BVVG* EU:C:2015:470, para. 24; Case C-524/14 P *Commission v. Hansestadt Lübeck* EU:C:2016:971, para. 40; Joined Cases C-20 and 21/15 P *World Duty Free Group*, para. 53; Case C-203/16 P *Andres*, para. 82; Case C-374/17 *A-Brauerei* EU:C:2018:1024, para. 19. Emphasis added by the author.
19. Case C-75/97 *Belgium v. Commission* EU:C:1999:311, para. 23; Case C-143/99 *Adria-Wien Pipeline*, para. 38; Case C-53/00 *Ferring* EU:C:2001:627, para. 15; Case C-66/02 *Italy v. Commission* EU:C:2005:768, para. 77; Joined Cases C-182 and 217/03 *Belgium and Forum 187*, para. 86; Case C-222/04 *Cassa di Risparmio di Firenze* EU:C:2006:8, para. 131; Joined Cases C-78 to 80/08 *Paint Graphos and Others* EU:C:2011:550, para. 45; Joined Cases C-106 and 107/09 P *Commission and Spain v. Government of Gibraltar and United Kingdom* EU:C:2011:732, para. 71; Case C-522/13 *Ministerio de Defensa and Navantia* EU:C:2014:2262, para. 22.
20. *See* on the applicable principles, e.g., Kelyn Bacon, *European Union Law of State Aid* (3rd edn 2017), paras 2.142ff. Calling for restriction of fiscal State aid relying on the criterion of a distortion of competition, e.g., Juliane Kokott, *Das Steuerrecht der Europäischen Union*, §3, para. 211 (2018).
21. *See* n. 73 *infra*.
22. Case C-156/98 *Germany v. Commission* EU:C:2000:467, para. 30; emphasis added by the author.

107(1) TFEU aside from selectivity in the future, it has thus far not indicated a willingness to do so for fiscal aid schemes.[23] We will therefore make the criterion of 'selective advantage' the focus of our analysis.

Unlike positive aid, the assessment of fiscal aid as a form of negative aid requires a determination of the *normal* level of tax that an undertaking should have borne in the absence of the State intervention mitigating the tax burden. To this end, the identification of a selective advantage for fiscal aid is ordinarily carried out by applying a three-step test, which is phrased in recent case law in the following terms:

> In the context of tax measures, in order to classify a national tax measure as 'selective', the Commission must begin by identifying the ordinary or 'normal' tax system applicable in the Member State concerned, and thereafter demonstrate that the tax measure at issue is a derogation from that ordinary system, in so far as it differentiates between operators who, in the light of the objective pursued by that ordinary tax system, are in a comparable factual and legal situation. [...] It should, however, be borne in mind, in the second place, that, according to the settled case-law of the Court, the concept of 'State aid' does not cover measures that differentiate between undertakings which, in the light of the objective pursued by the legal regime concerned, are in a comparable factual and legal situation, and are, therefore, a priori selective where the Member State concerned is able to demonstrate that that differentiation is justified since it flows from the nature or general structure of the system of which the measures form part [...].[24]

Thus, in a first step, the reference system of taxation has to be identified. In a second step, there has to be a derogation therefrom, which then leads to prima facie selectivity. Finally, in a third step, selectivity can still be avoided where this derogation is justifiable.

In our analysis, we will point out the tax-specific features for each step. Admittedly, given that the 1998 Commission Notice on direct business taxation[25] is no longer in force and was replaced by the 2016 Commission Notice that applies to all types of aid,[26] it might at first glance appear more plausible to extend our analysis to all aid measures as opposed to fiscal aid or at least all types of measures that mitigate the burdens that an undertaking would ordinarily have to bear. Indeed, the overarching principles of State aid law should be identical irrespective of the type of aid.

Nevertheless, there is a case for analysing the application of State aid law to tax measures as there are particularities of taxation that should not be overlooked. Taxes are one of the core areas of a State's sovereignty and are therefore a highly sensitive area of State aid control. Particularly in the area of direct taxation, the need to safeguard

---

23. *See* Kokott, *Steuerrecht*, *supra* n. 20, at §3, paras 210ff. for indications of a stronger role of these criteria in the decisional practice of the Commission.
24. Case C-88/03 *Portugal v. Commission*, paras 56, 81; Joined Cases C-78 to 80/08 *Paint Graphos*, paras 49, 65; Joined Cases C-20 and 21/15 P *World Duty Free Group*, paras 57f.; Case C-374/17 *A-Brauerei*, paras 36, 44.
25. Commission Notice on the application of the State aid rules to measures relating to direct business taxation [1998] OJ C 384/3.
26. Commission Notice on the notion of State aid as referred to in Article 107(1) of the Treaty on the Functioning of the European Union [2016] C 262/1.

the goals of State aid control has to be weighed against tax sovereignty, so that neither of them is undermined.[27]

Taxes are multi-faceted as a policy instrument. They can have various steering purposes ('special purpose levies'). Moreover, distinctions within taxes can have a variety of goals - tax benefits can, for example, serve to promote research and development (R&D), maintain competitiveness or employment, contribute to the protection of the environment or prop up companies in difficulty. Tax benefits can also be relied upon to attract particularly mobile forms of investment or support national industries. Fiscal State aid may come in a variety of guises, such as special deductions, exemptions, tax amnesties or deferrals. This makes the analysis extremely rich.

Fiscal aid also boasts particularities regarding the economics of taxation. For positive aid, remedying a breach of State aid law restores a situation where there is no State intervention. In the area of taxation, on the other hand, this is not the case, but for the rare cases where a tax as a whole is eliminated as a result of a breach of State aid law. This means that both in a situation with and without aid, there is a State intervention, which distorts the behaviour of economic actors. While this goes far beyond what a legal analysis such as ours can verify, it would theoretically be necessary to ascertain whether it is always desirable to eliminate the aid, i.e., whether the elimination of aid always achieves a less distortive situation. Questions on tax incidence and the identification of the beneficiary of aid arise - particularly in the area of indirect taxation.[28]

All this implies that while the overarching principles of State aid law as applied to tax measures are and should indeed not be particular to taxation, there is merit in examining tax measures as a particular category of aid. In doing so, we are not overly concerned with the exact definition of a tax under EU or national law. Instead, we give a wide meaning to the term of fiscal aid. It thus generally makes no difference for our purposes whether a levy qualifies as a tax or as a parafiscal levy.[29]

§1.02 FOCUS ON AID SCHEMES RATHER THAN INDIVIDUAL AID

Fiscal State aid can take the form of individual decisions by tax authorities or courts, i.e., a tax assessment, a tax ruling or a judgment, or derive directly from the law or other types of abstract provisions. It can thus either derive from rules themselves (or the lack thereof) or their application. Rules in this context should be defined broadly. We thus do not confine the term to provisions with legal value that have been issued by the legislator. Instead, we understand it to comprise all abstract-general ways of granting State aid. For example, this could also refer to Circulars issued by a Member State's tax authorities. In detail, it may nevertheless matter whether rules are issued by

27. *See* Ch. §1.03 *infra*.
28. *See* Ch. §2.02[A] *infra*.
29. Thomas Jaeger, *Fehlstellungen im Verhältnis von Steuer- und Beihilferecht: Ein Plädoyer für mehr Ausgewogenheit* 23 EuZW 92, 98 (2012) argues that the two should be clearly distinguished since it is particularly the use of the funds in question that can lead to State aid problems for parafiscal levies. However, for our purposes, parafiscal levies can be understood as special purpose levies.

the legislative or the executive branch, since there may be constitutional law implications that have to be considered.

The distinction of where aid derives from is not always straightforward. Typically, a taxpayer's tax burden is laid down in their tax bill, which is an individual decision. Yet the assessment under State aid law depends on the function of the tax bill in a concrete constellation: The tax liability normally derives from abstract tax rules – generally laws. These general rules are concretized in the tax assessment, which is the basis for the taxpayer's obligation to pay taxes. In the majority of cases, the tax authorities are not afforded discretion in tax law. This is to say that the individual tax burden can at least theoretically be derived directly from the applicable tax laws. Where this is the case, the State aid problem does not lie with the tax assessment but arises directly from the abstract rules.[30]

Alternatively, fiscal aid can arise from a (mis)application of national law. In such cases, it is not the rules themselves that are problematic, but the individual decision. This can either be a tax ruling or a tax assessment, or even a lack thereof. These types of aid measures lead to particular challenges. Indeed, not all misapplications of tax law that lead to a favourable tax treatment can and should be tackled from a State aid law perspective. This is primarily because of Member States' tax sovereignty and the division of competences between Member States and the EU. The Commission has neither the capacities nor is it designed to serve as a 'super'-tax authority.[31] Therefore, State aid control has to be limited to cases of gross misapplication.[32] The exact limits of this are not yet clear but are beyond the scope of our analysis.

This difference between aid deriving from rules in the widest sense and from individual decisions is mirrored in the fact that the State aid assessment varies depending on whether aid is granted through an aid scheme or individual aid. According to Article 1(d) of Procedural Regulation 2015/1589,[33] the term aid scheme refers to 'any act on the basis of which, without further implementing measures being required, individual aid awards may be made to undertakings defined within the act in a general and abstract manner and any act on the basis of which aid which is not linked to a specific project may be awarded to one or several undertakings for an indefinite period of time and/or for an indefinite amount' whereas individual aid under Article

30. *See also* the judgment in Case C-362/19 P *Commission v. Fútbol Club Barcelona* EU:C:2021:169, paras 68ff. on the delimitation. In this case, it was sufficient for the Commission to demonstrate from an *ex ante*-perspective that the scheme could lead to an advantageous treatment. It did not have to demonstrate that the football clubs in question actually benefitted from the exemptions from an *ex post* perspective, *see* Christian Pérez Merino, *The Commission's Burden of Proof in Respect of Fiscal State Aid Following the ECJ Decision in the Spanish Sports Clubs Case* 61 European Taxation 485, 488f. (2021) https://doi.org/10.59403/28fx38p.

31. Kokott, *Steuerrecht, supra* n. 20, at §3, para. 179; Wolfgang Schön, *State Aid in the Area of Taxation*, in Hancher et al. (eds), EU State Aids, para. 13-040 (5th edn 2016).

32. Stephen Daly, *The Power to Get It Wrong* 137 Law Quarterly Rev. 280ff. (2021). *See also* Opinion of AG Kokott in Case C-454/21 P *Engie Global LNG Holding and Others v. Commission* EU:C:2023:383, paras 92ff.

33. Council Regulation (EU) 2015/1589 of 13 July 2015 laying down detailed rules for the application of Article 108 of the Treaty on the Functioning of the European Union [2015] L 248/9, hereinafter Procedural Regulation 2015/1589.

1(e) refers to 'aid that is not awarded on the basis of an aid scheme and notifiable awards of aid on the basis of an aid scheme'.

On the level of the existence of aid, there are significant differences in the determination of the selective advantage as the most important criterion of fiscal State aid, depending on whether there is an aid scheme or individual aid. Moreover, it is settled case law that for aid schemes, the Commission may confine itself to examining the characteristics of the scheme at issue to assess its State aid quality rather than carrying out an analysis of each instance in which aid has been granted under the scheme. The latter is only necessary for the recovery of aid.[34] This difference can affect the legality of Commission decisions. In the Belgian Excess Profits case, the General Court annulled the decision of the Commission, reasoning that the measure at issue had been wrongly classified as an aid scheme.[35] However, upon appeal, the CJEU confirmed that the measure at issue was indeed an aid scheme.[36] Essentially, the Commission had argued that a systematic *contra legem* application by the tax authorities of a Member State which amounts to a consistent administrative practice in itself can lead to the existence of an aid scheme.[37] The CJEU also held that the General Court (GC) had committed an error of law in finding that the measure required further implementing measures, since the granting of the tax rulings involved discretion.[38] The consistent administrative practice of the Belgian tax authorities would also have led to a definition of the beneficiaries of the scheme in a general and abstract manner.[39] This means that the abstract and general manner of a tax measure can also be derived from a consistent administrative practice, even where this practice diverges from applicable law.

In the following, we will focus on aid schemes, i.e., abstract-general ways of granting aid. We do so for a host of reasons: First, by their very nature, aid schemes are less fraught with particularities and complexities of individual cases. Their analysis is less burdened with facts, which promises easier access to the legal issues. Second, aid schemes often strongly affect core aspects of Member States' sovereignty, namely their legislative powers and their scope for implementing public policy objectives in areas where they have not conferred their taxing powers to the EU.[40] This is at least the case,

34. Case C-310/99 *Italy v. Commission* EU:C:2002:143, paras 89-91; Joined Cases C-71, 73 and 76/09 P *Comitato 'Venezia vuole vivere' and Others v. Commission* EU:C:2011:368, para. 63.
35. Joined Cases T-131 and 263/16 *Belgium and Magnetrol International v. Commission* EU:T:2019:91.
36. Case C-337/19 P *Commission v. Belgium and Magnetrol International* EU:C:2021:741. On this: Benedikt Freund & Moritz Seiler, *Magnetrol v. Commission: When Do Advance Tax Rulings Become an Aid Scheme under Article 1(d) Regulation (EU) 2015/1589 – Case C-337/19 P Magnetrol v. Commission* 21 EStAL 302ff. (2022) https://doi.org/10.21552/estal/2022/3/8; Bob Michel, *ECJ Determines 'Only in Belgium' Excess Profit Ruling Practice Constitutes Aid Scheme, But Did It Provide Illegal Aid?* 62 European Taxation 95ff. (2022) https://doi.org/10.59403/1h73hrx.
37. Case C-337/19 P *Commission v. Belgium and Magnetrol International*, paras 71ff.
38. *Ibid.*, paras 104ff.
39. *Ibid.*, paras 120ff.
40. Wolfgang Schön, *Tax Legislation and the Notion of Fiscal Aid*, in Richelle et al. (eds), State Aid Law and Business Taxation 3, 5 (2016) therefore deems the application of State aid rules to tax legislation the most problematic area of fiscal State aid control.

where the aid scheme derives from Member States' legislation as opposed to a consistent administrative practice as was the case for the Belgian Excess Profits scheme. Aid schemes thus often lead to interesting questions regarding the interaction between national constitutional law and EU law. These questions become even more pressing against the background that the enforcement is very much driven by the European Commission, which thereby fulfils executive functions under Article 17(1), (5) TFEU. Finally, aid schemes raise specific questions both on the legal consequences of an infringement of State aid law and the role of private actors, i.e., beneficiaries and competitors, in enforcement.

§1.03 THE WIDER CONTEXT

As a backdrop to our analysis of the legal framework of fiscal State aid law, we will now take a step back and look at the bigger picture. We will briefly explore the objectives of fiscal State aid control as well as factors limiting enforcement. In our view, many of the developments of fiscal State aid law over the past years can be explained by taking a closer look at these opposing forces and the dynamics underlying State aid control.

What are thus the objectives of fiscal State aid control? Taking the wording and structure of the TFEU as a point of departure, State aid control is first and foremost an instrument of competition law. As such, State aid control certainly serves to protect and promote the internal market.[41] The underlying idea is that advantages granted to only some economic actors, such as national champions or particularly mobile types of undertakings, can be highly distortive and produce negative cross-border externalities.[42] State aid law promotes the competition between undertakings, which should compete on their own merits instead of being artificially propped up, and prevents State interventions as a means of protecting the internal market as a whole.[43] Different nuances are stressed within contributions advocating such internal market logic.

---

41. Ioannis Ganoulis & Reiner Martin, *State Aid Control in the European Union: Rationale, Stylised Facts and Determining Factors* 36 Intereconomics 289, 290f. (2001) https://doi.org/10.1007/bf02930146; Bartłomiej Kurcz & Dimitri Vallindas, *Can General Measures Be ... Selective? Some Thoughts on the Interpretation of a State Aid Definition* 45 CMLR 159 (2008) https://doi.org/10.54648/cola2008007; Franz Jürgen Säcker, *Introduction*, in Säcker & Montag (eds), European State Aid Law, para. 1 (2016); Arne Schnitger, *Der Einfluss des Beihilferechts auf die direkten Steuern in Deutschland* 26 IStR 421 (2017); Phedon Nicolaides, *The Economics of State aid*, in Hancher et al. (eds), EU State Aids, paras 2-014ff. (5th edn 2016); Emily Forrester, *Is the State Aid Regime a Suitable Instrument to Be Used in the Fight Against Harmful Tax Competition?* 27 EC Tax Rev. 19, 24f. (2018) https://doi.org/10.54648/ecta2018003; Sandra Marco Colino, *The Long Arm of State Aid Law: Crushing Corporate Tax Avoidance* 44 Fordham Int. Law J. 397, 407ff. (2020) https://doi.org/10.2139/ssrn.3692504; Mason, *Tax Competition and State Aid*, *supra* n. 9, at 3 (fiscal discipline would be an incidental benefit). Vincent Verouden & Philipp Werner, *Introduction: The Law and Economics of EU State Aid Control*, in Werner & Verouden (eds), EU State Aid Control: Law and Economics, 7, 11f. (2017) explain that the rationale for supranational State aid control would also relate to the fact that single Member States would not consider the negative cross-border externalities of granting aid.
42. *See* Bacon, *European Union Law of State Aid*, *supra* n. 20, at paras 1.16ff. for the different dimensions and Verouden & Werner, *supra* n. 41, at 11f.
43. *See*, for example, Richard Lyal, *State Aid, Tax Integration and State Sovereignty*, in Panayi et al. (eds), Research Handbook on European Union Taxation Law, 410 (2020).

Instead of focusing on the economics underlying the internal market and the competition law rationale of State aid law, some authors have, for example, stressed the parallels with the fundamental freedoms as both sets of rules establish a prohibition against Member States influencing and affecting the market, i.e., the free flow of trade.[44] Somewhat similarly, Buendía Sierra & Smulders in rejecting a more economic approach stress that the State aid provision does not only regulate the competition between undertakings but also the competition between Member States. The latter could resort to State aid to counter the effects of free movement in the internal market that they perceive as disadvantageous.[45] Such internal market perspective – regardless of the exact interpretation – is certainly inherent to the State aid provision and has to be considered in interpreting Article 107(1) TFEU.

Particularly for fiscal State aid control, additional justifications have been considered.[46] For example, the Commission has consistently stressed the goal of promoting fair taxation in its statements on its tax ruling cases.[47] This can be understood as an acknowledgement of the objective of contributing to equity between taxpayers – not necessarily as competing undertakings, but as contributors to the public budget.[48] However, this goes beyond the scope of our analysis as the analytical framework of State aid law focuses solely on the equal treatment of undertakings as economic actors as opposed to contributors to the public budget.

Somewhat related, the objective of combatting harmful tax competition has been discussed.[49] From the outset, it is not altogether clear how harmful tax competition can

44. Andrea Biondi, *The Rationale of State Aid Control: A Return to Orthodoxy* 12 Camb. Yearb. Eur. Leg. Stud. 35, 42f. (2010) https://doi.org/10.1017/s1528887000001749.
45. José Luis Buendía Sierra & Ben Smulders, *The Limited Role of the 'Refined Economic Approach' in Achieving the Objectives of State Aid Control: Time for Some Realism*, in EC State Aid Law: Liber Amicorum Francisco Santoalalla Gadea, 1, 8f. (2008).
46. Mason, *Tax Competition and State Aid*, *supra* n. 9 discusses the potential enforcement goals of promoting free trade within the EU, preventing tax competition, promoting fiscal discipline, and fairly distributing the tax burden among EU taxpayers. *See also* for potential tax specific goals that have been brought forward in the literature: Ruth Mason, *Tax Rulings as State Aid: Part 4: Whose Arm's-Length Standard?* TNI 947, 963 (2017).
47. Commission, Press Release of 18 December 2017, IP/17/5343: 'All companies, big or small, multinational or not, should pay their fair share of tax. Member States cannot let selected companies pay less tax by allowing them to artificially shift their profits elsewhere. [...] .'
48. *See* on this dimension: Moritz Scherleitner & Tomi Viitala, *EU State Aid Rules as a Means of Promoting Equity Within International Taxation* 8 Nordic Tax Journal 20ff. (2021) with extensive references to the literature https://doi.org/10.2478/ntaxj-2021-0003.
49. *See* on this, e.g.,: Forrester, *supra* n. 41, at 30; de Cecco, *State Aid and the European Economic Constitution*, *supra* n. 5, at 131ff.; Christian Koenig, *Where Is State Aid Law Heading To?* 13 EStAL 611, 612 (2014); Kyriazis, *Fiscal State Aid Law as a Tool Against Harmful Tax Competition in the EU: déjà vu?*, *supra* n. 12; Patricia Lampraeve, *Harmful Tax Competition and Fiscal State Aid: Two Sides of the Same Coin?* 59 European Taxation 197ff. (2019) https://doi.org/10.59403/1344jka; Raymond Luja, *Tax Incentives, Harmful Tax Competition and State Aid Considerations in the EU*, in Richelle et al. (eds), State Aid Law and Business Taxation 65ff. (2016); Marco Colino, *supra* n. 41, at 455ff.; Mason, *Tax Competition and State Aid*, *supra* n. 9; Monti, *supra* n. 7; Saturnina Moreno González, *State Aid and Tax Competition: Comments on the European Commission's Decisions on Transfer Pricing Rulings* 15 EStAL 556ff. (2016) https://doi.org/10.21552/estal/2016/4/7; Francesco Nanetti & Giovanni Mameli, *The Creeping Normative Role of the EC Commission in the Twin-Track Struggle Against State Aids and Harmful Tax Competition* 11 EC Tax Rev. 185ff. (2002) https://doi.org/10.1023/a:1021807400018; Gabriella Perotto, *How*

be defined.[50] A myriad of studies have examined tax competition from an economic point of view with a focus on empirical evidence.[51] Other contributions have explored the upsides and downsides of tax competition.[52] Yet there appears to be no clear-cut picture of the very phenomenon of harmful tax competition.

Regardless, addressing harmful tax competition is high on the agenda of the EU. State aid law and the EU Code of Conduct, which was specifically designed to combat harmful tax competition, are not identical in scope.[53] Yet there are overlaps where measures of tax competition fulfil the criteria of State aid under Article 107(1) TFEU.[54]

In particular, the Commission in its investigations of Member States' tax rulings expressly referred to the objective of combatting harmful tax competition. This could have implied that a new objective of fiscal State aid control might have emerged.[55] However, in our view, while State aid law *can* in some cases tackle certain forms of harmful tax competition, it is not designed to do so.[56] In other words, as Mason puts it, the possibility to tackle some ways of engaging in tax competition appears to be nothing but a by-product of the internal market logic of State aid law.[57]

---

to Cope with Harmful Tax Competition in the EU Legal Order: Beyond the Elusive Quest for a Definition and the Misplaced Reliance on State Aid Law 13 EJLS 309ff. (2021); Schön, *Taxation and State Aid Law, supra* n. 7, at 913ff.; Edoardo Traversa & Alessandra Flamini, *Fighting Harmful Tax Competition through EU State Aid Law: Will the Hardening of Soft Law Suffice?* 14 EStAL 323ff. (2015); Edoardo Traversa & Pierre M. Sabbadini, *State-Aid Policy and the Fight Against Harmful Tax Competition in the Internal Market: Tax Policy in Disguise?*, in Haslehner et al. (eds), EU Tax Law and Policy in the 21st Century 107ff. (2017); Frans Vanistendael, *Fiscal Support Measures and Harmful Tax Competition* 9 EC Tax Rev. 153ff. (2000) https://doi.org/10.54648/269555.

50. Lilian V. Faulhaber, *The Trouble with Tax Competition: From Practice to Theory* 71 Tax L. Rev. 311, 312f. (2018) https://doi.org/10.2139/ssrn.2912477. Mason, *Tax Competition and State Aid, supra* n. 9, at 4 with further references on the ambiguities. *See*, for example, Monti, *supra* n. 7, at 209 who points to the desirability of certain types of tax competition.
51. Michael Devereux & Simon Loretz, *What Do We Know about Corporate Tax Competition* 66 NTJ 745ff. (2013) https://doi.org/10.17310/ntj.2013.3.08 conduct an extensive literature review. *See also* David C. Elkins, *The Merits of Tax Competition in a Globalized Economy* 91 Indiana Law Journal 905ff. (2016).
52. Elkins, *supra* n. 51; Faulhaber, *supra* n. 50, at 314ff. with extensive further references; Mason, *Tax Competition and State Aid, supra* n. 9, at 17f.; Julie Roin, *Competition and Evasion: Another Perspective on International Tax Competition* 89 Georgetown Law Journal 543ff. (2001) points out that tax harmonization is not the right way to proceed to tackle tax competition.
53. Lampraeve, *supra* n. 49, at 203ff. on the convergence and divergence of the respective criteria. *See* Anna Beckers, *The Creeping Juridification of the Code of Conduct for Business Taxation: How EU Codes of Conduct Become Hard Law* 37 YEL 569, 587ff. (2018) https://doi.org/10.1093/yel/yey006 for indications that a juridification of the Code of Conduct by means of fiscal State aid law is taking place.
54. Monti, *supra* n. 7, at 209. Traversa & Sabbadini, *State-Aid Policy and the Fight Against Harmful Tax Competition, supra* n. 49, at 108ff. trace the different phases of the fight against harmful tax competition relying on State aid law.
55. Traversa & Flamini, *supra* n. 49, at 329.
56. A different view is held by Pierpaolo Rossi-Maccanico, *Fiscal State Aids, Tax Base Erosion and Profit Shifting* 24 EC Tax Rev. 63, 64ff. (2015) ttps://doi.org/10.54648/ecta2015008; Francesco de Cecco, *A Constitutional View of State Aid*, in Piernas López et al. (eds), The Future of EU State Aid Law: Consolidation and Expansion 25, 31 (2023).
57. Mason, *Tax Competition and State Aid, supra* n. 9, at 13 and 17ff. for the arguments supporting her conclusion. Similarly, but pointing to positive integration as the appropriate tool, Benedikt Ellenrieder, *Die materielle Selektivität steuerlicher Beihilfen* 46 (2020).

For one, the Commission has been largely unsuccessful in its agenda as evidenced by the crucial loss in the *FIAT* case.[58] Moreover, several arguments speak against the view that combatting harmful tax competition can be considered an objective of fiscal State aid control: The State aid rules were from the outset never meant to become a tool to tackle harmful tax competition.[59] Such objective cannot be inferred from the wording of the Treaties or past case law.[60] Vanistendael had early on pointed out that two different dimensions of competition are concerned. Whereas tax competition refers to the competition for tax revenue between (Member) States, Article 107 TFEU and the case law focus on free competition among market players in the traditional sense.[61] The State aid rules would be inappropriate to tackle harmful tax competition which would constitute a systemic issue, whereas State aid law could only ever be applied to singular cases.[62] Moreover, it has been noted that State aid law focuses on the measure of a particular Member State and the effect on the internal market, whereas tax competition is characterized by a strong cross-border dynamic that State aid law would not be designed to catch.[63] Mason brings forward that the legal consequence of recovery would be inconsistent with the objective of addressing tax competition and cites the example of *Apple*. Recovery of the presumed aid in Ireland would disregard the fact that the tax should never have accrued to Ireland and would instead substantively have belonged to the USA or to the EU States where Apple's customers resided.[64] It has also been pointed out that erasing tax incentives as tools of tax competition may not necessarily be desirable as this could be detrimental to the investment climate in Europe vis-à-vis third countries.[65]

58. Joined Cases C-885 and 898/19 P *Fiat Chrysler Finance Europe and Others v. Commission* EU:C:2022:859, para. 94. For example, Kyriazis, *Fiscal State Aid Law as a Tool Against Harmful Tax Competition in the EU: déjà vu?, supra* n. 12, at 35 has pointed out that at least in the second wave of State aid control of the Commission tackling harmful tax competition, the Commission has overstretched the State aid provision.
59. Forrester, *supra* n. 41, at 30; Koenig, *supra* n. 49, at 612; Mason, *Tax Competition and State Aid, supra* n. 9; Lorenzo Panci, *Latest Developments on the Interpretation of the Concept of Selectivity in the Field of Corporate Taxation* 17 EStAL 353, 367 (2018) https://doi.org/10.21552/estal/2018/3/5; Perotto, *supra* n. 49, at 321; Henk van Arendonk, *The European Cooperation Project, Tax & Sovereignty* 25 EC Tax Rev. 242, 245 (2016) https://doi.org/10.54648/ecta2016026. Similarly: Lampraeve, *supra* n. 49, at 205, according to whom the two sets of rules are complementary.
60. Mason, *Tax Competition and State Aid, supra* n. 9, at 7ff.
61. Vanistendael, *Fiscal Support Measures, supra* n. 49, at 156. Similarly Nanetti & Mameli, *supra* n. 49, at 188.
62. In this vein: Pinto, *supra* n. 7, at 193. Similarly Moreno González, *State Aid and Tax Competition, supra* n. 49, at 573. By contrast, this would not prevent the Commission from tackling at least the types of harmful tax measures it can: Traversa & Sabbadini, *State-Aid Policy and the Fight Against Harmful Tax Competition, supra* n. 49, at 128f. A different view appears to be held by Hugo López López, *General Thought on Selectivity and Consequences of a Broad Concept of State Aid in Tax Matters* 9 EStAL 807, 818 (2010) who is, however, critical due to the effect on the competitiveness of European Member States vis-à-vis third countries.
63. Perotto, *supra* n. 49, at 324.
64. Mason, *Tax Competition and State Aid, supra* n. 9, at 22. De Broe adds that recovery may lead to economic double taxation where the Commission tackles transfer pricing rulings or mismatches since taxation might already have taken place elsewhere, Luc De Broe, *The State Aid Review Against Aggressive Tax Planning: 'Always Look a Gift Horse in the Mouth'* 24 EC Tax Rev. 290, 293 (2015) https://doi.org/10.54648/ecta2015030.
65. Schön, *Taxation and State Aid Law, supra* n. 7, at 936.

Further problems result from the lack of coherence between what State aid law can achieve and what is perceived to be harmful tax competition: State aid law would be overinclusive if it truly sought to tackle harmful tax competition since it can effectively strike down distinctions that do not amount to harmful tax competition, even if understood very widely.[66] Inversely, State aid law is an inadequate tool to *comprehensively* tackle tax competition. For example, the fact that corporate tax rates differ between Member States is bound to cause distortions, where the freedom of establishment allows undertakings to freely choose their location.[67] Moreover, mismatches that cannot be attributed to one single Member State are outside the scope of State aid control.[68] Such imperfections will inevitably lead to circumvention strategies.

In light of these disadvantages and shortcomings, many contributions have pointed out that instead of relying on State aid law to address harmful tax competition, positive integration should be pursued.[69] Indeed, while the Commission's recent efforts to tackle harmful tax competition relying on State aid law have more often than not failed, this may ultimately not matter as they have simultaneously resulted in significant advances in positive integration. These advances can certainly at least partly be attributed to the pressure that had been created due to the increased reliance on fiscal State aid law.[70]

The core objective of State aid law therefore appears to be the objective of promoting the internal market. Admittedly, the case law of the European courts on fiscal aid is not very clear on this. At least the competition law logic of State aid does not always clearly emerge. There is generally no in-depth analysis of the distortive effects and the effect on the trade between Member States in the case law on fiscal aid schemes.[71] This may perhaps be explained by the fact that the CJEU in its long-standing case law assumes that operating aid – as opposed to investment aid – is presumed to have a distortive effect.[72] Tax benefits will most often qualify as operating aid since

66. In this vein: Faulhaber, *supra* n. 50, at 331f.
67. In this vein: Joachim Englisch, *Das Beihilfenverbot im Steuerrecht*, in Schaumburg & Englisch (eds), Europäisches Steuerrecht, para. 9.17 (2nd edn 2020).
68. De Broe, *The State Aid Review against Aggressive Tax Planning*, *supra* n. 64, at 291; Raymond Luja, *Will the EU's State Aid Regime Survive BEPS?* BTR 379, 387f. (2015).
69. Perotto, *supra* n. 49, at 336; Traversa & Flamini, *supra* n. 49, at 331. Conor Quigley, *European State Aid Law and Policy*, 149 (3rd edn 2015), points to Art. 116 TFEU. The ambiguities in even defining the very notion of harmful tax competition would appear to indicate that any attempts to address it should be made relying on legislation rather than the Commission in its executive function, Mason, *Tax Competition and State Aid*, *supra* n. 9, at 18. Thomas Jaeger, *Schwächen der Prüfung von Steuerbeihilfen am Beispiel der Urteile Fiat und Starbucks* 31 EuZW 18, 19 (2020) refers to the democratic principle and the separation of powers in rejecting an executive approach.
70. Moreno González, *State Aid and Tax Competition*, *supra* n. 49, at 574.
71. Critical, e.g., José Luís da Cruz Vilaça, *Material and Geographic Selectivity in State Aid: Recent Developments* 8 EStAL 443, 444 (2009) https://doi.org/10.21552/estal/2009/4/150; Cristina Romariz, *Revisiting Material Selectivity in EU State Aid Law: Or the Ghost of Yet-to-Come* 13 EStAL 39, 47 (2014).
72. Case C-86/89 *Italy v. Commission* EU:C:1990:373, para. 18; Case C-288/96 *Germany v. Commission* EU:C:2000:537, para. 77; Case C-156/98 *Germany v. Commission*, para. 30.

they allow undertakings to reduce their running costs.[73] Moreover, some contributions have more generally questioned the distinction between general measures and selective measures for lack of a clear rationale that would prescribe only tackling the latter due to their detrimental effect on competition.[74] Nevertheless, a basis for the understanding that only *selective* tax benefits are considered problematic under the Treaties can be found in the wording of Article 107 TFEU.

However, this still does not answer the question of what types of tax measures should be forbidden under such internal market logic. If the distortive effects of a tax measure as well as its effect on the trade between Member States are generally presumed to exist under the current case law, this question can only be answered by resorting to the criterion of 'selective advantage'. The wording of Article 107(1) TFEU shows that there has to be a discrimination of some kind. Yet the Treaties do not provide further explicit guidance in this respect.

What type of discrimination is thus relevant from a State aid law perspective?[75] The case law shows that fiscal State aid control now effectively amounts to a control of the internal consistency of Member States' tax laws, i.e., a rationality review.[76] This is because the point of departure for the assessment of selectivity is the reference system of taxation, i.e., in principle the entire levy as designed by the Member State, which includes elements, such as the tax rate and the taxable object.[77] Prima facie selectivity is then present, where undertakings that are in a legally and factually comparable situation in light of the objective of this reference system are treated differently.[78] In other words, the prohibition of granting *selective* tax advantages leads to Member

73. Thomas Jaeger, *Tax Measures*, in Säcker & Montag (eds), European State Aid Law, para. 93. (2016) with further references. *See* in particular Case C-156/98 *Germany v. Commission*, para. 30. Nevertheless, some authors have called for a stronger emphasis of the distortive effects of aid, *see*, for example, Kokott, *Steuerrecht*, *supra* n. 20, at §3, para. 211. Whether this would be a viable option to reasonably restrict State aid control is beyond the scope of our analysis.
74. Cees Peters, *Tax Policy Convergence and EU Fiscal State Aid Control: In Search of Rationality* 28 EC Tax Rev. 6, 13 (2019) https://doi.org/10.54648/ecta2019002 with further references; Vanistendael, *Fiscal Support Measures*, *supra* n. 49, 156. A different view is held by de Cecco, *A Constitutional View of State Aid*, *supra* n. 56, at 31; Phedon Nicolaides, *Fiscal State Aid in the EU: The Limits of Tax Autonomy* 27 W. Comp. 365, 369 (2004) https://doi.org/10.54648/woco2004021.
75. Biondi, *The Rationale of State Aid Control*, *supra* n. 44, at 51 refers to the fundamental freedoms which could be used as interpretative tools.
76. Of course, this can only promote the rationality of a particular levy at issue at a time. Whether tackling tax benefits under State aid law makes the tax system as a whole more rational is doubtful.
77. *See* on this Ch. §3.02[B], [2] and §3.02[C], [1] *infra*. In detail Roland Ismer & Sophia Piotrowski, *The Selectivity of Tax Measures: A Tale of Two Consistencies* 43 Intertax 559ff. (2015) https://doi.org/10.54648/taxi2015055; Roland Ismer & Sophia Piotrowski, *Selectivity in Corporate Tax Matters after World Duty Free: A Tale of Two Consistencies Revisited* 46 Intertax 156, 158ff. (2018) https://doi.org/10.54648/taxi201801; Moreno González, *State Aid and Tax Competition*, *supra* n. 49, at 573 alludes to the 'internal coherence' of tax laws. A number of alternative legitimation narratives have been discussed in the literature. For an overview *see* Jaeger, *Tax Measures*, *supra* n. 73, at paras 4ff.; Ruth Mason, *Identifying Illegal Subsidies* 69 American University L. Rev. 479ff. (2020); Cees Peters, *The Legitimacy of EU Fiscal State Aid Control: What Is Your Legitimation Narrative*, in De Pietro (ed.), New Perspectives on Fiscal State Aid 5ff. (2019).
78. Commission Notice on the notion of State aid, *supra* n. 26, at para. 128.

States being held to their own fundamental charging decision which has to be implemented in an internally consistent manner,[79] i.e., without resorting to unjustified discriminations.[80]

Such an approach has a role model in the German constitutional law tradition, where it is dubbed *Folgerichtigkeitsgebot* (coherence or consistency requirement).[81] It started to make inroads into the case law of the *Bundesverfassungsgericht* (BVerfG) (Federal Constitutional Court) in the 1990s.[82] It is derived from the equality principle under Article 3 *Grundgesetz* (German Basic law).[83] Similarly to the approach under EU State aid law, the legislator is free in its choice of the taxable object and tax rates.[84] Deviations from this fundamental charging decision, however, can only be justified on grounds of a particularly good reason. Tracing the debate on the principle under German constitutional law would go beyond the scope of our analysis.[85] Suffice it to say that the consistency requirement under German national law imposes upon the legislator the obligation to draft rational laws.[86] The debate on the *Folgerichtigkeitsgebot* shows that an internal consistency requirement can – at least under the case law of the German *Bundesverfassungsgericht* – be traced back to the principle of equality and is not at odds with the logic of State aid law which monitors tax laws for positive discriminations.[87]

79. Note the difference in terminology relied on by Humbert Drabbe, *The Test of Selectivity in State Aid Litigation: The Relevance of Drawing Internal and External Comparisons to Identify the Reference Framework*, in Rust & Micheau (eds), State Aid and Tax Law 87ff. (2013).
80. *See* on this in detail Ch. §3.03 *infra*.
81. Similarly pointing out the similarities: Benedikt Ellenrieder, *Verhandlung der Grundsätze der beihilferechtlichen Selektivität: Grundlegende Gedanken im Nachgang zur mündlichen Verhandlung des EuG in den Rechtssachen World Duty Free und Banco Santander und Santusa* 27 IStR 480, 485 (2018); Englisch, *Das Beihilfenverbot im Steuerrecht, supra* n. 67, at para. 9.33; Jaeger, *Tax Measures, supra* n. 73, at para. 5. *See also* Stefan Rode, *Steuervergünstigungen, Beihilfen und Steuerwettbewerb: Zur Relevanz des europäischen Beihilfenrechts für das nationale Steuerrecht der Mitgliedstaaten*, 98ff. (2006) proposing such approach. *Rode* also presents a number of alternative narratives, pp. 74ff.
82. BVerfG, Case 2 BvR 1493/89, BVerfGE 84, 239; paras 118ff.; Case 2 BvL37/91, BVerfGE 93, 121, para. 58; Case 2 BvR 552/91, BVerfGE 93, 165, para. 20.
83. Paul Kirchhof, *Art. 3 Abs. 1 Gleichheit vor dem Gesetz*, in Dürig et al. (eds), Grundgesetz-Kommentar (100th edn 2023), para. 408.
84. *See* only BVerfG, Case 1 BvL 21/12, BVerfGE 138, 136, para. 135 with further references.
85. On this, e.g., Roland Ismer, *Judicial Review of Tax Laws: The Coherence Requirement (Folgerichtigkeitsgebot)*, in Meßerschmidt & Lalana (eds), Rational Lawmaking under Review 209ff. (2016) and Paul Kirchhof, *§181 Der allgemeine Gleichheitssatz*, in Isensee & Kirchhof (eds), Handbuch des Staatsrechts für die Bundesrepublik Deutschland, paras 209ff. (3rd edn 2010, vol. 8) with further references. Naturally, the coherence requirement is not undisputed in the German scholarly literature. It has, for example, been held to not have a sufficient constitutional basis, Oliver Lepsius, *Zur Neubegründung des Rückwirkungsverbots aus der Gewaltenteilung* 69 Juristenzeitung 488, 495f. (2014). *See* for further criticism, e.g., Mehrdad Payandeh, *Das Gebot der Folgerichtigkeit: Rationalitätsgewinn oder Irrweg der Grundrechtsdogmatik* 136 AöR 578ff. (2011) https://doi.org/10.1628/000389111798369834.
86. BVerfG, Case 2 BvL 1/00, BVerfGE 123, 111, para. 32. Critical, e.g.,: Payandeh, *supra* n. 85, at 591.
87. Englisch, *Das Beihilfenverbot im Steuerrecht, supra* n. 67, at para. 9.33 rejects a discrimination approach and instead contends that the selectivity test is limited to monitoring the internal consistency of Member States' tax laws (without this being rooted in considerations of

This then leads to the question of why the European courts resorted to (only) monitoring the internal consistency of tax laws – an approach which diverges from the fundamental freedoms, for example. In our view, the answer to this question lies in the fiscal sovereignty of Member States as a limit to fiscal State aid control.[88]

Fiscal sovereignty refers to the inherent prerogative of a State to tax.[89] It is a crucial dimension of sovereignty as a whole since taxation provides the main source of financing that States require to provide public goods and services.[90] Fiscal sovereignty has been discussed in a number of areas of international tax law.[91] Within the EU, the

---

non-discrimination). Ellenrieder, *Verhandlung der Grundsätze der beihilferechtlichen Selektivität, supra* n. 81, at 485 points out that the third step of the selectivity test does not allow for external grounds for justification, which would, however, be the case if a discrimination approach was applicable. *See* in more detail: Ellenrieder, *Die materielle Selektivität steuerlicher Beihilfen, supra* n. 57 at 439ff. and 457ff.

88. Peters, *Tax Policy Convergence, supra* n. 74, at 13 describes the current state of affairs as a 'rather unstable balancing act between the autonomy of the Member States and the harm of specific tax measures to the welfare of the EU'.
89. *See,* for example, René Barents, *The Single Market and National Tax Sovereignty,* in Jansen (ed.), Fiscal Sovereignty of the Member States in an Internal Market: Past and Future 51, 58 (2011); Allison Christians, *Sovereignty, Taxation and Social Contract* 18 Minnesota Journal of International Law 99, 105f. (2009) https://doi.org/10.21759/caulaw.2009.11.1.583 with further references.
90. Christians, *supra* n. 89, at 104.
91. *See* for a critical view: Yariv Brauner, *An Essay on BEPS, Sovereignty, and Taxation,* in Rocha & Christians (eds), Tax Sovereignty in the BEPS Era 73ff. (2017). *See* on an overview of the impact of globalization: Charles E. McLure, *Globalization, Tax Rules and National Sovereignty* 55 BIT 328ff. (2001). On tax sovereignty concerns in the context of automatic information exchange Luzius U. Cavelti, *Automatic Exchange Versus the Withholding Tax Regime Globalization and Increasing Sovereignty Conflicts in International Taxation* 5 WTJ 172ff (2013) https://doi.org/10.59403/3a7s4sw. Fiscal sovereignty is regularly brought forward in the context of tax treaty arbitration as arbitration is often held to imply a loss of sovereignty Spyridon E. Malamis, *The Future of OECD Tax Arbitration: The Relevance of Investment Treaty and WTO Dispute Settlement Practice in Promoting a Gradual Evolution of the International Tax Dispute Resolution System* 48 Intertax 966ff. (2020) https://doi.org/10.54648/taxi2020099. Fiscal sovereignty is also regularly brought forward in the fight against (harmful) tax competition on an international level. Tax competition and base erosion due to tax arbitrage are often discussed as potential threats to tax sovereignty: Peter Dietsch & Thomas Rixen, *Tax Competition and Global Background Justice* 22 The Journal of Political Philosophy 150, 151 (2014) https://doi.org/10.1111/j.1467-9760.2012.00419.x; António Carlos dos Santos & Cidália Mota Lopez, *Tax Sovereignty, Tax Competition and the Base Erosion and Profit Shifting Concept of Permanent Establishment* 25 EC Tax Rev. 296, 298 (2016) https://doi.org/10.54648/ecta2016030; Diane Ring, *One Nation Among Many: Policy Implications of Cross-Border Tax Arbitrage* 44 Boston College L. Rev. 79ff. (2002) https://doi.org/10.2139/ssrn.417560. It is also discussed in relation to the sovereignty of other States or international efforts to reallocate taxing rights or modify the international tax system more generally: Luis Calderon Gomez, *Transcending "Tax" Sovereignty and Tax Standardization: Three Questions* 45 The Yale Journal of International Law 191ff. (2020); Christians, *supra* n. 89; Martin F. de Wilde, *Some Thoughts on a Fair Allocation of Corporate Tax in a Globalizing Economy* 38 Intertax 281ff. (2010) https://doi.org/10.54648/taxi2010032; Sissie Fung, *The Questionable Legitimacy of the OECD/G20 BEPS Project* 11 Erasmus L. Rev. 76ff. (2017) https://doi.org/10.5553/elr.000085; Stjepan Gadžo, *The Principle of 'Nexus' or 'Genuine Link' as a Keystone of International Income Tax Law: A Reappraisal* 46 Intertax 194ff. (2018) https://doi.org/10.54648/taxi2018022; Andrew P. Morriss & Lotta Moberg, *Cartelizing Taxes: Understanding the OECD's Campaign Against 'Harmful Tax Competition'* 4 Columbia Journal of Tax Law 1ff. (2012) https://doi.org/10.2139/ssrn.1950627; Diane Ring, *Democracy, Sovereignty and Tax Competition: The Role of Tax Sovereignty in Shaping Tax Cooperation* 9 Florida Tax Review 555ff. (2009) https://doi.org/10.5744/ftr.2009.1053; *Dagan* elaborates on

role of fiscal sovereignty has a particularity in that Member States have transferred at least certain competences related to their fiscal sovereignty to the EU which to this extent yields supranational powers.[92] Yet there is a second dimension that is more relevant for our purposes, namely the impact of 'neutral' provisions, i.e., EU law that does not apply to only taxation, on Member States' tax systems. Particularly the fundamental freedoms and State aid law can have a profound impact on Member States' tax design.

Both the fundamental freedoms and State aid law certainly *factually* limit the exercise of fiscal sovereignty. This phenomenon has been subject to intense scrutiny in the scholarly literature on the fundamental freedoms.[93] More recently, fiscal sovereignty has also been discussed in the context of fiscal State aid,[94] albeit rarely in relation to aid schemes.[95]

---

tax sovereignty as the exclusive power of the state to tax its subjects based on the social contract and how this power is transformed by globalization, Tsilly Dagan, *Klaus Vogel Lecture 2021: Unbundled Tax Sovereignty – Refining the Challenges* 76 BIT 318ff. (2022) https://doi.org/10.59403/4b430e.

92. *See* on fiscal sovereignty in the internal market in general, e.g., B.H. ter Kuile, *Legal Aspects of Fiscal Sovereignty Within the Internal Market* 19 Intertax 503ff. (1991) https://doi.org/10.54648/taxi1991080; H. Onno Ruding, *Fiscal Sovereignty in the Internal Market* 19 Intertax 249ff. (1991) https://doi.org/10.54648/taxi1991041; van Arendonk, *supra* n. 59. Gianluigi Bizioli, *Building the EU Tax Sovereignty: Lessons from Federalism* 14 WTJ 407, 408 (2022) https://doi.org/10.59403/25ztn44 explains that only the competences related to sovereignty, not fiscal sovereignty itself can be surrendered to the EU.
93. In the wake of an increased application of the fundamental freedoms to Member States' tax measures many contributions have discussed the relationship with fiscal sovereignty, often describing it as a balancing act: María Cruz Barreiro Carril, *National Tax Sovereignty and EC Fundamental Freedoms: The Impact of Tax Obstacles on the Internal Market* 38 Intertax 105ff. (2010) https://doi.org/10.54648/taxi2010010; Sylvia Elwes, *The Internal Market Versus the Right of Member States to Levy Direct Tax: A Clash of Fundamental Principles* 41 Intertax 15ff. (2013) https://doi.org/10.54648/taxi2013002; Mathieu Isenbaert, *EC Law and the Sovereignty of the Member States in Direct Taxation* (2010); Moris Lehner, *Limitation of the National Power of Taxation by the Fundamental Freedoms and Non-discrimination Clauses of the EC Treaty* 9 EC Tax Rev. 5ff. (2000) https://doi.org/10.54648/261251; Frans Vanistendael, *The ECJ at the Crossroads: Balancing Tax Sovereignty Against the Imperatives of the Single Market* 46 European Taxation 413ff. (2006); Frans Vanistendael, *Denkavit Internationaal: The Balance Between Fiscal Sovereignty and the Fundamental Freedoms?* 47 European Taxation 210ff. (2007); Dennis Weber, *In Search of a (New) Equilibrium Between Tax Sovereignty and the Freedom of Movement Within the EC* 34 Intertax 585ff. (2006) https://doi.org/10.54648/taxi2006086. *See* for more recent contributions: Bizioli, *Building the EU Tax Sovereignty*, *supra* n. 92; Edoardo Traversa, *Tax Incentives and Territoriality Within the European Union: Balancing the Internal Market with the Tax Sovereignty of Member States* 6 WTJ 315ff. (2014) https://doi.org/10.59403/mfddv0. Many of the contributions have focused on the tax-specific dogmatic regarding a potential justification of discriminations, *see* only Gianluigi Bizioli, *Balancing the Fundamental Freedoms and Tax Sovereignty: Some Thoughts on Recent ECJ Case Law on Direct Taxation* 48 European Taxation 133, 140 (2008).
94. *See* for an early contribution addressing the conflict between State aid law and fiscal sovereignty and identifying potential threats to sovereignty: Christiana HJI Panayi, *State Aid and Tax: The Third Way?* 32 Intertax 283ff. (2004) https://doi.org/10.54648/taxi2004048.
95. *See*, however, e.g., Chiara Balbinot, *Europäisches Beihilfeverbot vs. Mitgliedstaatliche Steuersouveränität: eine kritische Untersuchung der Anwendung des Art. 107 Abs. 1 AEUV im Steuerrecht* 100 FR 729ff. (2018) https://doi.org/10.9785/fr-2018-1001603; Jens Ekkenga & Javid Safaei, *Bedroht die EU-Beihilfenaufsicht die Steuerautonomie der EU-Mitgliedstaaten: Zweifel sind*

For example, some authors have argued that the recent developments in State aid law – in particular the Commission's efforts to tackle Member States' tax rulings relying on an autonomous arm's length standard – would unduly limit Member States' sovereignty.[96] In this vein, the CJEU has recently explicitly relied on the division of competences and fiscal sovereignty in annulling the Commission decision in *Fiat*. The Commission in its decision had relied on an autonomous EU arm's length standard:

> In addition, by accepting, in paragraph 113 of the judgment under appeal, that the Commission may rely on rules which were not part of Luxembourg law, even though it recalled, in paragraph 112 of that judgment, that that institution did not, at that stage of development of EU law, have the power autonomously to define the 'normal' taxation of an integrated company, disregarding national tax rules, *the General Court infringed the provisions of the FEU Treaty relating to the adoption by the European Union of measures for the approximation of Member State legislation relating to direct taxation, in particular Article 114(2) TFEU and Article 115 TFEU. The autonomy of a Member State in the field of direct taxation [...] cannot be fully ensured if, in the absence of any such approximation measure, the examination carried out under Article 107(1) TFEU is not based exclusively on the normal tax rules laid down by the legislature of the Member State concerned.*[97]

Tax sovereignty has also sometimes been brought forward by commentators sceptical of the judgment of the CJEU in *Gibraltar* since in this judgment, the CJEU found that the proposed tax system of Gibraltar was selective even though it did not formally contain exceptions for certain operators.[98] Luja has examined a variety of aspects in which fiscal sovereignty is curtailed by State aid law.[99] More generally, others have voiced the concern that the imprecision of the criteria of Article 107 TFEU has enabled the Commission to curtail Member States' remaining policy spaces by

angebracht – Ein Gegenplädoyer am Beispiel von Steuererleichterungen in Krisen- und Insolvenzfällen 56 DStR 1993ff. (2018); Raymond Luja, *Do State Aid Rules Still Allow European Union Member States to Claim Fiscal Sovereignty* 25 EC Tax Rev. 312ff. (2016) https://doi.org/10.54648/ecta2016031; Rita Szudoczky & Balázs Károlyi, *The CJEU's Approach to the Objectives of Progressive Turnover-Based Taxes: Respect for the Member States' Fiscal Sovereignty or Authorization for Circumventing EU Law?* 50 Intertax 82ff. (2022) https://doi.org/10.54648/taxi2022007.

96. *See* only Rita de la Feria, *Pillar 2, Fiat, and the EU Unanimity Rule on Tax Matters* 32 EC Tax Rev. 1, 6f. (2023) https://doi.org/10.54648/ecta2023001; Forrester, *supra* n. 41, at 32f.; Edouard Fort, *EU State Aid and Tax: An Evolutionary Approach* 57 European Taxation 370, 382 (2017) https://doi.org/10.59403/386n1ka; Ricardo André Galendi Júnior, *State Aid and Transfer Pricing: The Inherent Flaw under a Supranational Reference System* 46 Intertax 994ff. (2018) https://doi.org/10.54648/taxi2018105; Dimitrios Kyriazis, *From Soft Law to Soft Law to Hard Law: The Commission's Approach to the State Aid Assessment of Tax Rulings* 15 EStAL 428, 436 (2016) https://doi.org/10.21552/estal/2016/3/10; Leopoldo Parada, *Between Apples and Oranges: The EU General Court's Decision in the 'Apple Case'* 30 EC Tax Rev. 55, 62 (2021) https://doi.org/10.54648/ecta2021007.
97. Joined Cases C-885 and 898/19 P *Fiat*, para. 94; emphasis added by the author.
98. Raymond Luja, *(Re)shaping Fiscal State Aid: Selected Recent Cases and Their Impact* 40 Intertax 120, 131 (2012) https://doi.org/10.54648/taxi2012013; John Temple Lang, *The Gibraltar State Aid and Taxation Judgment: A Methodological Revolution* 11 EStAL 805, 809ff. (2012) https://doi.org/10.21552/estal/2012/4/315. *See* on de facto-selectivity below [D].
99. Luja, *Fiscal Sovereignty*, *supra* n. 95.

enabling it to enforce its vision of State aid control.[100] It has also been argued that State aid would have to take the particularities of taxation into account as there would otherwise be a risk of trespassing into areas of national tax sovereignty.[101] Advocate General (AG) Kokott has pointed out that national tax laws often contain ambiguities and leeway for varying interpretations which can only be settled by a national Supreme Court – and not by the European institutions.[102]

Moreover, some contributions have stressed the importance of fiscal sovereignty for the de jure-selectivity of aid schemes and particular certain steps of the selectivity test: It is commonly accepted that as an emanation of fiscal sovereignty, the reference system of taxation is for the Member State to design. For example, Schön has therefore stressed that fiscal sovereignty implies that any taxation has to have a legislative basis by a democratically elected legislative body. As a consequence, the benchmark for fiscal State aid necessarily has to be the tax legislation of the Member State in question. This also means that in the absence of such a benchmark there could be no State aid.[103]

By contrast, others have gone so far as to argue that tax sovereignty within the internal market and the special role of taxation as opposed to other areas of law in this context would be nothing but a false paradigm since the CJEU has consistently stressed that where there is no harmonization, direct taxes are subject to State aid control (and an application of the fundamental freedoms).[104]

Against this background, we aim to demonstrate that fiscal sovereignty has played a pivotal role in the interpretation of the State aid provision which has become even more prominent in light of the recent developments of the case law. Indeed, the CJEU has always stressed that Member States' tax laws are not exempt from State aid control (and an application of the fundamental freedoms).[105] The case law has also never acknowledged a special role in the area of taxation. However, it seems as though this is not the complete picture. Instead, inversely, fiscal sovereignty also limits the enforcement of primary law. Neither of the two aspects necessarily takes precedence over the other, at least where primary law is open to interpretation. Jaeger has thus rightly pointed out that the interplay between the two concepts requires a balancing of interests as well as the exercise of mutual consideration.[106]

100. Romariz, *supra* n. 71, at 46, particular with reference to the judgment in *Gibraltar*.
101. Jaeger, *Fehlstellungen im Verhältnis von Steuer- und Beihilferecht*, *supra* n. 29, at 92. *See also* Thomas Jaeger, *Tax Incentives under State Aid Law: A Competition Law Perspective*, in Richelle et al. (eds), State Aid Law and Business Taxation 39, 55f. (2016).
102. Juliane Kokott, *Tax Harmonisation Through the Prohibition of State Aid?* 21 EStAL 462, 464 (2022) https://doi.org/10.21552/estal/2022/4/19.
103. Schön, *Tax Legislation and the Notion of Fiscal Aid*, *supra* n. 40, at 5 and 7. Based on the latter, *Luja* argues that a lack of anti-avoidance legislation, such as transfer pricing rules, cannot lead to State aid. In other words, State aid law cannot serve to replace the lack of implementation of such rules by Member States. If, however, the anti-avoidance rules are flawed in that they lead to selective exemptions of certain sectors, there could still be State aid, Luja, *Fiscal Sovereignty*, *supra* n. 95, at 323.
104. Barents, *supra* n. 89, at 59. Similarly: Kyriazis, *Fiscal State Aid Law as a Tool Against Harmful Tax Competition in the EU: déjà vu?*, *supra* n. 12, at 5.
105. Case C-562/19 P *Commission v. Poland* EU:C:2021:201, para. 26 with further references.
106. Jaeger, *Tax Measures*, *supra* n. 73, at para. 2.

We aim to demonstrate that the recent developments of the notion of material selectivity for fiscal aid schemes embody the conflict between fiscal sovereignty and European State aid law. This is not limited to the finding that the benchmark for the analysis is designed by the Member State.[107] Instead, fiscal sovereignty in our view has had a profound impact on the tax-specific approach to assessing material selectivity in a number of respects that will be pointed out throughout this book.[108] Fiscal sovereignty as a limit to State aid control is also underlying the judgment in *Gibraltar* since the threshold for disregarding the fundamental charging decision of the Member State is very high and reserved for extreme cases of 'external inconsistency'.[109] Most recently, fiscal sovereignty tends to be favoured over effective State aid control in the ongoing balancing process between the two opposing considerations. This is evidenced by indications of a rollback in the case law on selectivity.

This then brings us back to the question of why the discrimination test that was developed by the European courts to test for selectivity is limited to monitoring tax laws for internal inconsistencies. In our view, an obligation to design internally consistent taxes may be the maximum of what can be achieved by relying on fiscal State aid law without infringing upon fiscal sovereignty. A wider interpretation that tackles any kind of differentials in Member States' tax laws would fundamentally put into question their freedom to design direct taxes where there has not been a transfer of competences.[110]

A second important limiting factor to fiscal State aid control that should be considered is the position of taxpayers in the State aid procedure. In this, we focus on an individual taxpayer rights perspective.[111] While the first limit to State aid control – fiscal sovereignty – primarily impacts the material State aid law provision, the taxpayer rights dimension primarily concerns the legal consequences of a Member State granting unlawful aid, i.e., recovery. Despite the recent rollback in the case law of the CJEU,[112] the weak position of taxpayers in a climate of ongoing legal uncertainty[113] remains

107. Schön, *Taxation and State Aid Law, supra* n. 7, at 924.
108. By contrast, we will not address another important source of friction, namely the question of the burden of proof in light of fiscal sovereignty. The Commission has the burden of proof in establishing that a measure is prima facie selective. This requires an interpretation of national tax laws which for the purposes of the State aid procedure are factual, not legal issues, Josef Azizi, *The Tension Between Member States' Autonomy and Commission Control in State Aid Matters: Selected Aspects*, in Kanninen et al. (eds), EU Competition Law in Context, 307, 316 (2009).
109. *See* Ch. §4.01 *infra*.
110. This is in contrast to the fundamental freedoms. Their ambit is from the outset more limited because they only require equal treatment of domestic and cross-border scenarios.
111. In the literature on taxpayer rights under international law, a distinction is made between individual taxpayer rights and collective taxpayer rights. *See* on the distinction Juliane Kokott & Pasquale Pistone, *Taxpayers in International Law*, 70ff. (2022) https://doi.org/10.5771/9783748913443.We focus on the first dimension of taxpayer rights. Suffice it to say that the acknowledgement of the existence of collective taxpayer rights further strengthens the internal market objective of State aid law. In other words, State aid law promotes the collective rights dimension of taxpayer rights because it prevents Member States from forgoing tax revenue that would otherwise accrue to the public budget.
112. *See* on the evolution of the case law Ch. §3.01 *infra*.
113. *See*, for example, Peters, *Tax Policy Convergence, supra* n. 74, at 6; Romariz, *supra* n. 71, at 46; Katharina Schlücke, *Der Referenzrahmen selbst unterliegt nur einer eingeschränkten beihilferechtlichen Kontrolle* 9 ISR 439, 441 (2020) https://doi.org/10.9785/isr-2020-091206.

problematic. The role of third parties, which includes both beneficiaries of aid and other interested parties, such as competitors, in the State aid procedure was traditionally weak[114] but has been strengthened over time.[115] Nevertheless, the underlying administrative State aid procedure from notification to recovery is bilateral in nature, as it only involves the Commission on the one hand and the Member State that grants aid on the other hand.[116] Taxpayers are not in a position to notify potential aid to the Commission.[117]

In this book, we are primarily interested in the legal consequence of recovery and its connection with the notification requirement. Taxpayer rights in relation to recovery cannot only be promoted by creating or strengthening procedural rights. Instead, we consider any limit to recovery motivated (at least partly) by individual rights.[118] First, the legal consequence of recovery could be modified or abolished for fiscal aid schemes due to their specific characteristics, which make recovery particularly problematic from the perspective of taxpayers.[119] An explicit legal source of individual rights

114. Azizi, *supra* n. 108, footnote 1 with further references; Marc Barennes, *The Standing of the Competitors of the Aid Recipient in State Aid Cases,* in Kanninen et al. (eds), EU Competition Law in Context 321, 322f. (2009); Leigh Hancher, *State Aid Recovery: A New Public Order?* 12 EStAL 1, 3 (2013); Ana Pošćić, *Procedural Aspects of EU State Aid Law* 1 EU and Comparative Law Issues and Challenges 490, 494 (2017) https://doi.org/10.25234/eclic/6542; Anne Van de Vijver, *National Courts as 'Guardians' of Commission Recovery Decisions,* in De Pietro (ed.), New Perspectives on Fiscal State Aid, 131, 132 (2019).
115. José Luis Buendía Sierra, *Judicial Control and the Recovery Phase* 18 EStAL 173 (2019) https://doi.org/10.21552/estal/2018/2/2. *See* Fernando Pastor-Merchante, *The Protection of Competitors under State Aid Law* 15 EStAL 527ff. (2016) https://doi.org/10.21552/estal/2016/4/5 for a break-down of competitors' options for influencing the State aid procedure. François-Charles Laprévote, *A Missed Opportunity? State Aid Modernization and Effective Third Parties Rights in State aid Proceedings* 13 EStAL 426, 436f. (2014) identifies missed opportunities with regard to third-party rights in comparison to anti-subsidy law.
116. Pošćić, *supra* n. 114, at 494. Critical, e.g., Andreas Bartosch, *Procedural Rights Denied for Too Long: Is Legal Conservativism Finally Heading for Its 'Götterdämmerung'?* 10 EStAL 579 (2011) https://doi.org/10.21552/estal/2011/4/256; Buendía Sierra, *Judicial Control and the Recovery Phase, supra* n. 115, at 173ff.; Jeremy Lever, *EU State Aid Law: Not a Pretty Sight* 12 EStAL 5, 8 (2013) https://doi.org/10.21552/estal/2013/1/327; Kristina Nordlander & David Went, *Checks and Balances in EU State Aid Procedures: Should More Be Done to Protect the Rights of Aid Recipients and Third Parties?* 11 ERA Forum 367, 368 (2010) https://doi.org/10.1007/s12027-010-0171-y with a focus on the principle of good administration; Henrik Petyz & Thomas Mygind, *Direct Action in State Aid Cases: Tightropes and Legal Protection* 9 EStAL 617, 626 (2010) https://doi.org/10.21552/estal/2010/2/178; Oana Stefan, *General Principles in EU State Aid Law,* in Ziegler et al. (eds), Research Handbook on General Principles in EU Law, 441, 459 (2022).
117. *See* on this in particular Ch. §7.01 *infra.*
118. The recent literature on taxpayer rights in the EU primarily focuses on the fundamental rights as enshrined in the ChFR: Katerina Perrou, *Fundamental Rights in EU Tax Law,* in Panayi et al. (eds), Research Handbook on European Union Taxation Law (2020) 511ff. with further references. Others have relied on a comparative law approach: Philip Baker & Pasquale Pistone, *General Report* 100B IFA Cahiers 17ff. (2015).
119. *See* on this Chs §5.01[C] and §6.01[D] *infra.* For example: Johanna Hey, *EU-Beihilfen und Steuervergünstigungen: Gemeinsamkeiten und Unterschiede* 92 StuW 331, 336 (2015) https://doi.org/10.9785/stuw-2015-920404; Kokott, *Steuerrecht, supra* n. 20, at §3, para. 232. Similarly Ruben Martini, *Rechtsfolgen unionsrechtswidriger Beihilfen im Steuerrecht* 94 StuW 101, 107f. (2017); Kokott, *Tax Harmonisation, supra* n. 102, at 466f.

limiting recovery could be the general principles of EU law. Under Article 16(1) of Procedural Regulation 2015/1589, recovery is excluded, where it would lead to an infringement of the general principles of EU law. The principle of legal certainty, the principle of protection of legitimate expectation and the principle of proportionality may not immediately be obvious embodiments of the rights of taxpayers in the EU. Yet even though the scholarly literature often distinguishes rules from principles[120] and the principles we refer to here are not laid down in the Charter of Fundamental Rights (ChFR), the general principles of EU law that can be of relevance in State aid law have a strong individual rights dimension.[121]

In theory, these principles could play a significant role in State aid law since they are explicitly enshrined in secondary law as limits to recovery and can thus be invoked in legal proceedings. Yet the general principles of EU law currently have but limited significance for fiscal aid schemes due to the case law of the CJEU which establishes a firm link with the notification requirement.[122] As a result, two constellations have to be distinguished in examining the potential of the general principles of EU law to limit recovery. Where the taxpayer was not – and did not have to be – aware that a measure may conceivably amount to State aid, the exact portent of the general principles of EU law has to be analysed. By contrast, where taxpayers are aware of the potential of there being State aid, the bilateral nature of the State aid procedure and the impossibility of notifying aid is the real issue that has to be addressed.

In any case, simply referring to the restrictive case law of the CJEU on the general principles of EU law and the status quo of the State aid procedure does not suffice since taxpayer rights in relation to recovery could also derive from other sources of individual rights, such as the EU ChFR,[123] the fundamental freedoms, or even the constitutional laws of Member States. While the latter have only limited legal value in relation to EU law,[124] much of the backlash against the Commission's State aid agenda has been informed by principles, such as the principle of legal or the prohibition of

120. Critical of such distinction Chris Hilson, *Rights and Principles in EU Law: A Distinction Without Foundation?* 15 Maastricht Journal of Comparative Law 193ff. (2008) https://doi.org/10.1177/1023263x0801500203.
121. Hans Dieter Jarass, *Schutz durch rechtsstaatliche Grundsätze des Unionsrechts* 133 Deutsches Verwaltungsblatt 1249f. (2018) https://doi.org/10.1515/dvbl-2018-1331903; Hans Dieter Jarass, *Einleitung: Grundlagen und Bedeutung der Grundrechte*, in Jarass (ed.), Charta der Grundrechte der EU, para. 37 (4th edn 2021); Kokott, *Steuerrecht*, *supra* n. 20, at §2, para. 27; Takis Tridimas, *The General Principles of EU Law*, 47 (2nd edn 2006). *See also* in particular Kokott & Pistone, *supra* n. 111, at 83ff.
122. *See* Ch. §5.01[A] and §5.02[A] *infra*.
123. Charter of Fundamental Rights of the European Union [2007] OJ C 303/1.
124. Constitutional law traditions often act as role models for the interpretation of the principles in the European legal order, Tridimas, *supra* n. 121, at 23ff. In some legal orders, such as Germany, constitutional law principles can even override European law in exceptional cases, *see* Klaus Gärditz, *§11 Verfassungsidentität und Schutz der Verfassung*, in Stern et al. (eds), Das Staatsrecht der Bundesrepublik Deutschland im europäischen Staatenverbund, paras 10ff. (2nd edn 2022, vol. 1) with further references.

retroactive taxation as understood under Member States' constitutions.[125] Understanding and answering these national objections is important to ensure the acceptability of EU (State aid) law.

§1.04 OVERVIEW OF THE LITERATURE ON FISCAL STATE AID SCHEMES

Although the majority of the most recent literature on fiscal aid focuses on the Commission's investigations into tax rulings and the resulting case law,[126] there is still

---

125. *See, e.g.*, Kokott, *Tax Harmonisation, supra* n. 102, at 466 on the notion of fiscal aid that is imposed on the taxpayer leading to retroactive taxation and legislation as a source of a protection of legitimate expectation. *See* on this Chs §5.01[C], [1] and §6.01[D] *infra.*

126. *See* only: Giulio Allevato, *Judicial Review of the State Aid Decisions on Advance Tax Rulings: A Last Resort to Safeguard the Rule of Law* 62 European Taxation 86ff. (2022) https://doi.org/10.59403/238pb0p; Philip Baker, *The Week of the 10 May 2021: A Week of State Aid, Transfer Pricing and Tax Rulings* 49 Intertax 602ff. (2021) https://doi.org/10.54648/taxi2021062; Nieves Bayón Fernández, *The Selective Advantage Criterion in Tax Rulings: The Path Towards a More Coherent and Thorough Analysis of Selectivity* 12 JECLAP 200ff. (2021) https://doi.org/10.1093/jeclap/lpab018; Franklin Cachia, *Analysing the European Commission's Final Decisions on Apple, Starbucks, Amazon and Fiat Finance & Trade* 26 EC Tax Rev. 23ff. (2017) https://doi.org/10.54648/ecta2017003; Stefano Castagna, *On the European Commission's Understanding of the Arm's Length Principle in International Taxation versus State Aid Matters: Treaty Violations and High Stakes in Play* 13 WTJ 481ff. (2021) https://doi.org/10.59403/1gcnvw7; Adrien Giraud & Sylvain Petit, *Tax Rulings and State Aid Qualification: Should Reality Matter* 16 EStAL 233ff. (2017) https://doi.org/10.21552/estal/2017/2/9; Stephen Daly, *The Constitutional Implications of an EU Arm's Length Principle* 60 European Taxation 70ff. (2020) https://doi.org/10.59403/1k885s0; Tony Joris & Wout De Cock, *Is Belgium and Forum 187 v. Commission a Suitable Legal Source for an EU 'At Arm's Length Principle'?* 16 EStAL 607ff. (2017) https://doi.org/10.21552/estal/2017/4/10; Jeffery M. Kadet, *Thoughts on Treasury's White Paper on EU State Aid* TNI 877ff. (2016); James Kavanaugh & Nicole Robins, *Corporate Tax Arrangements under EU State Aid Scrutiny* 14 EStAL 358ff. (2015); Kyriazis, *From Soft Law to Soft Law to Hard Law: The Commission's Approach to the State Aid Assessment of Tax Rulings, supra* n. 96; Liza Lovdahl Gormsen, *EU State Aid Law and Transfer Pricing: A Critical Introduction to a New Saga* 7 JECLAP 369ff. (2016) https://doi.org/10.1093/jeclap/lpw040; Liza Lovdahl Gormsen & Clement Mifsud-Bonnici, *Legitimate Expectation of Consistent Interpretation of EU State Aid Law: Recovery in State Aid Cases Involving Advanced Pricing Agreements on Tax* 8 JECLAP 423ff. (2017) https://doi.org/10.1093/jeclap/lpx028; Timothy Lyons, *Luxembourg v. European Commission; Amazon EU Sarl and Amazon.com Inc v. European Commission: The Issue of Competence Again* BTR 470ff. (2021); Raymond Luja, *State Aid Benchmarking and Tax Ruling: Can We Keep It Simple?*, in Richelle et al. (eds), State Aid and Business Taxation, 111ff. (2016); Marco Colino, *supra* n. 41; Mason, *Tax Rulings as State Aid, supra* n. 46; Ruth Mason, *Ding-Dong! The EU Arm's Length Standard Is Dead* TNI 1249ff. (2022); Michel, *supra* n. 36; Phedon Nicolaides, *State Aid Rules and Tax Rulings* 15 EStAL 416ff. (2016) https://doi.org/10.21552/estal/2016/3/9; Parada, *Between Apples and Oranges, supra* n. 96; Dionysios Pelekis, *The Burden and Standard of Proof in the Tax Ruling Cases: A Practical Limit to the EU's Arm's Length Principle?* 12 JECLAP 669ff. (2021) https://doi.org/10.1093/jeclap/lpab038; Marc Rasch & Pawel Wroblewski, *Fiat State Aid Coming to a Positive End?* 29 ITPJ 216ff. (2022) https://doi.org/10.59403/2es9z7w https://doi.org/10.59403/2es9z7w; Pierpaolo Rossi-Maccanico, *A New Framework for State Aid Review of Tax Rulings* 14 EStAL 371ff. (2015); Jean Schaffner & Sophie Balliet, *BEPS, EU State Aid Investigations and LuxLeaks: And What about Luxembourg?* 23 ITPJ 279ff. (2016) https://doi.org/10.59403/343m109; Daniel Shaviro, *The U.S. Response to OECD-BEPS and The EU State Aid Cases*, Law & Economics Research Paper Series, Working Paper Nos 16-27 (2016); Bruce Sewell, *In Need of an Economic Reality Check: The Commission's State Aid Decision Regarding Ireland and Apple*

a vast and highly complex body of scholarly literature on aid schemes. Any attempt at a comprehensive overview would be futile. Nevertheless, the literature can be categorized with a broad brush.

While there is some disagreement as to the function of the necessary advantage in the literature on fiscal aid schemes, most contributions advocate a stand-alone significance of the advantage.[127] The main focus of the literature, however, is the notion of selectivity. A variety of different, often overlapping approaches to identifying selectivity have been advocated in this regard, with representatives emphasizing various aspects simultaneously. This reflects the variety of different approaches that could have been deduced from the earlier case law of the CJEU, which still lacked clear contours.[128]

For example, Schön has stressed the aspect of fiscal sovereignty[129] which would mean that where economic incentives are available to all actors there could be no State aid. State aid law would only cover state measures that address 'certain undertakings' in the sense that they introduce distinctions, for example, by sector or horizontal criteria.[130]

---

7 JECLAP 649ff. (2016) https://doi.org/10.1093/jeclap/lpw086; Anja Taferner & Jurjan Wouda Kuipers, *Tax Rulings: In Line with OECD Transfer Pricing Guidelines, but Contrary to EU State Aid Rules?* 56 European Taxation 134ff. (2016) https://doi.org/10.59403/1tn5qtq; Romero J.S. Tavares et al., *The Intersection of EU State Aid and U.S. Tax Deferral: A Spectacle of Fireworks, Smoke, and Mirrors* 19 Florida Tax Review 121ff. (2016) https://doi.org/10.5744/ftr.2016.1031; Fausta Todhe, *The Rise of an (Autonomous) Arm's Length Principle in EU State Aid Rules* 18 EStAL 249ff. (2019) https://doi.org/10.21552/estal/2019/3/5; Tim Van Helfteren, *A Restriction on the Commission's State Aid Enforcement in Fiscal Aid Cases: Fiat and Ireland V Commission* 14 JECLAP 168ff. (2023) https://doi.org/10.1093/jeclap/lpad011; Apurva Vats, *Tax Rulings and EU State Aid: Lessons to Be Learnt from the Apple-Ireland Case* 42 ECLR 80ff. (2021); Hans Verhagen, *State Aid and Tax Rulings: An Assessment of the Selectivity Criterion of Article 107(1) of the TFEU in Relation to Recent Commission Transfer Pricing Decisions* 57 European Taxation 279ff. (2017) https://doi.org/10.59403/3brh1ye; Peter J. Wattel, *Stateless Income, State Aid and the (Which?) Arm's Length Principle* 44 Intertax 791 (2016) https://doi.org/10.54648/taxi2016071.

127. *See, e.g.*, Svitlana Buriak & Ivan Lazarov, *Between State Aid and the Fundamental Freedoms: The Arm's Length Principle and EU Law* 56 CMLR 1, 8 (2019) https://doi.org/10.54648/cola2019076; Kyriazis, *From Soft Law to Soft Law to Hard Law: The Commission's Approach to the State Aid Assessment of Tax Rulings*, *supra* n. 96, at 432; López López, *General Thought on Selectivity*, *supra* n. 62, at 808; Joris Luts, *Compatibility of IP Box Regimes with EU State Aid Rules and Code of Conduct* 23 EC Tax Rev. 258, 269f. (2014) https://doi.org/10.54648/ecta2014025; Juan Jorge Piernas López, *Revisiting Some Fundamentals of Fiscal Selectivity* 17 EStAL 274, 277 (2018) https://doi.org/10.21552/estal/2018/2/11; Schön, *Tax Legislation and the Notion of Fiscal Aid*, *supra* n. 40, at 8. A different view is held by Jaeger, *Tax Measures*, *supra* n. 73, at para. 75, according to whom no comprehensive advantage test would be performed for tax measures. Miro Prek & Silvère Lefèvre, *The Requirement of Selectivity in the Recent Case-Law of the Court of Justice* 11 EStAL 335, 337 (2012) https://doi.org/10.21552/estal/2012/2/285 hold that the two notions are closely related in practice.
128. *See, e.g.*, Kurcz & Vallindas, *supra* n. 41, at 159ff.
129. *See also* Schön, *Taxation and State Aid Law*, *supra* n. 7, at 924 as to the general tax system of the Member State as the only possible point of departure.
130. Schön, *State Aid in the Area of Taxation*, *supra* n. 31, at para. 13-085.

Many contributions have understood the notion of selectivity – and the State aid provision as a whole – as a non-discrimination provision.[131] Within the latter group, some authors have argued that the reference system of taxation is generally the levy itself,[132] whereas others have argued that the reference system of taxation can also be made up of a sub-system of rules within a tax,[133] such as a Member State's tax rules that apply to group companies.

There is also disagreement as to the precise function of the reference system. Some authors consider the identification of the reference system to be superfluous. The continued reliance on this first step would be a mere remnant of an outdated 'rule-exception-logic'.[134] Others have claimed that the reference system would become relevant in cases where no reference system can be relied upon as a benchmark or where it is not clear what the benchmark is. Where this is the case, there could be no State aid.[135] Sometimes, it has also been argued that the relevance of the reference system lies in the fact that its objective is to determine whether there is a derogation from the reference system from taxation, i.e., the question of whether there is an unequal treatment of undertakings in a legally and factually comparable situation, would have to be ascertained in light of the objective of the reference system of taxation.[136] By contrast, before the clarifications in recent case law, many contributions

131. *See* only José Luis Buendía Sierra, *Finding Selectivity or the Art of Comparison* 17 EStAL 85ff. (2018) https://doi.org/10.21552/estal/2018/1/10; Buriak & Lazarov, *supra* n. 127, at 2; Axel Cordewener, *Asymmetrical Tax Burdens and EU State Aid Control* 21 EC Tax Rev. 288ff. (2012) https://doi.org/10.54648/ecta2012029; Lars Dobratz, *Artikel 107 AEUV*, in Musil & Weber-Grellet (eds), Europäisches Steuerrecht, paras 72f. (2022); Ismer & Piotrowski, *Selectivity in Corporate Tax Matters, supra* n. 77; Michael Lang, *State Aid and Taxation: Selectivity and Comparability Analysis*, in Richelle et al. (eds), State Aid Law and Business Taxation, 27ff. (2016); Richard Lyal, *Transfer Pricing Rules and State Aid* 38 Fordham Int. Law J. 1017ff. (2015) https://doi.org/10.4337/9781788110846.00029; Rita Szudoczky, *Convergence of the Analysis of National Tax Measures under the EU State Aid Rules and the Fundamental Freedoms* 15 EStAL 357ff. (2016) https://doi.org/10.21552/estal/2016/3/6; Marta Villar Ezcurra, *State Aids and Energy Taxes: Towards a Coherent Reference Framework* 41 Intertax 340, 343 (2013) https://doi.org/10.54648/taxi2013030. Critical, albeit finding that the case law amounts to a non-discrimination approach: Balbinot, *Europäisches Beihilfeverbot vs. Mitgliedstaatliche Steuersouveränität, supra* n. 95, at 732f. A discrimination approach has been rejected by Ellenrieder, *Verhandlung der Grundsätze der beihilferechtlichen Selektivität, supra* n. 81, at 485 and Englisch, *Das Beihilfenverbot im Steuerrecht, supra* n. 67, at para. 9.33; who, however, both argue that there is a monitoring for internal consistency.
132. Roland Ismer & Sophia Piotrowski, *Selektivität von Beihilfen: Dogmatische Grundfragen am Beispiel von IP-Boxen* 24 IStR 257, 260 (2015); Fabian Mang, *The (In)Compatibility of IP Box Regimes with EU Law, the Code of Conduct and the BEPS Initiatives* 55 European Taxation 78, 81 (2015) https://doi.org/10.59403/mwbb9s; Szudoczky, *Convergence of the Analysis of National Tax Measures, supra* n. 131, at 367.
133. Lovdahl Gormsen, *supra* n. 126, at 377. Somewhat similarly: Nicolaides, *State Aid Rules and Tax Rulings, supra* n. 126, at 425.
134. Lang, *State Aid and Taxation: Selectivity and Comparability Analysis, supra* n. 131, at 27ff. Also doubting the stand-alone significance of the reference system of taxation: Dobratz, *Artikel 107 AEUV, supra* n. 131, at para. 74.
135. Schön, *Tax Legislation and the Notion of Fiscal Aid, supra* n. 40, at 11ff.; Balbinot, *Europäisches Beihilfeverbot vs. Mitgliedstaatliche Steuersouveränität, supra* n. 95, at 733 advocates a return to the rule-exception logic.
136. Ismer & Piotrowski, *Selectivity in Corporate Tax Matters, supra* n. 77, at 159; Paul-John Loewenthal, *Fiscal Selectivity: A Notion in Need of Clarity*, in De Pietro (ed.), New Perspectives

had contended that the objective of the measure should be relied upon to assess whether there is a derogation from the reference system of taxation in the second step.[137]

As to the required unequal treatment, it has been asserted that abstract selectivity suffices, which means that based on recent case law it is not necessary to identify certain undertakings or a group of undertakings that are benefitting from a tax measure as opposed to others that are not.[138] By contrast, others had argued that there has to be concrete selectivity, which means that the fact that theoretically, all undertakings can make use of a tax benefit would be sufficient to rule out selectivity.[139] Some authors had advocated a rule of reason approach or an objectives-based approach respectively, which could be derived from current CJEU case law.[140]

Particularly following the judgment of the CJEU in *World Duty Free Group*,[141] several commentators have criticized an overly broad notion of material selectivity in fiscal aid schemes.[142] Most likely due to these concerns, some contributions have stressed the fact that Article 107(1) TFEU is a competition law provision, which would mean that a stronger emphasis should be put on the question of whether aid is truly

---

on Fiscal State Aid, 31, 46 (2019); Lyal, *supra* n. 131, at 1036; Michael Sánchez Rydelski, *Distinction Between State Aid and General Measures* 19 EC Tax Rev. 149, 151 (2010) https://doi.org/10.54648/ecta2010020; Chu Shi, *IP Boxes in Light of the BEPS Project and EU Law: Part II* 56 European Taxation 371, 372 (2016) https://doi.org/10.59403/a8bfmq; Szudoczky, *Convergence of the Analysis of National Tax Measures, supra* n. 131, at 367; Szudoczky & Károlyi, *The CJEU's Approach to the Objectives of Progressive Turnover-Based Taxes, supra* n. 95, at 84.

137. *See, e.g.*, Cécile Brokelind, *Intellectual Property, Taxation and State Aid Law,* in Richelle et al. (eds), State Aid Law and Business Taxation, 221, 228f. (2016); Michael Honoré, *Selectivity,* in Werner & Verouden (eds), EU State Aid Control: Law and Economics, 119, 128f. (2017); Kurcz & Vallindas, *supra* n. 41; Luts, *supra* n. 127, at 269; Mang, *supra* n. 132, at 81.

138. Andreas Bartosch, *Spanish Goodwill: A Textbook on Material Selectivity Awaiting a Second Edition* 21 EStAL 65, 69 (2022) https://doi.org/10.21552/estal/2022/1/8; De Broe, *The State Aid Review Against Aggressive Tax Planning, supra* n. 64, at 291; Dobratz, *Artikel 107 AEUV, supra* n. 131, at paras 74f.; Adrien Giraud & Sylvain Petit, *Bury Them Deep: The Court of Justice Annuls the Autogrill and Banco Santander Judgments of the General Court* 16 EStAL 310, 314 (2017); Ismer & Piotrowski, *Selektivität von Beihilfen, supra* n. 132, at 261f.; Ismer & Piotrowski, *The Selectivity of Tax Measures, supra* n. 77, at 562f.; Ismer & Piotrowski, *Selectivity in Corporate Tax Matters, supra* n. 77, at 159f.; Loewenthal, *supra* n. 136, at 39; Lyal, *supra* n. 131, at 1031f.

139. John Temple Lang, *EU State Aid Rules: The Need for Substantive Reform* 13 EStAL 440, 446 (2014); John Temple Lang, *Autogrill Espana and Banco Santander: The Concept of 'General' Tax Measures Clarified for State Aid* 40 European L. Rev. 763; 764f. (2015); Phedon Nicolaides, *New Limits to the Concept of Selectivity: The Birth of a 'General Exception' to the Prohibition of State Aid in EU Competition Law* 6 JECLAP 315, 322 (2015) https://doi.org/10.1093/jeclap/lpu124; Phedon Nicolaides, *Excessive Widening of the Concept of Selectivity* 16 EStAL 62, 69f. (2016) https://doi.org/10.21552/estal/2017/1/9.

140. Andreas Bartosch, *Is There a Need for a Rule of Reason in European State Aid Law? Or How to Arrive at a Coherent Concept of Material Selectivity?* 47 CMLR 729ff. (2010) https://doi.org/10.54648/cola2010032.

141. Joined Cases C-20 and 21/15 P *World Duty Free Group.*

142. Jacques Derenne, *Commission v. World Duty Free Group a.o.: Selectivity in (Fiscal) State Aid, quo vadis Curia?* 8 JECLAP 311, 313 (2017) https://doi.org/10.1093/jeclap/lpx018; Nicolaides, *Excessive Widening, supra* n. 139, at 69ff.; Kokott, *Steuerrecht, supra* n. 20, at §3 paras 169ff.

distortive or whether it has an effect on trade between Member States.[143] Some have even questioned the distinction between selective and general measures and have pointed to a lack of a clear rationale underlying State aid control.[144] Others have called for a stronger emphasis on the particularities of tax law in the State aid assessment.[145]

There is furthermore little common ground in the scholarly literature on the particular issue of de facto-selectivity as derived from the CJEU's judgment in *Gibraltar*.[146] While it is now often acknowledged that there are two separate forms of selectivity, namely de jure-selectivity on the one hand and de facto-selectivity on the other hand and that the applicable tests diverge,[147] some contributions have been extremely sceptical towards the notion of de facto-selectivity since it disregards the fundamental charging decision of Member States.[148] By contrast, more recently, others have criticized that particularly in light of the judgments on progressive turnover-based taxation, the judgment in *Gibraltar* is now interpreted too narrowly by the CJEU. As a consequence, some highly distortive tax measures could fall entirely through the cracks.[149]

Other contributions have examined the abstract conceptualization of the notion of selectivity. For example, Peters has explored three different narratives, namely a tax

143. Kokott, *Steuerrecht, supra* n. 20, at §3, para. 211; Stefan Trencsik & Jesko Thiede, *Beihilferecht und Entscheidungsspielräume der Verwaltung bei Gesetzesauslegung und Ermessensausübung: Am Beispiel des Steuererlasses für internationale Kunst- und Sportveranstaltungen* 95 StuW 170, 182 (2018). Somewhat similarly: Johanna Hey, *Steuerbefreiung für Sanierungsgewinne und EU-Beihilferecht: Zum Notifizierungsverfahren* 99 FR 453, 457 (2017) has argued that a tax benefit that is open to all undertakings could not have an effect on trade between Member States. Ekkenga & Safaei, *supra* n. 95, at 1997f. agree that a stronger emphasis is warranted, but find that such new approach is unlikely. Critical of a stronger role for economics Buendía Sierra & Smulders, *supra* n. 45.
144. Peters, *Tax Policy Convergence, supra* n. 74.
145. Jaeger, *Fehlstellungen im Verhältnis von Steuer- und Beihilferecht, supra* n. 29.
146. Joined Cases C-106 and 107/09 P *Gibraltar*. On this judgment, e.g., Maarten Aalbers, *Gibraltar: A Rock Solid Interpretation of the Selectivity Criterion* 16 EStAL 495ff. (2017); Ismer & Piotrowski, *The Selectivity of Tax Measures, supra* n. 77, at 566ff.; Ismer & Piotrowski, *Selectivity in Corporate Tax Matters, supra* n. 77, at 163ff.; Michael Lang, *State Aid and Taxation: Recent Trends in the Case Law of the ECJ* 11 EStAL 411, 414ff. (2012) https://doi.org/10.21552/estal/2012/2/281; Luja, *(Re)shaping Fiscal State Aid, supra* n. 98, at 129ff.; Pasquale Pistone, *Smart Tax Competition and the Geographical Boundaries of Taxing Jurisdictions: Countering Selective Advantages Amidst Disparities* 40 Intertax 85ff. (2012) https://doi.org/10.54648/taxi2012009; Conor Quigley, *Direct Taxation and State Aid: Recent Developments Concerning the Notion of Selectivity* 40 Intertax 112, 117ff. (2012) https://doi.org/10.54648/taxi2012012; Pierpaolo Rossi-Maccanico, *Gibraltar: Beyond the Pillars of Hercules of Selectivity* 11 EStAL 443ff. (2012) https://doi.org/10.21552/estal/2012/2/277; Peter Staviczky, *De Facto Selectivity in the Light of the Recent Case Law of the General Court* 14 EStAL 332ff. (2015); Temple Lang, *The Gibraltar State Aid and Taxation Judgment, supra* n. 98.
147. *See* only Ismer & Piotrowski, *Selectivity in Corporate Tax Matters, supra* n. 77; Szudoczky, *Convergence of the Analysis of National Tax Measures, supra* n. 131.
148. Luja, *(Re)shaping Fiscal State Aid, supra* n. 98, at 131; Temple Lang, *The Gibraltar State Aid and Taxation Judgment, supra* n. 98, at 809ff.
149. Maciej Bernatt & Łukasz Grzejdziak, *Selectivity of State Aid and Progressive Turnover Taxes: Leaving the Door (Too) Wide Open? – Commission v. Poland* 59 CMLR 187ff. (2022) https://doi.org/10.54648/cola2022009; Federico Fichera, *Digital Service Taxes under State Aid Scrutiny* 20 EStAL 479, 490 (2021) https://doi.org/10.21552/estal/2021/4/4; Szudoczky & Károlyi, *The CJEU's Approach to the Objectives of Progressive Turnover-Based Taxes, supra* n. 95.

expenditure narrative, a discrimination narrative, and a democracy narrative.[150] In an earlier contribution, we have argued that the notion of selectivity can be interpreted as an obligation to design internally and externally consistent taxes. This is essentially an emanation of a discrimination narrative.[151] Yet as laid out above, this narrative is rooted in the internal market logic of State aid law as limited by fiscal sovereignty.[152] Again others have relied on a competition law narrative.[153] Jaeger has held that the CJEU and the Commission would have applied both a tax expenditure approach and the theory of the exceptional character (*Theorie vom Ausnahmecharakter*) in practice.[154] Mason has also drawn a comparison with the US tax expenditure approach which reveals similar structural problems as the three-step selectivity regarding the identification of the correct benchmark for the analysis. She has therefore proposed that the US law concept of internal consistency that is relied on in the context of the assessment of state income-allocation rules under the dormant Commerce Clause would yield more exact results when adapted to State aid law.[155]

A host of contributions has sought to comprehensively illustrate the issues of State aid law as applied to tax measures.[156] A variety of contributions instead focus on specific questions, such as selectivity in certain types of taxes, such as progressive turnover-based taxes,[157] the newly emerging national digital service taxes,[158] or

150. Peters, *The Legitimacy of EU Fiscal State Aid Control*, *supra* n. 77.
151. Ismer & Piotrowski, *Selectivity in Corporate Tax Matters*, *supra* n. 77.
152. *See* Ch. §1.03 *supra*.
153. Jaeger, *Tax Incentives under State Aid Law*, *supra* n. 101.
154. Jaeger, *Tax Measures*, *supra* n. 73, at para. 6.
155. *See*, *e.g.*, Mason, *Identifying Illegal Subsidies*, *supra* n. 77, at 535ff.
156. Englisch, *Das Beihilfenverbot im Steuerrecht*, *supra* n. 67; Dobratz, *Artikel 107 AEUV*, *supra* n. 131; Jaeger, *Tax Measures*, *supra* n. 73; Schön, *State Aid in the Area of Taxation*, *supra* n. 31.
157. Irene Agnolucci, *Turnover-Based Taxes in EU State Aid Control: The 'Hypothecation Test' and Its Relationship with Free Movement* 19 EStAL 193ff. (2020) https://doi.org/10.2139/ssrn.3660401; Bernatt & Grzejdziak, *supra* n. 149; Daniel Deák, *Cloaking Member State Objectives Through Legislative Instruments* 30 EC Tax Rev. 111ff. (2021) https://doi.org/10.54648/ecta2021013; Stephan Eilers & Stefan Schmitz, *Indirekte Steuern und EU-Beihilfenrecht: Europäische Kommission verbietet (teilweise) den Vollzug der ungarischen Werbesteuer/Krisensteuer* 4 ISR 211ff. (2015); Balázs Károlyi, *Progressive Turnover-Based Taxes and Their Legal Repercussions under EU Law* 29 EC Tax Rev. 271ff. (2020) https://doi.org/10.54648/ecta2020055; Michael Lang, *Taxation and State Aid: Recent Case Law on Progressive Turnover Taxes* 61 European Taxation 516ff. (2021) https://doi.org/10.59403/3e62rye; Ruth Mason, *What the CJEU's Hungarian Cases Mean for Digital Taxes*, TNI 161ff. (2020) https://doi.org/10.2139/ssrn.3550757; Danish Mehboob, *Turnover Taxes Do Not Violate EU State Aid Law, Finds CJEU* 32 Intertax 69f. (2021); Jörg Manfred Mössner, *Umsatzbasierte direkte Steuern* 9 ISR 162ff. (2020); Phedon Nicolaides, *Multi-rate Turnover Taxes and State Aid: A Prelude to Taxes on Company Size?* 18 EStAL 226ff. (2019); Leopoldo Parada, *How the Vodafone Magyarország Opinion Affects EU Debate on Turnover-Based Digital Taxes* TNI 399ff. (2019); Julia Sinnig, *Turnover Taxes under State Aid Spotlight* 59 European Taxation 106ff. (2019) https://doi.org/10.59403/36a9rh3; Dario Stevanato, *Are Turnover-Based Taxes a Suitable Way to Target Business Profits* 59 European Taxation Issue 538ff. (2019) https://doi.org/10.59403/mfvjb1; Rita Szudoczky & Balázs Károlyi, *The Troubled Story of the Hungarian Advertisement Tax: How (Not) to Design a Progressive Turnover Tax* 48 Intertax 46ff. (2020) https://doi.org/10.54648/taxi2020004; Szudoczky & Károlyi, *The CJEU's Approach to the Objectives of Progressive Turnover-Based Taxes*, *supra* n. 95.
158. Maria Carro Pitarch, *Analysis of the (In)compatibility of Digital Services Taxes with State Aid Rules* 31 EC Tax Rev. 326ff. (2022) https://doi.org/10.54648/ecta2022031; Fichera, *supra* n.

'asymmetric' taxes.[159] Englisch has authored an in-depth examination of the particularities in the assessment of the existence of aid in indirect taxes.[160] Again others have examined the interactions of State aid law and domestic anti-abuse provisions[161] or the relationship with double taxation conventions (DTCs).[162] Some authors have examined the State aid compatibility of examples of national tax measures.[163] Several

---

149; Georg Kofler, *The Future of Digital Services Taxes* 30 EC Tax Rev. 50 (2021) https://doi.org/10.54648/ecta2021006; Ruth Mason & Leopoldo Parada, *Digital Battlefront in the Tax Wars*, TNI 1183ff. (2018).

159. Cordewener, *supra* n. 131; Guilherme Galdino, *Special Charges, Free Movement and State Aid* 18 EStAL 510ff. (2019) https://doi.org/10.21552/estal/2019/4/7; Phedon Nicolaides & Antonis Metaxas, *Asymmetric Tax Measures and EU State Aid Law* 13 EStAL 51ff. (2014); Begoña Pérez-Bernabeu, *The Spanish Hydroelectric Tax: Asymmetrical Taxation with Environmental Flavour* 19 EStAL 352ff. (2020) https://doi.org/10.21552/estal/2020/3/12; Wolfgang Schön, *Special Charges: A Gap in European Competition Law* 5 EStAL 494ff. (2006) https://doi.org/10.21552/estal/2006/3/82.

160. Joachim Englisch, *EU State Aid Rules Applied to Indirect Tax Measures* 22 EC Tax Rev. 9ff. (2013) https://doi.org/10.54648/ecta2013002. *See also*: Sebastian Pfeiffer, *Asymmetrically Relying on the EU VAT Directive: Is VAT a Picnic?* 24 Int. VAT Monitor 158ff. (2015) https://doi.org/10.59403/28kmcdd; Joep Swinkels, *State Aid and VAT* 14 Int. VAT Monitor 311ff. (2005); Ben Terra, *Value Added Tax and State Aid Law in the EU* 40 Intertax 101ff. (2012) https://doi.org/10.54648/taxi2012011.

161. Luc De Broe & Mélanie Massant, *The General Court's Judgment in Engie: The Non-Application of a National GAAR Confers State Aid* 31 EC Tax Rev. 6ff. (2022) https://doi.org/10.54648/ecta2022002; Joachim Englisch, *State Aid Prohibition: The New GAAR in Town* 30 EC Tax Rev. 144, 145f. (2021) https://doi.org/10.54648/ecta2021016; Daniël S. Smit, *State Aid and Domestic Anti-tax Avoidance Rules: Who Is in Charge? – A Preliminary Analysis*, in De Pietro (ed.), New Perspectives on Fiscal State Aid, 87ff. (2019); Edoardo Traversa, *State Aid and Taxation: Can an Anti-avoidance Provision be Selective* 13 EStAL 518ff. (2014); Edoardo Traversa & Pierre M. Sabbadini, *Anti-avoidance Measures and State Aid in a Post-BEPS Context: An Attempt at Reconciliation*, in Richelle et al. (eds), State Aid Law and Business Taxation, 85ff. (2016).

162. Luc De Broe, *Can Tax Treaties Confer State Aid?* 26 EC Tax Rev. 228ff. (2017) https://doi.org/10.54648/ecta2017025; Raymond Luja, *Tax Treaties and State Aid: Some Thoughts* 44 European Taxation 234ff. (2004); Rita Szudoczky, *Double Taxation Relief, Transfer Pricing Adjustments and State Aid Law: Comments*, in Richelle et al. (eds), State Aid Law and Business Taxation, 163ff. (2016); Christiana HJI Panayi, *Limitation on Benefits and State Aid* 44 European Taxation 83ff. (2004); Šime Jozipović, *Die Anwendung des EU-Beihilferechts auf das internationale Steuerrecht* (2018).

163. Janina Brandau et al., *Brennpunkt Beihilferecht: Das deutsche Steuerrecht auf dem Prüfstand* 72 BB 1175ff. (2017). *See* in particular on the German Sanierungsklausel Luc De Broe, *The State Aid Selectivity-Test in Corporate Tax Matters: CJEU Applies Common Sense in Its Judgments on the German 'Sanierungs'-Clause, but Do We Have All Pieces of the Puzzle Now?* 27 EC Tax Rev. 285ff. (2018) https://doi.org/10.54648/ecta2018031; Jan de Weerth, *Sanierungsklausel, Sanierungserlass und andere Steuererleichterungen im Fokus des EU-Beihilferechts* 52 DStR, 2485ff. (2014); Tim Hackemann & Sabine Sydow, *Richtungsentscheidung des EuGH in der Rs. C-6/12, P Oy für die Voraussetzungen der Einstufung einer Sanierungsklausel als staatliche Beihilfe; Auswirkungen auf die suspendierte deutsche Sanierungsklausel des §8c Abs. 1a KStG* 22 IStR 786ff. (2013); Felix Klemt, *Richtungsentscheidung für Kompetenzen in Europa: lässt das Beihilferecht die Sanierungsklauseln in §8c Abs. 1a KStG zu?* 51 DStR 1057ff. (2013); Roman Seer, *Insolvenz, Sanierung und Ertragsteuern: verfassungs- und europarechtliche Überlegungen* 96 FR 721ff. (2014). Other contributions have focused on the German *Sanierungserlass*: Roland Ismer & Sophia Piotrowski, *Falsche Begründung: richtiges Ergebnis? – Zur beihilferechtlichen Argumentation im Vorlagebeschluss zum Sanierungserlass* 53 DStR 1993ff. (2015); André Wehner, *Der Sanierungserlass des BMF vom 27.3.2003: Ein Verstoß gegen EU-Beihilferecht?* 15 Neue Zeitschrift für Insolvenz- und Sanierungsrecht 537ff. (2012). On section 3a *Einkommensteuergesetz*: Marc Desens, *Die neue Besteuerung von Sanierungserträgen* 99 FR 981, 982

contributions have addressed the relationship between the criterion of selective advantage and the analysis under the fundamental freedoms.[164] Recently, the implications of the crisis triggered by COVID-19 that has led to enormous amounts of aid being granted have been discussed.[165]

When it comes to the legal consequences of State aid law, there is a vast body of literature that does not focus on the tax-specific aspects but addresses aspects, such as recovery,[166] the role of private actors (i.e., beneficiaries and competitors) in the State aid procedure,[167] and the role of general principles of EU law in recovery[168] without

(2017); Hey, *Steuerbefreiung für Sanierungsgewinne, supra* n. 143; Robert Hinz, *Sanierungserträge: §3a EStG – eine zulässige Beihilfe?* 104 FR 1021ff. (2022); Andreas Möhlenkamp, *Steuerfreie Sanierungsgewinne, EU-Beihilfenverbot und Wettbewerb* 39 ZIP 1907ff. (2018). *See* for a list of provisions of German tax law that could potentially infringe upon EU law, including State aid law: Wolfgang Kessler & Christoph Spengel, *Checkliste potenziell EU-rechtswidriger Normen des deutschen direkten Steuerrechts* 73 Beilage 02 Der Betrieb 1ff. (2020).

164. Frank Engelen, *State Aid and Restrictions on Free Movement: Two Sides of the Same Coin?* 52 European Taxation 204ff. (2012) https://doi.org/10.59403/3mfg5gv; Englisch, *Das Beihilfenverbot im Steuerrecht, supra* n. 67, at paras 9.53ff.; Roland Ismer & Sophia Piotrowski, *Relationship of Fiscal State Aid and the Fundamental Freedoms*, in Panayi et al. (eds), Research Handbook on European Union Taxation Law 450ff. (2020); Juliane Kokott, *Steuerrecht und unionsrechtlicher Beihilfebegriff*, in Lang (ed.), Europäisches Steuerrecht 535, 550ff. (2018); Michael Lang, *Seminar J: Steuerrecht, Grundfreiheiten und Beihilfeverbot* 19 IStR 570ff. (2010); Claire Micheau, *Fundamental Freedoms and State Aid Rules under EU Law: The Example of Taxation* 52 European Taxation 210ff. (2012) https://doi.org/10.59403/5gskyg; Martha O'Brien, *Company Taxation, State Aid and Fundamental Freedoms: Is the Next Step Enhanced Cooperation* 30 European L. Rev. 209ff. (2005); Pierpaolo Rossi-Maccanico, *EU Review of Direct Tax Measures: Interplay Between Fundamental Freedoms and State Aid Control* 22 EC Tax Rev. 19ff. (2013) https://doi.org/10.54648/ecta2013003; Mélanie Staes, *The Combined Application of the Fundamental Freedoms and the EU State Aid Rules: In Search of a Way Out of the Maze* 42 Intertax 106ff. (2014) https://doi.org/10.54648/taxi2014010; Szudoczky, *Convergence of the Analysis of National Tax Measures, supra* n. 131; Peter J. Wattel, *Forum: Interaction of State Aid, Free Movement, Policy Competition and Abuse Control in Direct Tax Matters* 5 WTJ 128ff. (2013) https://doi.org/10.59403/1rxxhrw; Peter J. Wattel, *Comparing Criteria: State Aid, Free Movement, Harmful Tax Competition and Market Distorting Disparities*, in Richelle et al. (eds), State Aid Law and Business Taxation 59ff. (2016).

165. *See* only Raymond Luja, *EU Fiscal State Aid Rules and COVID-19: Will One Survive the Other?* 29 EC Tax Rev. 147ff. (2020) https://doi.org/10.54648/ecta2020043; Carole Maczkovics, *How Flexible Should State Aid Control Be in Times of Crisis?* 19 EStAL 271ff. (2020) https://doi.org/10.21552/estal/2020/3/4.

166. Lucyne Ghazarian, *Recovery of State Aid: The Obligations of Member States, National Courts and National Authorities in State Aid Recovery and Recent Developments in the Case-Law of the Court of Justice of the European Union* 15 EStAL 228ff. (2016) https://doi.org/10.21552/estal/2012/3/309; Hancher, *State Aid Recovery, supra* n. 114.

167. José Luis Buendía Sierra, *The Role of Competitors in State Aid Procedures* 14 EStAL 451f. (2015); Edoardo Gambaro & Francesco Mazzocchi, *Montessori v. Commission: A New Frontier for Competitors of Beneficiaries to Bring Action Against a Commission Decision on Aid Schemes?* 10 JECLAP 91ff. (2019) https://doi.org/10.1093/jeclap/lpz006; Martin Köhler, *Private Enforcement of State Aid Law: Problems of Guaranteeing EU Rights by Means of National (Procedural) Law* 11 EStAL 369ff. (2012) https://doi.org/10.21552/estal/2012/2/279; Pastor-Merchante, *supra* n. 115.

168. Eve Fink, *The Possibility of Protection of Legitimate Expectations in Recovery of Unlawful State Aid* 20 Juridica International 133ff. (2013); Adrien Giraud, *A Study of the Notion of Legitimate Expectations in State Aid Recovery Proceedings: 'Abandon All Hope Ye Who Enter Here'?* 45 CMLR 1399ff. (2008) https://doi.org/10.54648/cola2008096; Krzysztof Jaros & Nicolai Ritter, *Pleading Legitimate Expectations in the Procedure for the Recovery of State Aid* 3 EStAL 573ff. (2004) https://doi.org/10.21552/estal/2004/4/48; Antonio Papi Rossi, *Recovery of Unlawful*

referring to the specificities of fiscal aid schemes. Some contributions, by contrast, analyse tax-specific aspects,[169] with some authors examining the difficulties surrounding the recovery of fiscal aid and in some cases questioning whether in light of this recovery is the appropriate legal consequence for fiscal aid schemes.[170] Some contributions have suggested alternative legal consequences altogether.[171] Again others have examined whether State aid may exceptionally result in a refund of tax instead of recovery.[172] A number of contributions have examined the role of the general principles of EU law either as a case-by-case limit or as a general obstacle to the recovery of fiscal aid.[173] Some authors have addressed different procedural options that would

and Incompatible Aid, in Santa Maria (ed.), Competition and State Aid: An Analysis of EU Practice 141, 155ff. (2nd edn 2015); Marek Rzotkiewicz, *The General Principles of EU Law and Their Role in the Review of State Aid Put into Effect by Member States* 12 EStAL 464, 467ff. (2013) https://doi.org/10.21552/estal/2013/3/365; Cláudia Saavedra Pinto, *The Narrow Meaning of the Legitimate Expectation Principle in State Aid Law Versus the Foreign Investor's Legitimate Expectations* 15 EStAL 270ff. (2016); Eleanor Sharpston, *Legitimate Expectations and Economic Reality* 15 European L. Rev. 103ff. (1990); Eleanor Sharpston, *European Community Law and the Doctrine of Legitimate Expectations: How Legitimate, and for Whom?* 11 Northwestern Journal of International Law and Business 87ff. (1990); Wolfgang Weiß & Markus Haberkamm, *Legitimate Expectations in State Aid and the CFI* 9 EStAL 531 (2010) https://doi.org/10.21552/estal/2010/2/187. In favour of a special case for tax rulings: Pieter Van Cleynenbreugel, *Recovering Unlawful Advantages in the Context of EU State Aid Tax Ruling Investigations* 1 Market and Competition L. Rev. 15 (2017) https://doi.org/10.7559/mclawreview.2017.307.

169. On national perspectives: Marc Fierstra, *Ex-Officio Application of EU State Aid Rules by National Courts*, in De Pietro (ed.), New Perspectives on Fiscal State Aid: Legitimacy and Effectiveness of Fiscal State Aid Control, 117ff. (2019); Julie Leroy, *Recovery of Fiscal State Aid in the Netherlands and the Role of the National Judge*, in De Pietro (ed.), New Perspectives on Fiscal State Aid, 159ff. (2019); Hugo López López, *Recent Developments in Spanish Legislation on State Aid Recovery of a Tax Nature* 14 EStAL 382ff. (2015); Saturnina Moreno González, *Recovery of Tax-Related State Aid in Spain: Current Scenario and Legislative Initiatives for Immediate and Effective Recovery* 14 EStAL 391ff. (2015); Bruno Peeters, *Recovery Procedures and National Issues: The Belgian 'Excess Profit Exemption' Scheme*, in De Pietro (ed.), New Perspectives on Fiscal State Aid, 143ff. (2019).
170. Maarten Aalbers & Paul Adriaanse, *Recovery of Unlawful Aid*, in Hancher et al. (eds), EU State Aids, para. 30-004 (5th edn 2016); Lever, *supra* n. 116; Claire Micheau, *Récupération des aides d'État illegals et incompatibles sous forme fiscale* 50 Revue trimestrielle de droit européen 343, 349ff. (2014); Moreno González, *Recovery of Tax-Related State Aid in Spain*, *supra* n. 169, at 392.
171. Hanno Kube et al., *Tax Policy: Trends in the Allocation of Powers Between the Union and Its Member States* 25 EC Tax Rev. 247ff. (2016) https://doi.org/10.54648/ecta2016027; Alexandre Maitrot de la Motte, *The Recovery of the Illegal Fiscal State Aids: Tax Less to Tax More* 26 EC Tax Rev. 75ff. (2017) https://doi.org/10.54648/ecta2017009.
172. Ismer & Piotrowski, *Relationship of Fiscal State Aid and the Fundamental Freedoms*, *supra* n. 164; Kokott, *Steuerrecht*, *supra* n. 20, at §3 para. 234; Rita Szudoczky, *The Sources of EU Law and Their Relationships: Lessons for the Field of Taxation*, 697ff. (2014).
173. Heribert Anzinger, *Stand und Perspektiven der positiven und negativen Integration des materiellen Steuerrechts in der EU* 6 HFSt 123ff. (2017); Carla De Pietro, *The EU Notion of Legitimate Expectations in the Context of State Aid Law: What Role for National Judges*, in De Pietro (ed.), New Perspectives on Fiscal State Aid: Legitimacy and Effectiveness of Fiscal State Aid Control, 103, 108ff. (2019); Christian Dorenkamp, *Seminar G: EU-Vorschläge zur Besteuerung der Digitalwirtschaft sowie EU-Beihilfenrecht und Verrechnungspreise* 27 IStR 640ff. (2018); Englisch, *Das Beihilfenverbot im Steuerrecht*, *supra* n. 67, at paras 9.69ff.; Hey, *EU-Beihilfen und Steuervergünstigungen*, *supra* n. 119; Rudolf Mellinghoff, *Europäisches Steuerrecht und grenzüberschreitender Rechtsschutz* 6 HFSt 221ff. (2017); Marcel Krumm,

aim to create legal certainty, such as the publication of comfort letters[174] or a right for taxpayers to notify aid to the European Commission.[175]

There have also been quite a few monographs in recent years: Jozipović in his dissertation examined the interactions of State aid law and international taxation.[176] Micheau in her dissertation took a comparative approach and examined fiscal State aid law on the one hand and subsidy law under World Trade Organization (WTO) law on the other hand.[177] Piernas López traced the evolution of the concept of State aid Law under EU law without relying on a tax-specific perspective. Instead, he saw the case law of the fiscal aid cases as a part of the overall body of case law and identified different periods in the case law of the European courts.[178]

Szudoczky in her doctoral thesis addressed the relationship between the different sources of EU law. Relying on a case law approach, she comprehensively addressed the relationship between fundamental freedoms and fiscal State aid law as part of her thesis. She contrasted the material law requirements of the two sets of rules and addressed ways to solve potential overlaps, thereby contributing significantly to the understanding of the dogmatics of fiscal State aid law.[179]

Finally, Ellenrieder in his extensive monograph explored the material selectivity of both fiscal aid schemes and individual aid. He traced the evolution from a rule-exception approach towards a comparison approach in the case law on material selectivity and touched upon a multitude of issues, such as indirect selectivity, the selectivity of complex tax measures, selectivity in international tax law as well as selectivity in procedural law. He particularly explored potential redefinitions of the notions of advantage and selectivity, suggesting what he dubs a 'factor-approach' ('*Faktor-Ansatz*') to assessing selectivity. A measure would be general, and thus not selective, where it serves to distribute the tax burden to different production factors and where it coherently pursues a permissible objective of general economic policy.[180]

Verfahrensrechtliche Aspekte steuerlicher Beihilfen, in Lang (ed.), Europäisches Steuerrecht, 561, 575ff. (2018); Julia Kühn, *Die Rückforderung unionsrechtswidrig gewährter Steuerbeihilfen nach deutschem Recht* 7 ISR 360ff. (2018); Lovdahl Gormsen & Mifsud-Bonnici, *supra* n. 126; Martini, *supra* n. 119; Ruth Mason, *State Aid Special Reports: Part 2: Legitimate Expectations,* TNI 615ff. (2017); Juan Salvador Pastoriza, *The Recovery Obligation and the Protection of Legitimate Expectations: The Spanish Experience,* in Richelle et al. (eds), State Aid Law and Business Taxation, 247ff. (2016); Jens Schönfeld & Benedikt Ellenrieder, *Vertrauensschutz bei steuerlichen Beihilfen* 27 IStR 444ff. (2018).

174. Daniel Reich, *Rechtsfolgen steuerlicher Verstöße gegen das Beihilferecht* 8 HFSt 219ff. (2018); Ulrich Soltész, *EU State Aid Law and Taxation: Where Do We Stand Today* 41 ECLR 18, 25 (2020).
175. Brandau et al., *supra* n. 163, at 1187; Reich, *supra* n. 174, at 239f.; Krumm, *supra* n. 173, at 611.
176. Jozipović, *supra* n. 162.
177. Claire Micheau, *State Aid, Subsidy and Tax Incentives under EU and WTO Law* (2014).
178. Juan Jorge Piernas López, *The Concept of State Aid under EU Law* (2015).
179. Szudoczky, *The Sources of EU Law, supra* n. 172.
180. Ellenrieder, *Die materielle Selektivität steuerlicher Beihilfen, supra* n. 57.

§1.05 AIM OF THIS BOOK AND KEY FINDINGS

Against this background, the present book seeks to further contribute to an overall understanding of the architecture of State aid law as applied to fiscal aid schemes by considering the particularities of taxation both on the level of material State aid law and on the level of the legal consequences of infringements thereof. It aims to understand the current state of play after nearly 25 years of an ever more significant role of fiscal State aid law. Though there are still many uncertainties as to the way forward in fiscal State aid law, the main principles and trends have in our view – at least for now – emerged quite clearly.[181] In this endeavour, we will seek to address the two main (groups of) objections that have frequently been raised against the application of State aid law to abstract-general tax measures, namely: (i) an allegedly overly broad reading of material State aid law; and (ii) the supposedly unjust consequences of infringements of State aid law. We believe that these objections do have some merit, but they can be or have already been convincingly addressed without putting the increased application of State aid law to fiscal aid schemes as such into question.

We rely on a case law approach and find that the objectives of State aid control cannot be pursued in a vacuum; instead, two core concepts are limiting any excessive application of fiscal State aid law, namely first Member States' fiscal sovereignty and second taxpayer rights.

This results in the following key findings: The notion of advantage has stand-alone significance [A]. Tax sovereignty implies different tests for de jure- and de facto-selectivity [B]. Recent case law by the CJEU avoids an overly broad interpretation of selectivity by deriving limits from fiscal sovereignty [C]. Particularities may apply for harmonized and indirect taxes, but uncertainties remain [D]. The different objectives that Member States can pursue in levying taxes have to be distinguished [E]. Contrary to scholarly criticism, recovery is at least in general the appropriate legal consequence of State aid control [F]. The general principles of EU law can only rarely serve as limits to recovery [G]. Rather than through limits to recovery, the protection of taxpayer rights should take the form of procedural rights and in particular a right to notification [H].

[A] Advantage Has Stand-Alone Significance

The notion of advantage has stand-alone significance. State aid control only applies to advantages as opposed to disadvantages. There is a link between the necessary advantage and the identification of the beneficiary of aid. The beneficiary of aid has to be identified on a case-by-case basis for each type of tax and every tax measure at issue. While the taxable person will generally be the beneficiary of aid for direct taxes, this may particularly be problematic for indirect taxes. We develop some criteria to allow for an identification of the beneficiaries of aid.

181. Bartosch, *Spanish Goodwill*, *supra* n. 138, at 70 describes material selectivity as 'the ever-lasting jelly-fish' meaning that the developments would be far from over.

[B] Tax Sovereignty Implies Different Tests for De Jure- and De Facto-Selectivity

We show that two different selectivity tests can be applicable depending on the design of the tax measure in question. Where a tax measure constitutes an exception to the general system, a three-step test is applicable. This test verifies whether there is a derogation from the reference system of taxation and whether this derogation is justified (de jure-selectivity). This test generally takes the entire levy as a point of departure. The reference system of taxation serves as the benchmark for the analysis. There has to be a different treatment of undertakings that are in a legally and factually comparable situation in light of the objective of the levy. The test for prima facie de jure-selectivity amounts to an obligation for Member States to design internally consistent taxes. Beyond that, an obligation not to design manifestly inconsistent taxes exists, even though this will be limited to exceptional circumstances. It becomes relevant where there is no formal derogation, but where the boundaries of the reference system itself are designed in an arbitrary manner. Where this leads to a factual discrimination, the measure may be de facto selective. Since there is no deviation from the benchmark that has been set by the Member State itself, this form of selectivity has to be handled very restrictively. Both selectivity tests in tax matters are by nature discrimination tests.

[C] Restrictive Tendencies in the Case Law and Remaining Uncertainties

We argue that the case law on the notion of selectivity had initially appeared to point towards an overly broad interpretation of selectivity. It had seemed as though each and every distinction in national tax laws could potentially amount to aid. Yet the problem has in the meantime been addressed in what can be understood as a rollback in the case law of the European courts. The case law on turnover-based taxes and the judgment in *Andres* have shown that tax measures will often not be selective since they are considered to form part of the reference system of taxation rather than derogating from it. This means they cannot be de jure selective. This approach shows a high degree of deference to a Member State's fundamental charging decision. Since the notion of de facto-selectivity is handled restrictively, many measures will then fall through the cracks altogether. Moreover, with its judgment in *A-Brauerei,* the CJEU has indicated that it now appears to favour a lenient approach in the third step of the selectivity test, not entering into a stringent analysis of the proportionality of the measure. There are, however, still uncertainties which result in legal uncertainty. First, this pertains to the delimitation of elements that form part of the reference system of taxation and rules that can lead to derogations. Second, it is still not entirely clear what is the exact approach to determining the rule and exception in tax measures with complex structures. Third, the third step of the selectivity test is not yet entirely fleshed out.

[D] The Selectivity Test Requires a Distinction Between Different Types of Taxes

Although State aid law in principle applies regardless of the type of tax and the framework for the State aid analysis is generally the same, particularities of different types of taxes have to be considered. More precisely, some technical distinctions are warranted, namely first between harmonized and non-harmonized taxes, and second between direct and indirect taxes. These distinctions are closely related: While harmonization in the area of direct taxation is limited to but a few instruments, Article 113 TFEU provides for an EU competence 'for the harmonization of legislation concerning turnover taxes, excise duties and other forms of indirect taxation to the extent that such harmonization is necessary to ensure the establishment and the functioning of the internal market'.

The analysis of harmonized (in)direct taxes and non-harmonized taxes may diverge in some key points: The partial harmonization of a tax may impact the definition of the reference system because the decision on what to tax does not solely lie with the Member State levying the tax. Where harmonizing legislation exists, the reference system of taxation will at least partly be defined by such legislation. For partially harmonized taxes, selectivity may be excluded. For (fully) harmonized taxes, there may even be no State measure that could qualify as aid in the first place.

Beyond the aspect of harmonization, indirect taxes may also warrant special attention in the context of the notion of advantage. This is because the underlying assumption is that the taxable person and the tax burden diverge. The tax is thus fully or partly passed on to the consumer. This gives rise to problems in assessing the advantage.

[E] Importance of Objectives of the Tax

Moreover, the objectives that Member States can pursue in levying taxes have to be differentiated. Schön distinguishes fiscal taxes on the one hand and taxes with a primarily regulatory goal on the other hand. In the former case, the benchmark is set by the ability to pay principle in combination with the legislator's choice of a suitable indicator for the ability to pay. In the latter case, the benchmark for the selectivity analysis would be defined by the achievement of this regulatory goal.[182] We argue that the latter category should be defined more broadly since the special purpose of a tax cannot only refer to regulatory taxes. In line with the terminology relied upon by the Commission, we therefore distinguish levies that have some sort of special purpose - be it behavioural steering or the remuneration of certain public services through parafiscal levies - and others that do not have such purpose and merely serve to raise funds for the public budget.

In practice, a further distinction between broad- and narrow-based levies has to be made for fiscal levies. Examples of the former are income taxes or Value Added Tax

182. Schön, *Tax Legislation and the Notion of Fiscal Aid*, *supra* n. 40, at 11.

(VAT). The latter are levies that merely serve to levy funds but have a significantly narrower base.

We thus distinguish three categories of levies, namely first broad-based (fiscal) levies, second special purpose levies, and third narrow-based fiscal levies. For broad-based taxes, the starting point of the analysis is fairly straightforward. Since all actors or relevant economic processes are comparable, the reference system of taxation is the levy itself. For fiscal taxes with a narrower base, the case is less clear as the choice of the relevant economic process itself could theoretically be put into question. Yet the scope of such levies could very well fall through the cracks. The approach to assessing selectivity for special purpose levies in principle does not significantly differ from other tax measures. Yet there are some particularities that boil down to the question of what the exact objectives of such a tax are, how they can be identified and monitored, and how they have to be translated into taxes, so as not to run the risk of constituting State aid. We will elaborate on the underlying principles drawing on the example of fiscal taxes and point out relevant differences regarding special purpose levies separately.

[F] Recovery as the Appropriate Legal Consequence of State Aid Law

Many scholarly articles have raised concerns as to the enforcement of State aid law. The main reproach is an alleged infringement of the principle of protection of legitimate expectation where aid is recovered from the beneficiaries of aid for ten years. We argue that no general modification of the legal consequence of recovery is warranted. The competition law logic primarily requires recovery rather than sanctions against the Member State – even though this can be considered an additional legal consequence.

There may be special constellations where the infringement of State aid law can be addressed both by recovery and by a retroactive abolishment of the tax in question. This can be the case both when the Commission orders recovery and when State aid law is enforced by a national court. We point out the pivotal role of Article 108(3), (3) TFEU, which is the deciding factor on how infringements of State aid law can be remedied on the level of the Member States. The provision also allows for private enforcement of State aid law by competitors, where this would not lead to a widening of the recourse to unnotified aid measures.

[G] General Principles of EU Law Can Only Rarely Serve to Exclude Recovery

The principle of protection of legitimate expectation can regularly not serve to exclude recovery. Under EU law, it is generally only applicable where expectations are caused by an EU institution. EU law does not work with an abstract understanding of the principle of protection of legitimate expectation in the sense that the legitimate expectation in the continuity of laws would be protected. The principle will hardly ever come into play due to its link to the requirement of notification. The principle of legal certainty could in rare cases serve to exclude recovery, where an interpretation of the State aid provision by the European courts was not foreseeable for taxpayers. However, as the principle is also linked to the obligation to notify aid, this could not be the case where there is simply a situation of legal uncertainty and the aid could simply have been notified. There is no room for a tax-specific approach for either of these principles.

[H] Stronger Procedural Rights Are Required

In light of the narrow reading of the principle of protection of legitimate expectation, the link with the notification requirement and remaining uncertainties in fiscal State aid law, there is a significant structural weakness, namely the fact that taxpayers are currently not in a position to notify aid. At the same time, they cannot necessarily escape an advantageous tax treatment that could later on be rescinded through recovery. There should be an enforceable right to have potential aid measures notified to the Commission. Moreover, comfort letters and pre-notification letters should be published.

§1.06 OUTLINE

This book is structured in two parts. Part I will deal with the existence of aid under Article 107(1) TFEU, and in particular the third criterion of Article 107(1) TFEU, i.e., the notion of 'selective advantage'. We start by examining the limited impact of the notion of advantage (Chapter 2), before we analyse the concepts of de jure- and de facto-selectivity respectively, with a focus on de jure-selectivity (Chapter 3 and Chapter 4).

In Part II, we will address the legal consequences of an infringement of State aid law. We will first elaborate on the legal consequence of recovery and potential modifications thereto (Chapter 5). We will then focus on the role of the general principles of EU law as case-by-case limits to State aid enforcement (Chapter 6). Finally, we will address the structural problem that taxpayers are not in a position to notify aid to the Commission, so as to achieve legal certainty (Chapter 7).

Our analysis ends with a Conclusion and an Outlook (Chapter 8).

PART I

The Criterion of 'Selective Advantage'

This Part deals with what is currently the only relevant criterion of fiscal State aid under Article 107(1) TFEU – the selective advantage. The two aspects – advantage and selectivity – will be distinguished, even though they are admittedly not always clearly separated in the case law. Nevertheless, the notion of advantage is not superfluous and has – limited – stand-alone significance.

The State aid provision only covers positive derogations from the reference system of taxation. Thus, where a tax measure amounts to a special disadvantage, there can be no State aid. Furthermore, the notion of advantage is connected with the identification of the beneficiaries of aid, which is particularly problematic for indirect taxes. The beneficiary of aid will generally be the taxable person despite the legal assumption that indirect taxes are borne by the consumer. Yet in some constellations, namely where the tax contains an inherent pass-on mechanism, the consumer may be the actor that actually benefits from a tax advantage, which would often rule out the existence of aid. Additionally, indirect advantages can arise (Chapter 2).

Nevertheless, it will become apparent that the existence of an advantage is not at the core of the analysis. Instead, the focus has to lie on the selectivity of such advantage, which underlines the fact that the European courts interpret the State aid provision as a non-discrimination provision. Within the notion of selectivity, the terminology that the Commission relies upon in its Notice on the notion of State aid will be applied. Thus, a distinction has to be made between material selectivity on the one hand and regional selectivity on the other hand. The former refers to distinctions by aspects such as size or sector.[183] Regional selectivity by contrast means that the selectivity results from the geographical scope of a measure.[184] Regional measures can escape the classification as selective where the criteria laid down in the CJEU's

183. Commission Notice on the notion of State aid, *supra* n. 26, at paras 120ff.
184. *Ibid.*, paras 142ff.

judgment in *Portugal v. Commission* are met.[185] The assessment is then restricted to the tax treatment within the relevant area.[186]

Within the notion of material selectivity, one can further distinguish between de jure-selectivity and de facto-selectivity.[187] The Commission describes the distinction as follows:

> *De jure selectivity* results directly from the legal criteria for granting a measure that is formally reserved for certain undertakings only (for instance: those having a certain size, active in certain sectors or having a certain legal form; companies incorporated or newly listed on a regulated market during a particular period; companies belonging to a group having certain characteristics or entrusted with certain functions within a group; ailing companies; or export undertakings or undertakings performing export-related activities). *De facto selectivity* can be established in cases where, although the formal criteria for the application of the measure are formulated in general and objective terms, the structure of the measure is such that its effects significantly favour a particular group of undertakings (as in the examples in the preceding sentence).[188]

A measure is thus de jure selective where it constitutes a formal exception from the normal tax treatment. To identify this form of selectivity, the CJEU relies on a three-step test, which seeks to ascertain whether a measure derogates from the reference system of taxation and whether this derogation is justifiable. By contrast, a measure may be de facto selective where it is formally applicable to every undertaking, but where the result is nevertheless a factual advantage in favour of a particular (group of) undertaking(s). The test for de jure-selectivity is more significant since it respects Member States' tax sovereignty by taking their own fundamental charging decision as a point of departure. Our focus will thus lie on the decidedly more relevant notion of de jure-selectivity.

For the notion of de jure-selectivity, we will first provide a brief overview of the development of the case law of the CJEU on the three-step test for selectivity, before addressing each of the three steps of the selectivity test, namely the reference system of taxation, the derogation from the reference system, and the possibility of justifications of derogations (Chapter 3).

Finally, we examine the second form of selectivity. De facto-selectivity applies where there is no formal derogation from the reference system but where the boundaries of a levy are designed in an arbitrary manner. The potential significance of de facto-selectivity is limited, as has become apparent from the case law on progressive turnover-based taxes (Chapter 4).

---

185. Case C-88/03 *Portugal v. Commission*.
186. Yet the mere fact that regional selectivity is excluded does not mean the measure can escape from State aid scrutiny altogether. Within the relevant geographical area, there may still be a materially selective treatment of certain actors.
187. *See* Commission Notice on the notion of State aid, *supra* n. 26, at paras 121ff.
188. *Ibid*., at paras 121f.; emphasis added by the author.

CHAPTER 2

The Notion of Advantage

While this does not always emerge clearly from the case law, the notion of advantage has stand-alone significance. State aid law only ever covers an advantageous treatment. This means that the benchmark, i.e., the normal case, has to be taxation as opposed to non-taxation. State aid law can only apply where there is a positive derogation from the reference system. The notion of advantage is also closely related to the identification of the beneficiary of aid. Neither the distinction between direct and indirect taxes nor the actual economic incidence are appropriate indicators to identify the beneficiary of aid. Instead, the beneficiary has to be determined case-by-case not only for each type of tax but also for each tax measure. For direct taxes, this is mostly straightforward since the beneficiary of aid will generally be the taxable person. By contrast, the case law shows that several factors have to be relied on for indirect taxes. These include the question of legislative intent, whether there is a tax-inherent mechanism to pass on the tax or the method of granting the advantage (i.e., automatic or through a rebate). The beneficiary of aid will generally be the final consumer for VAT. Therefore, State aid can generally only exist if the principle of neutrality is infringed upon or if the mechanism of passing on the tax is hindered for whatever reason. Beyond this, additional indirect advantages may be relevant. However, unless they can be easily identified and quantified, they will most likely fall through the cracks of State aid control. By contrast, mere secondary effects that would require an in-depth economic analysis, such as windfall effects from an increased level of demand, cannot be subject to State aid control.

The existence of an advantage under Article 107(1) TFEU is closely related to the obligation of recovery. To determine the amount to be recovered, the advantage has to be quantified. For fiscal aid measures, this requires a benchmark. The advantage is determined by comparing the situation with and without the state measure in question[189] but treating all other circumstances as a given.

The advantage is often not clearly separated from the selectivity test. Yet we will show in the following that while the two concepts are logically intertwined to a certain extent, the advantage is not superfluous.[190] In particular, the notions of advantage and disadvantage (or more specifically discrimination) are not necessarily congruent. State aid law is an instrument of privilege control. This implies that State aid law can only remedy unequal treatment where the reference scenario is taxation – rather than non-taxation. The concept of negative aid as proposed by Schön[191] would be based on an analogy (§2.01).

Moreover, the notion of advantage is closely related to the identification of the beneficiary of aid. The advantage accrues to the beneficiary of aid and has to be recovered from them. Complex questions arise in particular for indirect taxes. The findings on real tax incidence are inconclusive and cannot be relied upon. Ultimately, the identification of the beneficiary of aid in indirect tax cases requires consideration of a number of factors. Additionally, indirect advantages can arise that – if hard to quantify – may be relevant from a State aid law perspective. Mere secondary effects, however, do not amount to State aid (§2.02).

§2.01 STATE AID LAW ONLY APPLICABLE TO ADVANTAGES: NOT DISADVANTAGES

State aid law is an instrument of privilege control. Rather than examining whether some undertakings are treated *worse* than others, State aid law asks the question of whether some undertakings are treated *better* than others. At first glance, this may appear to be a somewhat superfluous distinction, because the two dimensions could be regarded as two sides of the same coin. Yet such a view would disregard the stand-alone significance of the necessary advantage. It does not solely serve as the starting point for the correction of an infringement of State aid law (i.e., recovery from the beneficiaries rather than reimbursement to the actors that had been discriminated against). The notions of discrimination and selective advantage are not necessarily congruent. An advantage is only present, where the normal case is taxation and the beneficiary is not taxed at the appropriate level. While this issue is closely related to the three-step selectivity test, there is nevertheless merit in examining the problem separately.

189. Loewenthal, *supra* n. 136, at 34.
190. Similarly: Buriak & Lazarov, *supra* n. 127, at 8; Kyriazis, *From Soft Law to Soft Law to Hard Law: The Commission's Approach to the State Aid Assessment of Tax Rulings, supra* n. 96, at 432; López López, *General Thought on Selectivity, supra* n. 62, at 808; Luts, *supra* n. 127, at 269f.; Piernas López, *Revisiting Some Fundamentals, supra* n. 127, at 277; Schön, *Tax Legislation and the Notion of Fiscal Aid, supra* n. 40, at 8. A different view is held by Jaeger, *Tax Measures, supra* n. 73, at para. 75 (no comprehensive advantage test would be performed for tax measures). Prek & Lefèvre, *supra* n. 127, at 337 hold that the two notions are closely related in practice.
191. *See* Schön, *Special Charges, supra* n. 159.

The fact that the State aid provision requires an exact delimitation of advantages and disadvantages became particularly apparent in the CJEU's judgment in *GIL Insurance*.[192] The case concerned a tax on the receipt of insurance premiums by an insurer or taxable insurance intermediary (IPT) in the United Kingdom. With the Finance Act 1997, the standard rate of the IPT was increased to 4%. A second rate of 17.5% was introduced. This latter rate - which was equal to the then standard rate of VAT in the United Kingdom - only applied to insurance premiums relating to domestic appliances (where they were not sold through insurance brokers or directly by insurance companies), motor cars and travel insurance sold through travel agents.[193] The objective underlying the introduction of the higher rate of IPT was to counteract tax arbitrage: There had been a trend of replacing service contracts for repair and maintenance with insurance contracts ancillary to the respective contract of sale or rental to benefit from the VAT exemption for insurance transactions. The introduction of the higher rate of IPT indeed resulted in suppliers relying on service contracts rather than insurance contracts.[194]

In its judgment, the CJEU examined whether the IPT constituted State aid. Regarding the verification of whether the levy contained an advantage, it stated the following:

> In the present case, *even on the assumption* that the *introduction of the higher rate involves an advantage* for operators offering contracts subject to the standard rate, it must be examined whether the application of the higher rate of IPT to a specific part of the insurance contracts previously subject to the standard rate is justified by the nature and the general scheme of the system of which that tax forms part. [...] That rate was introduced to counteract the practice of taking advantage of the difference between the standard rate of IPT and that of VAT by manipulating the prices of rental or sale of appliances and of the associated insurance. Such conduct had given rise to a loss of income in terms of VAT receipts and to shifts in the conditions of competition in the domestic appliance sector. As the Advocate General suggests in point 84 of his Opinion, in view of its purpose and effect, *the higher rate of IPT has the appearance of a regulatory charge intended specifically as a deterrent to the conclusion of connected insurance contracts. The introduction of a higher rate of IPT on certain contracts was not intended to confer an advantage on all operators who offer contracts of insurance subject to the standard rate of IPT, in application of the general system of taxation of insurance.* It should be observed that standard rate IPT *does not constitute a derogation from the general system of taxation of insurance* in the United Kingdom. It is not a tax scheme favouring a specified sector, since it is a system of taxation of insurance premiums intended to compensate for the fact that insurance transactions are not subject to VAT.[195]

The implications of this passage are not entirely clear. The CJEU does not make a definite call on whether the measure constitutes an advantage. Nevertheless, it later relies on the lack of an advantage to reject the assumption that there is a derogation. At the same time, the CJEU seems to anchor its argument on the level of justification.

192. Case C-308/01 *GIL Insurance and others* EU:C:2004:252.
193. For a description of the facts of the case, *see ibid.*, paras 6ff.
194. *Ibid.*, para. 17.
195. *Ibid.*, paras 73-76; emphasis added by the author.

Regardless of the exact interpretation, the CJEU appears to view the higher rate of IPT as a stand-alone measure, which would not have to be assessed in relation to the standard rate of IPT. In this, the CJEU refers to the legislative purpose that the higher rate was meant to serve as a deterrent.

The CJEU's stance would then either seem to imply that there is a special disadvantage as such or as compared to the standard rate of IPT. In any case, the CJEU indeed makes a distinction between a special advantage - which may lead to the existence of State aid - on the one hand, and special disadvantages on the other hand, which may not, denying the existence of an advantage in the case at hand. Regardless of the question of how the CJEU defines the reference system of taxation, it thus clarifies that only positive derogations from the reference system can qualify as State aid. The question of whether there is an advantage has to be answered from a normative point of view: Considering the objective of the tax, should a specific situation be taxed or not? In other words, it is necessary to ascertain whether taxation or non-taxation is the normal case. We will deal with this latter aspect in the context of the identification of the reference system of taxation.[196]

The notion that it is always necessary to identify an advantageous treatment is sometimes challenged in the scholarly literature. Schön describes the existence of what he dubs 'negative State aid'. He thereby does not question that Article 107(1) TFEU explicitly requires an advantage. Instead, he refers to specifically burdensome tax rules that could amount to State aid by analogy.[197] Schön argues that for taxes that affect a range of events or situations a special burden may amount to aid, citing the hypothetical example of a disadvantageously high corporate tax rate for operators of nuclear power plants, which would not fall within the ambit of the State aid provision as it stands. The legal consequence of the existence of such negative aid, according to Schön, should not be recovery from the undertakings engaged in the production of non-nuclear energy. Instead, the special burden as such would require justification. Otherwise, disadvantaged undertakings could be granted a restitution claim.[198]

Schön bases his analogy partly on the legislative history - Article 4 lit. c ECSC covered both subsidies or aids and special charges. He further argues that special charges are the logical counterpiece of aid and can cause similar distortions.[199] These distortions could not be tackled through reliance on other Treaty provisions.[200] He furthermore cites the judgments of the CJEU in *GIL Insurance* and *AEM SpA*[201] as an indication that the CJEU itself diverges from the requirement of identifying an advantageous treatment.[202] As one of the objectives of the treaties is ensuring

196. *See* on this in detail Ch. §3.02[B], [1] & [2] *infra*.
197. Schön, *Tax Legislation and the Notion of Fiscal Aid*, *supra* n. 40, at 14. *See* on this also Galdino, *supra* n. 159, at 511ff.
198. Schön, *Tax Legislation and the Notion of Fiscal Aid*, *supra* n. 40, at 14f.
199. Schön, *Special Charges*, *supra* n. 159, at 497.
200. *Ibid.*, at 502 with reference to what are now Arts 30, 116f., 110 TFEU as well as the fundamental freedoms.
201. Joined Cases C-128 and 129/03 *AEM SpA* EU:C:2005:224.
202. Schön, *Special Charges*, *supra* n. 159, at 502. Galdino, *supra* n. 159, at 512 cites the judgments in *Ferring* and *Laboratoires Boiron* as an implicit acknowledgement of negative State aid.

undistorted competition,[203] he consequently proposes an analogy to the State aid provision to deal with such measures, all the while cautioning that Article 5(1) Treaty on European Union (TEU) requires a narrow interpretation of EU competences.[204]

A detailed analysis of the proposal goes beyond the scope of our book. The principles of legality and protection of legitimate expectation do not appear to pose a major problem, since the proposed legal consequences are beneficial for the taxpayers concerned. From a tax sovereignty perspective, an extension of the State aid provision by analogy nevertheless fails to convince. An analogy on the level of European law appears more problematic than in a domestic law context due to the supranational dimension and the principle of conferral. Moreover, the historical argument could also very well be seen as an indication that the legislator specifically sought to exclude special disadvantages from the scope of the State aid provision.

§2.02 IDENTIFICATION OF THE BENEFICIARY OF AID

The notion of advantage is inextricably linked with the question of who is the beneficiary of aid. The beneficiary is the person to whom the advantage accrues and whom the aid has to be recovered from. Article 107(1) TFEU specifies that the beneficiary of aid can only be an undertaking. The notion of undertaking under European State aid law is not specific to tax matters. According to long-standing case law of the CJEU, an undertaking in the context of competition law refers to any entity engaged in an economic activity, regardless of its legal status and the way in which it is financed.[205] This definition also applies to State aid law as one area of competition law.[206] Where tax measures result in a tax advantage for individuals that do not fall within the ambit of this definition, there can be no State aid. A tax advantage for individuals which simultaneously amounts to an indirect advantage for undertakings, however, may constitute State aid.[207]

The identification of the beneficiary of aid may raise particular issues in taxation, since the taxable person and the person bearing the tax burden may not always be identical.[208] For example, the identification of the beneficiaries of aid becomes problematic where entities are fiscally transparent. In this case, the advantage may accrue to the shareholders of the transparent entity.[209]

However, these cases concern parafiscal levies and thus should be understood as special purpose levies, *see* Chs §3.03[C] and §5.02[C] *infra*.

203. Schön, *Special Charges, supra* n. 159, at 503 with reference to Art. 3(1)(g) EC Treaty.
204. *Ibid.*, at 502f.
205. Case C-180 to 184/98 *Pavlov and Others* EU:C:2000:428, para. 74 with further references; Commission Notice on the notion of State aid, *supra* n. 26, at para. 7.
206. Case C-222/04 *Cassa di Risparmio di Firenze and others*, paras 107f.
207. *See* Ch. §2.02[C] *infra* and Commission Notice on the notion of State aid, *supra* n. 26, at paras 115f.
208. Ellenrieder, *Die materielle Selektivität steuerlicher Beihilfen, supra* n. 57, at 587ff. presents a sophisticated proposal relying on his 'factor-approach' which treats system immanence as an integral part of the notion of advantage.
209. *See* on this Joined Cases C-649, 658 and 662/20 P *Spain and Others v. Commission* EU:C:2023:60, para. 118, albeit in the context of an infringement of the obligation to state reasons.

In the following, we will approach the problem by taking different types of taxes as a point of departure. A distinction is commonly made between indirect and direct taxes. Yet relying on presumptions underlying the respective types of taxes fails to convince. Neither can the actual incidence of a tax be referred to [A]. Instead, the beneficiary of aid should be determined based on several criteria that can create rebuttable legal presumptions: These include the question of whether the aid is granted automatically or upon application by the final consumer; the existence of an obligation to pass on the tax as opposed to such pass on depending on the subsequent choices of the taxable person; the targeting or intent of an aid measure; or the determination of whether the tax is reflected in the price the consumer pays in its entirety. For VAT, there is a mechanism to pass on the tax that is inherent to the tax. Consequently, there is a presumption that the consumer bears the tax. For State aid law purposes, this presumption breaks down if there is an infringement of the principle of neutrality or where the pass-on mechanism is otherwise hindered [B]. Indirect secondary effects, such as an increase in demand or output due to the granting of State aid, should be irrelevant. (Additional) indirect advantages, by contrast, may accrue to other actors, such as shareholders that are undertakings or to the final consumer where they are an undertaking [C].

[A] Actual Economic and Legally Presumed Incidence Not Decisive

The most intuitive approach to identifying the beneficiary of aid would at first glance be to resort to the incidence of a given tax. One could then refer to studies on the economic incidence of taxes to identify the beneficiary of aid.[210] This would at least be under the assumption that tax measures that reduce the tax burden of a taxpayer are directly passed on to the economic actor that bears the burden of the tax in question.

Ultimately, this fails to convince. First, while there is extensive research on the economic incidence of taxes, the results on, for example, the incidence of corporate tax are somewhat inconclusive.[211] Many studies, moreover, focus on the overall incidence of a tax, not on isolated changes in tax measures within the framework of a tax. Second, one has to keep in mind that State aid control prescribes an *ex ante* monitoring mechanism for any aid a Member State seeks to introduce. Studying the actual

---

210. *See* Don Fullerton & Gilbert E. Metcalf, *Tax Incidence*, in Auerbach & Feldstein (eds), Handbook of Public Economics, vol. 4, 1788ff. (2002) on the study of tax incidence from an economic point of view in general.

211. *See* for corporate tax, e.g.,: Alan J. Auerbach, *Who Bears the Corporate Tax? A Review of What We Know*, in Poterba (ed.), Tax Policy and the Economy, 1ff. (2006) for an overview; Kimberly A. Clausing, *Who Pays the Corporate Tax in a Global Economy* 66 NTJ 151ff. (2013) https://doi.org/10.17310/ntj.2013.1.06; Martin Feldstein, *Incidence of a Capital Income Tax in a Growing Economy with Variable Saving Rates* 41 Review of Economic Studies 505ff. (1974) https://doi.org/10.2307/2296700; Arnold C. Harberger, *The Incidence of the Corporation Income Tax* 70 Journal of Political Economy 215ff. (1962) https://doi.org/10.1086/258636; Kevin A. Hassett & Aparna Mathur, *A Spatial Model of Corporate Tax Incidence* 47 Applied Economics 1350ff. (2015) https://doi.org/10.1080/00036846.2014.995367; Li Liu & Rosanne Altshuler, *Measuring the Burden of the Corporate Income Tax under Imperfect Competition* 66 NTJ 215ff. (2013) https://doi.org/10.17310/ntj.2013.1.08.

economic effects of a tax measure that may amount to an aid scheme from an *ex ante* perspective would be close to impossible. This particularly holds true for new types of special purpose levies, for which no empirical evidence on tax incidence exists. Just as in other areas of competition law, it will thus be necessary to rely on certain assumptions and simplifications.

An approach relying on the true economic incidence of tax benefits is also unconvincing from a normative point of view. It is incompatible with the very wording of the State aid provision according to which an advantage in the sense of Article 107 TFEU can only accrue to undertakings. Moreover, it has to be seen that while the State aid provision is located in the chapter on competition law and is therefore concerned with the threat of distortions of competition, Article 107(1) TFEU as applied to fiscal aid measures is now often justified relying on a discrimination narrative.[212] The principle of equality is primarily concerned with distinctions between taxpayers, i.e., the immediate effect of a certain tax treatment. At best, the fact that the economic incidence of taxes does not play a role in fiscal State aid control points towards a structural deficit in a State aid provision that is in practice understood as a non-discrimination provision. Perhaps there may therefore indeed be a case for a stronger focus on the criteria of an effect on trade between Member States and distortion of competition to determine whether aid is truly distortive.

An alternative, equally intuitive approach to identifying the beneficiary of aid could be to refer to the legal presumption as to who bears the burden of a given tax. A distinction is commonly made between direct and indirect taxes. There is a general legal presumption that indirect taxes are passed on from the taxable person, while no such mechanism exists for direct taxes.[213] Transferring this finding to fiscal State aid law, one may argue that the beneficiary of aid for direct taxes would generally be the taxable person. By contrast, for indirect taxes, the taxable persons, who only collect and remit the tax due, could not be considered the beneficiary of State aid, unless they derive some kind of additional indirect benefit from the aid. In all other cases, any advantageous tax measure would not benefit them, but the final consumer. All this implies that there could often be no State aid in the area of indirect taxation unless the final consumer qualifies as an undertaking.

However, the distinction between indirect and direct taxes described above is now commonly questioned. Atkinson early on argued that the only difference between direct and indirect taxation is that direct taxes can be adjusted for the personal characteristics of the taxpayer.[214] The distinction between indirect and direct taxes has recently become ever blurrier as States increasingly rely on hybrid taxes, which cannot clearly be classified as indirect or direct taxes.[215] Legal presumptions along the

212. *See* Ch. §1.03 *supra*.
213. Joachim Englisch, *Umsatzsteuer*, in Tipke & Lang (eds), Steuerrecht, para. 17.12 (24th edn 2020).
214. *See* Anthony B. Atkinson, *Optimal Taxation and the Direct versus Indirect Tax Controversy* 4 Canadian Journal of Economics 590, 592 (1977) https://doi.org/10.2307/134292.
215. *See* on this Roland Ismer & Christoph Jescheck, *Taxes on Digital Services and the Substantive Scope of Application of Tax Treaties: Pushing the Boundaries of Article 2 of the OECD Model?* 46 Intertax 573ff. (2018) https://doi.org/10.54648/taxi2018059 with further references.

vanishing demarcation line between direct and indirect taxes would then appear not to be convincing. In any case, even if one only took the traditional distinction into account, the legal presumption is not necessarily indicative of who the beneficiary of aid is. The example of VAT shows that the legal presumption of who bears an indirect tax can at best be the point of departure for the identification of the beneficiary of aid because many constellations are conceivable where the mechanism of passing on the tax does not work.[216]

[B] Criteria for Identifying the Beneficiary of Aid for Indirect Taxes

Given that neither the presumptions underlying the distinction between indirect and direct taxes, nor the actual incidence of such taxes can therefore be relied on to identify the beneficiary of aid, additional criteria have to be found in the case law. The judgments in *Adria-Wien Pipeline*[217] on the one hand and *Aer Lingus and Ryanair*[218] on the other hand at first glance appear to be contradictory [1]. However, a number of different criteria to identify the beneficiary of aid can be derived from contrasting these two judgments. Such criteria ultimately help to determine whether the taxable person merely serves as an intermediary that collects and remits the tax due or whether they can profit from the tax measure themselves [2] For VAT, there is the assumption of a tax inherent pass on, unless the principle of neutrality is infringed upon [3].

[1] Seemingly Contradictory Case Law

The irrelevance of the normative incidence of the tax for State aid purposes appears to be reflected in the case law of the CJEU. The question of the passing on of tax advantages to the final consumer in the area of indirect taxation arose in the CJEU's judgment in *Aer Lingus and Ryanair*.[219] The case dealt with two different tax rates of the Irish Air Travel Tax (ATT).[220] For shorter flights (for flights to an airport located no more than 300 km from Dublin airport), the tax due was EUR 2 per passenger, whereas for longer flights, the tax due was EUR 10 per passenger. The Commission found that this rate structure amounted to State aid for the operators of shorter flights, which was then contested in front of the European courts.[221]

Aer Lingus had argued that at least part of the advantage had been passed on to the passengers.[222] The issue underlying this argument relates to the identification of the beneficiary of aid. The General Court in its judgment held that the ATT as an excise duty is 'by definition, an indirect tax levied on the consumption of a particular good or service, by contrast with direct taxes such as taxes on income or on profits, which are

216. *See* Ch. §2.02[B], [3] *infra*.
217. Case C-143/99 *Adria-Wien Pipeline*.
218. Joined Cases C-164 and 165/15 P *Commission v. Aer Lingus and Ryanair* EU:C:2016:990.
219. Joined Cases C-164 and 165/15 P *Aer Lingus and Ryanair*.
220. *See* furthermore on this case Ch. §3.02[B], [2] *infra*.
221. Joined Cases C-164 and 165/15 P *Aer Lingus and Ryanair*, paras 8ff. for the facts of the case.
222. Case T-473/12 *Aer Lingus v. Commission* EU:T:2015:78, paras 78ff.

paid directly by the undertakings'[223] It noted that the ATT was formally intended to be passed on through the price of the flight ticket as the tax had to be indicated separately in the price of each ticket sold.[224] Yet from an economic perspective, this would not necessarily be the case. It would therefore be necessary to determine the extent of economic passing on, i.e., 'to what extent the airline bore the economic cost of the ATT by possibly adjusting the ticket price exclusive of the ATT according to the rate of the ATT actually applicable, or, in the case of application of the ATT at the reduced rate of EUR 2, to what extent they actually retained the economic advantage arising from the application of that lower rate'.[225]

It cited the Commission in stating that the choice of whether the tax should be passed on was for the airline to make since there was no formal mechanism that ensured that the tax was passed on.[226] It held that the economic advantage arising from the application of the reduced tax rate did not necessarily have to amount to the difference between the two rates as it could at least have been passed on to the passengers of the airline. This would only be the case if the airline had systematically increased the price of the tickets that were subject to the lower rate of ATT.[227] It held that this was unlikely in light of the competitive constraints of the market in question.[228]

As a result, it contended that 'although the advantage resulting from the application of a lower rate could consist in the improvement of the competitive position of airlines, because they could offer more competitive prices, the Commission should have merely ordered the recovery of the amounts actually corresponding to that advantage or, if it proved impossible to determine those amounts accurately in the decision, to confer that task to the national authorities and provide the necessary information in that respect [...]'.[229]

Upon appeal, however, the CJEU rejected the reasoning of the General Court. It held that the advantage for the airlines did not consist in the opportunity for airlines subject to the lower rate to offer more competitive prices to their customers. Instead, it merely amounted to paying a lower rate of ATT. Any further potential benefits (e.g., being able to offer more competitive prices or increasing ticket prices by the difference between the two rates) that the airline then derives from this advantage would be irrelevant to the assessment of the amount to be recovered.[230] It was also irrelevant that the airlines could not recover the advantage from their customers where they had passed it on. In the view of the CJEU, the normative or presumed incidence of the tax as an excise duty was thus entirely irrelevant. This would even hold true if the airline

223. *Ibid.*, para. 89.
224. *Ibid.*, para. 90.
225. *Ibid.*, para. 91.
226. *Ibid.*, para. 94.
227. *Ibid.*, paras 97ff.
228. *Ibid.*, para. 102.
229. *Ibid.*, para. 105.
230. Joined Cases C-164 and 165/15 P *Aer Lingus and Ryanair*, paras 102, 104.

itself did not derive any benefit from this advantage, passing it on entirely to the customers.[231]

The CJEU thus distinguishes between the advantages inherent to a tax measure on the one hand and the additional benefits derived therefrom on the other hand. The normative incidence only plays a role in the second aspect, which is, however, irrelevant for State aid law purposes. It did not even touch upon the aspect of the 'economic incidence' that had been the principal focus of the General Court's reasoning.

In contrast to this, the CJEU's judgment in *Adria-Wien Pipeline* appears to contradict the finding that the taxable person is the beneficiary of aid.[232] The judgment case concerned the area of energy taxation. Major energy users whose activity was shown to consist primarily of the production of goods could apply for a rebate of energy taxes in Austria.[233] Instead of the suppliers of electricity – and thus the taxable persons – the CJEU appeared to consider the customers of those undertakings, i.e., the major energy users that could make use of the rebates, the beneficiaries of the aid scheme.[234]

[2] Relevant Criteria for the Identification of the Beneficiary of Aid

In our view, the two judgments can nevertheless be reconciled as they provide distinguishing criteria for the identification of the beneficiary of aid: The respective tax advantages granted relied on different mechanisms. The reduction of the tax rate of the ATT was automatic, i.e., the respective airlines only had to remit the lower rate for the shorter flights. The energy tax rebates, however, were not granted automatically. Every undertaking first had to pay the tax to the respective energy supplier, but the beneficiaries of the scheme could then apply for the rebate, which would result in a reimbursement of the tax. While technical distinctions in the legislative technique should generally be irrelevant from a State aid law point of view, they can in our view be relevant for the identification of the beneficiary of aid. This is because the existence of a specific advantage for a beneficiary leads to recovery where aid has already been granted. Recovery is meant to re-establish the situation that would have existed had the aid not been granted. This means that in certain cases, the mere fact that there is a formalistic distinction as to who has to pay a tax or receives a refund can make a difference. It is therefore convincing to consider the undertakings that received the rebates from the beneficiaries of aid in *Adria-Wien Pipeline* because the tax burden of the taxable person was not actually reduced.[235] In a similar vein, Englisch cites the example of a deferment of tax where such formal distinction leads to a rather

231. *Ibid.*, paras 115.
232. *See* Case T-473/12 *Aer Lingus v. Commission*, para. 121.
233. Case C-143/99 *Adria-Wien Pipeline*, paras 3ff.
234. *Ibid.*, para. 55.
235. Similarly Englisch, *Indirect Tax Measures, supra* n. 160, at 14, who contends that it is particularly the aspect of the rebate of tax in *Adria-Wien Pipeline* that was relevant for determining the beneficiary of aid. Similarly, a deferment of tax will normally only benefit the taxable person, with reference to Case T-67/94 *Ladbroke Racing v. Commission* EU:T:1998:7.

straightforward determination of the beneficiary of aid. Such deferment will normally only benefit the taxable person, not the consumer.[236]

Yet this formal criterion cannot provide a solution for all cases. In the majority of cases, the taxable person remits the amount of tax due, which may be reduced by tax benefits. Further criteria then have to be relied upon.

A comparison with positive subsides is not helpful. For such subsidies, the question of the identification of the beneficiary of aid will generally not arise. The beneficiary of aid will generally be the direct recipient of the funds save for exceptional circumstances. One case where such exceptional circumstances were found was the CJEU's judgment in *Belgium v. Commission*.[237] The pertinent aspect of the case concerned loans which were granted by the *Société régionale d'investissement de Wallonie* to *Heye*, a private investor that acquired a majority shareholding in *Verlipack*. The latter was an undertaking in difficulty. The terms of the loan included financial allocation clauses, which provided that the full amount of the loan was to be used to finance the recapitalization of *Verlipack*.[238] Under these circumstances, the CJEU held that it was not *Heye*, which had obtained the funds, but *Verlipack*, which was the beneficiary of the aid.[239] Such cases are the exception. Yet in the area of taxation, intricate mechanisms of a potential passing on of the tax burden have to be considered.

An additional criterion for the identification of the beneficiary of aid may be whether there is an explicit obligation to pass on the tax burden.[240] In this context, it first has to be noted that the competition law 'passing on-defence' cannot play a role. Ryanair in the proceedings on the ATT had brought forward that for infringements of Articles 101f. TFEU, the EU Damages Directive 2014/104/EU[241] in its Article 13 provides for the so-called passing on defence.[242] This provision allows the defendant in an action for damages for overcharges due to a competition law infringement to invoke the fact that the claimant passed on the whole or part of the overcharge to their customers. Ryanair had held that it would be illogical not to investigate the effect on customers of the advantage obtained by the aid beneficiary in light of the possibility of invoking the passing on defence in other areas of law.[243] The CJEU clarified that the Damages Directive concerns the compensation for the harm individuals suffer from a competition law infringement. It contrasts this with the objective of the recovery of aid

236. Englisch, *Indirect Tax Measures, supra* n. 160, at 14, with reference to Case T-67/94 *Ladbroke Racing*.
237. Case C-457/00 *Belgium v. Commission* EU:C:2003:387.
238. *Ibid.*, paras 23f.
239. *Ibid.*, para. 61.
240. In the judgment on the Spanish Tax Leasing Scheme, the scheme in question also partly benefitted shipping companies which had not been identified as beneficiaries in the Commission Decision as there was an obligation to transfer part of the tax advantage, *see* Joined Cases C-649, 658 and 662/20 P *Spain and Others v. Commission*, paras 127ff.
241. Directive 2014/104/EU of the European Parliament and the Council of 26 November 2014 on certain rules governing actions for damages under national law for infringements of the competition law provisions of the Member States and of the European Union [2014] OJ L 349/1.
242. On the passing on defence in State aid law: Edouard Louis Jean-Baptiste Bruc, *Passing-on and Recoverable Unlawful State Aid under European Union Law,* 17 EStAL 54 (2018) https://doi.org/10.21552/estal/2018/1/7.
243. Joined Cases C-164 and 165/15 P *Aer Lingus and Ryanair*, para. 84.

as a public enforcement mechanism, which seeks to re-establish the situation without the State's intervention in the market in question.[244]

However, this does not mean that an obligation to pass on a tax is irrelevant to the identification of the beneficiary of aid. For the ATT, there was no obligation to pass on the tax and the tax advantage for shorter flights. Although, given the competitive market conditions, the airlines were likely to do so, they could still decide not to. The fact that the levy qualified as an excise duty merely raised the probability that the benefit could be passed on.[245] As Bruc notes, the same can hold true for any direct tax, yet one will only ever consider the taxpayer as a potential beneficiary of aid for such cases.[246] The obligation to indicate the amount of tax on the tickets does not change the assessment either, since that obligation did not affect the choice as to whether the tax is passed on. The reasoning of the General Court was furthermore somewhat inconsistent as it also distinguished the benefit received from the aid from the aid itself. Bruc rightly considers this distinction a subjectivization of the notion of advantage as the benefit received depends on the choice of the airlines.[247] AG Mengozzi in his opinion also rejected merging the concept of advantage with the subsequent choices of the undertakings. He held that a variety of mechanisms exist for passing on benefits or burdens to other actors, which are irrelevant for State aid purposes and gave a rise in the corporate tax rate, which leads to an increase in prices, as an example.[248] The Austrian rules in question, by contrast, explicitly provided for an obligation to pass on the tax to the recipient of the supply.[249] Where this is the case, the most obvious beneficiary of a tax advantage appears to be not the taxable person, but the consumer, be it an undertaking or an individual that is not an undertaking. In the latter case, there could be no State aid.

Where there is no obligation to pass on the tax, it could be relevant whether the passing on of the tax burden is inherent to the tax system or whether it is a mechanism that is external to the tax system. The German Federal Financial Court brought forward a similar argument in the context of the assessment of the German electricity tax. The case concerned the question of whether it was unjust to levy electricity tax if the consumer did not pay for the electricity consumed. The Court denied this and held that while the electricity tax was an indirect tax, which is generally supposed to be borne by the consumer of electricity, this passing-on mechanism is carried out outside of the realm of tax law. Instead, the amount of tax is merely taken into account when calculating the price that the consumer has to pay.[250] This criterion also appears to be useful for State aid purposes.

244. *Ibid.*, para. 105; *see* in detail Ch. §5.01[A] *infra*.
245. Similarly Bruc, *supra* n. 242, at 54.
246. *Ibid.*, at 60.
247. *Ibid.*, at 59.
248. Opinion of AG Mengozzi in Joined Cases C-164 and 165/15 P *Commission v. Aer Lingus and Ryanair* EU:C:2016:515, para. 76.
249. Case C-143/99 *Adria-Wien Pipeline*, para. 5.
250. *Bundesfinanzhof*, Case VII R 8/12, BFHE 244, 184 paras 16f. with reference to Case VII R 56/72, BStBL II 1975, 462.

The two tax measures can also be distinguished by who they were targeting. The tax advantage in the case of the ATT did not bear any relation with the identity of the passenger. What 'triggered' the tax advantage was the decision of the airline to offer short-distance flights. While the tax was only due where tickets were sold, the intended beneficiaries were nevertheless the airlines because they could derive a competitive advantage from the tax advantage. In *Adria-Wien Pipeline,* however, the tax benefit was not targeted at the taxable persons remitting the tax, but it was dependent on the activity and the level of energy consumption of the undertaking. It did not depend on the identity of the energy supplier. This could potentially also be underlined by a subjective element, i.e., the question of which actor is meant to profit from the advantageous tax measure. For example, where the legislator intends to promote the competitiveness of a certain sector the taxable person is active in through reduced rates, this may indicate that this taxable person should be identified as the beneficiary of aid.

Another potential argument can be derived from the area of energy taxation and in particular the CJEU's judgment in *Kernkraftwerke Lippe-Ems.* While the pertinent section did not relate to State aid law, the CJEU stated the following on the German duty on the use of nuclear fuel:

> Furthermore, [...] the tax introduced by KernbrStG is not levied directly on the consumer of the excise product but on the electricity producer. It is true that the financial burden of that tax could, in principle, [...] be borne indirectly in its entirety by the final consumer if the producer included the amount of that tax in the price charged for each amount of the product released for consumption, thus rendering the tax neutral for the producer. However, it is apparent from the analysis carried out by the referring court on that point that the tax introduced by KernbrStG cannot be passed on in its entirety to the final electricity consumer in view of, inter alia, the particular nature of that product, it not being possible to determine the origin of any given amount of electricity, and of the pricing mechanism for electricity applied in Germany, which is characterised by the fact that the price of electricity is, essentially, a single price arrived at by negotiation on the energy exchange market. [...] Nor can the duty at issue be regarded as being calculated directly or indirectly on the quantity of electricity at the time of release for consumption of that product [...].[251]

This criterion can be transferred to European State aid law. Where the tax is not reflected in its entirety in the price that the consumer pays, there should be a presumption that the beneficiary of the aid is the taxable person instead of the consumer (regardless of whether the consumer is an undertaking or not under the state aid law definition).

The identification of the beneficiary of aid in indirect tax cases thus depends on a variety of factors. The criteria we have identified – the question of whether the aid is granted automatically or upon application by the final consumer; the existence of an obligation to pass on the tax as opposed to the pass-on depending on the subsequent choices of the taxable person; the targeting or intent of an aid measure; or whether the

251. Case C-5/14 *Kernkraftwerke Lippe-Ems* EU:C:2015:354, paras 64f.

tax is reflected in the price the consumer pays in its entirety – should be understood as legal presumptions that are rebuttable in exceptional cases.

[3] Tax Inherent Pass On of VAT

The considerations above have shown that the identification of the beneficiary of aid in indirect tax cases always requires an examination of the tax as well as the tax measure in question. In this context, one may wonder how tax measures within VAT should be assessed. State aid law in the area of VAT has so far not played a significant role in the case law of the CJEU. This is primarily because of the extent of harmonization of VAT.[252] Full harmonization would rule out the existence of State aid for lack of imputability.[253] Nevertheless, as there is no full harmonization, the existence of a selective advantage is not ruled out.[254]

Yet who does this advantage accrue to? There is a legal presumption that VAT is borne by the final consumer due to the mechanism of VAT input deduction.[255] The mechanism of input tax deduction, which ensures neutrality for the taxable person, is inherent to VAT. Moreover, the VAT is reflected in the price of the final product. This means that as a rule, VAT will be passed on in its entirety, so there should be a presumption that the tax is indeed borne by the final consumer. This is in contrast to the examples from the case law in the area of energy taxation cited above where the passing on of the tax burden was a mechanism that was not inherent to the tax itself and the determination of the price for the consumer was subject to a variety of factors beyond tax.

This finding appears to be at odds with the CJEU's judgment in *Heiser.*[256] The case dealt with a transitional rule in the Austrian VAT code, which exempted medical practitioners from the obligation to adjust input tax deductions where there was a subsequent changeover from taxable to exempt status in terms of the purpose of goods and services acquired. In this context, Austria brought forward that this measure promoted solidarity between sickness insurance bodies because it benefitted such bodies in practice.[257] However, the CJEU held that medical practitioners were the only beneficiaries as there was no indication that the benefit was systematically passed on and thus cancelled out for medical practitioners.[258] The CJEU thus considered the taxable person the relevant beneficiary of aid and denied a systematic passing on of the advantage. However, Englisch convincingly argues that this should not lead to a general presumption that a tax advantage under VAT benefits the taxable person. He considers the identification of the beneficiary an emanation of the CJEU's case law

252. *See* Council Directive 2006/112/EC of 28 November 2006 on the common system of value added tax [2006] OJ L 347/1, last amended by Council Directive (EU) 2022/890 of 3 June 2022 [2022] L 155/1.
253. *See* Commission Notice on the notion of State aid, *supra* n. 26, at paras 44ff.
254. *See* Ch. §3.04[B], [4] *infra*.
255. Englisch, *Umsatzsteuer, supra* n. 213, at paras 17.12, 15.
256. Case C-172/03 *Heiser* EU:C:2005:130.
257. *Ibid.*, para. 44.
258. *Ibid.*, para. 47.

according to which taxable persons who avail themselves of an exemption are not in a position to pass any charge to the person next in line in the chain of supply and are thus similar to a final consumer, which he, however, finds unconvincing.[259] He argues that the *Heiser* judgment would only demonstrate that evidence as to the real economic incidence must be admitted to identify the typical effective recipient of aid. This would take precedence over the legally intended recipient. Nevertheless, as a rebuttable presumption, the beneficiary of aid would generally be the final consumer. A contrary presumption would apply where a tax measure 'is linked to certain production processes or to certain producer categories in order to compensate for competitive cost disadvantages of such processes or producers'.[260]

The general presumption that VAT is normatively borne by the final consumer – which is ensured through a tax inherent mechanism, i.e., the right to deduct input tax – appears convincing for State aid law purposes as long as an exemption is within the ambit of this mechanism. However, the presumption, for example, breaks down where exemptions entail the forfeiture of the right to deduct input tax. In the *Heiser* case, the presumption was convincingly rebutted. There was indeed no means to pass on the advantage in the specific constellation so that the taxable person had to be considered the beneficiary of the aid. This was not a reliance on the true economic incidence, but a rebuttal of the legal presumption underlying VAT.

[C] Additional Indirect Advantages Rather Than Mere Secondary Effects

Englisch addresses secondary effects that could lead to State aid, even where there is a tax-inherent passing-on mechanism and the final consumer is not an undertaking. In these cases, there may be an indirect advantage for the taxable persons because the original tax measure – even though it may not directly qualify as aid to the consumer for lack of an undertaking as a direct beneficiary – may affect market mechanisms.[261] For example, he refers to the potential of an increased sales volume and thus increased market share due to the possibility to lower prices.[262] This would amount to an indirect advantage that is relevant for State aid law purposes. In some cases, this would be rather obvious, for example, where a tax advantage depends on the use of a particular good or service from a particular undertaking. In other cases, it would be necessary to carry out an economic analysis of cross-price elasticity between privileged and non-privileged goods or services.[263]

Although interesting from a legal point of view, the problem does not appear overly relevant in practice. What Englisch deems the obvious cases, namely where a tax advantage depends on the use of a specific good or service from a particular undertaking, will often amount to a breach of the principle of fiscal neutrality. In these

259. Englisch, *Indirect Tax Measures, supra* n. 160, at 12f. with reference to Case 8/81 *Becker* EU:C:1982:7, para. 44; Case C-460/07 *Puffer* EU:C:2009:254, para. 59.
260. Englisch, *Indirect Tax Measures, supra* n. 160, at 13.
261. *Ibid.*, 13f.
262. *Ibid.*, 14.
263. *Ibid.*

cases, the direct beneficiary of aid would in our view presumably be the taxable person.[264] While there are certainly secondary effects where an advantage is completely passed on from the taxable person to the consumer, a reliance on a macroeconomic analysis to determine the increase in market share and demand appears to go beyond what State aid control can accomplish. In particular for aid schemes, this would amount to the analysis of hypothetical market scenarios. State aid law merely contrasts a situation with and without aid, disregarding other factors. Moreover, such analysis would be impossible to conduct from an *ex ante* perspective, which is an indication that such secondary effects are not covered by State aid law in the first place. Consequently, distortive effects that are not foreseeable with sufficient certainty before the introduction of aid should be irrelevant for State aid law purposes.

Instead, in our view, there could only be State aid where the taxable person (also) receives an indirect advantage. On this, the Commission Notice on the notion of State aid states the following:

> An advantage can be conferred on undertakings other than those to which State resources are directly transferred (*indirect advantage*). A measure can also constitute both a direct advantage to the recipient undertaking and an indirect advantage to other undertakings, for instance, undertakings operating at subsequent levels of activity. The direct recipient of the advantage can be either an undertaking or an entity (natural or legal person) not engaged in any economic activity. Such *indirect advantages should be distinguished from mere secondary economic effects that are inherent in almost all State aid measures (for example through an increase of output)*. [...].[265]

The CJEU has, for example, accepted the presence of an indirect advantage in its judgment in *Germany v. Commission*, which dealt with a provision in the German income tax code which allowed for the carrying forward of hidden reserves:[266] Up to 100% profit made on the sale of shares in capital companies could be set off against the costs of purchasing new shares in capital companies through holding companies, provided that the purchase was connected to an increase in capital or the setting-up of new capital companies in one of the new *Länder* or in Berlin and that these companies had no more than 250 employees.[267] According to the Commission, the investors (i.e., the holding companies) had to be considered the direct beneficiaries of the aid. Yet additionally, the companies established in the new *Länder* and Berlin whose shares were being acquired had to be considered indirect beneficiaries, as investors would be prepared to acquire holdings in East Germany on more favourable terms as compared to a situation without these benefits. As a result, the volume of holdings in such companies would rise or the terms of the acquisition would be shifted, which would ultimately benefit the companies being acquired.[268] The CJEU agreed with this

264. *See* Ch. §2.02[B], [3] *supra*.
265. Commission Notice on the notion of State aid, *supra* n. 26, at paras 115f.; emphasis added by the author.
266. Case C-156/98 *Germany v. Commission*. *See* for another example: Case C-382/99 *Netherlands v. Commission* EU:C:2002:363.
267. *See* Case C-156/98 *Germany v. Commission*, paras 8f. for a description of the measure.
268. *Ibid.*, para. 12.

reasoning and held that it was irrelevant whether investors make independent decisions as to the acquisition of holdings. The mere decision to renounce tax revenue by the State enabled investors to acquire holdings in these undertakings on more advantageous terms, which then benefitted the undertakings being acquired.[269]

In this case, the fact that there is an additional indirect beneficiary of the aid was quite intuitive. Yet as far as can be seen, the CJEU has not established clear criteria to distinguish an indirect advantage from the secondary effects that any aid measure will entail. There also appears no explicit clarification of what an indirect advantage could be in indirect tax matters.

According to the Commission, an indirect advantage is present where a measure is designed to channel secondary effects towards identifiable undertakings or groups of undertakings. This should be examined from an *ex ante* perspective.[270] Secondary effects can thus amount to an indirect advantage where there is a close link between the aid granted to the beneficiary and the then more or less automatically resulting advantage for the indirect beneficiary.

269. *Ibid.*, paras 26f.
270. Commission Notice on the notion of State aid, *supra* n. 26, at para. 116.

CHAPTER 3
The Notion of De Jure-Selectivity

The case law on de jure-selectivity shows that an initially ever-wider understanding of selectivity has now been replaced by a rollback that emphasizes fiscal sovereignty – sometimes at the expense of the effectiveness of State aid control. While the selectivity test amounts to a non-discrimination test, it also has elements of a benchmark approach. This has two main dimensions. First, such a benchmark has to exist at all, otherwise, there can be no State aid. Second, the reference system of taxation is for the Member State to design. This includes elements, such as the taxable base and the tax rate. The reference system of taxation is generally the entire levy, in which a tax measure is embedded. Beyond that, the elements of the reference system of taxation have to be identified either normatively or, where this is not possible, relying on an empirical approach. Technical provisions that are necessary for the functioning of the levy generally cannot amount to a derogation. The CJEU appears to consider a growing number of types of rules, such as progressive rate structures, to form part of the reference system of taxation, which significantly restricts State aid control. While such restriction was certainly warranted, the distinction between technical rules and potential derogations lacks a clear methodology or theoretical foundation. The ambiguities are particularly apparent where complex tax measures are suspected of amounting to aid. In the second step, there has to be a derogation from the reference system which leads to a different treatment of undertakings that are in a situation that is legally and factually comparable. The case law shows that abstract selectivity suffices. Moreover, comparability has to be ascertained in light of the objective of the reference system of taxation. This results in a wide notion of prima facie selectivity for broad-based fiscal levies. For special purpose levies, selectivity cannot only be derived from an explicit derogation from the reference system of taxation. Instead, by normatively identifying the reference system of taxation, it is also possible to monitor the boundaries of such levies for their consistent implementation, i.e., an implementation that is in line with the stated objectives of the tax. In light of this objective, all comparable situations have to fall within the ambit of the tax in the first place. There are significant uncertainties regarding the identification of the objective of special purpose levies. In any case, tax sovereignty requires a low standard of control both regarding the objectives and the boundaries of such levies. For narrow-based fiscal levies, such comparability analysis on the level of the reference system of taxation is generally not possible or will at least not yield meaningful results. In a third step, a derogation from the reference system of taxation can still be justified. The third step has stand-alone significance as the relevant yardstick in this respect is the objective of the measure. The grounds for justification must be internal to the tax system, which means that in some cases the distinction between the permissible grounds in the second and in the third step may be blurry. This chapter explores the examples of the avoidance of international double taxation as grounds for justification as well as the aspect of harmonization. No particularities apply for special purpose levies, even though the potential internal grounds of justification will naturally be very different from fiscal levies. Finally, the proportionality test under State aid law is underexplored. A low standard of control appears to be applicable. The narrow reading of the third step of the selectivity test means that there is but limited potential for this step to serve as a general rule of reason to limit the notion of selectivity. At best, justifications in line with EU objectives could be recognised.

Even more important than the advantage is the notion of selectivity. According to Article 107(1) TFEU, the existence of State aid requires that 'certain undertakings or the production of certain goods' are favoured. The CJEU has developed the concepts of de jure-selectivity and de facto-selectivity to concretize this Treaty passage. In this section, we will discuss de jure-selectivity, which is far more significant in practice than de facto-selectivity.

In its case law, the CJEU relies on a three-step selectivity test to assess whether a tax measure formally derogates from the normal tax treatment in a way that cannot be justified, i.e., whether it is de jure selective. In the words of the CJEU:

> In order to classify a domestic tax measure as 'selective', it is necessary to begin by identifying and examining the common or 'normal' regime applicable in the Member State concerned. It is in relation to this common or 'normal' tax regime that it is necessary, secondly, to assess and determine whether any advantage granted by the tax measure at issue may be selective by demonstrating that the measure derogates from that common regime inasmuch as it differentiates between economic operators who, in light of the *objective assigned to the tax system of the Member State concerned, are in a comparable factual and legal situation [...].*[271]

271. Joined Cases C-78 to 80/08 *Paint Graphos*, para. 49; emphasis added by the author.

Then as to the third step, the CJEU has held the following:

> It should also be recalled that a measure which creates an exception to the application of the general tax system *may be justified if it results directly from the basic or guiding principles of that tax system.* In that context, a distinction must be made between, on the one hand, the objectives *attributed to a particular tax regime and which are extrinsic to it and, on the other, the mechanisms inherent in the tax system itself which are necessary for the achievement of such objectives [...].*[272]

While at least the abstract approach to identifying selectivity – if not every detail thereof – is now quite clearly fleshed out in the case law, this was not always the case. This led to a significant degree of legal uncertainty and terminological confusion: For example, Schön identifies two main approaches that would be represented in the literature, namely the discrimination approach and the benchmark approach. He holds that the former would forego the quest for a benchmark altogether and instead ask whether existing differentials in national tax laws are justified by carrying out a rule of reason examination. The benchmark approach, of which Schön is a proponent, instead refers to the assumption that a tax measure can only be selective where there is a benchmark that can be relied upon. This is because Member States' tax sovereignty prescribes that Member States are free to design their tax system. Selectivity can therefore only ever derive from a Member State's tax legislation.[273] According to Schön, the distinction would only become relevant where a benchmark does not exist. An example would be domestic legislation that is so fragmented or chaotic that it is impossible to define a benchmark.[274] He argues that the benchmark approach would be superior as it allows to identify the direction in which a breach of State aid law should be remedied as well as the amount to be recovered.[275]

Meanwhile, the authors that Schön refers to as proponents of the discrimination approach[276] in our view follow different avenues. For example, Lang indeed holds that the reference system is irrelevant altogether and argues that what he dubs the traditional 'rule-exception-approach' would be outdated.[277] Cordewener notes that the CJEU's approach boils down to a non-discrimination test.[278] He holds that it is necessary to rely on a comparability analysis and particularly derives this from the CJEU's *Gibraltar* judgment.[279] Yet, for example, Lyal stresses the significance of the reference system of taxation, albeit in a different dimension than Schön.[280]

272. *Ibid.*, para. 69; emphasis added by the author.
273. Schön, *Tax Legislation and the Notion of Fiscal Aid*, *supra* n. 40, at 9ff. He cites the judgments in *British Aggregates*, *Regione Sardegna* and particularly *Gibraltar* as examples of where the CJEU did not strictly follow a benchmark approach.
274. *Ibid.*, at 11.
275. *Ibid.*, at 13f.
276. Andrea Biondi, *State Aid Is Falling Down, Falling Down: An Analysis of the Case Law on the Notion of Aid* 50 CMLR 1719ff. (2013) https://doi.org/10.54648/cola2013164; Cordewener, *supra* n. 131; Lang, *Recent Trends in the Case Law of the ECJ*, *supra* n. 146, at 418; Lyal, *supra* n. 131, at 1032f.
277. Lang, *State Aid and Taxation: Selectivity and Comparability Analysis*, *supra* n. 131, at 33.
278. Cordewener, *supra* n. 131, at 288.
279. Lang, *State Aid and Taxation: Selectivity and Comparability Analysis*, *supra* n. 131, at 32f.
280. Lyal, *supra* n. 131, at 1017ff.

Haslehner distinguishes between the 'comparability approach' on the one hand and the 'derogation approach' on the other hand. He contends that the two approaches would differ only in the function that is assigned to the reference system. For the latter, the reference system would solely be relied upon to determine whether there is a derogation or in other words an exception to the general rule. By contrast, the second approach would require the identification of the objective of the reference system to assess whether there is a discrimination of comparable actors in light of this objective.[281]

Szudoczky similarly refers to a 'derogation approach' on the one hand and a 'comparison approach' on the other hand, albeit with a slightly different connotation than Haslehner.[282] In her view, both approaches are relied upon in the assessment of selectivity. She holds that where a tax measure is integrated into a broader system that has been appropriately defined, the derogation approach should be applied. Yet this derogation approach incorporates elements of a comparison test. It is thus necessary to identify a reference system as this determines the comparator (the objective of the reference system)[283] in relation to which the derogatory measure has to be assessed.[284] Haslehner would presumably dub this the comparability approach. Szudoczky further contends that where selectivity may arise from the fact that the tax regime in question is not defined appropriately, so as to encompass all undertakings which should be covered by it, there is no need to identify a common system and a derogation therefrom. Instead, the correct method of assessment would be only the comparison test. She cites both sub-systems existing parallel with the general tax system, such as environmental tax regimes, and the *Gibraltar* case as examples.[285]

We will refer to the two approaches that have been convincingly identified by Szudoczky as abstract and concrete selectivity respectively to avoid the terminological confusion laid out above. For de jure-selectivity, abstract selectivity suffices - or, in other words: a benchmark approach applies in the guise of the three-step test of selectivity. In this context, it is not necessary to identify a group of undertakings that are the only ones to be able to profit from a tax measure.[286] A tax measure may thus be selective, even where it is theoretically open to all undertakings. For this type of selectivity, it is crucial to identify a benchmark in the reference system of taxation. This is because the legislator is held to its own fundamental charging decision which it has to implement in an internally consistent manner. De jure-selectivity combines elements of a discrimination and a benchmark approach. By contrast, de facto-selectivity requires concrete selectivity, i.e., the demonstration that some clearly defined (groups

281. Werner Haslehner, *Double Taxation Relief, Transfer Pricing Adjustments and State Aid Law*, in Richelle et al. (eds), State Aid Law and Business Taxation, 133, 139 (2016).
282. Szudoczky, *Convergence of the Analysis of National Tax Measures*, *supra* n. 131, at 361f. Similar terminology is relied on by Shi, *supra* n. 136, at 371. The 1998 Commission Notice would rely on a derogation approach whereas the case law of the CJEU would rely on a comparative approach.
283. Szudoczky, *Convergence of the Analysis of National Tax Measures*, *supra* n. 131, at 366f.
284. *Ibid.*, at 362.
285. *Ibid.*
286. *See* Ch. §3.03[A] *infra*.

of) undertakings are the only ones to profit from the tax measure in question. The applicable standard in this respect is manifest inconsistency.[287] In substance, our understanding of selectivity thus very much coincides with Szudoczky's stance.

We will first briefly trace the evolution of the case law, only highlighting some cases that demonstrate the Courts' interpretation over time. This shows that the CJEU has been consistent in its interpretation, but that the interpretation of the notion of selectivity was only gradually clarified in detail. Initially, the notion of de jure-selectivity appeared to be very wide. Most recently, however, a rollback[288] that significantly limits selectivity - but may very well be in line with the particularities of taxation - can be observed. The CJEU now considers many features of a tax system to form part of the reference system of taxation and has widened the recourse to a justification in the third step of the selectivity test (§3.01).

We will then analyse the different steps of the selectivity test. Admittedly, separating the analysis of the first and the second step of the selectivity test may appear somewhat artificial, since the scope of the reference system of taxation is impacted by the objective of a levy, which also becomes relevant in the second step. Consequently, we will deal with the objective of levies in the second step. However, the reference system also has a stand-alone significance, since there are uncertainties as to the delimitation of derogations and integral elements of the reference system of taxation that will be addressed in the context of the elaborations on the first step. The reference system of taxation has three functions. It is primarily identified by relying on a normative approach, although in exceptional cases, an empirical approach could be applicable. Problems arise in the distinction between derogations on the one hand and technical rules that form part of the reference system of taxation on the other hand. Finally, the case law on tax measures with complex structures has shown that there is a potential for circumvention of State aid law (§3.02).

As to the derogation from the reference system of taxation in the second step, the case law has shown that abstract selectivity suffices for de jure-selectivity. The relevant benchmark that is relied upon to determine whether there is derogation is the objective of the reference system of taxation. At least for broad-based fiscal levies, this leads to a wide notion of selectivity. We will then focus on special-purpose levies. For such levies, the boundaries of a levy have to be designed in accordance with the objective of the levy. By contrast, narrow-based fiscal levies have no special purpose that could be monitored, so the boundaries of such levies are generally treated as a given (§3.03).

For the third step, we will first address the function and stand-alone significance of the possibility of a justification. We will then address permissible grounds for justification in fiscal levies, before highlighting some aspects of the justification of distinctions within special purpose levies. Perhaps the most relevant aspect of the third step is the necessity of derogations being proportionate. A low standard of control appears applicable. The third step has but limited potential to serve as a rule of reason,

287. *See* Ch. §4.01 *infra*.
288. Similarly Michael Honoré, *State Aid and Taxation: All Clear* 14 EStAL 306, 308 (2015).

even though it is conceivable that the case law could allow for a justification on grounds of objectives that are in line with EU law (§3.04).

§3.01 THE EVOLUTION OF THE CASE LAW ON SELECTIVITY

The three-step test for de jure-selectivity is not new.[289] It had emerged from the case law as early as 1974. The CJEU's *Italy v. Commission* case dealt with reductions in social security contributions in the Italian textile sector.[290] While the three-step test that was applied in the judgment was not as clearly contoured as nowadays, the case nevertheless seems to constitute the origin of the three-step test.

It was not long after this first judgment acknowledging the three-step test that the CJEU started to apply the test to fiscal aid measures. One of the first landmark judgments was the CJEU's *Adria-Wien Pipeline* decision.[291] The case concerned rebates of energy taxes charged on supplies of natural gas and electricity under Austrian law. Such taxes had to be reimbursed upon application in so far as they exceeded 0.35% of net production value. The rebate was paid after deduction of a maximum amount of the first ATS 5,000. The rebate was only granted to undertakings whose activity was shown to consist primarily of the production of goods.[292]

As to selectivity, the CJEU stated:

> The only question to be determined is whether, under a particular statutory scheme, a State measure is such as to favour 'certain undertakings or the production of certain goods' within the meaning of Article 92(1) of the Treaty in comparison with other undertakings *which are in a legal and factual situation that is comparable in the light of the objective pursued by the measure in question [...].* According to the case-law of the Court, a measure which, although conferring an advantage on its recipient, is justified by the nature or general scheme of the system of which it is part does not fulfil that condition of selectivity [...].[293]

In the second step, the CJEU relied on the 'objective pursued by the measure in question'. This appears to be at odds with later case law where the CJEU refers to the objective of the reference system as the appropriate yardstick for the second step. However, from the ensuing elaborations in *Adria-Wien Pipeline*, it is not altogether clear which objective the CJEU truly intends to refer to. This is because it then brings forward the following argument:

> For one thing, undertakings supplying services may, just like undertakings manufacturing goods, be major consumers of energy and incur energy taxes above 0.35% of their net production value – the threshold above which undertakings manufacturing principally goods are eligible for the energy tax rebate.[294]

289. The evolution of the case law is traced by Juan Jorge Piernas López, *The Concept of State Aid Under EU Law* (2015).
290. Case 173/73 *Italy v. Commission* EU:C:1974:71.
291. Case C-143/99 *Adria-Wien Pipeline*.
292. *Ibid.*, paras 7ff. *See* already on the identification of the beneficiary of aid Ch. §2.02 *supra*.
293. *Ibid.*, paras 41f.; emphasis added by the author.
294. *Ibid.*, para. 50.

This appears to be a reference to the objective of the measure. However, as to a potential justification it goes on to state that:

> For another thing, the ecological considerations underlying the national legislation at issue do not justify treating the consumption of natural gas or electricity by undertakings supplying services differently than the consumption of such energy by undertakings manufacturing goods. Energy consumption by each of those sectors is equally damaging to the environment.

Without explicitly clarifying this, the CJEU thus also appears to refer to the objective of the reference system instead of the objective of the measure in question.

The CJEU's *GIL Insurance* case then dealt with insurance taxation. The CJEU ultimately did not find that there was State aid. However, concerning selectivity it stated:

> Article 87(1) EC requires it to be determined whether, under a particular statutory scheme, a State measure is such as to favour 'certain undertakings or the production of certain goods' in comparison with others which, *in the light of the objective pursued by the system in question, are in a comparable legal and factual situation* [...]. If that is the case, the measure concerned satisfies the condition of selectivity which is a constituent of the concept of State aid under that provision [...].[295]

There is thus already a reference to the objective of the system as opposed to the objective of the tax measure as the correct yardstick.

The case *Portugal v. Commission*[296] concerned a case of regional selectivity: The Azores Region intended to introduce reductions in the rates of income and corporation tax for all economic operators. They were meant to allow undertakings in the Azores to compensate for the structural handicaps resulting from being located in an insular region. The reductions were considered State aid by the Commission.[297] As to the selectivity of such tax measures, the CJEU held:

> It is clear from the foregoing that in order to determine whether the measure at issue is selective it is appropriate to examine whether, within the context of a particular legal system, that measure constitutes an advantage for certain undertakings in comparison with others which are in a comparable legal and factual situation. The determination of the reference framework has a particular importance in the case of tax measures, since the very existence of an advantage may be established only when compared with 'normal' taxation. The 'normal' tax rate is the rate in force in the geographical area constituting the reference framework.[298]

It then went on to state:

> In such a case it is the area in which the infra-State body responsible for the measure exercises its powers, and not the country as a whole, that constitutes the

295. Case C-308/01 *GIL Insurance*, para. 68; emphasis added by the author. Similarly Case C-172/03 *Heiser*, para. 40.
296. Case C-88/03 *Portugal v. Commission*.
297. *Ibid.*, paras 8ff. for the facts of the case.
298. *Ibid.*, para. 56.

> relevant context for the assessment of whether a measure adopted by such a body favours *certain undertakings in comparison with others in a comparable legal and factual situation, having regard to the objective pursued by the measure or the legal system concerned.*[299]

In this case, the CJEU already referred to the objective pursued by the reference system, albeit only as one of two options.

Perhaps one of the most significant clarifications came with the CJEU's *Paint Graphos* judgment, which concerned tax benefits for cooperative societies.[300] This case was significant in several respects. First, it demonstrated that the case law that had initially primarily been limited to the area of indirect taxation and/or special purpose levels was similarly applicable to direct taxation. Second, it clarified that – contrary to what had often been deduced from the CJEU's *Adria-Wien Pipeline* judgment – the relevant objective in the second step of the selectivity test is the objective of the reference system as opposed to the objective of the measure in question. Third, it contained the first mention of the principle of proportionality as a pivotal part of the analysis in the third step. As to prima facie selectivity, the CJEU explained:

> In order to classify a domestic tax measure as 'selective', it is necessary to begin by identifying and examining the common or 'normal' regime applicable in the Member State concerned. It is in relation to this common or 'normal' tax regime that it is necessary, secondly, to assess and determine whether any advantage granted by the tax measure at issue may be selective by demonstrating that the measure derogates from that common regime inasmuch as it differentiates between economic operators who, in light of the *objective assigned to the tax system of the Member State concerned, are in a comparable factual and legal situation [...].*[301]

As to the justification, the CJEU elaborated:

> It should also be recalled that a measure which creates an exception to the application of the general tax system may be justified if it results directly from the *basic or guiding principles of that tax system.* [...] In any event, in order for tax exemptions such as those at issue in the main proceedings to be justified by the nature or general scheme of the tax system of the Member State concerned, *it is also necessary to ensure that those exemptions are consistent with the principle of proportionality* and do not go beyond what is necessary, in that the legitimate objective being pursued could not be attained by less far-reaching measures.[302]

Only a few months later, the CJEU's Grand Chamber published its judgment in *Gibraltar.*[303] The ruling fundamentally challenged the notion of selectivity in that it deemed the planned Gibraltar corporate tax system selective even though there was no formal derogation from the reference system of taxation. However, the *Gibraltar* case concerned another form of selectivity, namely de facto-selectivity.[304]

---

299. *Ibid.*, para. 58; emphasis added by the author.
300. Joined Cases C-78 to 80/08 *Paint Graphos*.
301. *Ibid.*, para. 49; emphasis added by the author.
302. *Ibid.*, paras 69, 75; emphasis added by the author.
303. Joined Cases C-106 and 109/09 P *Gibraltar*.
304. *See* on this Ch. §4.01 *infra*.

The broad notion of de jure-selectivity as it had emerged in *Paint Graphos* was reiterated in the CJEU's *P Oy* judgment.[305] Finally, the Grand Chamber decision in *World Duty Free Group* cemented this interpretation of selectivity.[306] The judgment concerned a Spanish tax measure that allowed undertakings that acquired a shareholding of at least 5% in a foreign company and retained it for at least one year, to deduct the goodwill resulting therefrom as an amortization from their basis of assessment for corporate tax. A foreign company under the provision was defined as a company that was liable to pay a tax that was identical to the tax applicable in Spain and whose income was derived mainly from business activities carried out abroad.[307] The Commission's decision declaring the measure incompatible with the internal market was annulled by the General Court.[308] Upon appeal, the CJEU made some important clarifications on the exact interpretation of the selectivity test,[309] In its judgment, the CJEU endorsed the three-step test as established particularly in *Paint Graphos* and confirmed that the *Gibraltar* case indeed concerned a separate form of selectivity. Moreover, it clarified that abstract selectivity suffices for de jure-selectivity.[310]

However, this did not settle the debate on the correct interpretation of selectivity. The CJEU's Grand Chamber decision in *A-Brauerei* concerned the German real property transfer tax, and in particular exemptions therein.[311] Since the AG in his Opinion had again questioned the approach to identifying selectivity,[312] the CJEU again reiterated its stance on de jure-selectivity as it had emerged in *World Duty Free Group*[313] as well as the delimitation from cases of de facto-selectivity.[314] At the same time, the Court significantly developed the possibilities for a justification in the third step and explicitly accepted a justification, while applying a rather low standard of control.[315]

There has thus been a consistent development in the CJEU's case law on selectivity. After doubts as to the correct yardstick in the second step of the analysis, there is now clarity that it is the objective of the reference system that has to be referred to. It also appears to be clear that the reference system of taxation for aid schemes is generally the levy itself. Moreover, the three-step selectivity test is applicable regardless of which type of tax is concerned, be it an indirect or a direct tax. All this results in a very wide notion of selectivity.

Most recently, however, the CJEU's case law has shown more restrictive tendencies. There is no explicit deviation from the prior case law. Yet in areas that had not been clarified before, the CJEU is now increasingly adopting a more restrictive

305. Case C-6/12 *P Oy* EU:C:2013:525.
306. Joined Cases C-20 and 21/15 P *World Duty Free Group*.
307. *Ibid.*, para. 5.
308. Case T-219/10 *Autogrill España v. Commission* EU:T:2014:939. *See* Case T-219/10 RENV *World Duty Free Group v. Commission* EU:T:2018:784 for the judgment upon renvoi.
309. Joined Cases C-20 and 21/15 P *World Duty Free Group*, paras 53ff.
310. *See* on this Ch. §3.03[A] *infra*.
311. Case C-374/17 *A-Brauerei*.
312. Opinion of AG Saugmandsgaard Øe in Case C-374/17 *A-Brauerei*, EU:C:2018:741.
313. Case C-374/17 *A-Brauerei*, paras 35ff.
314. *Ibid.*, paras 32ff.
315. *See* on this Ch. §3.04[B], [2] *infra*.

approach.[316] This has particularly emerged in the judgment of *Andres*. In this judgment, the CJEU denied that the German restructuring clause was selective.[317] Moreover, there has recently been a stronger emphasis on the integral elements of the reference system of taxation that are solely for the national legislator to determine. This has particularly emerged in the judgments on the Polish and Hungarian progressive turnover-based taxes where the CJEU found that progressivity is an integral part of the reference system of taxation itself.[318]

§3.02 THE REFERENCE SYSTEM OF TAXATION

We will now zoom in and focus on the reference system as the first step of the selectivity analysis. We will show that given its three closely related functions, the reference system is pivotal to the analysis [A]. Subsequently, we will demonstrate that the reference system is primarily identified normatively, although in exceptional cases, an empirical approach can be applied [B]. Problems arise in the distinction between derogations on the one hand and technical rules that form part of the reference system of taxation on the other hand. Such technical rules are generally exempt from State aid control as they are solely for the national legislator to determine. Progressivity has been identified as a feature that is generally inherent to the reference system [C]. Finally, the case law on tax measures with complex structures has shown that the case law as it stands opens up possibilities for circumvention of State aid law that are particularly relevant for the design of anti-abuse provisions [D].

[A] Three Functions of the Reference System of Taxation

One may first wonder whether it is truly always necessary to identify the reference system of taxation to identify selectivity. Indeed, this seems futile at first glance for broad-based fiscal taxes. This is because, in light of the objective to levy funds, almost all actors would in principle appear to be comparable. This in turn means that regardless of the type of distinction within a national law, there would be a derogation from the reference system.[319] Some authors had furthermore argued that instead of identifying a reference system of taxation, the approach taken in the context of the fundamental freedoms – that is the identification of comparators – could be relied on. Lang has derived this from the judgment of the CJEU in *Gibraltar*. He contended that

316. Soltész, *supra* n. 174, at 24 argues that the recent developments do not amount to a rollback, but that the Commission's failures were due to technical deficiencies in the decisions underlying the cases. The CJEU would have repeatedly confirmed the wide notion of selectivity.
317. Case C-203/16 P *Andres*, paras 101ff.
318. *See* Ch. §3.02[C], [2] *infra*.
319. *See* on this case law Ch. §3.03[B], [2] *infra*.

the approach of identifying comparators could be generalized. The traditional approach that follows a 'rule-exception-logic' would have been outdated.[320] Yet while the CJEU relied on a comparison approach in *Gibraltar*, it does not appear convincing to generalize this finding because the CJEU has since clarified that the judgment concerned de facto-selectivity, not de jure-selectivity.[321]

Admittedly, even the CJEU does not always emphasize the identification of the reference system.[322] For one, this is of course because the legal question at issue does not in all cases concern the first step of the selectivity test. In other cases, the identification of the reference system will not be relevant for procedural reasons.[323] The identification of the exact elements of the reference system thus now typically (only) becomes relevant in rather complex cases or for atypical types of levies. Nevertheless, in our view, this step is crucial – at least from a dogmatic point of view.

Three functions can be attributed to the reference system of taxation. First, there needs to be a derogation, i.e., an exception from the general rule of the reference system. This means that where there is no benchmark, for example, because of fragmentation, which does not permit an identification of a general system of taxation, there can be no selectivity.[324] Related to this is the question of what are the elements of the reference system of taxation. Technical rules that are inherent to the functioning of the tax system cannot lead to a derogation from the reference system of taxation.[325] This first function corresponds with a benchmark approach to assessing selectivity. In this dimension, the reference system of taxation has stand-alone significance vis-à-vis the second step.

Second, the reference system is required to identify a different treatment of undertakings that are in a comparable situation in light of the objective of the reference system.[326] This is the first step to testing for discrimination, which leads to a derogation in the second step.[327] The identification of the circle of comparable undertakings is

320. Lang, *State Aid and Taxation: Selectivity and Comparability Analysis*, *supra* n. 131, at 36. Similarly dubbing the identification of the reference system of taxation 'illustrative only', whereas in fact the principle of equality would be applied Prek & Lefèvre, *supra* n. 127, at 344.
321. *See* Ch.§4.01 *infra*.
322. Loewenthal, *supra* n. 136, at 38 with reference to the judgments in Case C-74/16 *Congregación de Escuelas Pías Provincia Betania* EU:C:2017:496, paras 68-72; Joined Cases C-234 and 235/16 *ANGED* EU:C:2018:281, para. 35.
323. This was, for example, the case in Joined Cases C-20 and 21/15 P *World Duty Free Group* but was later remedied after the renvoi, *see* Ch. §3.02[B], [1] *infra*.
324. This is a function that *Schön* relies on extensively in contrasting benchmark and discrimination approaches, Schön, *Tax Legislation and the Notion of Fiscal Aid*, *supra* n. 40, at 9ff. *See also* Ellenrieder, *Die materielle Selektivität steuerlicher Beihilfen*, *supra* n. 57, at 168; Leigh Hancher, *The Role of Presumptions and the Burden of Proof in Recent State Aid Cases: Some Reflections* 18 EStAL 470, 484 (2019) https://doi.org/10.21552/estal/2019/4/5.
325. *See* Ch. §3.02[C], [1] *infra*.
326. *See* in more detail Ch. §3.03 *infra*.
327. Ismer & Piotrowski, *Relationship of Fiscal State Aid and the Fundamental Freedoms*, *supra* n. 164, at 455f. Rather than relying on the objective of the reference system itself as a benchmark, *Lang* considers all companies that are in considerable competitive relationships comparable. The intensity of competition would have to be examined in the scope of proportionality, Lang, *Recent Trends in the Case Law of the ECJ*, *supra* n. 146, at 421; Lang, *State Aid and Taxation: Selectivity and Comparability Analysis*, *supra* n. 131, at 35f. Yet this approach would lead to considerable legal uncertainty and does not appear workable in practice.

crucial since selectivity lacks a specific discrimination criterion, and thus also a 'standard' comparator that can be relied upon.[328] From a tax sovereignty perspective, it is necessary to acknowledge that Member States may assign objectives to taxation that go beyond the mere levying of funds. The only possible starting point of the analysis is therefore the fundamental charging decision of the Member State which has to be relied upon as a yardstick.[329] Within a reference system of taxation, all actors in principle have to be treated equally.

Both of these functions can ultimately be traced back to the fiscal sovereignty of Member States. In its judgment in *Fiat,* the CJEU stated:

> In the second place, outside the spheres in which EU tax law has been harmonised, *it is the Member State concerned which determines, by exercising its own competence in the matter of direct taxation and with due regard for its fiscal autonomy, the characteristics constituting the tax, which define, in principle, the reference system or the 'normal' tax regime,* from which it is necessary to analyse the condition relating to selectivity. This includes, in particular, the determination of the basis of assessment and the taxable event [...].[330]

This shows the direct link between the fiscal sovereignty of Member States and the identification of the reference system of taxation. This passage concerns the first function of the reference system identified above, but the same ultimately also holds true for the second function.

Third, the reference system of taxation is also relied on to determine what types of grounds for justification are permissible in the third step of the selectivity test. A justification can only be derived from the basic and guiding principles of the reference system of taxation.[331]

[B] Identification of the Reference System

The reference system of taxation is generally the entire levy in which the tax measure is embedded [1]. Difficulties may exist concerning the identification of the elements of the reference system of taxation. They may either be determined normatively or in exceptional constellations empirically [2].

[1] Reference System of Taxation Generally the Entire Levy

It has rightfully been noted that the CJEU's guidance on the identification of the reference system of taxation has lacked clarity and consistency.[332] This explains the

328. Ismer & Piotrowski, *Relationship of Fiscal State Aid and the Fundamental Freedoms*, *supra* n. 164, at 454f. with further references.
329. Loewenthal, *supra* n. 136, at 41.
330. Joined Cases C-885 and 898/19 P *Fiat*, para. 73; emphasis added by the author.
331. *See* Ch. §3.04 *infra*.
332. Loewenthal, *supra* n. 136, at 42. Similarly: Phedon Nicolaides, *Can Selectivity Result from the Application of Non-selective Rules?* 18 EStAL 15, 28 (2019) https://doi.org/10.21552/estal/2019/1/4.

fundamentally diverging opinions in the scholarly literature on how to identify the reference system of taxation. This is particularly because the specifics of the selectivity test have only emerged fairly recently.

It had therefore sometimes been argued that the reference system of taxation would be made up of a subset of rules within a levy.[333] For example, it had been suggested that the rules on transfer pricing in a Member State could constitute a reference system of taxation.[334] Others had instead argued that the reference system would generally be the entire levy.[335] The underlying assumption is that in drafting such a levy the legislator assumes that all actors or situations that fall within the scope of such tax - which is again defined by relying on the objective of the tax in question - are comparable.

Recent case law has now confirmed that the reference system of taxation is indeed - at least generally - the entire levy rather than a subset of rules therein. This holds true regardless of the levy in question. For example, in its judgment in *Paint Graphos,* the CJEU identified corporate taxation as the point of departure.[336] In its judgment in *A-Brauerei,* the CJEU identified the German real property transfer tax as the appropriate reference system of taxation.[337]

The *World Duty Free Group* judgment further clarified the notion of selectivity for broad-based fiscal taxes, also regarding the identification of the reference system of taxation. The judgment dealt with a Spanish rule that allowed undertakings taxable in Spain that acquired a shareholding in a foreign country of at least 5 % of that company's capital to deduct the goodwill from the shareholding in the form of an amortization.[338]

When the Grand Chamber of the CJEU first dealt with the case, it mainly clarified the overall approach to assessing selectivity clearly fleshing out the different notions of de facto and de jure-selectivity. In its first judgment, the CJEU in fact did not answer the question of whether the Commission had correctly determined the reference system of taxation. It did not have to. The main issue of the case at that time was whether the Commission had to demonstrate that the measure in question favoured a group of undertakings which could be clearly defined by their characteristics and which distinguish them from other undertakings that cannot benefit from the aid. This was rejected by the CJEU.[339] However, in the original judgment, the CJEU had repeatedly referred to the fact that the reference system of taxation is comprised of the ordinary tax system, which would appear to imply that corporation tax is the reference system of taxation.[340]

333. Buriak & Lazarov, *supra* n. 127, at 21.
334. Giraud & Petit, *Tax Rulings and State Aid Qualification, supra* n. 126, at 238 - stand-alone and group companies would not be comparable; Lovdahl Gormsen, *supra* n. 126, at 377. Somewhat similarly: Nicolaides, *State Aid Rules and Tax Rulings, supra* n. 126, at 425.
335. Ismer & Piotrowski, *Selektivität von Beihilfen, supra* n. 132, at 260; Mang, *supra* n. 132, at 81; Szudoczky, *Convergence of the Analysis of National Tax Measures, supra* n. 131, at 367.
336. *See* only Joined Cases C-78 to 80/08 *Paint Graphos*, para. 50.
337. Case C-374/17 *A-Brauerei*, para. 37.
338. Joined Cases C-20 and 21/15 P *World Duty Free Group*, para. 5.
339. *Ibid.*, para. 78.
340. E.g., *Ibid.*, para. 57.

The case was referred back to the General Court, which then determined that the Commission was right in finding that Spain had granted State aid.[341] The judgment was again appealed. In this second judgment, the CJEU appears to divert from the prior case law – and in particular the first judgment of the CJEU on the same Commission decision. The CJEU stated that the General Court had correctly interpreted the Commission decision which had in essence used the tax treatment of goodwill – as opposed to only financial goodwill – within the Spanish corporate tax system as the reference system of taxation.[342]

Without clearly defining the objective of the rules on the tax treatment of goodwill, the CJEU held that a measure which is designed to facilitate exports may be regarded as selective as it benefits undertakings carrying out cross-border transactions, in particular investment transactions. It in turn disadvantages other undertakings which are in a comparable factual and legal situation in light of the objective pursued by the tax system concerned and carry out comparable transactions within the national territory.[343]

Did the CJEU thereby acknowledge that the reference system can be made up of a subset of rules within the corporate tax system? From the outset, the case demonstrates that scholars have to take care in interpreting the judgments of the CJEU. More explicitly, one has to remember not to interpret judgments of the CJEU the same way as judgments of national courts. The CJEU is under no obligation to clarify points that aren't the explicit subject of the case at issue. This is to say that one may never assume that the CJEU tacitly takes a stance due to the mere fact that it does not clarify the contrary. While this is particularly relevant for references for preliminary rulings, the same holds true for appeals against Commission decisions.

Indeed, the CJEU in its first judgment did not take a definite stance on the corporate tax system making up the reference system of taxation. The second judgment appears to put into question the finding that the point of departure for the selectivity test is the whole levy, since the rules that the Court tests against are a subset of the entire corporation tax. Yet one could nevertheless interpret the judgment as a mere concretization of the notion that broad-based fiscal levies generally require an equal treatment of all company profits. The treatment of financial goodwill is a matter of the determination of a company's profits. In the case at issue, companies were able to deduct financial goodwill only for certain types of acquisitions, whereas the same was not possible for acquisitions within Spain. This means that the case clarifies that the State aid law in principle not only requires an equal treatment of all types of profit but also a coherent and internally consistent method of calculating profits in the first place. Thus, where rules within a corporate tax system not only introduce technical guidelines for the calculation of profits but also distinctions which lead to discriminations, they may be selective. The direct comparison with domestic transactions that the CJEU makes could merely be for simplification purposes.

341. Case T-219/10 RENV *World Duty Free Group v. Commission*.
342. Joined Cases C-51 and 64/19 P *World Duty Free Group v. Commission* EU:C:2021:793, paras 72, 80.
343. *Ibid.*, paras 127f.

[2] Identification of the Elements of the Reference System of Taxation

An error in the determination of the reference system of taxation necessarily vitiates the whole of the analysis of selectivity.[344] The relevant reference framework can only be the prevailing national law and not hypothetical or notional law. Anything else would permit the Commission to replace the respective national legislature and to determine its favoured tax system as the reference framework.[345] For example, the General Court in its judgment on the Polish turnover-based tax rightly found that the Commission chose the incorrect reference framework in referring to a hypothetical single-rate tax system as the relevant benchmark.[346]

While the reference system of taxation is now known to generally be the levy itself, this is only helpful in so far as this provides the correct yardstick for the discrimination analysis in the second step, namely the objective of the levy in question. Yet beyond that, it is also necessary to determine the exact elements of the reference system of taxation as well as the exact scope of the reference system as an added dimension for special purpose levies. This is not always straightforward. Accordingly, De Broe has described the identification of the reference system of taxation as 'replete with uncertainty' in light of the complexities of corporate tax regimes and the multitude of legal techniques that Member States rely on to design such systems.[347]

There are two different approaches to determining the exact elements of the reference system of taxation. Primarily, the reference system of taxation should be determined normatively through an interpretation of the rules in question.

For example, this is the case for the objective of a levy. Technically, the objective of the tax only becomes relevant in the second step of the three-step selectivity test. However, it will be shown that particularly for special purpose levies, the objective of a tax determines the circle of comparable undertakings and thus the necessary scope of a tax.[348] This is to say that the scope of a tax has to be derived from the objectives the legislator intends to pursue with its tax. It is necessary to understand the objectives of the legislator, perhaps also taking into account the general context of the rules or legislative documents. In this, the decisions of the national legislator cannot be substituted with value judgments derived from European law, unless there is some sort of harmonization. We will focus on this issue in more detail below in the context of special-purpose levies.

Of course, such normative analysis is not always straightforward and leads to some issues in practice. For example, the problem arises that the legislator will not always comprehensively explain the exact motivations behind a tax. Under national law, a similar conflict can exist between the legislator and the judiciary. Yet under State aid law, there is an additional dimension to the problem because the conflict is between

344. Case C-203/16 P *Andres*, para. 107.
345. *See* Opinion of AG Kokott in Case C-562/19 P *Commission v. Poland* EU:C:2020:834, para. 66.
346. Joined Cases T-836/16 and 624/17 *Poland v. Commission* EU:T:2019:338.
347. De Broe, *The State Aid Selectivity-Test in Corporate Tax Matters*, *supra* n. 163.
348. Englisch, *Das Beihilfenverbot im Steuerrecht*, *supra* n. 67, at para. 9.32: this implies that there is no room for a separate comparability test in the second step as it is already part of the identification of the reference system.

the Member State's tax sovereignty on the one hand and supranational State aid control on the other hand. It is thus even more important that legislative discretion be safeguarded and that the Commission does not substitute its own interpretation of the motivations behind a tax. Such a normative approach also applies to the distinction between technical rules and derogations, but may sometimes yield ambiguous results at best.[349]

Furthermore, there are still uncertainties as to the determination of the rule and the exception within a tax system. In such cases, it is necessary to determine which of several measures amounts to the 'rule' which makes up the reference system of taxation.

In its judgment in *Aer Lingus and Ryanair*, the CJEU at least did not reject the view that it is also possible to define the standard tax treatment from an empirical perspective.[350] To verify the existence of an advantage – rather than a disadvantage which could not amount to State aid – it was necessary to determine which of the two rates of the ATT was the normal tax rate. A normative determination was not possible, since the tax was not explicitly designed as a regulatory tax. The Commission adopted an empirical approach and found that the lower rate applied to only some 10% to 15% of all flights that were subject to the tax. Consequently, the higher rate was deemed the standard rate, and the lower rate constituted a positive derogation from the reference system, i.e., an advantage for some operators.[351] These points were mentioned in the subsequent decision of the CJEU, but they were neither discussed nor explicitly rejected. The CJEU did find, however, that the appeals relating to the identification of the reference system of taxation brought by Aer Lingus and Ryanair were unfounded.[352]

In our view, the normative determination of the reference system of taxation has to take precedence over the empirical approach.[353] This is because the former is an assessment of the objectives of the legislator and is thus in conformity with tax sovereignty. By contrast, conformity with the objectives of the legislator can only be assumed for an empirical determination. In any case, such an 'empirical' approach will but rarely be workable. It requires clear-cut percentages. As soon as there are more than two rates or other types of variations in the tax treatment of the same element of the tax system, it will most often be difficult to determine a standard rate. Where the standard tax treatment can neither be determined relying on a normative, nor an

349. *See* Ch. §3.02[C] *infra*.
350. Ismer & Piotrowski, *Relationship of Fiscal State Aid and the Fundamental Freedoms*, *supra* n. 164, at 457. Schön, *Tax Legislation and the Notion of Fiscal Aid*, *supra* n. 40, at 13f. refers to this case as a demonstration of the necessity of a benchmark approach. Critical: Ellenrieder, *Die materielle Selektivität steuerlicher Beihilfen*, *supra* n. 57, at 170ff. according to whom the logic of the tax would have implied taxing all passengers departing from Ireland, making an empirical approach obsolete.
351. Commission Decision 2013/199/EU of 25 July 2012 on State aid case SA.29064 (11/C, ex 11/NN) – Differentiated air travel tax rates implemented by Ireland [2013] OJ L 119/30, para. 45.
352. *See* Joined Cases C-164 and 165/15 P *Aer Lingus and Ryanair*, paras 47ff.
353. In a similar vein: Schön, *State Aid in the Area of Taxation*, *supra* n. 31, at para. 13-076.

empirical approach, i.e., where it is impossible to identify a benchmark, there can be no de jure-selectivity.

Finally, the reference system of taxation may be partly influenced by European law where there is harmonizing legislation. In this context, the aspect of tax sovereignty plays a limited role. The design of the reference system of taxation, as well as the principles underlying such tax, are then shaped by the underlying secondary law.[354] Yet while selectivity is not excluded for partly harmonized taxes,[355] there is presumably a certain degree of restraint in reviewing legislation that implements European secondary law from a State aid law perspective. In other words, it is reasonable to assume that the Directive itself has been designed in accordance with primary law, which may limit State aid control in practice. Of course, this also implies that State aid vulnerabilities may particularly arise where the Directive has not been correctly transposed into national law.[356]

[C] Distinction Between Technical Rules as Emanations of Fiscal Sovereignty and Derogations

Ambiguities that have still not been satisfactorily resolved arise from the distinction between technical rules that are part of the reference system of taxation on the one hand and rules that can indeed lead to derogations on the other hand. There appears to be a trend to include more and more types of rules in the first category, which is presumably informed by a desire to promote fiscal sovereignty [1]. An example of this is a progressive tax structure, even where the progressivity is designed along turnover thresholds [2].

[1] Integral Elements of the Reference System of Taxation

Every tax system necessarily contains a number of technical provisions, whether they apply on the level of determining what profits are or at a later stage. Such technical rules lay down the general principles or parameters of a comprehensive tax system.[357] These technical rules that by default form part of the reference system have to be distinguished from rules that can indeed lead to a derogation.[358] Where technical rules that are inherent to the reference system itself are facially neutral, there can be no de jure-selectivity. This means that they can only confer State aid if they are designed in a manifestly inconsistent manner, i.e., if they are de facto selective.[359]

354. According to Pfeiffer, *supra* n. 160, at 161, the VAT Directive itself would be the reference system itself, where Member States asymmetrically rely on it.
355. *See* Ch. §3.04[B], [4] *infra* for a possible justification in the third step.
356. Swinkels, *supra* n. 160, at 315.
357. Schön, *Taxation and State Aid Law, supra* n. 7, at 928.
358. Balbinot, *Europäisches Beihilfeverbot vs. Mitgliedstaatliche Steuersouveränität, supra* n. 95, at 730.
359. Kelyn Bacon, *State Aids and General Measures* 17 YEL 269, 299ff. (1997) https://doi.org/10.1093/yel/17.1.269 makes a distinction between direct and indirect discrimination.

The distinction between technical rules and potential derogations is all the more relevant since the CJEU has underlined the significance of the technical elements of any tax system in its recent case law and established a connection with fiscal sovereignty. This has most clearly emerged in the judgments on the Polish and Hungarian progressive turnover-based taxes. The CJEU stated the following:

> As regards the fundamental freedoms of the internal market, the Court of Justice has held that, given the current state of harmonisation of EU tax law, the Member States are free to establish the system of taxation which they deem most appropriate, meaning that the application of progressive taxation falls within the discretion of each Member State [...]. It follows that, *outside the spheres in which EU tax law has been harmonised, the determination of the characteristics constituting each tax falls within the discretion of the Member States, in accordance with their fiscal autonomy, that discretion having, in any event, to be exercised in accordance with EU law. This includes, in particular, the choice of tax rate, which may be proportional or progressive, and also the determination of the basis of assessment and the taxable event.* Those characteristics constituting the tax therefore, in principle, define the reference system or the 'normal' tax regime, from which it is necessary, [...] to analyse the condition relating to selectivity.[360]

The CJEU thus understood progression as an integral feature of the tax itself. It has furthermore recently decided that unilateral rules for the avoidance of double taxation form part of the reference system of taxation.[361] Yet no clear dividing line between the two types of rules has emerged from the case law.

The conceptual difficulties in drawing a line between potential derogations and technical rules have also been subject to extensive debate in the US on tax expenditure theory.[362] The notion of tax expenditures as a way to quantify what would be negative aid under European State aid law had first been brought forward by Surrey according to whom 'deliberate departures from accepted concepts of net income and through various special exemptions, deductions and credits, our tax system does operate to affect the private economy in ways that are usually accomplished by expenditures – in effect to produce an expenditure system described in tax language'.[363] Surrey described tax expenditures as consisting of two elements, namely first the imputed tax payment that would have been due in the absence of the special provision and second the simultaneous expenditure of the payment as a direct subsidy to the beneficiary.[364] He acknowledged the difficulty in distinguishing tax rules that were integral to a tax system and which served to provide a balanced tax structure and an exact measurement of income and departures therefrom, which would qualify as tax expenditures. There would also be problems in the computation of the expenditure equivalent.[365] The distinction between tax expenditures and rules that constitute the basic structure of

360. Case C-562/19 P *Commission v. Poland*, paras 37ff.; emphasis added by the author.
361. Case C-705/20 *Fossil (Gibraltar)* EU:C:2022:680.
362. Mason, *Tax Competition and State Aid, supra* n. 9, at 10.
363. Stanley S. Surrey, *Pathways to Tax Reform*, 3 (1973).
364. *Ibid.*, at 6f.
365. *Ibid.*, at 4.

income tax would depend on the definition of 'income' for income tax purposes.[366] The starting point of his analysis is the Haig-Simons approach, according to which personal income is defined as the sum of the market value of rights exercised in consumption and the change in the value of the store of property rights between the beginning and the end of the period in question.[367]

The theory has been criticized in the scholarly literature for the very reasons that we are concerned with here. The identification of the applicable baseline would remain unresolved.[368] In particular, it has been noted that there is no general agreement on what constitutes an ideal or correct tax structure that could serve as a benchmark.[369] Neither a historical approach nor an approach relying on the consensus of experts would convince.[370] The tax expenditure approach would consequently be subjective and ambiguous.[371]

The parallels to the dogmatic shortcomings of fiscal State aid law have, for example, been pointed out by Mason. The three-step selectivity test could be understood as an application of a tax expenditure approach where the benchmark is the Member State's domestic law.[372] She argues that an approach that includes all 'structural' tax rules into the baseline would be under-inclusive.[373] By contrast, benchmarking by (external) norms[374] would replace policy preferences enacted by a Member State's legislator with policy preferences of the Commission and would be overinclusive because it mistakes mismatches for State aid.[375] Benchmarking would work well in two types of cases, namely either for special tax provisions that benefit only members of selective classes or derogating provisions that do not benefit selective classes. The former would amount to State aid, while the latter would not.[376] Yet there would be a number of categories of 'hard cases' that could not be solved by relying on tax expenditure analysis.[377]

366. *Ibid.*, at 7.
367. *Ibid.*, at 12 with reference to Henry C. Simons, *Personal Income Taxation,* 50 (1938). Critical of *Surrey's* point of departure Victor Thuronyi, *Tax Expenditures: A Reassessment* 37 Duke Law Journal 1155f. (1988) https://doi.org/10.2307/1372533.
368. Mason, *Identifying Illegal Subsidies, supra* n. 77, at 497ff.
369. Boris I. Bittker, *Accounting for Federal 'Tax Subsidies' in the National Budget* 22 NTJ 244, 247 (1969) https://doi.org/10.1086/ntj41792208; *see* for a focus on the intrinsic objectives of the tax William D. Andres, *Personal Deductions in an Ideal Income Tax* 86 Harvard L. Rev. 309, 312ff. (1972) https://doi.org/10.2307/1339894, which could fall through the cracks in applying tax expenditure analysis.
370. Thuronyi, *supra* n. 367, at 1166.
371. Bruce Bartlett, *The End of Tax Expenditures as We Know Them?* 84 IRET policy Bulletin, 7 (2001). Similarly Boris L. Bittker, *The Tax Expenditure Budget: A Reply to Professors Surrey & Hellmuth* 22 NTJ 538, 542 (1969) https://doi.org/10.1086/ntj41791687; Douglas A. Kahn & Jeffery S. Lehman, *Tax Expenditures: A Critical View* 54 Tax Notes 1661, 1664 (1992).
372. Mason, *Identifying Illegal Subsidies, supra* n. 77, at 501.
373. *Ibid.*, at 482.
374. *See* Ch. §4.01 *infra.*
375. Mason, *Identifying Illegal Subsidies, supra* n. 77, at 485.
376. *Ibid.*, at 502. An example for the latter would be a one-year-only expensing rule that is available to all companies.
377. *Ibid.*, at 505ff.

Indeed, the problems that arise in the context of the selectivity test are very similar. The case law has sought to address this issue by developing the two tests for selectivity. Both types of benchmarking as described by Mason are applied. De jure-selectivity tests for internal consistency and relies on the fundamental charging decision of the Member State as the point of departure, whereas de facto-selectivity tests for external consistency. The problem of the over-inclusiveness of relying on external benchmarks has at least theoretically - if not necessarily in practice - been solved by applying a very low standard of control for de facto-selectivity.[378] By contrast, the potential of under-inclusiveness has not been addressed, since the current case law emphasizes promoting fiscal sovereignty by considering more and more rules to form part of the reference system of taxation itself. In any case, the very reason that the point of departure for the selectivity test is the domestic tax system is an emanation of the fiscal sovereignty of Member States in light of the multi-polar enforcement structure of State aid law. Therefore, there appears to be little room for an altogether different approach to identifying selectivity that does not rely on benchmarking.

What types of rules are thus 'characteristics constituting a tax'? Some contributions in the scholarly literature have provided valuable indicators for the identification of technical rules. Schön points out that such technical rules often concern certain 'events', such as the accrual of losses, instead of undertakings.[379] He provides the example of diverging depreciation rules for different assets that are intended to approximate the financial situation of the taxpayer.[380] This is not to say that within such technical rules, there cannot be distinctions that can lead to State aid. This was, for example, the case in the CJEU's judgment in *World Duty Free Group.*[381] According to Mason, the first type of structural rule would be tax-mix questions. A second type would be rules arising from practical necessity. Examples would be progressive rates, definitions of debt and equity, or methods for dividing income from cross-border transactions among States with jurisdiction to tax.[382] Jaeger refers to the distinction made by tax expenditure theory and considers norms that contribute to the functioning of a system and whose system is logical technical norms.[383]

Yet beyond that, there is little clarity.[384] When making the distinction, one should avoid a fallacy: The identification of a technical rule is not necessarily related to the definition of the tax base in the sense that any rule that has an impact on the tax base could not amount to State aid. Furthermore, it is clear that technical rules themselves cannot pursue a policy objective. This may allow for a negative delimitation of technical rules in some cases.

378. *See* Ch. §4.01 *infra.*
379. Schön, *Taxation and State Aid Law, supra* n. 7, at 928.
380. Bacon, *State Aids and General Measures, supra* n. 359, at 302 points to the definition of what a corporation is as an example; *see also* Schön, *Taxation and State Aid Law, supra* n. 7, at 924.
381. *See* on this Ch. §3.02[B], [1] *supra.*
382. Mason, *Identifying Illegal Subsidies, supra* n. 77, at 500 with further examples.
383. Jaeger, *Tax Measures, supra* n. 73, at para. 5.
384. The case law on the German *Sanierungsklausel* ultimately dealt with the same issue with the added dimension of a complex structure of the pertinent legal provisions, *see* Ch. §3.02[D], [1] *infra.*

For more or less standardized taxes, the classification of technical rules may in some cases be fairly obvious, even where certain ambiguities are hard to explain from a dogmatic point of view. For such taxes, one could, for example, rely on a comparative law approach to determine features that are common to most tax systems. This could, for example, be the case for participation exemptions which are meant to ensure that profits are only taxed once within a group.[385] Nevertheless, even for 'typical' taxes, the distinction will often be blurry, since technical rules - even where they are neutral - will not affect each taxpayer equally.[386] Moreover, as an emanation of fiscal sovereignty, a comparative law approach can only lead to certain types of standard rules being considered technical rules. By contrast, the lack of consensus among Member States cannot exclude a rule from nevertheless being considered a technical element of the tax system of the Member State in question. The same reasoning applies to making a historical argument or referring to internationally accepted accounting standards to conclude that a rule should be considered technical in nature. Where Member States design atypical taxes, the boundary becomes even less clear.[387] This particularly holds true for special-purpose levies, since these taxes are designed to achieve some specific goal of public policy. The technical rules of such tax would be aligned with this special purpose.

All this means that the identification of the technical elements of the reference system of taxation indeed involves value judgments. Perhaps the growing impact of State aid law in the area of corporate taxation that could be observed for some years was due to the (flawed) assumption that there is an 'ideal' corporate tax system that could be taken as a point of departure. While the latter assumption has meanwhile been rejected, the case law has not yet defined clear criteria for the distinction and legal uncertainty remains.

Pointing to these difficulties of drawing the line, some contributions have instead suggested a global examination of national tax systems that would imply a limited impact of State aid control. For example, it would be common to combine a high nominal tax rate with a narrow taxable base, the latter being obtained through deductions, exemptions or deferrals. Rather than considering the high nominal rate the benchmark, the rate and the exemptions reducing the tax base would be inextricably linked. The State aid provision should then be understood as a non-discrimination provision where the focus lies on the justification of differences in the treatment of taxpayers.[388] However, even uniform rules that minimize the tax base can be designed

385. In this vein: Opinion of AG Kokott in Case C-454/21 P *Engie Global LNG Holding and Others v. Commission*, para. 181. Against such understanding and assuming an evident inconsistency of the Luxembourg law: Pierpaolo Rossi-Maccanico, *AG Kokott Tries to Bring Clarity to the Selectivity Test for Individual Tax Rulings* 32 EC Tax Rev. 183, 187 (2023) https://doi.org/10.54648/ecta2023023.

386. Balbinot, *Europäisches Beihilfeverbot vs. Mitgliedstaatliche Steuersouveränität, supra* n. 95, at 730.

387. Similarly, albeit in the context of tax expenditure theory, Bittker, *The Tax Expenditure Budget, supra* n. 371, at 540. According to Jaeger, *Tax Measures, supra* n. 73, at para. 5 the criticism that tax expenditure theory cannot be transferred to other types of taxes would be unfounded.

388. Traversa & Sabbadini, *Anti-avoidance Measures and State Aid in a Post-BEPS Context, supra* n. 161, at 87f.

with the intention of affording advantages to certain undertakings under the guise of technical rules.

Therefore, it appears to us as though it is still necessary to examine each tax measure in isolation and determine whether it is truly just a technical rule rather than an explicit derogation from the reference system. Thus, it seems preferable to maintain the – albeit blurred – distinction.

[2] *Progressivity as an Inherent Element of the Reference System*

Many tax systems do not work with a single rate for a given tax but provide for different rates depending on aspects, such as a taxpayer's ability to pay or the regulatory purpose of the tax. While different rates (as opposed to full exemptions or a zero rate) may be one of the most obvious ways of providing privileged treatment to certain groups of actors, it is notoriously difficult – and perhaps not always desirable – to tackle such differentiations under State aid law. Multi-rate tax systems can fall outside the scope of State aid control altogether for one of two reasons, namely either because it is impossible to determine what the standard rate is or because the respective rate structure can be considered a technical rule that forms part of the reference system and is thus – as an emanation of tax sovereignty – at least generally not subject to State aid control. The two aspects cannot always be separated.

This difficulty had first become apparent in the CJEU's judgment in *Aer Lingus and Ryanair.* In this case, the problem was that it was not clear which of the two rates was the standard rate. Had the Commission not been able to resort to an empirical approach to determining the standard tax treatment in this case, State aid law would have fallen short.[389]

Similar issues may arise in the context of progressive tax systems. In contrast to the constellation at issue in the judgment in *Aer Lingus and Ryanair,* the issue may then not so much be the delimitation of advantages and disadvantages. Instead, it appears as though progressivity – while leading to a differentiated tax treatment of undertakings – is a matter of the definition of the reference system itself. Therefore, there can be no derogation.

Admittedly, such a view of progressivity as an element of the reference system of taxation may be at odds with the Commission's interpretation: In its Notice on the notion of State aid, the Commission lists the following conceivable grounds for justification: 'the need to fight fraud or tax evasion, the need to take into account specific accounting requirements, administrative manageability, the principle of tax neutrality, the progressive nature of income tax and its redistributive purpose, the need to avoid double taxation, or the objective of optimising the recovery of fiscal debts'.[390] This appears to indicate that the progressivity of tax systems would lead to a derogation from the reference system of taxation that has to be justified in the third step. This in turn would mean that a proportionality test would have to be applied. It is moreover

389. *See* Ch. §3.02[B][2] *supra.*
390. Commission Notice on the notion of State aid, *supra* n. 26, at para. 139.

striking that the Commission only explicitly acknowledges the progressive nature and redistributive purpose of income tax. This would appear to suggest that progressivity in other types of taxes could not be justified.

Yet in our view, this fails to convince: It has been argued that progressivity should not be assessed in the third step because progression as a general feature of a tax system bears no particular relationship to certain undertakings or the production of certain goods (as per the wording of the TFEU). Progression could not be understood as a tax incentive for small earners, but rather as a surcharge for high-income taxpayers.[391] Szudoczky similarly argues that the progressivity of a tax system would not be prima facie selective in the first place. It would be an emanation of the objective of the income tax system – the implementation of the ability to pay principle – itself.[392]

This result is certainly convincing for the area of personal income taxation since such taxes are imposed on the ability to pay off the taxpayer, which is expressed in personal income.[393] Where the taxable person is not a natural person, the case becomes somewhat less clear.[394] It is not altogether clear whether the ability to pay principle can be applied at all for corporations – a debate which goes beyond the scope of this book.[395] The CJEU does not share these concerns and has held that progressive taxation could in principle be relied upon to take account of the ability to pay of legal persons, in particular undertakings.[396]

State aid law can furthermore only apply where it is possible to identify a 'normal' tax rate, and where there is a favourable derogation from this normal tax rate. In a progressive tax system, this will most often not be possible. Since all taxpayers regardless of their overall income pay the same rate for the portion of income not exceeding a certain threshold, it will be almost impossible to determine a standard rate. As long as it is not possible to unambiguously determine such a standard rate, the impact of State aid control has to be limited by default.

The CJEU had to answer the question of whether these arguments can be transferred to progressive turnover-based income taxes.[397] For these taxes, the debate shifts to the chosen proxies for the ability to pay as the basis for progressivity.[398] These

391. Schön, *State Aid in the Area of Taxation*, *supra* n. 31, at para. 13-074.
392. Szudoczky, *Convergence of the Analysis of National Tax Measures*, *supra* n. 131, at 371.
393. *See* Sinnig, *supra* n. 157, at 110 with further references.
394. *See* on the different applicable dimensions of the ability to pay principle for individuals and for corporations Johanna Hey, *Steuersystem und Steuerverfassungsrecht*, in Tipke & Lang (eds), Steuerrecht, paras 3.50f. (24th edn 2020).
395. *See* on the discussion with further references Sinnig, *supra* n. 157, at 110ff.
396. *See* Case C-562/19 P *Poland v. Commission*, para. 40.
397. *See* on this, e.g.: Agnolucci, *supra* n. 157; Bernatt & Grzejdziak, *supra* n. 149; Deák, *supra* n. 157; Eilers & Schmitz, *supra* n. 157; Lang, *Recent Case Law on Progressive Turnover Taxes*, *supra* n. 157; Károlyi, *supra* n. 157; Ruth Mason, *What the CJEU's Hungarian Cases Mean for Digital Taxes* TNI 161ff. (2020) https://doi.org/10.2139/ssrn.3550757; Mehboob, *supra* n. 157, at 69f.; Nicolaides, *Multi-rate Turnover Taxes and State Aid*, *supra* n. 157; Parada, *Vodafone Magyarország Opinion*, *supra* n. 157; Sinnig, *supra* n. 157; Stevanato, *supra* n. 157; Szudoczky & Károlyi, *The Troubled Story of the Hungarian Advertisement Tax*, *supra* n. 157; Szudoczky & Károlyi, *The CJEU's Approach to the Objectives of Progressive Turnover-Based Taxes*, *supra* n. 95.
398. *See* on this Chs §3.03[D] and §4.02 *infra*.

taxes can be qualified as narrow-based fiscal levies. For example, a number of such progressive turnover-based taxes were levied on grounds of the same law in Hungary ('Law No XCIV of 2010 on the special tax on certain sectors'). This was the case for the tax on telecommunications and the tax on the store retail trade sector. The preamble of the law in question stated that the tax was meant to raise revenue from taxpayers whose ability to contribute to the costs of public expenditure exceeds the general obligation to pay tax.[399] These taxes could thus not be qualified as a special-purpose levy as understood here. Additionally, the Hungarian government justified the taxes by arguing that MNEs tend to be able to avoid paying corporate income tax through tax planning, which is not possible to the same extent where turnover-based taxes are in place.[400] As such, the Hungarian taxes are very similar to the digital services taxes that have been introduced in several Member States. However, digital services taxes more specifically aim to address the perceived inadequacies of the concept of source and residence for digitalized business models.[401]

The first judgments on these taxes did not address their State aid compatibility for procedural reasons. The judgments in *Vodafone Magyarország*[402] and *Tesco-Global Áruházak*[403] dealt with the special taxes on telecommunications activities and in the store retail trade sector in Hungary respectively. The Grand Chamber decisions were issued on the same day and are very similar since the logic of both taxes was the same.

The taxable amount for the tax on telecommunication activities was defined as the net turnover of the taxable person resulting from the telecommunications activities. The tax rate depended on turnover thresholds (no tax for a taxable amount not exceeding HUF 500 million; 4.5% for a taxable amount of HUF 5 billion, and 6.5% for any taxable amount exceeding this threshold).[404] The retail tax, in turn, was levied on the net turnover of store retail trade. Again, the tax rate increased along the lines of turnover thresholds. Both Vodafone and Tesco challenged their own tax burden in front of a national court, which referred questions on the interpretation of the fundamental freedoms, other non-discrimination provisions and Article 107 to the CJEU.[405] The questions of the referring court show that it considered particularly contentious the fact that although not directly discriminatory, the actual tax burden for the highest tax band fell mainly on foreign-owned persons.[406]

399. Case C-75/18 *Vodafone Magyarország*, para. 4.
400. Szudoczky & Károlyi, *The Troubled Story of the Hungarian Advertisement Tax, supra* n. 157, at 46.
401. Similarly Szudoczky & Károlyi, *The Troubled Story of the Hungarian Advertisement Tax, supra* n. 157, at 50.
402. Case C-75/18 *Vodafone Magyarország*.
403. Case C-323/18 *Tesco-Global Áruházak*.
404. *See* Case C-75/18 *Vodafone Magyarország*, para. 17; Case C-323/18 *Tesco-Global Áruházak*, paras 4ff. for the facts of the case.
405. Case C-75/18 *Vodafone Magyarország*, para. 17; Case C-323/18 *Tesco-Global Áruházak*, para. 19.
406. *See* in particular questions (1) and (2).

Infringements of the fundamental freedoms were denied by the CJEU in substance.[407] The questions relating to State aid law were inadmissible.[408] While unsatisfying in terms of a desired clarification of the State aid compatibility of such taxes, this was very much in line with the long-standing case law of the CJEU.[409] The fact that a tax exemption amounts to State aid does not affect the legality of the tax itself.[410] The question would not be inadmissible if the dispute concerned the rules relating to that tax as a matter of EU law itself.[411]

In parallel, these same taxes were subject to investigations by the Commission. This resulted in two Commission decisions finding that the Polish tax on the retail sector and the Hungarian advertisement tax amounted to State aid.[412]

The Polish case concerned a tax on the retail sector, namely on the sale of goods to consumers who are natural persons.[413] The basis of the assessment was the monthly turnover above ZLT 17 million. The tax rate was 0.8%, for the portion of monthly turnover between ZLT 17 million and ZLT 170 million and 1.4% for the portion of monthly turnover above that.[414] The stated objective of the legislator was to introduce a sectoral tax with a redistributive purpose on retailers' turnover.[415]

The Hungarian Advertisement Tax, which was also tackled by the Commission, is perhaps an even more striking example of why State aid suspicions arose in the first place due to its steep rate structure and actual effects.[416] Taxable persons under this law were those making advertisements public (as opposed to the advertisers themselves or advertising agencies). The applicable rates ranged from 0% to 40% and later on even 50%, depending on the taxable amount. There was also the possibility to deduct 50% of the losses carried forward from the 2014 taxable amount for taxable persons whose pre-tax profits for the financial year 2013 were zero or negative.[417] Hungary subsequently amended the tax, introducing only two tax rates (0% and 5.3% for the taxable amount above HUF 100 million).[418] In its Decision, the Commission

407. Case C-75/18 *Vodafone Magyarország*, para. 56; Case C-323/18 *Tesco-Global Áruházak*, para. 76.
408. Case C-75/18 *Vodafone Magyarország*, para. 32; Case C-323/18 *Tesco-Global Áruházak*, para. 44.
409. *See* Ch. §5.02[A], [2], [a] *infra*.
410. Case C-75/18 *Vodafone Magyarország*, para. 24; Case C-323/18 *Tesco-Global Áruházak*, para. 36.
411. Case C-75/18 *Vodafone Magyarország*, para. 25; Case C-323/18 *Tesco-Global Áruházak*, para. 37.
412. Commission Decision (EU) 2017/329 of 4 November 2016 on the measure SA.39235 implemented by Hungary on the taxation of advertisement turnover [2017] OJ L 49/36; Commission Decision (EU) 2018/160 of 30 June 2017 on the State aid SA.44351 (2016/C) (ex 2016/NN) implemented by Poland for the tax on the retail sector [2017] OJ L 29/38.
413. Joined Cases T-836/16 and 624/17 *Poland v. Commission*.
414. *Ibid.*, para. 3.
415. *Ibid.*, para. 76.
416. On this tax: Szudoczky & Károlyi, *The Troubled Story of the Hungarian Advertisement Tax*, *supra* n. 157.
417. Case T-20/17 *Hungary v. Commission* EU:T:2019:448, paras 2ff. The latter aspect will not be dealt with in detail here.
418. *Ibid.*, para. 7.

ordered Hungary to recover the aid or to abolish the tax retroactively.[419] Hungary chose the latter option.

Nevertheless, the Commission decision was later annulled by the General Court.[420] The General Court identified the sectoral tax itself as the reference system of taxation.[421] It held that the rates of taxation were an inherent part of the reference system of taxation. In this respect, it would not matter whether a tax is levied at a progressive or a single rate.[422] According to the General Court, neither the Polish government nor the Hungarian government had explicitly designated a standard rate.[423] However, only if the standard rate was the highest applicable tax rate, could there be an advantage for undertakings with a lower turnover, thus profiting from a lower tax rate. Simply choosing the higher tax rate as the normal rate in a system of progressive taxation would amount to a merely hypothetical system which could not be sustained. Failing to make such a determination would mean that the reference system of taxation is incomplete.[424]

Both judgments were upheld by the CJEU. The impact of these judgments goes beyond the applicability of State aid law to progressive turnover-based taxes. The CJEU thereby fundamentally reaffirmed Member States' fiscal sovereignty, which exempts certain features of tax systems from State aid control almost altogether.[425] In particular, it stated:

> As regards the fundamental freedoms of the internal market, the Court of Justice has held that, given the current state of harmonisation of EU tax law, the Member States are free to establish the system of taxation which they deem most appropriate, meaning that the application of progressive taxation falls within the discretion of each Member State [...]. It follows that, outside the spheres in which EU tax law has been harmonised, *the determination of the characteristics constituting each tax falls within the discretion of the Member States, in accordance with their fiscal autonomy, that discretion having, in any event, to be exercised in accordance with EU law.* This includes, in particular, the choice of *tax rate, which may be proportional or progressive, and also the determination of the basis of assessment and the taxable event.* Those characteristics constituting the tax therefore, in principle, define the reference system or the 'normal' tax regime, from which it is necessary, in accordance with the case-law referred to in paragraph 31 of the present judgment, to analyse the condition relating to selectivity.[426]

It then clarified that this is also the case if the progressivity is based on turnover, 'including where such taxation is not intended to offset the negative effects likely to be

419. *See* on the latter option Ch. §5.01[D], [2] *infra.*
420. Case T-20/17 *Hungary v. Commission.*
421. *Ibid.*, para. 79.
422. *Ibid.*, para. 80.
423. Joined Cases T-836/16 and 624/17 *Poland v. Commission*, para. 66.
424. Case T-20/17 *Hungary v. Commission*, paras 81f.
425. Bernatt & Grzejdziak, *supra* n. 149, at 194. The CJEU would have given priority to tax sovereignty over the Treaty competition rules. All the considerations on progressivity should have been dealt with in the second and third step of the selectivity test.
426. Case C-596/19 P *Commission v. Hungary* EU:C:2021:202, paras 43ff.; Case C-562/19 P *Commission v. Poland*, paras 37ff.; emphasis added by the author.

caused by the activity being taxed' (i.e., for fiscal taxes).[427] This is in principle convincing and this clarification was very much warranted to counter an overly wide notion of selectivity.

The argument of the General Court that it is problematic to identify a standard rate for such taxes also has merit.[428] To address this problem, Nicolaides took the objective of the tax as the point of departure. He referred to the Polish tax and argued that in light of the objective of the reference system of taxation the zero rate for turnover up until ZLT 17 million would certainly constitute a derogation from the reference system. This is because a zero rate would not be consistent with the objective of raising revenue.[429] Indeed, such full exemption cannot be derived from the ability to pay principle, since it also benefits high turnover undertakings. Nevertheless, the problem remains that there would then still be two tax rates that could potentially constitute the standard rate.

Finally, the case law on progressivity in the context of the fundamental freedoms appears transferrable. The CJEU has decided that the establishment of a progressive tax system is within Member States' discretion.[430] It does not constitute a relevant discrimination.

All this means that the progressivity of tax systems is generally a matter of the definition of the reference system of taxation and thus does not lead to de jure-selectivity.[431] This holds true for any kind of fiscal tax, regardless of whether it is profit or turnover-based. Therefore, the question of whether there is a derogation does not arise in the first place. Despite this convincing result, the judgments clarifying these principles could potentially be problematic, since it is currently not clear what other types of rules could amount to technical rules and because the CJEU categorically denied that there was de facto-selectivity. This may be giving Member States too much leeway to reverse-engineer taxes.[432]

[D] Selectivity in Tax Measures with Complex Structures

Uncertainties in the determination of the reference system of taxation still exist where a tax measure is structured in a complex manner, containing exceptions to exceptions. In its judgment in *Andres*, the CJEU has clarified some aspects of the determination of

427. Case C-596/19 P *Commission v. Hungary*, para. 47; Case C-562/19 P *Commission v. Poland*, para. 41.
428. Joined Cases T-836/16 and 624/17 *Poland v. Commission*, paras 65ff. A different view is apparently held by Eilers & Schmitz, *supra* n. 157, at 212.
429. Nicolaides, *Multi-rate Turnover Taxes and State Aid*, *supra* n. 157, at 232.
430. *See* Case C-75/18 *Vodafone Magyarország*, para. 49 with reference to Case 127/75 *Bobie Getränkevertrieb* EU:C:1976:95, para. 9; Case C-298/05 *Columbus Container Services* EU:C:2007:754, paras 51, 53.
431. Mössner, *supra* n. 157, at 166. Bernatt & Grzejdziak, *supra* n. 149, at 194 criticize that the CJEU did not explain why the CJEU departed from its approach in *ANGED*, where tax autonomy was analysed in the second step of the selectivity test. Moreover, the court would have introduced a subjective element into the analysis of the reference system with the need to consider operators' ability to pay.
432. *See* on this in detail Ch. §4.02 *infra*.

the reference system where a tax measure's structure is more complex than a single explicit exception from the reference system of taxation. The judgment, in which the CJEU has taken a lenient approach, has to be seen in the context of what can be described as a rollback in State aid law. It is bound to have wider significance for the design of anti-abuse rules.[433]

To demonstrate the remaining ambiguities, we will first briefly introduce the different approaches taken by the CJEU in its judgments in *Andres* on the one hand [1] and *A-Brauerei* [2] on the other hand. We will then discuss the wider impact of these judgments, in particular for anti-abuse legislation, arguing that it should be possible to establish an additional reference system of taxation for a subset of rules. There is otherwise room for reverse engineering [3]. We will contrast our findings with the Group Financing Exemption within the UK-controlled foreign corporation (CFC) rules, which had been tackled by the Commission. The latter does not fall within the ambit of the *Andres* case law. Instead, the CFC rules themselves constitute the relevant reference system of taxation [4].

[1] The Andres Case: Definition of the Scope of the Reference System

Many tax rules work with a rule-exception technique. The exceptions themselves may again be subject to exceptions – which means that the legal consequence of the general rule applies. In such cases, the complexities as to the identification of the elements of the reference system of taxation laid out above are even exacerbated.

Let us assume a tax measure is structured in three steps. A rule that is beneficial to the taxpayer is subject to an exception (i.e., detrimental to the taxpayer). To limit an overkill effect, the exception is again subject to an exception. The latter is again beneficial for the taxpayer. Two fundamental questions arise: Is what we assume to be the first step for whatever reason, such as regulatory technique, indeed the general rule? Of course, fiscal sovereignty prescribes that it is up to the national legislator to designate the fundamental charging decision that serves as a rule. Yet this will be very hard to verify, especially where the structure of the tax measure in question is not neatly organized as an explicit exception from an exception. An alternative reading could, for example, be that what at first glance appears the rule and exception respectively indeed should be read in conjunction and form the relevant benchmark.

Once such a three-step structure has been ascertained, the question is whether the exception to the exception can entail a selective advantage. This is problematic, since in our example the general rule, i.e., the legal consequence provided for by the reference system of taxation, is beneficial for the taxpayer. This would appear to imply that the exception of the exception can by definition not entail a selective advantage. Could selectivity then instead result from an additional reference system of taxation for

433. On the interplay of anti-abuse rules and State aid law: Smit, *State Aid and Domestic Anti-tax Avoidance Rules*, *supra* n. 161; Edoardo Traversa, *State Aid and Taxation: Can an Anti-avoidance Provision Be Selective* 13 EStAL 518ff. (2014); Traversa & Sabbadini, *Anti-avoidance Measures and State Aid in a Post-BEPS Context*, *supra* n. 161.

the subset of rules that is detrimental to the taxpayer? Or in other words, do exceptions from the general rule have to be implemented in an internally consistent manner?

The case law up until the CJEU's *Andres* case,[434] which dealt with the German restructuring clause, appeared to point towards a reading that a tax measure can be selective where it does not derogate from the levy itself, but where a provision within the corporate tax system provides for exceptions on a smaller scale. Such an approach would imply that even exceptions to exceptions could amount to State aid.

The CJEU's *P Oy* judgment[435] could be understood as supporting such interpretation to a certain extent, even though in this case, the CJEU contended that it was incapable of comprehensively assessing the selectivity of the measure in question:[436] Under Finnish income tax established losses could be deducted from the profits of the following tax years. Losses were not deductible if during the year in which they arose or thereafter more than half of the company's shares had changed ownership otherwise than through inheritance or will, or more than half of its members were replaced. The competent tax office could upon application authorize the deduction of losses for special reasons where this was necessary for the continuation of the activities of the company. Such special reasons could, for example, be changes of ownership within a group of companies, changes of ownership related to a rescue programme or a particular impact on employment.[437] The substantive law questions referred to the CJEU pertained to the identification of the reference system, the justifications of *a priori* selective measures as well as the role of discretion in the context of such justification.

The judgment appeared to imply that the provisions on forfeiture could serve as a subset of rules that can form a reference system of taxation in its own right. Upon closer inspection, however, the CJEU did not explicitly clarify how to identify the reference system of taxation. The CJEU stated that:

> such classification presupposes not only familiarity with the content of the provisions of relevant law but also requires examination of their scope on the basis of administrative and judicial practice and of information relating to the ambit ratione personae of those provisions. As the referring court has not submitted all that information, the Court considers that it is unable to adopt a position on that classification.[438]

At the same time, the CJEU also did not clarify that the reference system could not be made up of the rule on loss forfeiture. What's more, the CJEU dealt with the role of justification in the third step of the analysis, which would appear to point towards such understanding.

However, the judgment is another example that demonstrates the dangers of drawing conclusions from judgments delivered in the procedure under Article 267

434. Case C-203/16 P *Andres*.
435. Case C-6/12 *P Oy*.
436. Similarly Traversa & Sabbadini, *Anti-avoidance Measures and State Aid in a Post-BEPS Context*, *supra* n. 161, at 103f.
437. *See* Case C-6/12 *P Oy*, paras 4ff.
438. *Ibid.*, paras 20f.

TFEU. This is because the picture changed considerably with the CJEU's subsequent judgment in *Andres*.[439]

The case concerned the German *Sanierungsklausel* (restructuring clause), which was very similar to the Finnish provisions in the *P Oy* case, even though it didn't afford the tax authorities discretion. The rules on loss carry-forward were structured as follows:[440] German corporate tax law generally allowed for a carry-forward of losses for corporations. Due to increased trade in empty-shell companies, the German legislator restricted the loss carry-forward by introducing an anti-avoidance provision in section 8c(1) *Körperschaftsteuergesetz* (German Corporate Income Tax Act (KStG)) that excluded a loss carry-forward altogether where more than 50% of the share capital, membership rights, ownership rights or voting rights were transferred. The corporation was then not considered to be identical to the corporation that had originally incurred the losses. The loss carry-forward was excluded on a pro-rata basis where, within five years, more than 25%, but not more than 50% were transferred. This latter pro rata exclusion of the loss carry-forward was declared unconstitutional by the German Federal Financial Court in 2017 and later retroactively abolished.[441]

In 2009, the German legislator retroactively introduced an exception to section 8c(1) KStG in section 8c(1a) KStG (the restructuring clause or *Sanierungsklausel*). According to the Commission, the restructuring clause amounted to State aid.[442] Under the provision, a loss carry-forward is nevertheless possible where a company in difficulty is acquired for the purpose of restructuring provided it is or is likely to be insolvent or over-indebted at the time of the acquisition; the company's fundamental business structures are preserved; the company does not change the sector of activity for five years after the acquisition and the company had not ceased operation at the time of the acquisition. The losses can only be offset against the profits of the company that is being restructured. The acquiring company eventually benefits from the possibility of a loss carry-forward due to the decrease in tax liabilities of the acquired company as well as the possibility of a merger.[443]

Thus, it was necessary to determine whether the general rule in this case was the possibility of a loss carry-forward or the loss forfeiture. The Commission held that the reference system was made up of the German corporate income tax system, and in particular the rules on the denial of the tax loss carry-forward for companies, upon change in their shareholding.[444] The General Court upheld the Commission's decision

439. Case C-203/16 P *Andres*. On this case *see, e.g.*, Christoph Arhold, *The German Scheme on the Fiscal Carry-Forward of Losses: A Selected Case* 10 EStAL 71ff. (2011) https://doi.org/10.21552/estal/2011/1/220; De Broe, *The State Aid Selectivity-Test in Corporate Tax Matters*, *supra* n. 163; Hackemann & Sydow, *supra* n. 163; Seer, *supra* n. 163.
440. Case C-203/16 P *Andres*, paras 3ff. for the facts of the case.
441. BVerfG, Case 2 BvL 6/11, BVerfGE 145, 106.
442. Case C-203/16 P *Andres*, para. 8.
443. *Ibid.*, paras 17ff.
444. Commission Decision 2011/527/EU of 26 January 2011 on State aid C 7/10 (ex CP250/09 and NN 5/10) implemented by Germany – Scheme for the carry-forward of tax losses in the case of restructuring of companies in difficulty (Sanierungsklausel) [2011] OJ L 235/26, paras 66f.

deeming the scheme selective.[445] Upon appeal, however, the CJEU eventually found that there was, in fact, no selectivity as the Commission had erred in its identification of the reference system.[446] It argued that if the use of a certain regulatory technique cannot enable a tax measure to escape the finding of selectivity, it is also not sufficient to establish the reference system by mere reference to the use of a certain regulatory technique. It stated:

> If, on the basis of that case-law, the use of a regulatory technique cannot enable national tax rules to escape from the outset the scrutiny concerning State aid provided for under the FEU Treaty, resorting to the regulatory technique used is not sufficient to define the relevant reference framework for the purposes of assessing the condition relating to selectivity, except in order to ensure that the form of State intervention prevails decisively over its effects. Consequently, [...] the regulatory technique used cannot be decisive for the purposes of determining the reference framework.[447]

The CJEU went on to state that the General Court had incorrectly classified the rule governing the forfeiture of losses as the reference framework, and had excluded from the reference framework the general rule of loss carry-forward.[448] The effect of the restructuring clause would merely be to define a situation falling under the general loss carry-forward rule, while section 8c(1), i.e., the forfeiture of losses, constitutes a mere (negative) exception therefrom.[449] The CJEU then referred to the Opinion of the AG in stating that:

> the selectivity of a tax measure cannot be precisely assessed on the basis of a reference framework consisting of some provisions that have been artificially taken from a broader legislative framework. Therefore, by thus excluding from the relevant reference framework in the present case the general rule of loss carry-forward, manifestly the General Court defined it too narrowly.[450]

Finally, the CJEU referred to the *P Oy* judgment and rejected any argument based on the determination of the reference system of taxation in *P Oy:*

> In addition, any argument in support of the judgment under appeal cannot, in this case, be based on the judgment of 18 July 2013, P (C-6/12, EU:C:2013:525), since, in that judgment, the Court did not rule on what should constitute the reference framework in the case before it.[451]

As such, there is no open contradiction between the two judgments. Since according to the CJEU the GC had incorrectly upheld the identification of the reference

445. Case T-287/11 *Heitkamp BauHolding v. Commission* EU:T:2016:60; Case T-620/11 *GFKL Financial Services AG v. Commission* EU:T:2016:59. By contrast, the German government's action was dismissed as it was filed one day late, Case T-205/11 *Germany v. Commission* EU:T:2012:704 and Case C-102/13 P *Germany v. Commission* EU:C:2014:2054.
446. Case C-203/16 P *Andres.*
447. *Ibid.*, para. 92.
448. *Ibid.*, para. 101.
449. *Ibid.*, para. 102. Critical: Phedon Nicolaides, *The Definition of the Reference Tax System Is Still A Puzzle* 17 EStAL 419, 425 (2018) https://doi.org/10.21552/estal/2018/3/11.
450. *Ibid.*, para. 103.
451. *Ibid.*, para. 105.

system as carried out by the Commission, it did not have to examine the remaining parts of the appeal, which focused on the subsequent steps of the selectivity test.[452]

In its reasoning, the CJEU made no reference to either the objective of the reference framework (including the restructuring clause) or the rules on the forfeiture of losses, even though this was part of the pleas of the parties as well of the Commission decision. This is because if the restructuring clause is considered an integral part of the reference system, the second and third steps of the selectivity test are simply not relevant. The judgment thus could not clarify whether the State aid compatibility of anti-abuse rules, such as the rules on loss forfeiture, depends on how well-targeted such rules are.[453]

[2] The **A-Brauerei** *Case: Justification of a Derogation from the Reference System*

The CJEU's judgment in *A-Brauerei* also concerned a tax measure with a complex structure that had an anti-abuse aspect to it. Again, the German provision of section 6a *Grunderwerbsteuergesetz* (real property transfer tax) could be understood as being structured in three steps.[454] In a first step, the levy provides for the taxation of certain types of real property transfer. In case of restructuring within a group in which a controlling and a dependent party took part, transactions were in some cases exempted from taxation in what could be understood as a second step. However, in what could be understood as a third step, this exemption was subject to a minimum holding period of five years before and after the transaction in question.[455]

In this case, the CJEU deemed the German real property transfer tax the reference system of taxation and held that while there was indeed a derogation, it could be justified. It held that the minimum holding period was justified as it was intended to prevent abusive practices by excluding undesirable windfall effects where companies acquire a company solely to benefit from that exemption.[456] In contrast to the judgment on the restructuring clause, the CJEU did not consider the fact that the exemption was contingent on a minimum holding period a return to the normal rule of taxation, and thus a part of the definition of the scope of the reference system. Instead, it considered it a matter of the justification of the derogation. This means that in this constellation, there may, indeed, be selectivity. Admittedly, the minimum holding period was designed as a condition for the exemption which would make an alternative reading somewhat artificial.

Yet regardless of regulatory technique, the effect of the minimum holding period is a return to the general rule 'taxation', and thus the case is comparable to the

452. *Ibid.*, para. 107.
453. Traversa & Sabbadini, *Anti-avoidance Measures and State Aid in a Post-BEPS Context, supra* n. 161, at 104.
454. Case C-374/17 *A-Brauerei*. *See* on this case in the third step Ch. §3.04[B], [2] *infra*.
455. *See* Case C-374/17 *A-Brauerei*, paras 5ff. for a description of the facts of the case.
456. *Ibid.*, para. 51.

constellation at issue in *Andres* for our purposes. Moreover, the CJEU in its judgment treated the minimum holding as a separate distinctive feature.

[3] Possibility of an Additional Reference System of Taxation on a Smaller Scale

The judgment on the restructuring clause may have wider implications for the design of anti-abuse provisions since they are usually structured in a complex manner. From the outset, certain types of anti-abuse provisions, such as a General Anti-Abuse Rule (GAAR) could certainly be understood as distinctive technical features of the tax system in line with the recent case law on the wide ambit of the reference system.[457]

It also has to be seen that anti-abuse provisions as such, where they do not contain exceptions, will generally not be subject to State aid control: they are disadvantageous to the taxpayer and State aid control only extends to advantages.[458] Anti-abuse provisions always lead to a tax burden that would otherwise not be due.[459] By contrast, one may wonder whether the lack of (specific) anti-abuse rules limiting the ambit of certain advantageous provisions can conceivably be a matter of the proportionality of an exemption to the general rule of taxation, which could then lead to selectivity.[460] State aid concerns might also arise from an asymmetric application of general or specific anti-abuse rules.[461]

For other measures that are structured in several steps, the case is less clear which warrants a closer look at the conclusions that can be drawn from the judgment in *Andres*.

While some contributions had argued that the Commission's stance on the restructuring clause was correct,[462] the Commission's decision led to intense criticism, particularly in the German literature. The near consensus was that the general rules on the carry-forward of losses rather than the denial of the loss carry-forward had to be considered the general rule. This would mean that the restructuring clause would

457. *See* Ch. §3.01[C], [1] *supra.*
458. Similarly Smit, *State Aid and Domestic Anti-tax Avoidance Rules, supra* n. 161, at 92. For example, Traversa & Sabbadini, *Anti-avoidance Measures and State Aid in a Post-BEPS Context, supra* n. 161, at 105 wonder whether the general exclusion of a loss carry-forward in cases of restructuring was proportionate. Yet this question cannot be answered from a State aid law point of view, since regardless of the identification of the reference system, the exclusion of the loss-carry forward can only constitute a disadvantage.
459. Conversely, anti-abuse provisions also do not confer advantages onto undertakings conducting genuine, non-abuse economic activities, Traversa & Sabbadini, *Anti-avoidance Measures and State Aid in a Post-BEPS Context, supra* n. 161, at 106.
460. *See* Ch. §3.04[B], [3] *infra* on the prevention of double taxation as grounds for justification.
461. Rita Szudoczky, *The Future of Fiscal State Aid,* in Piernas López et al. (eds), The Future of EU State Aid Law: Consolidation and Expansion, 273, 278 (2023). *See* on this also the judgment of the GC in *ENGIE,* Joined Cases T-516 and 525/18 *Luxembourg and Others v. Commission* EU:T:2021:251. *See* on this De Broe & Massant, *supra* n. 161 condoning the approach taken in *ENGIE,* but calling for a limited review for manifest arbitrariness. Englisch, *State Aid Prohibition, supra* n. 161, at 145f. argues that the GC and the Commission overstepped authority in comprehensively monitoring the application of the Luxembourg GAAR in *ENGIE. See also* Nicolaides, *Non-selective Rules, supra* n. 332.
462. *See, e.g.,* Klemt, *supra* n. 163.

constitute a mere return to this general rule. The restructuring clause could not be selective for lack of a derogation from the reference system.[463] There was thus relief when the CJEU found that there was no selectivity.[464] The judgment nevertheless appears problematic and does not significantly contribute to promoting legal certainty as to the identification of the reference system of taxation.[465]

In both its judgments in *Andres* and *A-Brauerei,* the CJEU in essence held that the reference system of taxation was the levy itself. The difference was that in *Andres*, the legal consequence provided for by the reference system of taxation (possibility of a loss-carry forward) was beneficial to the taxpayer, while it was detrimental in the *A-Brauerei* case (taxation). In the former case, the implication would be that there can be no selectivity regardless of the type of exemption since derogations from the reference system of taxation can by definition only be disadvantageous. In the latter case, however, any derogation from the reference system can lead to selectivity as the legal consequence in the first step would lead to a tax burden for the taxpayer. This distinction does not appear altogether convincing.[466]

One could read the judgment in *Andres* as the CJEU merely being true to its former case law, according to which the reference system of taxation is generally the levy with the fundamental taxing decision laid down therein. As such, the judgment does not put into question the case law on selectivity. In particular, it confirms the notion that the reference system is normally not a subset of rules applicable to certain undertakings, but the entire levy.[467]

This also ties into the still problematic and unresolved distinction between technical rules on the one hand and potential derogations on the other hand. In this case, the loss carry-forward rule would certainly have to be considered a technical rule that forms an integral part of the reference system of taxation. However, was this truly also the case for the restructuring clause? It appears somewhat far-fetched to consider exemptions catering to special interests a return to the general rule.[468] It has rightfully

463. *See, e.g.,* Christian Brodersen & Norbert Mückl, *The German Restructuring Privilege (Section 8c(1a) of the Corporate Income Tax Act) and the EU State Aid Rules (Article 107(1) of the TFEU* 54 European Taxation 56, 61 (2014) https://doi.org/10.59403/2demq8k; de Weerth, *supra* n. 163, at 2487. Prior to the judgment of the GC: Hackemann & Sydow, *supra* n. 163, at 789f. Again others have considered s. 8c(1) KStG the reference system of taxation, but argued that the provision constituted an anti-abuse provision aimed at preventing shell company purchases. Due to the coherent implementation of this objective, there could be no aid, Seer, *supra* n. 163, at 729. According to Raymond Luja, *Andres: The Unfinished Business of a Seemingly Selective Non-Advantage* 20 EStAL 578, 580f. (2021) https://doi.org/10.21552/estal/2021/4/12 the restructuring clause did not lead to an advantage in the sense of Art. 107(1) TFEU.

464. *See* Chiara Balbinot, *§8c Abs. 1a KStG (Sanierungsklausel) doch keine unionsrechtswidrige Beihilfe? Schlussanträge des Generalanwalts Wahl in der Rs. Heitkamp (C-203/16 P)* 56 DStR 334, 336 (2018) on the Conclusions of AG Wahl.

465. *See* only Nicolaides, *The Definition of the Reference Tax System, supra* n. 449.

466. According to Soltész, *supra* n. 174, at 20 the judgments demonstrate the arbitrariness of a 'rule and exception' approach in State aid. Nicolaides, *The Definition of the Reference Tax System, supra* n. 449, at 425 calls the identification of the loss carry-forward rule arbitrary.

467. Reading the judgment in this context: Ellenrieder, *Die materielle Selektivität steuerlicher Beihilfen, supra* n. 57, at 626.

468. Critical as to the CJEU dubbing this a mere matter of regulatory technique: Nicolaides, *The Definition of the Reference Tax System, supra* n. 449, at 426.

been pointed out that while in such cases the general rule is reinstated, the objectives of the general system on the one hand and of the exception to the exception on the other hand may differ.[469]

By contrast, according to Luja, there would be no advantage, since the anti-abuse rule would have been overinclusive. The advantage has to be assessed in relation to the normal tax system. Therefore, a return to the normal rule of a loss carry-forward would not lead to an advantage.[470] Smit, in a similar vein, adds that the CJEU's judgment would be an example of the permissibility of the reduction of the ambit of an anti-abuse provision that would otherwise lead to an overkill effect. The remaining constellations that would fall within the ambit of the provision would be disadvantaged so that there could be no aid. State aid law should not preclude a gradual reduction of the overkill effect of an anti-abuse rule where the latter is brought more in line with its rationale. Considering the restructuring clause, an overkill would mean that all bone fide taxpayers would be in a worse-off situation.[471] While this is indeed a possibility, not all exceptions to anti-abuse provisions necessarily reduce an overkill effect of anti-abuse rules. Moreover, such an approach would not be necessary to address overkill effects: the distinction between abusive and non-abusive constellations (i.e., cases that would be considered an overkill) could still be taken into account on the level of the justification of the measure, even if there was a derogation.

The CJEU claims that its reasoning is an emanation of the fact that the effects of a measure generally prevail over the regulatory technique, i.e., the effects doctrine.[472] As such, the formal drafting style of a tax measure should not be decisive for its qualification as State aid.[473] Yet the CJEU actually also resorts to an argument that puts form over substance. More importantly, the judgment could undermine effective State aid control to a certain extent. This is because it appears as though any rule that merely re-establishes a legal consequence that is beneficial to the taxpayer regardless of its objectives would be State aid proof.[474] This opens the door to an arbitrary design of anti-abuse rules which exempts certain situations although they are prone to abuse or problematic for other reasons.[475] The only limit to this would be manifest inconsistency

469. Traversa & Sabbadini, *Anti-avoidance Measures and State Aid in a Post-BEPS Context*, *supra* n. 161, at 104.
470. Luja, *Andres*, *supra* n. 463, at 580f.
471. Smit, *State Aid and Domestic Anti-tax Avoidance Rules*, *supra* n. 161, at 95. De Broe, *The State Aid Selectivity-Test in Corporate Tax Matters*, *supra* n. 163, at 287f. argues that the purpose of the rule would be to reduce the overkill effect of the anti-abuse provision which would otherwise be disproportionate.
472. Case C-203/16 P *Andres*, para. 92.
473. Begoña Pérez-Bernabeu, *Refining the Derogation Test on Material Tax Selectivity: The Equality Test* 16 EStAL 582, 586 (2017) https://doi.org/10.21552/estal/2017/4/8.
474. Ellenrieder, *Die materielle Selektivität steuerlicher Beihilfen*, *supra* n. 57, at 626 points out that the CJEU merely rejected the Commission's approach but did not positively endorse a certain reference system. This would mean that there is a room for further clarifications of the case law.
475. In a similar vein: Traversa & Sabbadini, *Anti-avoidance Measures and State Aid in a Post-BEPS Context*, *supra* n. 161, at 104 (referring to the judgment in *P Oy*); Luja, *Andres*, *supra* n. 463, at 583f.

which results in de facto-selectivity. In light of the high threshold that appears to be applicable to this form of selectivity, this may result in unjustified loopholes.[476]

One may furthermore consider the judgment on the restructuring clause problematic as the CJEU thereby allowed for preferential treatment of companies in difficulty. Rescue and restructuring aid granted to undertakings in difficulty is generally subject to strict scrutiny due to the competition law rationale of State aid control.[477] It is not necessarily desirable to artificially prop up undertakings in difficulty.[478] Admittedly, the rationales of State aid control can only become a decisive factor where the criteria of State aid are otherwise met. They can therefore only serve to justify a higher (or lower) degree of scrutiny where there is, in fact, aid. Yet the considerations underlying the German restructuring clause, which – had it been selective – would have had to be considered rescue and restructuring aid, are nevertheless problematic. This consequence of a measure escaping State aid scrutiny for mere formalistic reasons is precisely what the CJEU's effects doctrine seeks to prevent.

Therefore, in our view, the notion of selectivity should be understood to have an additional dimension: The reference system would generally be made up of the levy itself. Within the scope of this levy, all actors or constellations are comparable. A definition of a special reference system for the taxation of group companies, for example, would not be appropriate. Yet additionally, it should be possible to define a reference system on a smaller scale, since the State aid assessment would otherwise depend on the legal drafting technique. The legislator would then also be required to enact such subsets of rules in an internally consistent manner.[479] If the anti-abuse provision then contains exemptions, this may amount to a derogation.

If, by contrast, an anti-abuse rule re-establishes the general rule of taxation – as was the case in the CJEU's judgment in *A-Brauerei,* the reference system of taxation is the levy itself. The fact that exemptions are subject to conditions or limited by anti-abuse provisions should be a matter of the proportionality of the exemption.

[4] UK CFC Rules: Separate Reference System Due to Lack of Comparability

The problem of a potentially arbitrary design of anti-abuse rules based on the CJEU's judgment in *Andres* can be further demonstrated by taking a closer look at the General Court's judgment on the Group Financing Exemption to the UK CFC rules.[480] While the UK is no longer subject to the EU State aid rules, the case nevertheless allows us to draw some general conclusions on the State aid compatibility of anti-abuse rules.

476. *See* on this Ch. §4.01 *infra.*
477. Luja, *Andres, supra* n. 463, at 579.
478. Bacon, *European Union Law of State Aid, supra* n. 20, at para. 15.02.
479. In a similar vein: Englisch, *Das Beihilfenverbot im Steuerrecht, supra* n. 67, at para. 9.29 who distinguishes this from an anti-abuse regime with a limited scope, so as to ascertain that it is sufficiently targeted and cites the example of the restructuring clause as an example of the latter. *See also* in detail Ellenrieder, *Die materielle Selektivität steuerlicher Beihilfen, supra* n. 57, at 628ff.
480. Joined Cases T-363 and 456/19 *United Kingdom and ITV v. Commission* EU:T:2022:349.

The Commission decision describes the measure as follows: UK corporate tax law generally did not tax companies based on the profits of their subsidiaries. The CFC rules contained in Part 9A of the Taxation (International and Other Provisions) Act (TIOPA) 2010 were an exception to this general rule. They were applicable under three cumulative conditions: First, the CFC had to derive chargeable profits. Such chargeable profits (Chapters 3 to 9) were profits that were generally considered to point towards an artificial diversion of profits as opposed to a genuine commercial activity (gateway rules). Second, no CFC entity level exemption (Chapters 10 to 14) applied. Third, there was a UK interest holder of at least 25% in the CFC.[481]

The Group Financing Exemption was laid down in Chapter 9. It limited Chapter 5, which applied to non-trading finance profits arising from 'qualifying loan relationships'. According to the Commission, the two Chapters had to be read in conjunction.[482] A qualifying loan relationship under Chapter 9 was a loan from the CFC to foreign group companies that were under the control of the same UK resident company controlling the CFC.[483] As a default rule, only 25% of the CFC's profits would then pass through the CFC charge gateway under Chapter 5. Where certain additional criteria were met, a full exemption was possible.[484]

According to the Commission, the exemption contained in Chapter 9 for qualifying loan relationships amounted to State aid. The appropriate reference system of taxation would be the UK CFC regime.[485] Despite forming part of the UK corporate tax system, the CFC regime would make up a specific set of rules with its own objective. This objective would be sufficiently distinct from the objective of the general corporate tax system to form a reference system in its own right.[486] The objective of the CFC regime would be to ensure the taxation of profits that are artificially diverted from the UK into UK-controlled non-resident-associated entities.[487] The general rule would be the CFC charge.[488] All companies that artificially divert profits by use of a CFC would be in a legally and factually comparable situation. A tax measure would thus derogate from the reference system of taxation where certain situations were exempted from the application of the CFC rules, even though there was a risk of an artificial diversion of profits. This would be the case for the Group Financing Exemption.[489] According to the Commission, the derogation was not justified which means that there was selectivity.[490]

The Commission decision was confirmed by the General Court which held that the CFC rules were indeed severable from the general tax system since they were a

481. *See* for a detailed description Commission Decision (EU) 2019/1352 of 2 April 2019 on the State aid SA.44896 implemented by the United Kingdom concerning CFC Group Financing Exemption C/2019/2526 [2019] OJ L 216/1, paras 13ff.
482. *Ibid.*, para. 24.
483. *Ibid.*, para. 36.
484. *Ibid.*, paras 33ff.
485. *Ibid.*, paras 103ff.
486. *Ibid.*, para. 106.
487. *Ibid.*, para. 103.
488. *Ibid.*, para. 109.
489. *Ibid.*, paras 124ff.
490. *Ibid.*, paras 152ff.

consistent body of rules that had its own legal logic that was distinct from the logic of the general corporate tax system which was based on territoriality.[491] The Court considered the CFC rules an extension of rather than an exception to the general tax system.[492] It furthermore ascertained that the tax base, the taxable person, the taxable event as well as the tax rate were defined in a way to form a complete body of rules.[493]

Had the logic from the judgment in *Andres* been applied, the outcome of the judgment might have been different.[494] If the entire corporate tax system was taken as a point of departure, the general rule could have been the non-taxation of the profits of CFCs. The exemption contained in Chapter 9, Part 9A TIOPA could then merely have constituted a 'return' to the original rule of non-taxation and thus formed part of the reference system of taxation. Nevertheless, the GC was right to distinguish the two cases. This is because there was a lack of comparability. This is rare in broad-based fiscal levies because the benchmark of the analysis is generally the entire levy.[495] Yet CFC rules capture profits that would ordinarily not be taxable within a jurisdiction. Such profits are reincorporated into the domestic tax base because they are considered to be artificially diverted to a low-tax jurisdiction. This goes beyond the taxation of worldwide income since the profits accrue on the level of the CFC rather than the UK resident company.

The nature of the reference system of taxation will then be fragmented, as CFC rules are by definition not all-encompassing. They generally contain thresholds for the application of the rules. Moreover, CFC rules are only meant to apply to artificially diverted profits. One will also have to grant the legislator a certain degree of discretion as to what types of profits it considers to be artificially diverted. In other words, the boundaries of the reference system can generally not be monitored.[496] In particular, the fact that anti-avoidance rules do not apply to undertakings conducting genuine economic activities cannot lead to the finding of State aid.[497] Yet the fundamental charging decision underlying the CFC rules nevertheless has to be implemented in an internally consistent manner.

Finally, it also has to be seen that the constellation of CFC rules, i.e., constellations where a separate reference system of taxation exists, will be relatively rare.[498] They are an example of anti-avoidance rules that recharacterize transactions or

491. Joined Cases T-363 and 456/19 *United Kingdom and ITV v. Commission*, paras 79ff.
492. *Ibid.*, para. 83.
493. *Ibid.*, paras 85ff.
494. *See also* Smit, *State Aid and Domestic Anti-tax Avoidance Rules*, *supra* n. 161, at 97f.
495. *See* Ch. §3.03[B], [2] *infra* for further constellations.
496. Similarly with reference to safe harbour rules in anti-avoidance legislation Smit, *State Aid and Domestic Anti-tax Avoidance Rules*, *supra* n. 161, at 99. In extreme cases, there may still be de facto-selectivity.
497. Traversa & Sabbadini, *Anti-avoidance Measures and State Aid in a Post-BEPS Context*, *supra* n. 161, at 104f. arguing that the prevention of abuse is an objective inherent to the tax system.
498. Englisch, *Das Beihilfenverbot im Steuerrecht*, *supra* n. 67, at para. 9.29 cites the example of transfer pricing adjustments.

reattribute income.[499] Perhaps Limitation on Benefits provisions would also fall into that category.

§3.03 DEROGATION FROM THE REFERENCE SYSTEM OF TAXATION

The second step of the three-step test for selectivity requires a derogation from the reference system of taxation. According to the case law, 'it is necessary, secondly, to assess and determine whether any advantage granted by the tax measure at issue may be selective, by demonstrating that the measure derogates from that common regime inasmuch as it differentiates between economic operators who, in the light of the objective attributed to the tax system of the Member State concerned, are in a comparable factual and legal situation'.[500]

While the second step had led to significant controversy in the scholarly literature, the CJEU has clarified in its judgment in *World Duty Free Group* that abstract selectivity suffices. It is not necessary to establish concrete selectivity. This in essence means that a measure can even be selective where it is (theoretically) open to all undertakings [A]. The relevant benchmark to ascertain whether there is derogation is the objective of the reference system, not the objective of the measure. In the example of broad-based fiscal levies, we demonstrate that almost all distinctions can lead to prima facie selectivity [B]. We will then address the particularities of special purpose levies, for which the scope of the reference system may be broader than the tax itself, and the issues that come along with the identification of the objective of a levy [C]. For fiscal levies, the boundaries of levies generally have to be treated as a given as it is close to impossible to ascertain comparability in such levies [D].

[A] Abstract Selectivity Rather Than Concrete Selectivity

Some authors in the scholarly literature had held that for there to be a derogation from the reference system, the Commission had to identify a particular group of undertakings that are the only ones that can benefit from a tax measure (concrete selectivity). It would thus always be necessary to identify a particular category of undertakings that can be distinguished by certain properties, common to and characteristic of them and that are the only ones to be able to profit from a fiscal aid scheme.[501]

499. Traversa & Sabbadini, *Anti-avoidance Measures and State Aid in a Post-BEPS Context*, *supra* n. 161, at 94.
500. Joined Cases C-78 to 80/08 *Paint Graphos*, para. 49; Case C-6/12 *P Oy*, para. 19; Case C-522/13 *Ministerio de Defensa and Navantia*, para. 35; Case C-524/14 P *Hansestadt Lübeck*, paras 54f. Joined Cases C-20 and 21/15 P *World Duty Free Group*, para. 57; Case C-203/16 P *Andres*, para. 86; Case C-374/17 *A-Brauerei*, para. 36.
501. E.g., Hey, *Steuerbefreiung für Sanierungsgewinne*, *supra* n. 143, at 455; Thomas Jaeger, *From Santander to LuxLeaks: And Back* 14 EStAL 345, 352f. (2015); Temple Lang, *EU State Aid Rules*, *supra* n. 139, at 446; Temple Lang, *Autogrill Espana and Banco Santander*, *supra* n. 139, at 764f.; Nicolaides, *New Limits to the Concept of Selectivity*, *supra* n. 139, at 322. According to Nicolaides, *Excessive Widening*, *supra* n. 139, at 69f., the judgment would disregard the fundamental logic of tax systems which result in companies bearing different tax burdens

This view was not, however, supported by prior case law.[502] The CJEU consequently rejected this notion in its judgment in *World Duty Free Group*:

> *However, the imposition of such a supplementary requirement to identify a particular category of undertakings, additional to the analytical method applicable to selectivity in tax matters that may be deduced from the Court's settled case-law, which essentially involves ascertaining whether the exclusion of certain operators from the benefit of a tax advantage that arises from a measure derogating from an ordinary tax system constitutes discrimination with respect to those operators, cannot be inferred from the Court's case-law* and, in particular, from the judgment of 15 November 2011, Commission and Spain v Government of Gibraltar and United Kingdom (C-106/09 P and C-107/09 P, EU:C:2011:732). [...] All that matters in that regard is the fact that the measure, irrespective of its form or the legislative means used, should have the effect of placing the recipient undertakings in a position that is more favourable than that of other undertakings, although all those undertakings are in a comparable factual and legal situation in the light of the objective pursued by the tax system concerned.[503]

The judgment in *Gibraltar,* which had been cited by the GC to support its view that concrete selectivity was necessary, concerned the second form of material selectivity, namely de facto selective. By contrast, it has now clearly emerged that for there to be de jure-selectivity, abstract selectivity suffices. The higher degree of scrutiny in the context of de facto-selectivity is because such selectivity is not contingent on a derogation from the reference system. There is thus no benchmark, which means that any factual differential treatment arising from otherwise neutral tax rules that leads to a favourable treatment - regardless of whether this is coincidental or not - could potentially fall within the ambit of State aid law. This would obviously go too far so that concrete selectivity is necessary.[504] However, where there is, in fact, a derogation, abstract selectivity suffices.

---

depending on their business decisions. Where tax measures are open to every undertaking, there could be no State aid. Similarly Balbinot, *§8c Abs. 1a KStG (Sanierungsklausel) doch keine unionsrechtswidrige Beihilfe?, supra* n. 464, at 336 citing the wording of Art. 107 TFEU and the purpose of State aid control; Nicola Chesaites, *Tax Incentives as State Aid,* in Tomljenović et al. (eds), EU Competition and State Aid Rules, 253, 265 (2017).

502. De Broe, *The State Aid Review against Aggressive Tax Planning, supra* n. 64, at 291; Dobratz, *Artikel 107 AEUV, supra* n. 131, at paras 74f.; Englisch, *Das Beihilfenverbot im Steuerrecht, supra* n. 67, at para. 9.18; Giraud & Petit, *Bury Them Deep, supra* n. 138, at 314; Ismer & Piotrowski, *Selektivität von Beihilfen, supra* n. 132, at 261. *See also* Ismer & Piotrowski, *The Selectivity of Tax Measures, supra* n. 77, at 562f.; Ismer & Piotrowski, *Selectivity in Corporate Tax Matters, supra* n. 77, at 159f.; Lyal, *supra* n. 131, at 1031f.; Loewenthal, *supra* n. 136, at 39 notes that an approach requiring concrete selectivity would shield virtually every tax scheme. Bartosch, *Spanish Goodwill, supra* n. 138, at 69 argues that there would nevertheless have to be a discrimination, even if it would not be necessary to define privileged group.

503. Joined Cases C-20 and 21/15 P *World Duty Free Group,* paras 71 and 79; emphasis added by the author.

504. *See* on this Ch. §4.01 *infra.*

[B] Objective of the Reference System Instead of Objective of the Tax Measure

There had also long been dissent as to which yardstick for comparability ought to be referred to in the second step.[505] The second step requires a discrimination analysis for all undertakings which are in a comparable factual and legal situation. But what yardstick has to be referred to in order to determine whether there is indeed a different treatment? There were two main approaches. Some authors were proponents of an approach which relies on the objective of the tax measure in question. Others argued instead that the objective of the reference system has to be relied upon. The latter has now been enshrined in the case law [1]. Particularly for broad-based levies, this has led to concerns as to an overly broad reading of selectivity, which may, however, not in all cases be justified as a lack of comparability is still conceivable [2].

[1] Objective of the Reference System Decisive in the Second Step

Particularly up until the CJEU's Grand Chamber Decision in *World Duty Free Group*, many authors had advocated an approach that resorts to the objective of the tax measure, i.e., the tax benefit itself, as a yardstick for comparability.[506] In this, they had often relied on the wording that the CJEU had used in its *Adria-Wien Pipeline* judgment:

> The only question to be determined is whether, under a particular statutory scheme, a State measure is such as to favour 'certain undertakings or the production of certain goods' within the meaning of Article 92(1) of the Treaty in comparison with other undertakings which are in a legal and factual situation that is comparable *in the light of the objective pursued by the measure in question [...].*[507]

The impact of such reading would be that the notion of selectivity would be relatively narrow depending on which kinds of objectives are permissible in the second step. If all types of objectives were permissible, it would suffice to include all actors that can potentially make use of a tax benefit. Selectivity would thus only rarely be met.[508]

505. Unlike the approaches laid out below, López López, *General Thought on Selectivity*, *supra* n. 62, at 813 argues that the situation of the companies from an internal or national perspective would be relevant.
506. Brokelind, *supra* n. 137, at 228f.; Cordewener, *supra* n. 131, at 288; Honoré, *Selectivity*, *supra* n. 137, at 128f.; Kurcz & Vallindas, *supra* n. 41; Luts, *supra* n. 127, at 269; Mang, *supra* n. 132, at 81.
507. Case C-143/99 *Adria-Wien Pipeline*, para. 41; emphasis added by the author. *See also* Case C-88/03 *Portugal v. Commission*, para. 54.
508. The extensive past debate on the compatibility of IP boxes with State aid law demonstrates the impact of such approach. *See, e.g.*, Brokelind, *supra* n. 137; Ismer & Piotrowski, *Selektivität von Beihilfen*, *supra* n. 132; Luts, *supra* n. 127; Mang, *supra* n. 132; Claire Micheau & Gauthier Charles de la Brousse, *Case Studies of Tax Issues on Selectivity: Analysis of the Patent Box Scheme and the Reduced Taxation of Foreign-Source Interest Income*, in Rust & Micheau (eds), State Aid and Tax Law, 153ff. (2013); Shi, *supra* n. 136. In this context, *Brokelind* contended that IP Boxes would have to be considered selective depending on their objective. If their

As to the permissible objectives in the second step, for example, *Honoré* argues that Member States would have a large degree of discretion in the determination of the objective of a tax measure. Judicial control would only cover manifest errors, for example, where the objective is inherently discriminatory. He points to the objectives listed in Article 107(2) and (3) TFEU as examples of objectives which would in all likelihood be considered permissible. Unlike in the third step of the selectivity test, only extrinsic objectives, such as the protection of the environment, could be relied on. By contrast, fiscal aims would not be permissible.[509]

Biondi was more restrictive and contended that only certain 'classic principles of European integration' would be permissible in the second step.[510] There would be no prima facie selectivity where a Member State sufficiently takes into account such principles. He based this on the different assessments in the *British Aggregates Association* (BAA) case on the one hand and in the *Paint Graphos* case on the other hand. As to the *British Aggregates Association* case, which concerned the definition of the scope of an environmental levy, Biondi held that the CJEU essentially sanctioned that the measure itself did not respect the EU competence in the regulation of environmental protection and thus found that parts of the measure were selective. He contrasted this with the *Paint Graphos* case, which concerned tax benefits for cooperative societies. In this case, the CJEU concluded that it might very well be possible that there was no derogation in the second step.[511]

There may indeed be some merit to the latter view in practice, i.e., regarding the likelihood of tax measures being tackled by the Commission. However, in our view, this cannot be derived from the judgment in *Paint Graphos*. The CJEU had indeed extensively relied on EU legislation namely Council Regulation No. 1435/2003 to support its arguments based on the particularities of cooperative societies as opposed to other entities subject to corporate tax in *Paint Graphos*.[512] However, Lyal convincingly notes that the CJEU's reasoning in *Paint Graphos* may have created confusion. This is because the particularities of cooperative societies that the CJEU described in its judgment have no relevance to the functioning of a Member State's corporate tax system. The CJEU presumably thereby did not seek to open the door to external

objective was the promotion of R&D, they could only be justified if IP Box was the only way to promote R&D. If, by contrast, their objective was to promote innovation, selectivity could only be ruled out if all undertakings carrying out an activity leading to innovation could make use of the regime and if all kinds of expenses were included. She therefore concluded that schemes that reserve the tax benefits to certain types of property rights would have to be considered selective, Brokelind, *supra* n. 137, at 228f. By contrast, Mang, *supra* n. 132, at 81 contended that none of the IP box regimes in force at the time of the publication of his article had to be considered selective. This is because he defines the objective of IP Box regimes as the promotion of R&D activities. The comparable undertakings for the second step of the analysis would then be companies that engage in R&D. As none of the regimes in force had a particular requirement regarding the exploitation of the IP, there would be no different treatment in light of the objective of the tax measure.

509. Honoré, *Selectivity*, *supra* n. 137, at 129.
510. Biondi, *State Aid Is Falling Down*, *supra* n. 276, at 1732.
511. Joined Cases C-78 to 80/08 *Paint Graphos*.
512. Council Regulation (EC) No. 1435/2003 on the Statute for a European Cooperative Society (SCE) [2003] OJ L 207/1.

motivations for tax benefits.[513] Moreover, these judgments can be distinguished, since *Paint Graphos* concerned a broad-based fiscal levy, while *British Aggregates Association* concerned a special purpose levy.[514]

By contrast, other authors had convincingly argued that rather than the objective of the tax measure, it would be the objective of the reference system that has to be referred to as the correct yardstick.[515] Moreover, (external) national policy objectives can neither play a role on the level of prima facie selectivity nor on the level of a possible justification. They can only be considered in the context of the compatibility of aid if there is a discrimination.[516] This view was confirmed most clearly in the CJEU's judgment in *World Duty Free Group*.[517] While the diverging reasoning in *Adria-Wien Pipeline* indeed appeared to indicate a different interpretation, this might be explained by the fact that the levy at issue was a special purpose levy. For such levies, the delimitation of the objective of the levy itself and the objective of the tax measure in question will not always be straightforward. Otherwise, one would have to understand this as a change in the case law.[518]

[2] Comparability and Lack Thereof in Broad-Based Fiscal Taxes: The Example of Corporate Tax

Relying on the objective of the reference system of taxation as the correct yardstick, as well as the rejection of a requirement of concrete selectivity, had brought about valid concerns as to an overly extensive reading of State aid law.[519] For example, Englisch strikingly described the State aid prohibition as 'a kind of Union Law super-GAAR'.[520] This is because at least for broad-based fiscal taxes, such as income tax, corporate tax

513. Lyal, *supra* n. 131, at 1036. Also sceptical Loewenthal, *supra* n. 136, at 48.
514. *See* on the significance Ch. §3.03[C], [1], [a] *infra*.
515. Ismer & Piotrowski, *Selectivity in Corporate Tax Matters, supra* n. 77, at 159; Loewenthal, *supra* n. 136, at 46; Lyal, *supra* n. 131, at 1036; Sánchez Rydelski, *supra* n. 136, at 151; Shi, *supra* n. 136, at 372; Szudoczky, *Convergence of the Analysis of National Tax Measures, supra* n. 131, at 367; Szudoczky & Károlyi, *The CJEU's Approach to the Objectives of Progressive Turnover-Based Taxes, supra* n. 95, at 84.
516. Piernas López, *Revisiting Some Fundamentals, supra* n. 127, at 280.
517. Joined Cases C-20 and 21/15 P *World Duty Free Group*, para. 68 and further consistent case law ever since.
518. In this vein: Ellenrieder, *Die materielle Selektivität steuerlicher Beihilfen, supra* n. 57, at 324ff.
519. *See* only: Derenne, *supra* n. 142, at 313; Kokott, *Steuerrecht, supra* n. 20, at §3, paras 169ff.; Nicolaides, *Excessive Widening, supra* n. 139, at 69ff.; Peters, *Tax Policy Convergence, supra* n. 74, at 9; López López, *General Thought on Selectivity, supra* n. 62, at 814; Soltész, *supra* n. 174, at 24. A different view is held by Giraud & Petit, *Bury Them Deep, supra* n. 138, at 314ff. since there would still be the question of comparability as a limiting factor. David Hummel, *Das nationale Steuergesetz unter der umfassenden Kontrolle des unionsrechtlichen Beihilferechts?* 110 GmbH-Rundschau 390, 392 (2019) argues that the judgment in *World Duty Free Group* would be correct in essence, but the reasoning of the Commission and the CJEU would be wrong. The aid would instead result from the fact that the measure at issue in the case amounted to export aid. Spain would have sought to circumvent the State aid prohibition with a seemingly general measure in an abusive fashion.
520. Englisch, *State Aid Prohibition, supra* n. 161, at 146 regarding the primary reasoning of the Commission in its decision on the tax ruling granted to ENGIE by Luxembourg. This reasoning would be in line with the now settled case law ever since *World Duty Free Group*.

and VAT, such interpretation will generally amount to a very wide notion of prima facie selectivity.[521]

For example, the CJEU has in its judgment in *Paint Graphos* held that the objective of corporate taxation is the taxation of company profits.[522] It is not entirely clear how it arrived at this conclusion, since the objective of a tax system in principle has to be determined by the Member State as an emanation of fiscal sovereignty. The fact that the objectives that are assigned to a levy by the Member State are crucial can best be understood in the context of special purpose levies.[523] Yet corporate taxes do not have a special purpose of any kind and are thus qualified as purely fiscal taxes. As such, the assumption appears to be that within a broad-based fiscal tax, regardless of the actual intentions of the national legislator, distinctions between different actors would go against the nature of this very tax and be inconsistent from the outset, so that all actors are in a comparable factual and legal situation.[524] In light of the objective to tax company profits, only very few differentiations within national tax laws would conceivably not lead to an unequal treatment.[525] Most distinctions, be it by size, type of income, or sector would in principle lead to a derogation in the second step.[526]

Even for narrow-based fiscal levies, only very few distinctions within the scope of a tax would not result in a derogation from the reference system. For example, in *A-Brauerei*, the CJEU held that the objective of real property transfer tax was 'to tax any change in owner of the rights (Rechtsträgerwechsel) attaching to a property or, in other words, to tax any transfer of the right of ownership in a property from one natural or legal person to another natural or legal person within the meaning of civil law'.[527] It is difficult to conceive of situations in which comparability would be ruled out.

While this notion of selectivity had been widely criticized due to its potential ramifications, the recent case law has shown that there is a rollback, since many types of rules have now been determined to be an integral part of the reference system of taxation. Fiscal sovereignty has thus been strengthened in the case law.[528]

521. Ismer & Piotrowski, *Selectivity in Corporate Tax Matters, supra* n. 77, at 160.
522. Joined Cases C-78 to 80/08 *Paint Graphos*, para. 54.
523. *See* Ch. §3.03[C] *infra*.
524. A different view is held by Nicolaides, *Non-Selective Rules, supra* n. 332, at 28 according to whom a variety of objectives could be pursued even in the area of corporate taxation.
525. Interestingly, the judgment in *Paint Graphos* appeared towards a lack of comparability, which, was however, for the national court to decide, Joined Cases C-78 to 80/08 *Paint Graphos*, paras 61ff.
526. Ismer & Piotrowski, *Selectivity in Corporate Tax Matters, supra* n. 77, at 160; Ekkenga & Safaei, *supra* n. 95, at 1996. A different view is held by Bartosch, *Spanish Goodwill, supra* n. 138, at 69 who argues that there would nevertheless have to be a discriminatory treatment, even if it would not be necessary to define privileged group. This could serve as a restriction. Buendía Sierra, *Finding Selectivity, supra* n. 131, at 88 argues that two different reference systems, a reference system latu sensu and a reference system strictu sensu would have to be identified. If the objective of the entire levy was relevant in the second step, looking for selectivity would amount to a self-fulfilling prophecy. Instead, a comparability test would have to be carried out in the second step. However, this does not appear to lead to a significant restriction.
527. Case C-374/17 *A-Brauerei*, para. 39.
528. *See* Ch. §3.02[C] *supra*.

There are moreover limits to the idea that under broad-based fiscal taxes, all undertakings are in principle comparable.[529] One such example of a lack of comparability has already been touched upon in the context of anti-abuse rules, namely the design of CFC rules. Such CFC rules can form their own reference system of taxation that is distinct from the general corporate tax system.[530]

Another example may be differences in the taxation of residents and non-residents. In many jurisdictions, non-residents' income is only taxed if it is sourced within this jurisdiction, whereas residents are often taxed on their worldwide income. The majority of jurisdictions still refer to the notion of residence to determine whether a corporation's tax liability is limited or unlimited.

Under such a system, national law typically contains a special set of rules applicable to the taxation of non-residents. Yet these rules are generally not comprehensive. Only certain types of income are covered. There will thus generally be a certain degree of fragmentation. If the source country is a Member State, one may then wonder whether this 'selective' taxation of only some types of income derived by non-residents – or inversely the non-taxation of all remaining types of income – can constitute aid. This hinges on the question of whether residents and non-residents are comparable. In our view, however, this is not the case, since the objective of corporate taxation has to be seen in connection with the common differences in the tax treatment of residents and non-residents that exist in a large number of jurisdictions. As a result, resident and non-resident undertakings are not comparable in light of the objective of corporate tax. The exact definition of who is considered a resident is an inherent technical feature of the reference system of taxation and is therefore only subject to limited review. The next question is then whether the rules for the taxation of non-residents as such have to be assessed as a system. This does not necessarily appear convincing, since source taxation is often fragmented by nature.

However, residents and non-residents are comparable if the Member State itself has created comparability[531] or where the notion of residence is not connected to the power to tax. For example, distinctions based on residence in destination-based taxes could not escape State aid scrutiny, since they are simply not relevant to the tax at issue.

[C] Assessment of Special Purpose Levies

The particularities in the assessment of the selectivity of regulatory levies have so far received little attention in the literature. Meanwhile, the CJEU has issued several important judgments on the application of State aid law to special purpose levies, such

529. Sánchez Rydelski, *supra* n. 136, at 154 cites Commission practice on a lack of comparability of related and unrelated companies. However, this stance does no longer appear valid with the later developments in the transfer pricing cases.
530. *See* Ch. §3.02[D], [4] *supra*.
531. De Broe, *Can Tax Treaties Confer State Aid?*, *supra* n. 162, at 229 with reference to constellations, such as the ones at issue in the judgment in Case C-169/08 *Presidente del Consiglio dei Ministri v. Regione Sardegna* EU:C:2009:709.

as *British Aggregates Association,*[532] *Adria-Wien Pipeline,*[533] *Regione Sardegna*[534] and the judgments in *ANGED.*[535] All these judgments concerned different types of environmental levies.

In our view, the overall case law on selectivity can be better understood acknowledging the particularities of special purpose levies. These come down to the fact that such levies have a purpose beyond the levying of funds. As such, the motivations of the legislator in introducing the levy in the first place are more important in the assessment of selectivity. At the same time, there may be – either in acknowledgement of fiscal sovereignty or just in practice – tendencies to vary the intensity of control depending on the objectives of such levies and the distinctions therein.

We will address the particularities of the prima facie selectivity of special-purpose levies in this chapter since the objective of such levy impacts both the analysis of the first and second step: In line with the general approach, the reference system for special-purpose levies generally has to be determined normatively relying on the objective of the levy as the point of departure. As a particularity of special purpose levies, this implies that it is also possible to monitor the scope or boundaries of the levy in question in the framework of the three-step test for de jure-selectivity [1]. The Member State has to be granted a significant degree of autonomy in the definition of the objective of its levy as well as its exact implementation. The limit is a control for manifest inappropriateness. We will then elaborate on some aspects of the identification of the objective of a levy [2]. By contrast, there are no particularities in the second step of the analysis [3].

[1] Normative Determination of the Reference System

Unlike other types of levies, the reference system of taxation of special purpose levies may be broader than the scope of the tax [a]. The same methodology can be applied to parafiscal levies [b].

[a] Reference System Broader Than the Scope of a Special Purpose Levy

The scope of a levy, i.e., the design of the outer bounds of the reference system of taxation, is ordinarily not an aspect that can be monitored by relying on the three-step test for de jure-selectivity. Unlike other types of taxes, the three-step test for selectivity as applied to special purpose levies, however, has an additional dimension. For such levies, the reference system of taxation may be wider than the actual tax because it is – at least in theory – possible to monitor the consistent 'translation' of the underlying

532. Case C-487/06 P *British Aggregates Association v. Commission* EU:C:2008:757.
533. Case C-143/99 *Adria-Wien Pipeline.*
534. Case C-169/08 *Regione Sardegna.*
535. Case C-233/16 *ANGED* EU:C:2018:280; Joined Cases C-234 and 235/16 *ANGED* and Joined Cases C-236 and 237/16 *ANGED* EU:C:2018:291.

policy objectives into a tax.[536] This is not in deviation from the general approach to determining selectivity. In theory, a similar verification would have to be conducted for fiscal levies.[537] Yet since such taxes do not have a special purpose, such verification yields no meaningful results, so the levy as is has to be relied upon as the point of departure.[538]

This dimension emerged in the CJEU's judgment in *British Aggregates Association* (BAA).[539] This rather complex case concerned a levy on aggregates (AGL) in the United Kingdom. The charge of GBP 1.60 per tonne of aggregate arose whenever taxable aggregate (e.g., rock, gravel or sand) was subjected to commercial exploitation within the United Kingdom. A tax credit was thus available where aggregate was exported or removed from the United Kingdom without further processing. There were some exempted processes which were related to certain materials. Furthermore, where the aggregate had previously been used for construction purposes, where it had already been subject to a charge to the AGL, or where – on the commencement date under the Act – it was not on its originating site, the exploitation was not taxable. Finally, the aggregates levy was only gradually phased in in Northern Ireland.[540]

The levy was meant to steer demand away from virgin aggregates, so as to reduce the need for their unnecessary extraction, simultaneously encouraging the use of the exempted products (recycled aggregate and other alternatives to virgin aggregate). The levy was designed to contribute to resource efficiency. These environmental objectives of the levy were in principle accepted by the CJEU. State aid law does not put the use of taxes for policy purposes as such into question – as long as a special purpose levy is not inherently discriminatory for another reason.

In its judgment, the CJEU addressed potential State aid problems concerning the design of the boundaries of the levy. Without explicitly stating so, it in practice endorsed an approach that the reference system of taxation may be wider than the tax. This is to say that the objective of a regulatory tax necessarily defines the scope of the reference system. To avoid selectivity, a tax has to include all comparable situations. In this vein, the CJEU stated the following in *British Aggregates Association*:

536. Similarly: Nicolaides & Metaxas, *supra* n. 159, at 56ff.; Conor Quigley, *European State Aid Law and Policy*, 138 (3rd edn 2015). For an earlier contribution prior to the judgment in *British Aggregates Association:* Brigitta Renner-Loquenz, *State Aid in Energy Taxation Measures: First Experiences from Applying the Environmental Aid Guidelines 2001* 2 EStAL 21, 24 (2003) https://doi.org/10.21552/estal/2003/1/17.
537. Ellenrieder, *Die materielle Selektivität steuerlicher Beihilfen*, *supra* n. 57, at 183ff. similarly takes such normative approach as a point of departure for all types of taxes and concludes that it could even be possible for a reference system to comprise more than one tax, citing *GIL Insurance*.
538. *See* for the problem in the context of narrow-based fiscal levies Ch. §3.03[D] *infra*.
539. Case C-487/06 P *British Aggregates Association*. Michael Honoré, *Selectivity and Taxation: Reflections in light of Case C-487/06 P, British Aggregates Association* 8 EStAL 527ff. (2009) https://doi.org/10.21552/estal/2009/4/155; Juan Jorge Piernas López, *The Concept of State Aid Under EU Law*, 135ff. (2015) argues that the main significance of this judgment would be the addition of a reference to the 'techniques used' to the effects doctrine and the clarification of the limited role national objectives should play in the identification of State aid.
540. Case C-487/06 P *British Aggregates Association*, paras 3ff.

> Article 87(1) EC does not distinguish between the causes or the objectives of State aid, but defines them in relation to their effects [...]. In the light of that case-law, the unavoidable conclusion is that the Court of First Instance disregarded Article 87(1)EC, as interpreted by the Court of Justice, by holding [...] that Member States are free, in balancing the various interests involved, to set their priorities as regards the protection of the environment and, as a result, to determine which goods or services they decide to subject to an environmental levy, with the result that the fact that such a levy does not apply to all similar activities which have a comparable impact on the environment does not mean that similar activities, which are not subject to the levy, benefit from a selective advantage. [...][T]hat approach, which is based solely on a regard for the environmental objective being pursued, excludes a priori the possibility that the non-imposition of the AGL on operators in comparable situations in the light of the objective being pursued might constitute a 'selective advantage', independently of the effects of the fiscal measure in question [...] The Court of First Instance also erred in distinguishing [...], the present case from the facts which gave rise to the judgment in Adria-Wien Pipeline and Wietersdorfer & Peggauer Zementwerke on the ground that the latter concerned, not the definition of the material scope of an environmental levy, as in the present case, but the partial exemption from payment of such a levy which was granted to a certain category of undertakings. [...].[541]

The judgment in *British Aggregates Association* has been interpreted as the effects-based approach under State aid law only yielding to core tax logic – rather than allowing Member States to pursue objectives connected with the use of resources. The CJEU would have ruled that the only applicable logic could be the taxation of commercial activity.[542] Such a reading would indeed be problematic as it would substitute the discretion of the legislator and exclude its freedom to use tax policy for behavioural steering and selecting tax bases accordingly.

Yet in our view, this is not the core of the judgment. The CJEU did not negate the possibility of pursuing environmental policy objectives. It merely rejected the notion that such objectives in a levy are excluded from State aid control altogether since they are 'valuable' and in the absence of harmonization remain a Member State competence. Member States are very well within their rights to pursue environmental objectives through taxation. While they have to do so in an internally consistent manner, the starting point is the objective as defined by the national legislator. If there had been a valid (environmental) reason to only tax one type of aggregate, the levy would not have amounted to State aid. The legislator is merely bound by its own fundamental charging decision. The CJEU's judgment was primarily concerned with the applicable methodology but remained silent on the exact objective and its implementation and referred the case back to the GC.

According to the CJEU, State aid can thus both derive from an explicit exemption, i.e., an exception to the general rule and from the fact that not all comparable situations are covered by the scope of a levy in the first place.[543] All this means that for

541. *Ibid.*, paras 85ff.; emphasis added by the author.
542. Jaeger, *Tax Incentives under State Aid Law, supra* n. 101, at 47.
543. Similarly: Cordewener, *supra* n. 131, at 291f.; Luja, *Fiscal Sovereignty, supra* n. 95, at 313. Honoré, *Selectivity, supra* n. 137, at 146ff. argues that the reference system would be relevant to identify and handle cases of 'asymmetrical taxation'. This is an acknowledgement of the

special-purpose levies, State aid control (additionally) involves an assessment of the boundaries of a levy. This does not amount to a departure from previous case law or even a separate selectivity test. It is merely an emanation of the normative determination of the reference system of taxation, relying on the stated objective of a levy.

Admittedly, the delimitation of comparable undertakings may not always be straightforward.[544] This is perhaps what motivated the Commission in its Notice on the Notion of State aid appears to grant Member States a certain degree of leeway in the design of special purpose levies. Accordingly, such verification – as was carried out in *British Aggregates Association* – is (only) necessary where the scope of such levy is designed in an arbitrary or biased way. Interestingly, the Commission in its Notice does not clarify that the verification that was carried out in *Gibraltar* was a matter of de facto-selectivity, while it is a matter of de jure-selectivity for special purpose levies.[545] Yet the distinction is crucial, as a review of the logical transposition of the objective of a tax into a consistent scope would be nearly impossible as well as highly intrusive from a tax sovereignty point of view for fiscal levies.[546]

Such a normative approach to identifying the reference system of taxation for special-purpose levies has since been relied on in several judgments. For example, this was the case in the *Regione Sardegna* judgment. The judgment concerned a regional tax on stopovers by aircraft or recreational craft for tourist purposes, which was only levied on operators whose tax residence was outside of Sardinia. The CJEU found that there was a simultaneous infringement of the fundamental freedoms and State aid law because Sardinian tax residents were not taxable under the levy.[547] There was no formal derogation from the reference system, but the tax was dubbed an environmental tax. In the context of its analysis of infringements of the fundamental freedoms, the CJEU stated that it would be necessary to take into account the specific characteristics of the tax. In light of the environmental objective of the tax, the tax domicile of the operators of the aircraft or recreational craft should be irrelevant.[548] The same point was made in the assessment of the selectivity of the measure. The levy should have comprised all stopovers regardless of the tax domicile of the operator in question. The

---

principles developed in the judgment. The possibility of a broader reference system than the scope of the tax based on the effects-based approach has again emerged in Joined Cases C-105 to 113/18 *Unesa and Others* EU:C:2019:935, paras 63f. A different view is held by Andreas Bartosch, *Differenzierungen im nationalen Steuerrecht und das Selektivitätsmerkmal des EU-Beihilfeverbots: Sind die Steuerregelungen betreffend den deutschen Mittelstand in Gefahr* 73 BB 2199 (2018) who argues that the reference system has to be identified in an abstract manner, not taking into account comparability.

544. Panci, *supra* n. 59, at 357f.; Pérez-Bernabeu, *Refining the Derogation Test, supra* n. 473, at 596 points to a potential of legal uncertainty when Member States pursue more than one objective. Phedon Nicolaides & Ioana Eleonora Rusu, *The Concept of Selectivity: An Ever Wider Scope* 11 EStAL 791, 796f. (2012) https://doi.org/10.21552/estal/2012/4/314 cite the example of a levy that seeks to abate noise pollution. The notion of substitutability which is relied on to define the relevant market would not be convincing.
545. Commission Notice on the notion of State aid, *supra* n. 26, at para. 129ff.
546. *See* for narrow-based fiscal levies Ch. §3.03[D] *infra*.
547. Case C-169/08 *Regione Sardegna*, paras 59ff.
548. *Ibid.*, paras 33ff.

narrow scope of the levy thus had the same effect as an exemption.[549] Under the effects-based approach as developed in earlier case law, there was thus selectivity.[550]

[b] Applicability to Parafiscal Levies

Finally, this approach also seems to apply to parafiscal levies. They can be considered special purpose levies because the revenue from such levies is earmarked for a specific purpose. An example was the levy at issue in *Ferring*. The judgment concerned a direct sales tax on medicines. In France, 2.5% of the pre-tax turnover achieved by pharmaceutical laboratories from wholesale sales of medicinal products to dispensing pharmacies, mutual pharmacies and pharmacies belonging to mining-friendly societies was taxed. By contrast, the tax was not levied on sales of medicines by wholesale distributors. The levy was introduced to help finance the National Sickness Insurance Fund and to restore the balance of competition between the different distribution channels for medicines. The relevant distortion of competition derived from the fact that wholesale distributors were under a duty of public service in that they were obliged to, for example, be able to deliver any medicine in its range within 24 hours of receipt of the order.[551]

The CJEU held that the special tax itself equated to granting a tax exemption – i.e., an advantage – to wholesale distributors.[552] However, provided that the tax on direct sales corresponds to the additional costs incurred by wholesale distributors, the tax may be considered compensation for the services they provide and therefore not amount to aid. If this was the case, the wholesale distributors would not enjoy a real advantage, but would merely be put on an equal competitive footing with other distribution channels.[553] This assessment was for the national court to make.[554] In *Ferring*, the reference system of taxation was hence found to be broader than the scope of the tax as it extended to all distribution channels.

The narrow scope of the levy at issue in *Ferring* was chosen deliberately so as to eliminate perceived distortions of competition. The two distribution channels were in direct competition, which means that it was possible to identify the beneficiaries of aid in a straightforward manner. It is, however, unclear whether there also has to be a subjective element – in this case, the purpose to compensate wholesale distributors for their general interest obligations – for there to be State aid. This would make the levy a special purpose levy.

549. *Ibid.*, para. 63.
550. Raymond Luja, *Revisiting the Balance Between Aid, Selectivity and Selective Aid in Respect of Taxes and Special Levies* 9 EStAL 161, 168 (2010) https://doi.org/10.21552/estal/2010/1/169 criticizes that it was unclear whether taxation – as opposed to non-taxation was actually the benchmark. The latter would be the case if the vast majority of operators were Sardinian residents. He thus proposes an analysis similar to the one carried out in the *Aer Lingus* and *Ryanair* judgment, *see* Ch. §3.02[B], [2] *supra*. However, this does not appear convincing here due to the environmental objective of the tax.
551. Case C-53/00 *Ferring*, paras 5ff. for a description of the facts of the case.
552. *Ibid.*, para. 21.
553. *Ibid.*, para. 27.
554. *Ibid.*, para. 28.

If a close competitive relationship were to suffice, the potential ambit of the State aid provision would be very wide. By contrast, if the objective to eliminate distortions of competition was what led to the existence of aid, the case would be even less clear. This objective is inherently discriminatory. This is only otherwise where the tax serves as compensation for general interest services as may have been the case in *Ferring*. Such a perspective introduces a subjective element into the analysis that is very hard to verify.[555]

[2] Objective of Special Purpose Levies and Standard of Control

There is a fundamental conflict between Member States' scope for the implementation of non-fiscal policies through special purpose levies on the one hand and the objectives of State aid control on the other hand. This conflict arises because the reference system of taxation is not necessarily treated as a given for special-purpose levies. A full commitment to competitive neutrality would require examining and evaluating the objectives underlying a tax as well as reviewing their fully consistent implementation, which would be problematic in light of the division of competences between the EU and the Member States. This conflict is currently resolved through judicial restraint and a low standard of control [a].

Nevertheless, fundamental problems may arise for the evaluation and identification of the objectives underlying a tax. A number of issues are still unresolved. We will briefly touch upon some selected problems. On the example of environmental taxes, we will demonstrate that the stated objective of a levy is generally taken at face value unless there is a manifest error [b]. Where a special purpose levy simultaneously aims to levy funds, the analysis will usually disregard the latter objective [c]. The analysis is in principle neutral, regardless of whether a special purpose is in line with EU objectives. At the same time where objectives are indeed in line with EU law, this may have a positive impact on the outcome of the assessment in practice [d]. Finally, the stated objectives of the Member State generally have to be taken at face value. This is in deference to tax sovereignty [e].

[a] Lenient Standard of Control

It has been noted that Member States may prefer to pursue national policy objectives through special taxes rather than within the general tax regime because it is possible to take into account special purposes, such as environmental objectives, on the level of the design of such levy.[556] Measures that would be considered State aid if they formed part of the general tax system may escape State aid scrutiny as part of a special purpose levy. This is mirrored in the case law of the CJEU, which has shown a large degree of

555. *See* Ch. §3.03[C], [2], [e] *infra* for the ambiguities in identifying the objective of a levy.
556. Ellenrieder, *Verhandlung der Grundsätze der beihilferechtlichen Selektivität, supra* n. 81, at 484; Piernas López, *Revisiting Some Fundamentals, supra* n. 127, at 279. Others have instead pointed to the difficulties in designing an adequate scope for such levy, Nicolaides & Rusu, *supra* n. 544, at 802.

deference to the implementation of national policy objectives – as long as they are not pursued within the framework of the general tax system, but through special levies.[557]

The CJEU's judgment in *ANGED* concerned a tax on large retail establishments within the territory of Catalonia.[558] Since several similar levies in other regions of Spain were challenged by the organization ANGED, a number of judgments with the same title were delivered at the same time.[559] The features of the respective laws in Asturias and Aragon as well as the arguments that the CJEU relied on were very similar, so we will only focus on the Catalonian law.

The law introducing the tax stated that it was chargeable on the exceptional financial capacity of large retail establishments. Due to their large sales area, such retail establishments may acquire a dominant position and produce adverse effects on the territory and the environment, which they do not ordinarily bear. The revenue from the levy was to be used for the modernization of local businesses and to implement action plans to counter the effects of large retail establishments. The chargeable event for the tax was the use of a sales area of more than 2,500 m^2 by individual large retail establishments regardless of whether or not it was situated within a large collective retail establishment. Individual large retail establishments that were garden centres or sold vehicles, construction materials, machinery, or industrial supplies were exempt. The taxable amount was reduced by 60% for retail establishments that sold furniture, sanitary wares, doors, and windows, as well as for do-it-yourself stores.[560] ANGED, a national association of large distribution companies brought an action for annulment of the decree implementing the tax before the High Court of Justice of Catalonia arguing that it was incompatible with the freedom of establishment and State aid law. The action was dismissed. ANGED appealed against the decision before the Supreme Court, which stayed the proceedings and referred questions on the interpretation of EU law to the CJEU.[561]

The CJEU decided that there was no infringement of the fundamental freedoms.[562] As to potential infringements of State aid law, the CJEU pointed out that the reference system of taxation does not necessarily have to extend to the entire territory of the Member State where a regional or local authority is sufficiently autonomous in relation to the central government and fundamentally designs the political and economic environment in which undertakings operate.[563]

557. This has, in our view, not convincingly been linked to a stronger emphasis on a socially oriented interpretation of the selectivity test, Delia Ferri & Juan Jorge Piernas López, *The Social Dimension of EU State Aid Law and Policy* 21 Camb. Yearb. Eur. Leg. Stud. 75, 86f. (2019) https://doi.org/10.1017/cel.2019.2, also referring to the judgment in *Paint Graphos*.
558. Case C-233/16 *ANGED*. On the *ANGED* judgments *see, e.g.*, Nicolas de Sadeleer, *Preliminary Ruling on the Compatibility of Taxation of Superstores with the Right to Freedom of Establishment and State Aid Law: Case C-233/16, ANGED* 27 RECIEL 341ff. (2018) https://doi.org/10.1111/reel.12266; Piernas López, *Revisiting Some Fundamentals*, *supra* n. 127; Marek Szydło, *Differential Tax Burdens of Undertakings and Internal Market Law: The Way Forward after ANGED* 56 CMLR 1093ff. (2019) https://doi.org/10.54648/cola2019081.
559. Joined Cases C-234 and 235/16 *ANGED* and Joined Cases C-236 and 237/16 *ANGED*.
560. Case C-233/16 *ANGED*, paras 6ff.
561. *Ibid.*, paras 14ff.
562. *Ibid.*, paras 28ff. *See* in more detail Szydło, *supra* n. 558, at 1101ff.
563. *Ibid.*, para. 41.

The CJEU addressed the threshold of a sales area of 2,500 m^2, which due to the design of the tax could be considered a matter of the design of the reference system of taxation itself. It stated:

> Next, although the tax criterion relating to the sales area *does not appear to formally derogate from a given legal reference framework, its effect is nonetheless to exclude retail establishments whose sales area is less than 2 500 m^2 from the scope of that tax*. Thus, the IGEC cannot be distinguished from a regional tax on retail establishments whose sales areas exceed a certain threshold.[564]

Szydło has interpreted this part of the judgment as an indication that the boundaries between de jure- and de facto-selectivity are blurry.[565] In our view, however, this is not the case. The judgment can be read as the CJEU taking into consideration the particularities of special-purpose levies. For such levies, the point of departure of the analysis has to be the objective of the tax itself.[566] The scope of the tax then has to extend to all comparable situations in light of this objective. Where this is not the case, it does not matter whether a provision formally derogates from the reference system or whether the scope of the levy was not sufficiently wide to include all comparable situations in the first place. Both cases can lead to de jure-selectivity. Accordingly, the CJEU in its judgment referred to the effects doctrine as developed in this context in its judgment in *British Aggregates Association*.[567] This means that for special purpose levies the notion of de facto-selectivity would appear to be mostly irrelevant, unless State aid is granted by facially neutral technical rules within such levy.

The CJEU went on to elaborate on the objective of the tax, which, according to the information provided by the referring court, was to contribute towards environmental protection and town and country planning. It was meant to correct and counteract the environmental impact and territorial consequences of the activities of large retail establishments resulting from issues, such as a rise in traffic flows, by having those establishments contribute to the financing of environmental action plans and making improvements to infrastructure networks.[568]

It further held that it is not disputed that the environmental impact of retail establishments largely depends on their size. Sales area thresholds would therefore be suitable to distinguish between undertakings with a greater or lesser environmental impact.[569] Such establishments would also have particular significance for town and country planning policies.[570] In light of the objective of the tax, retail establishments with lower and higher sales areas were not in a comparable situation. Consequently,

564. *Ibid.*, para. 46; emphasis added by the author.
565. Szydło, *supra* n. 558, at 1106f.
566. With a similar reasoning: Piernas López, *Revisiting Some Fundamentals*, *supra* n. 127, at 279.
567. Case C-233/16 *ANGED*, para. 47.
568. *Ibid.*, para. 52. Critical: Hummel, *Das nationale Steuergesetz*, *supra* n. 519, at 394, according to whom the purpose to levy funds was wrongly disregarded since it was not mentioned in the preamble of the law. Such an interpretation of national law by the European courts would be risky.
569. Case C-233/16 *ANGED*, para. 53.
570. *Ibid.*, para. 54 with reference to Case C-400/08 *Commission v. Spain* EU:C:2011:172, para. 80.

the tax exemption for retail establishments whose sales area is less than 2,500 m^2 would not be selective. In its judgments on the Asturian levy, the CJEU went further and stated that the determination of these thresholds comes within the discretion of the national lawmaker and is based on technical, complex assessments that the Court only has limited power to review. Such review would be limited to the thresholds being manifestly inappropriate in light of the objectives pursued.[571]

Perhaps the most surprising aspect of the judgment was the CJEU's rather lenient approach. It did not put into question the stated objectives of the tax, the suitability of the tax to achieve these objectives, or the somewhat arbitrary threshold that would exclude comparability. All factual assumptions underlying the design of the tax, such as the differing environmental impact of retail establishments depending on their sales area and the concrete threshold, were taken for granted without any requirement for proof.[572] Indeed, it appears far-fetched that the threshold would depend on 'technical, complex assessments'.[573]

As such, the judgments in *ANGED* do not define a new standard for all types of levies going forward.[574] They are merely indicative of a necessarily lenient approach for special-purpose levies. It would encroach upon Member States' fiscal sovereignty if the CJEU conducted a fact-finding mission in such cases and then substituted its own standards.[575] A control for manifest error and demonstrating logical or formal inconsistencies, of course, remains possible. For example, the levy at issue in the *ANGED* question also contained an exemption for collective retail establishments.[576] According to the CJEU, the complete exemption granted to collective retail establishments would lead to a distinction between two categories of establishments (collective and individual) that are objectively in a comparable situation in light of the objectives of environmental protection and town and country planning and would therefore be selective.[577] The underlying argument was presumably that the environmental impact (traffic flows, etc.) is similar regardless of whether individual or collective retail establishments are concerned, even though the CJEU did not elaborate on the reasons for its assessment.[578]

571. Joined Cases C-234 and 235/16 *ANGED*, para. 48; Joined Cases C-236 and 237/16 *ANGED*, para. 43.
572. Szydło, *supra* n. 558, at 1108f. Similarly Loewenthal, *supra* n. 136, at 50. De Sadeleer, *supra* n. 558, at 346 holds that in light of this judgment Member States retain a large measure of discretion in the field of environmental taxation.
573. *See* Luja, *Revisiting the Balance, supra* n. 550, at 166 for an example of how the redefinition of the objectives of an environmental levy can change the legal assessment. This appears to be the real problem the CJEU faces here as well.
574. A different view is held by Szydło, *supra* n. 558, at 1111ff. who contrasts this lenient approach with the Commission's approaches on progressive turnover-based taxes and the Hungarian tobacco tax.
575. Similarly Conor Quigley, *European State Aid Law and Policy*, 137 (3rd edn 2015) on narrow-based levies in general.
576. Joined Cases C-234 and 235/16 *ANGED*.
577. *Ibid.*, para. 61.
578. Similarly de Sadeleer, *supra* n. 558, at 346; Szydło, *supra* n. 558, at 1110.

[b] Definitional Issues: The Example of Environmental Taxes and Tobacco Taxes

The category of special purpose levies certainly comprises regulatory taxes, including Pigouvian taxes, i.e., taxes that implement a price signal to correct for negative externalities.[579] Yet the notion of special purpose levies goes further and includes any type of non-fiscal objective. On the one hand, the State aid assessment of special purpose levies has an additional dimension in that it can be verified whether the scope of the reference system of taxation has been appropriately defined. On the other hand, the standard of control appears to be lower than for fiscal levies. From the case law, it appears as though the European courts would simply accept the stated objective of a levy at face value without further examining how strong the link between the stated objective and the design of the tax is and consequently apply the standards of special purpose levies. This then goes along with wide discretion as to the design of such levy.

For example, this can be observed in the area of environmental taxation. The taxes that were the subject of the *ANGED* judgments were deemed to have an environmental purpose.[580] Such levies are a separate category in the context of the compatibility of aid. The General Block Exemption Regulation (GBER) defines the term environmental tax as such:

> 'environmental tax or parafiscal levy' means a tax or a levy applied on a specific tax base, products or services that have a clear negative effect on the environment or which seeks to charge certain activities, goods or services so that the environmental costs may be included in their price or so that producers and consumers are oriented towards activities which better respect the environment.[581]

This definition is very broad[582] since it apparently suffices that the tax base has a clear negative effect on the environment. It does not appear to be necessary for the tax to achieve an inclusion of the environmental costs in prices or to influence the choices of producers and consumers. It is unclear whether the objective element of this definition (specific tax base that has a clear negative effect on the environment) and the description of the purpose are truly to be understood as alternative or cumulative criteria. The taxes at issue in *ANGED* presumably only (if at all) fulfil the first condition.[583] The implication of disregarding the environmental objective under State

579. *See*, e.g., Stuart Adam et al., *Tax by design*, 231 (2011) for environmental taxation; Reuven S. Avi-Yonah, *Taxation as Regulation: Carbon Tax, Health Care Tax, Bank Tax and Other Regulatory Taxes* Accounting, Economics, and Law 1, 6 (2011).
580. *See* Ch. §3.03[C], [2], [a] *supra*.
581. Article 2 Commission Regulation (EU) No. 651/2014 of 17 June 2014 declaring certain categories of aid compatible with the internal market in application of Articles 107 and 108 of the Treaty [2014] OJ L 187/1, last amended by Commission Regulation (EU) 2023/1315 of 23 June 2023 [2023] OJ L 167/1.
582. Alice Pirlot, *Exploring the Impact of EU Law on Energy an Environmental Taxation*, in Panayi et al. (eds), Research Handbook on European Union Taxation Law, 359, 372 (2020).
583. The problem of the impact of environmental taxes not only exists on a national level but there has also been criticism in the literature as to the missing link between the EU legislative

aid law would presumably be that the sales area threshold entails State aid since the sales area is a manifestly inappropriate proxy for the ability to pay.

The alleged environmental objective of the levy in question emerged in two aspects, namely first in the choice of taxable undertakings – only retail establishments with a significant environmental impact (expressed by a large sales area) were covered by the tax. Second, the revenue was to be used for the modernization of local businesses and to implement action plans to counter the effects of large retail establishments.

The first aspect, while linked to environmental concerns to a certain extent, is unlikely to have a tangible regulatory impact. In other words, it is doubtful whether – and how – the tax could contribute to mitigating environmental problems caused by large retail establishments. This link is presumably meant to be ensured by the (somewhat fuzzy) notion of the implementation of action plans to counter the effects of large retail establishments, i.e., the use of funds. Yet one may wonder whether this should suffice to justify treating the tax as an environmental tax.

Related is the question of how strong the link between the stated objective and the levy is, i.e., the suitability of special-purpose levies to achieve their objective. Again, the potential impact of State aid law in this respect seems to be limited, unless the tax is inherently discriminatory and leads to benefits being granted to some actors. The impact of a special purpose levy – even where there is a link to externalities – may be hard to evaluate. This particularly holds true because State aid control is meant to be carried out from an *ex ante* perspective. Only where a Member State has failed to notify a measure, will the examination be carried out at a later stage. For example, where the objective of a tax is to discourage consumption, (*ex post*) empirical evidence may point to the fact that this is not the case as demand proves to be inelastic. Where consumers alter their behaviour, it may be towards an equally harmful consumption choice.

The link between the stated objective and the design of the tax was even more doubtful in the tax underlying the Commission's decision on the Hungarian tobacco tax.[584] In this Decision, the Commission convincingly took the stated objective of the tax at face value but found that the tax at issue involved State aid due to its manifestly arbitrary design. Hungary had planned to introduce a tax levied on the turnover derived from the production and trade of tobacco products in Hungary, which was labelled a 'health contribution'. The tax was meant to collect funds for the financing of the health system, so as to increase the quality of health services. The tax would have been levied on authorized warehouse keepers, importers, and registered traders of tobacco products. It was to be levied along turnover thresholds. The tax would have

instruments on environmental taxation and environmental objectives. *See* for a comprehensive overview *ibid.*, at 364f. For the related problem of the definition of energy taxes: Villar Ezcurra, *supra* n. 131, at 345ff.

584. Commission Decision (EU) 2016/1846 of 4 July 2016 on the measure SA.41187 (2015/C) (ex 2015/NN) implemented by Hungary on the health contribution of tobacco industry businesses [2016] OJ L 282/43.

allowed companies to reduce their tax liability by making certain eligible investments.[585]

The Commission opened an investigation into the tax due to these distinctions. It argued that the progressivity of the tax could not form part of the reference system.[586] It conceded that it was not possible to identify a standard tax rate.[587] However, the stated objective of the tax would be to collect funds for the health care system and to increase the quality of health services in Hungary. The progressive rate structure would not mirror the relationship between the generation of negative externalities and turnover.[588] In other words, a lower turnover of a producer or trader of tobacco products does not go along with the lower health risks of each cigarette sold.

In light of the objective of the reference system, all operators involved in the production and trade of tobacco products would be in a comparable legal and factual situation.[589] There would therefore be a derogation from the reference system both due to the progressive rate structure and the possibility to reduce an undertaking's tax liability by making certain eligible investments.[590] According to the Commission, these differentiations could also not be justified in the third step.[591] Moreover, the Commission held that the reduction of the tax base for eligible investments was contrary to the objective of the tax as it would lead to an increase of the negative externalities that the tax claimed to seek to tackle.[592]

The special purpose of the levy only became relevant in the choice of the sector to be taxed and the use of the funds that were to be collected through the tax. Yet there was no clear regulatory purpose. It was not evident that the tax sought to modify the behaviour of producers or consumers in any way. This holds all the more true since the tax was not designed to be borne by the consumer. In this case, labelling the tax a health contribution may have actually worked against the Hungarian legislator: While it may be true that the overall health impact caused by operators with a larger turnover is bigger, the link between the tax and negative externalities was very weak. If the levy was a regulatory tax, the implementation of differential rates along turnover thresholds would be counter-intuitive, since the impact on health for each additional unit sold does not vary. The levy would have presumably been at least partly State aid proof had it been deemed a purely fiscal levy. Unlike in *ANGED*, the distinguishing was thus manifestly inappropriate in light of the objective of the tax.

All this means that State aid law has to take the decision of a Member State to tax for granted even where it is doubtful whether a tax will achieve its (stated) objective or purpose or where there would be more suitable means to achieve the objective from a regulatory point of view. In deference to these objectives, State aid control will only apply if the design of the tax is logically or formally inconsistent in light of the stated

585. *Ibid.*, paras 5ff. for a description of the measure.
586. *Ibid.*, para. 29.
587. *Ibid.*, para. 31.
588. *Ibid.*, para. 33.
589. *Ibid.*, para. 37.
590. *Ibid.*, paras 36ff.
591. *Ibid.*, paras 42ff.
592. *Ibid.*, para. 47.

objectives of the tax. This is in line with the standard of control that is applied in monitoring the boundaries of a special purpose levy.[593] It is not clear under what circumstances the CJEU would disregard the alleged purpose of a tax altogether.[594] Where the objective of a tax is ostensible and is meant to disguise the true objective of the tax, it should be possible to objectively examine whether this is plausible.[595] The applicable standard should again be an examination for manifest error.

[c] Limited Significance of the Purpose of Revenue Generation in a Special Purpose Levy

Special purpose levies generally have a two-fold objective: the purpose to levy funds coexists with the special (steering) purpose. This dual objective becomes apparent for Member States' taxes on tobacco, alcoholic beverages, fuel, or energy taxes. The majority of special purpose levies will very likely at least partly serve to raise funds, as long as the tax rate is not factually prohibitive. The question is then which of these goals should take priority for the identification of the scope of the reference system of taxation.[596]

From the case law, it seems as though the CJEU focuses on the special purpose of a levy where taxes have more than one purpose.[597] The (additional) objective to levy funds is not touched upon in the seminal cases on special purpose levies.[598] Instead, the CJEU will only survey those cases from the point of view of the special steering purpose of the levy. Again, there may be demarcation issues, for example, where the steering purpose is a mere pretext or where such purpose is altogether subordinate to the purpose of levying funds. However, as far as can be seen, there is no case law on this aspect.

[d] More Leeway for Objectives Aligned with EU Law or Policies?

One may then wonder whether the analysis varies depending on how valuable the objective of a levy is considered to be. Inherently discriminatory objectives would certainly be problematic. Beyond this, the objectives that a Member State has in introducing a special purpose levy can generally not be monitored under State aid law.

593. *See* Ch. §3.03[C], [1], [a] *supra*.
594. Pérez-Bernabeu, *The Spanish Hydroelectric Tax, supra* n. 159 cites the judgment in Joined Cases C-105 to 113/18 *Unesa and Others* as an example, where the CJEU based its judgments on the wrong premise as to the environmental levy in question.
595. Similarly Szudoczky & Károlyi, *The Troubled Story of the Hungarian Advertisement Tax, supra* n. 157, at 46.
596. This has an impact on the outcome of the analysis, Loewenthal, *supra* n. 136, at 47f.
597. *See, e.g.*, Case C-143/99 *Adria-Wien Pipeline*; Case C-487/06 P *British Aggregates Association*; Case C-169/08 *Regione Sardegna*; Case C-233/16 *ANGED*. Similarly Pérez-Bernabeu, *Refining the Derogation Test, supra* n. 473, at 589. According to Loewenthal, *supra* n. 136, at 48 the case law would not be clear. Yet the judgments he cites all concern fiscal levies.
598. Critical: Hummel, *Das nationale Steuergesetz, supra* n. 519, at 394.

However, is selectivity also neutral for objectives that are considered valuable in the sense that they are in line with EU policies or objectives?

In principle, this aspect should play no role as is underlined by the case law of the CJEU. In its judgment in *British Aggregates Association* the CJEU held:

> It should also be borne in mind that *protection of the environment constitutes one of the essential objectives of the Community.* [...] However, the need to take account of requirements relating to environmental protection, however legitimate, cannot justify the exclusion of selective measures, even specific ones such as environmental levies, from the scope of Article 87(1) EC [...], as account may in any event usefully be taken of the environmental objectives when the compatibility of the State aid measure with the common market is being assessed pursuant to Article 87(3) EC.[599]

The CJEU thus acknowledges that the protection of the environment is an EU objective that is even laid down in Article 3(3) TEU. Yet this should not influence the assessment of the existence of aid under Article 107(1) TFEU.[600] Instead, this aspect should primarily play a role in the context of the assessment of the compatibility of aid.

Nevertheless, the Commission as the most important actor to enforce State aid law has a certain degree of discretion in taking up cases in the first place. Particularly where a tax is levied based on a multitude of objectives, the assessment of selectivity includes value judgments. In this assessment, EU objectives can very well come into play. The options for competitors to achieve enforcement are then limited and taxpayers themselves will but rarely succeed in arguing that a tax entails illegal State aid.[601] Therefore, this kind of bias will not necessarily be subject to judicial control. For example, the Commission has thus far refrained from monitoring Member States' unilateral digital taxes for infringements of State aid law even though it (albeit unsuccessfully) tackled the Polish and Hungarian turnover-based taxes that are quite similar in design. This may be because such taxes might pave the way for a harmonized digital services tax.[602]

[e] Identification of the Objectives of a Levy and Implementation

The main problem in the assessment of special purpose levies is the identification of the objective of the levy in question.[603] Depending on the exact objective of a tax, the State aid assessment can vary significantly. Tax sovereignty warrants that the definition of the objective of the tax should in principle come from the Member State concerned. It is necessary to rely on the considerations behind the introduction of a levy.[604] In the

599. Case C-487/06 P *British Aggregates Association*, paras 91f. emphasis added by the author.
600. Lόpez Lόpez, *General Thought on Selectivity, supra* n. 62, at 815 argues that the differentiation between 'good' and 'bad' goals leads to legal uncertainty.
601. *See* on this Ch. §5.02[A], [2] *infra.*
602. Mehboob, *supra* n. 157, at 70.
603. *See* on this Szudoczky & Károlyi, *The CJEU's Approach to the Objectives of Progressive Turnover-Based Taxes, supra* n. 95.
604. Szudoczky & Károlyi, *The CJEU's Approach to the Objectives of Progressive Turnover-Based Taxes, supra* n. 95, at 87 point out that it is close to impossible to attribute intent to a legislative

procedure under Article 267 TFEU, information on the objectives of a tax is submitted by the national court. In a recent judgment, the CJEU addressed the State aid compatibility of an environmental levy, which was, however, held to have a purely economic objective by the referring court:

> In that regard, it is apparent from the presentation of national law in the orders for reference, and, in particular, from Article 112 bis(1) of the Water Law and from Articles 12 to 14 of Royal Decree 198/2015, that the *tax on the use of inland waters for the production of electricity is aimed at the protection and improvement of public water resources. [...] While the referring court, which has sole jurisdiction to interpret national law, indicates that that tax – notwithstanding the wording of Article 112 bis of the Water Law and the provisions of Royal Decree 198/2015 implementing the tax – pursues, in the light of its essential characteristics and its structure, a purely economic objective, it should be observed that, in the absence of EU rules governing the matter, it falls within the tax competence of the Member States to designate bases of assessment and to spread the tax burden across the various factors of production and economic sectors* [...]. Consequently, a criterion for taxation connected with the source of production of electricity enables, as a rule, a Member State to apply a tax, such as that at issue in the cases in the main proceedings, only to electricity producers using water as the source of electricity production.[605]

The CJEU thus exercised restraint and merely held that taking the legislative materials at face value, there would be no State aid. However, it was for the national court to decide whether this stated objective had to be disregarded.

It may in some cases be nearly impossible to determine the objective of a tax. This is particularly problematic where no or not sufficient documentation of the legislative process exists. To determine these objectives, it should not be sufficient to rely on a formal criterion (i.e., a purpose that is documented in legislative documents or the preamble of a law). Beyond that, representations by the Member State that are not documented in the legislative process should also be relevant. Where doubts as to the objective of the reference system cannot be eliminated, Member States' tax sovereignty warrants a reading that does not result in selectivity. Of course, this should only hold true where it is, in fact, impossible to determine the exact objective of a tax and where the Member State does not disguise the true objective of a tax or does not provide the Commission with access to the legislative materials on a tax. This means that again there should only be some sort of monitoring for manifest errors.[606] Beyond that, one

body. Deák, *supra* n. 157, at 111f. proposes a broader perspective, not only relying on legislative materials but also the general context of the levy.

605. Joined Cases C-105 to 113/18 *Unesa and Others*, paras 66ff.; emphasis added by the author. *See* Pérez-Bernabeu, *The Spanish Hydroelectric Tax, supra* n. 159, at 353 for an explanation of the doubts regarding the environmental objectives of the levy.

606. According to Szudoczky & Károlyi, *The CJEU's Approach to the Objectives of Progressive Turnover-Based Taxes, supra* n. 95, at 85, 89f. the CJEU takes the objective that was submitted by the Member State as a point of departure and can carry out a 'consistency/appropriateness scrutiny'. This would be overly lenient.

may wonder to what extent a subjective analysis should be introduced into the analysis. However, such subjective elements are quite hard to administer in practice.[607]

Another problem in this respect is that the design of a special purpose levy will often be the result of the balancing of more than one objective. The balancing of objectives could already be carried out on the level of the definition of the objective of the tax and would not have to be tested for its justifiability and proportionality. It would appear as though the more multi-faceted the objectives a legislator cites for a levy, the less vulnerable the levy would be to State aid control as different features of or distinctions within a tax can be justified by the different objectives of the tax.[608] It is therefore paramount for the national authorities to precisely explain the motivations underlying the design of a tax. At the same time, this means that the outcome of the State aid assessment very much depends on how the design of the tax is represented by the national authorities. As a downside, such analysis is naturally vulnerable to value judgments, which is all the more problematic because the Commission bears the burden of proof in this respect. This issue can only be addressed by applying a low standard of control.

[3] Derogation from the Reference System of Taxation in Special Purpose Levies

There are no particularities for the second step of the selectivity test. Member States have to design special purpose levies in an internally (and externally) consistent manner. Perhaps the most prominent case dealing with a derogation from the reference system of taxation for a special purpose levy was the CJEU's *Adria-Wien Pipeline* judgment. The levy in question provided for the possibility of rebates for undertakings that were major consumers of energy provided they were manufacturing principally goods. Applications for rebates from undertakings supplying services were rejected. The CJEU found this to be a selective advantage for undertakings manufacturing goods as undertakings supplying services may similarly be major consumers of energy, but could not profit from the exemption.[609] This is to say that in light of the environmental objective of the tax, all undertakings were in a comparable factual and legal situation. As to the justification in the specific case, the CJEU only stated that the ecological considerations underlying the tax do not provide a justification for the differentiated

607. Parada, *Vodafone Magyarország Opinion, supra* n. 157, at 405 argues that legislative intent could play a role in the determination of whether there is an indirect discrimination. This argument could be transferred to State aid law. Schön, *State Aid in the Area of Taxation, supra* n. 31, at para. 13-063 argues that the 'subjective aims' of the legislator should be irrelevant. Instead the underlying principles would have to be determined, albeit with respect to the third step.

608. Michael Honoré, *Selectivity and Taxation: Reflections in Light of Case C-487/06 P, British Aggregates Association* 8 EStAL 527, 533 (2009) https://doi.org/10.21552/estal/2009/4/155 holds that Member States should describe the objective of a measures in as much detail as possible to ensure that the would-be beneficiaries of aid are in a unique legal or factual situation.

609. Case C-143/99 *Adria-Wien Pipeline*, para. 50.

treatment as the sector an undertaking operates in is irrelevant in terms of the damage to the environment incurred.[610]

One may then wonder what is the difference between the *Adria-Wien Pipeline* and *British Aggregates Association* judgments. The sole difference appears to be the formalistic difference between the two cases: The former involved a formal derogation from the reference system of taxation, whereas the latter concerned a design issue of the scope of the levy. In its decision in *British Aggregates Association*, the CJEU invoked its effects doctrine.[611] It is thus irrelevant whether a tax advantage is granted through an arbitrary design of the scope of a levy or whether there is a formal exemption. In fact, in some cases, it may be hard to distinguish between the two scenarios. In any event, an exact determination of which of the two constellations applies does not appear necessary.

[D] Scope of Narrow-Based Fiscal Levies Not Subject to State Aid Control

Finally, one may wonder how the prima facie selectivity of narrow-based fiscal levies is assessed in light of the two approaches laid out for broad-based fiscal levies and special purpose levies.[612] Such levies will often be excise or stamp duties. They can be both transaction and consumption taxes, just as long as such levies have a more or less narrow base.[613] Examples would be excise duties on coffee or real estate property transfer taxes. Where such levies do not have a steering purpose, they were at least originally often considered proxies for the ability to pay.[614] Such levies often target the consumption of what are – or once were – considered luxury products, which were presumed to be most often consumed by high-income individuals.

It has to be noted that State aid problems will often not arise in practice, since many such levies had existed before the entry into force of the TFEU in the respective Member State. They would thus have to be considered existing aid.[615] This means that where they have not been altered and therefore become new aid,[616] the aid measure can merely be tackled in the context of the constant review of existing aid under Article 108(1) TFEU.[617]

Just like special purpose levies, narrow-based fiscal levies are also vulnerable to an arbitrary design on the level of the scope of the levy, which does not formally amount to a derogation from the reference system of taxation. Yet the approach described above is not necessarily viable for narrow-based fiscal levies, since no special

610. *Ibid.*, para. 52.
611. *Ibid.*, para. 85.
612. On asymmetric taxation under State aid law: Cordewener, *supra* n. 131; Galdino, *supra* n. 159; Nicolaides & Metaxas, *supra* n. 159; Schön, *Special Charges*, *supra* n. 159.
613. On the distinction *see* Adam et al., *supra* n. 579, at 151f.
614. Critical as to this justification *see, e.g.*, Joachim Englisch, *Spezielle Verkehr- und Verbrauchsteuern*, in Tipke & Lang (eds), Steuerrecht, para. 18.123 (24th edn 2020) with further references.
615. *See* for a definition Art. 1(b) of Procedural Regulation 2015/1589.
616. *See* for the definition of new aid Art. 1(c) of Procedural Regulation 2015/1589.
617. Articles 21ff. of Procedural Regulation 2015/1589.

purpose could be relied on as a starting point. The fiscal objective itself cannot be relied upon either as it does not allow for meaningful distinctions. As a consequence, the starting point for the analysis of de jure-selectivity has to be the levy as is. An artificially narrow scope of such levies (which advantages actors that do not fall within the ambit of the tax) generally does not lead to de jure-selectivity.

Admittedly, it should make no difference whether an event is taxable but subject to an exemption or whether it is not covered by the scope of a levy in the first place.[618] Both can be distortive and the effects doctrine would appear to prescribe that the regulatory technique should be irrelevant. Indeed, treating the boundaries of such levy as a given runs the risk of a more or less arbitrary scope of such taxes. This holds all the more true since the choice of proxies for the ability to pay may not be appropriate (anymore).[619] However, such reading is nevertheless warranted in deference to Member States' fiscal sovereignty.[620] Moreover, it has to be seen that recovery would be close to impossible in most such cases since it would often be very hard to determine which actors *should* have been taxed. This is an indication that State aid control simply falls short in such cases.[621]

This limited standard of review has recently become apparent in the context of progressive turnover-based taxes.[622] Despite the objective of these levies to address profit shifting by MNEs, these levies are in our view fiscal levies, since this objective is not sufficiently precise to allow for an identification of undertakings that should be within the scope of such levies.[623] The judgments on these taxes did not even address the narrow scope of the levies. In this context, the question has been raised whether the reference system of taxation should only comprise the levy itself or whether it should also extend to all tax obligations of undertakings subject to that tax (including from different levies). The latter approach would imply a necessity to justify why it is precisely the undertakings that are subject to the special tax that are required to contribute to the public budget to an extent that exceeds their obligations under corporate income tax.[624] Indeed, part of the justification of such taxes is often that they would address the problem of international profit shifting through a parameter that cannot be easily shifted. Thus, traditional (corporate) income taxation and such

618. Cordewener, *supra* n. 131, at 289.
619. *See, e.g.*, for the German coffee tax and the dog tax: Englisch, *Spezielle Verkehr- und Verbrauchsteuern*, *supra* n. 614, at paras 18.121, 18.123. Such taxes would therefore no longer be justifiable from a constitutional perspective.
620. Similarly: Hummel, *Das nationale Steuergesetz*, *supra* n. 519, at 396, albeit also with respect to all types of narrow-based levies.
621. Galdino, *supra* n. 159, at 518 proposes to solve this problem by applying the notion of 'negative' State aid by analogy as proposed by *Schön*. *See* Ch. §2.01 *supra*.
622. *See* already Ch. §3.02[C], [2] *supra* and §4.02 *infra*.
623. Agnolucci, *supra* n. 157, at 196 with reference to the Opinion of AG Kokott points to social policy goals that would be comparable to the taxes at issue in *ANGED* which pursued environmental objectives. However, this nevertheless does not appear sufficiently precise to warrant a classification as a special purpose levy.
624. Szudoczky & Károlyi, *The Troubled Story of the Hungarian Advertisement Tax*, *supra* n. 157, at 49.

turnover taxes would at first glance appear to be complementary.[625] Yet the mechanics of the taxes are very different. The link between the two taxes is merely incidental. Therefore, the reference system of taxation should be only the levy itself.[626]

The assessment of whether there is a derogation from the reference system of taxation then follows the principles laid out in the context of fiscal levies. Difficulties may arise in the distinction of derogations from the reference system of taxation (which lead to prima facie selectivity) on the one hand and the definition of the scope of the reference system of taxation (which is generally not subject to State aid control) on the other hand.

§3.04 INTERNAL JUSTIFICATION

In a third step, a derogation from the reference system of taxation, i.e., a prima facie selective measure, may still be justified.[627] This possibility had first emerged in the judgment in *Italy v. Commission* (i.e., the Italian Textile case), even though the CJEU rejected a justification in this case.[628] The terminology used for this step varies. Sometimes, several different terms are used in the same judgment. In some cases, the CJEU speaks of the 'basic and guiding principles of its tax system'.[629] In other cases, it speaks of the 'internal logic' of the reference system or of 'the mechanisms inherent in the tax system itself which are necessary for the achievement of the objectives of a particular tax scheme'.[630] In other cases, the CJEU speaks of a justification 'by the

625. If both taxes were understood as a means to tax profits without a coordination mechanism, there may be an infringement of the ability to pay principle under national law, Stevanato, *supra* n. 157, at 540f.
626. Similarly Carro Pitarch, *supra* n. 158, at 332 on the comparable digital services levies introduced by Member States. Fichera, *supra* n. 149, at 486f. takes the aim of digital service taxes to tax revenue that would otherwise escape taxation based on some sort of physical nexus whatsoever and is derived by businesses that benefit from participation and value creation as a point of departure. He thus effectively interprets the levies as special purpose levies. However, that kind of objective does not appear sufficiently well defined to allow for an exact delimitation of which types of undertakings should be taxed. In our view, digital services taxes are fiscal levies.
627. *See* only Case 173/73 *Italy v. Commission*, para. 15; Case C-75/97 *Belgium v. Commission*, para. 34; Case C-143/99 *Adria-Wien Pipeline*, para. 42; Case C-53/00 *Ferring*, para. 17; Case C-159/01 *Netherlands v. Commission* EU:C:2004:246, para. 42; Case C-66/02 *Italy v. Commission*; Case C-88/03 *Portugal v. Commission*, para. 52; Case C-148/04 *Unicredito Italiano*, para. 51; Case C-222/04 *Cassa di Risparmio di Firenze*, para. 137; Joined Cases C-78 to 80/08 *Paint Graphos*, para. 65; Case C-279/08 P *Commission v. Netherlands* EU:C:2011:551, para. 62; Joined Cases C-106 and 107/09 P *Gibraltar*, para. 145; Case C-6/12 *P Oy*, para. 22; Case C-522/13 *Ministerio de Defensa and Navantia*, para. 42; Case C-524/14 P *Hansestadt Lübeck*, para. 41; Joined Cases C-20 and 21/15 P *World Duty Free Group*, para. 58; Case C-233/16 *ANGED*, para. 42; Case C-203/16 P *Andres*, para. 87; Case C-374/17 *A-Brauerei*, para. 44.
628. Case 173/73 *Italy v. Commission*, para. 15.
629. Case C-88/03 *Portugal v. Commission*, para. 81; Joined Cases C-78 to 80/08 *Paint Graphos*, para. 65; Case C-6/12 *P Oy*, para. 22.
630. Case C-88/03 *Portugal v. Commission*, para. 81.

nature or general scheme of the system of which they form part'.[631] The underlying principles appear to be identical regardless of the exact terminology.

In the following, we will show that while the delimitation of the second and third steps is not always straightforward, the latter nevertheless has stand-alone significance [A]. We examine permissible grounds for justification for fiscal levies [B], before addressing distinctions within special purpose levies [C]. The third step includes a proportionality test, the exact interpretation of which, however, remains underexplored. A low standard of control appears applicable [D]. Despite indications in the case law that the third step is gaining in importance, it has but limited potential to serve as a general rule of reason. At best, a justification on grounds of objectives that can be derived from EU law is conceivable [E].

[A] Stand-Alone Significance of the Third Step

In the first two steps of the selectivity test, the Member State is subject to a requirement of internal consistency. The third step then determines whether a justification is possible. To this end, only basic and guiding principles that can be derived from the reference system of taxation itself can be relied upon.

The third step is so far the least developed of the three steps of the selectivity test. It has been argued that it would lead to more or less arbitrary results and that it would create confusion.[632] The fact that only basic and guiding principles of a given tax are admissible as potential grounds for justification amounts to a narrow reading of the third step. Against this background, some authors have questioned the stand-alone significance of the third step.[633] For example, Schön contends that it would be unclear why the third and the second steps should be distinguished. For the second step, one has to refer to the intrinsic purpose of the reference system and in the third step, a derogation can be justified by the basic or guiding principles of the reference system. At best, this distinction would have heuristic value.[634]

Others have argued that the analysis of the third step should be absorbed by the analysis of whether there is a discrimination. The analysis of a justification would merely amount to an integral part of the equality test. The justifications accepted in the third step are emanations of the principles of internal taxation, such as progressive

631. Case C-143/99 *Adria-Wien Pipeline*, para. 42; Joined Cases C-78 to 80/08 *Paint Graphos*, para. 64. Similarly Case C-88/03 *Portugal v. Commission*, para. 81; Case C-222/04 *Cassa di Risparmio di Firenze*, para. 137; Case C-6/12 *P Oy*, para. 22; Case C-522/13 *Ministerio de Defensa and Navantia*, para. 42; Case C-203/16 P *Andres*, para. 87; Case C-374/17 *A-Brauerei*, para. 44.
632. Jaeger, *Tax Incentives under State Aid Law*, *supra* n. 101, at 45ff.
633. Biondi, *State Aid is Falling Down*, *supra* n. 276, at 1737; Prek & Lefèvre, *supra* n. 127, at 342ff.; Schön, *Tax Legislation and the Notion of Fiscal Aid*, *supra* n. 40, at 21. *Englisch* advocates a stronger role for the advantage, which would imply that the third step of the selectivity test has no more stand-alone significance, Englisch, *Das Beihilfenverbot im Steuerrecht*, *supra* n. 67, at para. 9.33.
634. Schön, *Tax Legislation and the Notion of Fiscal Aid*, *supra* n. 40, at 21.

taxation or the avoidance of double taxation. The relevant question would merely be whether a distinction is arbitrary.[635]

By contrast, Szudoczky convincingly explains that a distinction is possible and warranted. Different yardsticks should be relied upon for the second and third steps. For the second step, the correct yardstick is the objective of the reference system of taxation. For the third step, the objective of the tax measure is the relevant yardstick. This would allow a distinction between the second and the third step of the selectivity test. Furthermore, in the third step, it is necessary to test the proportionality of the derogating measure.[636]

Admittedly, the distinction between the two steps will not always be straightforward. It has therefore been pointed out that the analysis runs the risk of being circular.[637] However, in our view, the main problem appears to be that the standard case that is relied upon as a point of departure is the idea of a broad-based fiscal tax. For such taxes, the delimitation of the two steps will indeed be highly problematic, since the overall objective and the underlying principles of a tax may be very similar. By contrast, for other types of taxes, the delimitation may be clearer. For example, a special purpose levy may have an environmental objective. In the third step, a measure that treats some actors advantageously for reasons of administrative manageability could lead to a justification, provided it is implemented in a proportionate manner.

While the third step thus does have a stand-alone significance, its significance in practice is limited. This is because the third step in essence merely serves as a further implementation of the internal consistency test in the first two steps.[638] The potential of a justification is thus much more limited than in other areas of law where different iterations of the principle of equality are applied.

Moreover, it has been noted that the distinction between internal and external objectives would still be blurred and imprecise.[639] This can perhaps be explained by the fact that the permissible objectives in the third step have to be identified for each and every jurisdiction and tax. This also means that the findings from the case law of the CJEU cannot necessarily be generalized.

In terms of the burden of proof, it is for the Member State and/or the beneficiary of aid to show that a justification is possible.[640] In this context, the Member State has to support its claim with specific and detailed arguments.[641] It has been claimed that this would amount to a principle of '*in dubio contra reum*' – if in doubt, the tax norm

635. Biondi, *State Aid is Falling Down, supra* n. 276, at 1737.
636. Szudoczky, *Convergence of the Analysis of National Tax Measures, supra* n. 131, at 371f.
637. Loewenthal, *supra* n. 136, at 49.
638. Englisch, *Das Beihilfenverbot im Steuerrecht, supra* n. 67, at para. 9.33 rejects a discrimination approach due to this limitation.
639. Luis Moscoso del Prado & Tomás Arranz, *A New Step in Material Selectivity in Tax Measures* 12 EStAL 401, 406 (2013).
640. Case C-159/01 *Netherlands v. Commission*, para. 43; Case C-279/08 P *Commission v. Netherlands*, para. 62; Joined Cases C-106 and 107/09 P *Gibraltar*, paras 146ff.; Case C-452/10 P *BNP Paribas and BNL v. Commission* EU:C:2012:366, para. 121; Piernas López, *Revisiting Some Fundamentals, supra* n. 127, at 278.
641. Bacon, *European Union Law of State Aid, supra* n. 20, at para. 2.133.

would be quashed.[642] By contrast, in our view, the shift of the burden of proof can be understood in light of the aspect of fiscal sovereignty underlying the third step. The basic and guiding principles have to be derived from national law. Therefore, it only makes sense that the Member State has to survey its national law for the existence of such principles. The same holds true for the procedure under Article 267 TFEU where it is also for the Member State to bring forward arguments that would show that the tax measure may be justified. The final decision in this respect, nevertheless is up to the national court.[643] Therefore, it appears as though potential justifications could still be considered by the national court, even if they had not been brought forward in the procedure under Article 267 TFEU.

[B] Justification of Distinctions Within Fiscal Levies

The case law of the European courts had long resulted in a limited significance of the third step of the selectivity test. We demonstrate this by briefly examining the existing case law on potential grounds for justification [1]. In the wider context of indications of a rollback in fiscal State aid law, a more lenient approach has emerged in the CJEU's judgment in *A-Brauerei*. In this judgment, the CJEU based a justification of the measure in question on the principle of the avoidance of double taxation [2]. We then examine the avoidance of double taxation in international taxation as a potential basis for a justification [3]. Finally, we briefly address the aspect of harmonization and its impact on the selectivity analysis. Contrary to some contributions in the literature, harmonization does not completely rule out selectivity. However, where there is imputability, harmonization will often lead to a justification in the third step [4].

[1] Limited Significance of the Third Step in the Case Law

Only grounds for justification that are inherent to the tax system itself are permissible in the third step.[644] The third step could otherwise be relied upon to implement Member States' policy objectives.[645] Meanwhile, a justification in the third step of the selectivity test had long appeared to be more of a logical possibility for fiscal levies rather than a realistic option. This may partly be because in cases where the Commission finds that a derogation is justified, this will but rarely be subject to litigation. Until recently, the CJEU, while regularly pointing out the possibility of a justification, had never explicitly endorsed a justification in the third step. It had outright rejected justifications that were external to a fiscal tax system, such as

642. Jaeger, *Tax Incentives under State Aid Law, supra* n. 101, at 48. Hancher, *The Role of Presumptions, supra* n. 324, at 483 holds that the third step results in a *probatio diabolico* since attempts to justify measures generally fail.
643. *See, e.g.*, Case C-522/13 *Ministerio de Defensa and Navantia*, para. 44.
644. *See* only Case C-88/03 *Portugal v. Commission*, para. 81; Joined Cases C-78 to 80/08 *Paint Graphos*, para. 69; Case C-233/16 *ANGED*, para. 43; Case C-522/13 *Ministerio de Defensa and Navantia*, para. 43; Case C-374/17 *A-Brauerei*, para. 48.
645. Loewenthal, *supra* n. 136, at 51. Critical of an approach that only condones tax logics Jaeger, *Tax Incentives under State Aid Law, supra* n. 101, at 48f.

measures that promoted competitiveness.[646] In other judgments, it did not outright reject a justification, but qualified the conditions under which a justification would be excluded.

In *Belgium v. Commission*, the CJEU rejected a justification of reductions in social security contributions for employers employing manual workers in certain sectors, such as the chemical industry, that aimed at improving the competitive situation of the undertakings concerned. The scheme could not be justified by relying on the objectives of employment policy.[647] In this case, the CJEU did not reject a justification of the measure in principle but argued that the limitation to certain sectors was not in line with the stated objective.[648]

In *Italy v. Commission*, the CJEU rejected a justification, since the tax advantages at issue were explicitly put forward as a means of improving the competitiveness of certain undertakings. By contrast, they did not serve to adapt the general tax system to the special characteristics of banking undertakings.[649] Similarly, in *Cassa di Risparmio di Firenze*, the CJEU rejected a justification of derogations in favour of banking foundations, since they were not based on the logic or technique of taxation, and instead aimed at financially favouring organizations regarded as socially deserving.[650]

In its judgment in *Portugal v. Commission*, the CJEU had rejected a justification on grounds of regional development or social cohesion policy.[651] The case concerned reductions in rates of income and corporate tax in the autonomous region of the Azores, which were available to all operators. The CJEU found that the relevant reference system of taxation had to be defined for the whole of Portugal which meant that the reductions were prima facie selective. This was because the Azores were not sufficiently autonomous for the reference system to be limited to the Azores.[652] The CJEU examined whether a justification was possible.[653] It rejected a justification based on regional development or social cohesion policy. However, a closer reading of the judgment reveals that it did not categorically do so. Instead, it held that the measures that applied to all economic operators without any distinction as to their financial circumstances went too far. The fact that theoretically, all economic operators could suffer disadvantages due to the insularity of the Azores could not justify a blanket correction of such inequalities.[654] It therefore seems as though the CJEU did not reject the ground for justification as such, but implicitly held that the advantage was disproportionate.[655]

646. Case 143/99 *Adria-Wien Pipeline*, para. 54.
647. Case C-75/97 *Belgium v. Commission*, paras 38f.
648. Szudoczky, *Convergence of the Analysis of National Tax Measures*, *supra* n. 131, at 373f.
649. Case C-66/02 *Italy v. Commission*, para. 101. *See also* Case C-148/04 *Unicredito Italiano*, para. 51.
650. Case C-222/04 *Cassa di Risparmio di Firenze*, para. 137.
651. Case C-88/03 *Portugal v. Commission*, para. 82. The impact of the case has been likened to the judgment in *Keck et Mithouard* in that it creates an exclusion from the reach of the State aid rules for regional tax breaks, Wattel, *Comparing Criteria*, *supra* n. 164, at 66.
652. Case C-88/03 *Portugal v. Commission*, paras 58ff.
653. *Ibid.*, paras 80f.
654. *Ibid.*, para. 82.
655. *See* Ch. §3.04[D] *infra* on the principle of proportionality.

The CJEU's judgment in *P Oy* dealt with the deductibility of losses under Finnish income tax.[656] This case concerned the possibility of a loss carry-forward in cases of changes in ownership. While such loss carry-forward was generally not possible, the competent tax office could, for special reasons where it was necessary for the continuation of the activities of the company, authorize the deduction of losses upon application.[657] The Tax Directorate of Finland issued a guidance letter on these provisions. It listed examples for special reasons, among others a particular impact on employment. The authorization was further subject to special conditions and could be granted where the deduction was necessary for a company to continue its activities. The elaborations of the CJEU on a potential justification very much focused on the role of discretion, which is problematic where it enables the Member State to base its decision on criteria unrelated to the tax system. Yet while referring the case back to the national Finnish court, the CJEU also assessed potential grounds for justification.[658] While noting that the guidance letter was not legally binding, the CJEU held that if the competent authorities were able to determine the beneficiaries of the measure based on criteria unrelated to the tax system - such as maintaining employment - this could lead to selectivity.[659]

In *Paint Graphos,* while not clearly endorsing the view of the Commission on the justification of derogations in favour of cooperative societies, the CJEU cited the Commission notice on direct business taxation and referred the question back to the national court in stating:

> Next, as is apparent from paragraph 25 of the notice on direct business taxation, the Commission takes the view that the nature or general scheme of the national tax system *may properly be relied on as justification for the fact that cooperative societies which distribute all their profits to their members are not taxed themselves as cooperatives, provided that tax is levied on the individual members.* Finally, as submitted in its written observations, the Commission also takes the view that the nature or general scheme of the tax system in question can provide *no valid justification* for a national measure *if it provides that profits from trade with third parties who are not members of the cooperative are exempt from tax or that sums paid to such parties by way of remuneration may be deducted.*[660]

Again, the CJEU did not in principle reject a justification but appeared to exclude it under certain conditions (in not rejecting the Commission's assertions).

A justification on grounds of the prevention of double taxation of services provided within an international group of companies was rejected in *Belgium and Forum 187 v. Commission.* The interpretation of double taxation referred to in the judgment was not further clarified or even considered in substance since the applicant failed to provide further arguments.[661]

656. *See* on this judgment Ch. §3.02[D], [1] *supra.*
657. *See* Case C-6/12 *P Oy,* paras 4ff.
658. *Ibid.,* paras 28ff.
659. *Ibid.,* para. 27.
660. Joined Cases C-78 to 80/08 *Paint Graphos,* paras 71f.; emphasis added by the author.
661. Joined Cases C-182 and 217/02 *Belgium and Forum 187,* paras 125f.

This case law shows that thus far, the CJEU has taken a restrictive approach. However, the CJEU has only rarely outright rejected grounds for justification. Instead, it either claimed that the respective Member State failed to provide evidence that a measure was truly justified on grounds of the reason brought forward by the Member State or that it was disproportionate – even though the necessity for adhering to the principle of proportionality was not explicitly acknowledged until the CJEU's judgment in *Paint Graphos.*[662]

[2] More Lenient Approach in A-Brauerei

More recently, however, the CJEU has explicitly accepted a justification for a derogation from the reference system of taxation in its judgment in *A-Brauerei.* In its judgment, the CJEU identified the rules on the German real property transfer tax as the reference system of taxation.[663] It found a derogation in the second step since the objective of this tax was to 'tax any change in owner of the rights attaching to a property or, in other words, to tax any transfer of the right of ownership in a property from one natural or legal person to another natural or legal person within the meaning of civil law'.[664] The CJEU further held that the non-taxation of restructuring procedures in such group constellations was justified based on the fact that it serves to avoid taxation that is considered excessive as the transfer of the property is already taxed at the time when the company owning the property is integrated into the group. Taxing the transfer in the context of such restructuring would lead to the transfer being taxed twice.[665] This is not the case where less than 95% of a shareholding is transferred as such transactions are not taxable in the first place under section 1(2a) and (3) *Grunderwerbsteuergesetz.*[666]

The CJEU has thus seemingly recognized the avoidance of excessive or double taxation as a ground for justification for the derogation from the reference system. However, the case is problematic in several respects. For one, this is with respect to the division of competences between the European courts and national courts. It appears questionable that in its judgment, the CJEU was truly competent to decide on the interpretation of German law. It assessed the principles of German law as well as the principles thereof, which appears an overreach because it is only meant to rule on the interpretation of EU law. The decision on whether the measure in question truly constituted aid should have been up to the German national court.

In substance, the role of the ground of justification 'avoidance of excessive taxation' appears undefined for lack of a determination of when taxation would have to be considered excessive.[667] The CJEU accepted that taxing such transfers would be

662. *See* Ch. §3.04[D] *infra.*
663. Case C-374/17 *A-Brauerei*, para. 37.
664. *Ibid.*, 39.
665. *Ibid.*, paras 45f.
666. *Ibid.*, paras 47, 50.
667. Critical as to the CJEU's reasoning Englisch, *Spezielle Verkehr- und Verbrauchsteuern*, *supra* n. 614, at para. 18.51: The benefit would be contingent on qualified participation thresholds and

excessive since the transfer of such property is already taxed when the property is integrated into such a group of companies. As a result, the same transaction would be taxed twice were it not for the exemption. Already, it is questionable if this would truly be the 'same' transaction. It is also questionable whether this is really a form of double taxation, as stated by the CJEU. At best, there would be a form of economic double taxation.

Furthermore, the CJEU followed the AG in stating that the derogation was justified: Where the shareholding was smaller than 95%, the controlling company's acquisition of the shareholding was not taxable in the first place under section 1(2a) and (3) *Grunderwerbsteuergesetz* whereas the subsequent restructuring would not benefit from the exemption provided for in section 6a.[668]

[3] Avoidance of Double Taxation in DTCs as Ground for Justification

A number of judgments of the CJEU have dealt with different aspects of double taxation. Yet those judgments have so far failed to provide a clear picture of what types of measures this could encompass. One may, for example, wonder whether the avoidance of double taxation can justify measures for the avoidance of international double taxation. Such rules can either be implemented unilaterally or on a bi- or multilateral level.

Unilateral rules for the avoidance of double taxation have now been shown to be relatively straightforward to assess. As an emanation of tax sovereignty, they do not even lead to a derogation from the reference system of taxation. This has recently been clarified by the CJEU in its judgment in *Fossil (Gibraltar)*. The preliminary ruling concerned a unilateral rule aimed at the avoidance of double taxation, namely a set-off of tax paid abroad against income that was also taxed in Gibraltar. In its judgment, the CJEU stated that the decision on which foreign taxes may be set off against a domestic tax liability and under which conditions such set-off is possible is a decision of a general nature which falls within the discretion of the Member States in determining the characteristics constituting a tax.[669] The rules were thus considered to constitute technical rules as defined above by the CJEU.[670]

By contrast, the situation could potentially be more complex for DTCs.[671] DTCs are agreed upon bi- or multilaterally, which runs the risk of special privileges granted

would therefore not be available to every undertaking. Furthermore, it would be far-fetched to consider the avoidance of economic double taxation to be inherent to the system of property transfer taxation.

668. Case C-374/17 *A-Brauerei*, para. 47. *See* Ch. §3.02[D], [2] & [3] *supra* on the frictions with the judgment in *Andres*.
669. Case C-705/20 *Fossil (Gibraltar)*, para. 60.
670. *See* Ch. §3.02[C] *supra*.
671. On the criteria of state origin and imputability *see, e.g.*, De Broe, *Can Tax Treaties Confer State Aid?*, *supra* n. 162; Luja, *Tax Treaties and State Aid*, *supra* n. 162, at 234, Szudoczky, *Double Taxation Relief, Transfer Pricing Adjustments and State Aid Law*, *supra* n. 162, at 177ff. (double non-taxation would be attributable to the state of residence); Haslehner, *supra* n. 281, at 137f. Panayi, *Limitation on Benefits*, *supra* n. 162, at 89f. suggests an analogy to the case law on the indirect grant of aid, such as in Case C-156/98 *Germany v. Commission*, where the other State

to economic operators from certain countries or operating in certain countries. At the same time, it has to be seen that DTCs are often standardized in that DTC provisions are modelled after Model Conventions. In deference to internationally agreed-upon standards, DTC provisions should not be considered potential State aid if they are in line with the Organisation for Economic Co-operation and Development (OECD) model or the United Nations (UN) model as almost universally accepted models for tax treaties. Moreover, the CJEU has shown a certain degree of restraint regarding DTCs in the context of the fundamental freedoms.[672] It is well conceivable that this could also be the case for State aid control. In our view, there would thus be no derogation from the reference system for such rules in the first place. It also has to be seen that the international tax system is constantly evolving. For example, the widespread use of anti-abuse provisions in DTCs is a rather recent development. Therefore, one should not assume that a DTC provision amounts to State aid only because it does not yet reflect these more recent developments. Moreover, DTCs very much depend on cooperation by the other contracting State, so a time lag in implementing provisions that reflect the newer developments in anti-abuse legislation, should not lead to the suspicion of State aid.

This reasoning also applies to an application of the exemption method as opposed to the credit method. The other State is assumed to tax in such a constellation – even if it taxes at a lower rate.[673] Under the current understanding, there would be no derogation from the reference system of taxation. Yet while the exemption method is not problematic from a State aid law point of view as such, it is conceivable that it could perhaps in the future have to be tested for its State aid compatibility if the DTC does not provide for a subject-to-tax clause or another fall-back option, which ensures that the provision does not lead to double non-taxation.[674] The understanding that DTCs have to contain anti-abuse provisions has only started to make inroads into the international

gives up tax revenue. Arguing that such analogy is not altogether convincing: Jozipović, *supra* n. 162, at 137ff., instead contending that the concessions within a DTC are imputable to both States in any case. Further norms of the other State could also be imputed on grounds of the criteria developed in the context of the acts of public undertakings as well as autonomous territories. He distinguishes between the concepts of granting aid and making available aid through a DTC. The latter would be imputable as well, but it would only result in aid where the other State indeed does grant such concession (even it does not amount to aid, since the other contracting State is not a Member State). The hypothetical possibility would not suffice. This, however, appears to go too far, Roland Ismer, *Grundlagen*, in Vogel & Lehner (eds), DBA, para. 273c (7th edn 2021).

672. *See* in detail Ismer, *Grundlagen*, *supra* n. 671, at paras 265ff.

673. Similarly Luja, *Tax Treaties and State Aid*, *supra* n. 162, at 235 who argues that the exemption method is an internationally accepted method for the relief of double taxation. Schön, *State Aid in the Area of Taxation*, *supra* n. 31, at para. 13-081 argues that the combination of the credit and the exemption method could lead to State aid problems, where the exemption method is applied to only certain types of foreign income. Similarly, Ellenrieder, *Die materielle Selektivität steuerlicher Beihilfen*, *supra* n. 57, at 773 convincingly argues that an incoherent combination of the two methods could lead to State aid. However, both methods as such would be State aid proof, as long as they do not lead to a privileged treatment that is systematically not in line with the logic to prevent double taxation.

674. Critical as to such 'single tax' principle Szudoczky, *Double Taxation Relief, Transfer Pricing Adjustments and State Aid Law*, *supra* n. 162, at 176.

tax law landscape fairly recently. However, to the extent that the existence of such anti-abuse provisions indeed becomes an internationally accepted and required standard, an application of the exemption method without such safeguards in place could indeed be considered problematic.

Indeed, in such a constellation, the occurrence of double non-taxation would not just be a random consequence of a mismatch between the two tax systems but would be directly caused by the DTC, which had been concluded by the two contracting States. One could thus argue that DTCs have to contain safeguards that prevent double non-taxation arising for whatever reasons (e.g., conflicts of qualification or the other contracting State simply not making use of its taxing rights). The exemption would otherwise go too far and thus be disproportionate, which could rule out a justification.[675]

In any case, all this does not mean that DTCs are currently completely immune to State aid control.[676] DTCs could otherwise be relied on to grant generous tax benefits to multinationals in circumvention of the State aid rules, provided the Member State can achieve cooperation from the other contracting State.

The function of a DTC is merely the limitation of existing taxing rights. Thus, the DTC itself does not create a new reference system.[677] Instead, the reference system of taxation is the general system of taxation as it applies to either residents or non-residents.[678] This also means that if one DTC contains more favourable rules than another, this would not lead to the finding of State aid for lack of comparability.[679] Both the allocation rules and the method article can then lead to a derogation from the reference system of taxation where they limit the tax claim that would ordinarily exist under national law. Unlike unilateral rules for the avoidance of double taxation, atypical DTC provisions limiting the taxing rights of either the source state or the residence state cannot be understood to form part of the reference system of taxation themselves, even where there are no distinctions within these rules. They are thus not

675. In this vein, albeit taking unilateral relief measures as the point of departure Szudoczky, *Double Taxation Relief, Transfer Pricing Adjustments and State Aid Law*, *supra* n. 162, at 174ff. This would then mean that where the DTC does not diverge from the applicable unilateral rules, there could only be de facto-selectivity, which would, however, be ruled out. A different view on the permissibility of double non-taxation under State aid law is held by Schön, *State Aid in the Area of Taxation*, *supra* n. 31, at para. 13-078 who argues that both tax systems have to be seen in isolation. Also sceptical: Ellenrieder, *Die materielle Selektivität steuerlicher Beihilfen*, *supra* n. 57, at 780f. Leaving the question open De Broe, *Can Tax Treaties Confer State Aid?*, *supra* n. 162, at 231, Haslehner, *supra* n. 281, at 142. Similar problems can arise with respect to tax sparing, *see* Jozipović, *supra* n. 162, at 84ff.

676. Haslehner, *supra* n. 281, at 137.

677. Similarly Jozipović, *supra* n. 162, at 158; Szudoczky, *Double Taxation Relief, Transfer Pricing Adjustments and State Aid Law*, *supra* n. 162, at 175 who argues that the reference system would be the unilateral rules for the avoidance of double taxation.

678. The latter requires that a sufficiently homogenous system can be made out, *see* Ch. §3.03[B], [2] *supra*.

679. De Broe, *Can Tax Treaties Confer State Aid?*, *supra* n. 162, at 231f.; Luja, *Tax Treaties and State Aid*, *supra* n. 162, at 235; Szudoczky, *Double Taxation Relief, Transfer Pricing Adjustments and State Aid Law*, *supra* n. 162, at 174.

merely technical rules because they only apply to cross-border constellations as they relate to one particular country.[680]

The Member State on grounds of the DTC limits its own right to tax profits that would ordinarily be subject to corporate tax. In light of the objective of corporate tax – to tax company profits – it does not matter where the source of these profits is located – to the extent that the State subscribes to the system of source and residence. The fact that another State might have a tax claim and the taxpayer is thus faced with (potential) double taxation does not exclude comparability and can only become relevant in the third step because the DTC is again only limited to cross-border dealings with one particular country.[681]

For the taxation of non-residents, the reference system is made up of the rules that apply to the taxation of the respective source, since no general system can be established.[682] Nevertheless, there can be a derogation from the reference system where there are distinctions within these provisions.

A derogation from the reference system of taxation can, however, be justified in the third step on grounds of the avoidance of double taxation. The judgment of the CJEU in *A-Brauerei* has shown that the standard of control in the third step is relatively low, as long as differentiations are plausible – or in other words logically and formally plausible. For DTCs, the standard of control will be even lower, as they are a result of negotiations between the two contracting partners. The Member State will have to make certain concessions, which justifies a lower standard of control. Therefore, even if a DTC provision favourably diverges from unilateral relief mechanisms, a justification would in our view be possible.[683] This approach ensures that rules that aim to prevent international double taxation are only tackled if there are reasons to suspect that there is indeed an unjustified privileged treatment.

[4] The Role of Harmonizing Legislation in the Third Step

Some authors have argued that harmonization by the EU would generally rule out selectivity. The aspect of harmonization would lead to a justification in the third step since differences in treatment between economic operators could not be ascribed to

680. Similarly Haslehner, *supra* n. 281, at 138f. A different view is apparently held by Schön, *State Aid in the Area of Taxation*, *supra* n. 31, at paras 13-077ff., who argues that tax provisions that compensate for the disadvantageous effects of double taxation would not lead to State aid. He appears to treat this as a question of the benchmark rather than the third step of the selectivity test. This is in line with his understanding that in cases where a justification is possible, there is actually no advantage in the first place. Only provisions, which grant tax breaks that are limited to a selective group of taxpayers would be problematic.
681. A different view is held by Haslehner, *supra* n. 281, at 140 who argues that taxpayers with purely domestic income and those with foreign income are not comparable in a tax system that is based on the ability to pay principle. Szudoczky, *Double Taxation Relief, Transfer Pricing Adjustments and State Aid Law*, *supra* n. 162, at 167 discusses a participation exemption regime without a subject-to-tax clause. She takes the general corporate tax system as the point of departure, but argues that there is a lack of comparability for taxpayers that are subject to double taxation and others that are not. In any case, there would be a justification.
682. *See* on the lack of comparability Ch. §3.03[B], [2] *supra*.
683. *See also* Luja, *Tax Treaties and State Aid*, *supra* n. 162, at 235.

one particular Member State.[684] Other contributions have convincingly taken a more nuanced approach, distinguishing between imputability and selectivity.[685] A distinction has to be made between obligatory and optional provisions within harmonizing legislation. For the former, there is a lack of imputability, since Member States have no choice on whether they want to implement such exemptions. Thus, many tax benefits in the area of harmonized taxes constitute Union aid, which is not covered by the State aid provisions in the first place.[686]

Englisch contrasts such obligatory exemptions with optional tax relief measures where the Member State has a significant degree of discretion as to their adoption, which could then lead to imputability.[687] In support of this, he refers to the decision of the CJEU in *Denkavit Italiana*, which concerned the repayment of unlawfully levied public health charges on the importation of milk and milk products. The CJEU did not consider this repayment to constitute State aid as the State aid provision would only refer to 'decisions of Member States by which the latter, in pursuit of their own economic and social objectives, give, by unilateral and autonomous decisions, undertakings or other persons resources or procure for them advantages intended to encourage the attainment of the economic or social objectives sought'.[688] He nevertheless contends that optional tax benefits 'should not be subject to State aid control to the extent that they necessarily entail selective and distortive effects'.[689] Instead, such exemptions in a Directive should (only) be evaluated by an application of Article 20 of the ChFR because the legislative process is launched by the Commission, which would entail a 'pre-approval' of the measure contained therein.[690]

This does not appear altogether convincing. The Directive is secondary law, while the State aid provision is primary law. The fact that tax benefits are 'pre-approved' by the Union legislator, therefore, appears irrelevant as long as Member States can choose whether or not they introduce the tax benefit. While it is true that the Commission has a pivotal role in both procedures, this should not be relevant, as the Commission acts in different roles. The State aid procedure is a balanced procedure that monitors aid taking into account the factual and legal circumstances of the aid in

684. Terra, *supra* n. 160, at 109 with reference to the *Puffer* judgment.
685. Similarly: Traversa & Sabbadini, *Anti-avoidance Measures and State Aid in a Post-BEPS Context*, *supra* n. 161, at 107 for the ATAD provisions.
686. Englisch, *Indirect Tax Measures*, *supra* n. 160, at 15 with reference to Case C-460/07 *Puffer*, para. 70. For harmonized exemptions, which are by default obligatory, but can be amended or modified by the respective Member State, he also contends that they should be considered to constitute Union aid. This is because the Directive, for which the legislative process would in fact be initiated by the Commission. Through the Directive, the Commission would 'pre-approve' the selective and distortive effects of such tax exemptions. The remaining degree of political discretion of the Member State cannot play a significant role in such cases.
687. Englisch, *Indirect Tax Measures*, *supra* n. 160, at 15 with reference to Case-61/79 *Denkavit Italiana* EU:C:1980,100, para. 31.
688. Case 61/97 *Denkavit Italiana*, para. 31.
689. Englisch, *Indirect Tax Measures*, *supra* n. 160, at 15.
690. *Ibid.*, at 16. He makes an exception for energy tax measures as Art. 26(2) of the Energy Taxation Directive explicitly states that optional tax benefits may still constitute State aid. In such cases, not all distortive effects would have been pre-approved by the Union legislator. The e contrario conclusion does not appear altogether convincing, however, as the provision may just as well exist for clarification purposes.

a specific case and the Member State in question. Such detailed analysis is not possible in the context of the Commission's right to initiate the legislative procedure. Moreover, while such an approach may be warranted where a Member State makes complete use of a tax benefit, there are cases where it may not do so, which may lead to distortions. Thus, a distinction should be made. Where a Member State fully makes use of an exemption, this will most likely mean that the prima facie selectivity will be justified by the basic and guiding principles of the tax. By contrast, where this is not the case, there is still room for selectivity.

In this, the basic and guiding principles of VAT could be relied upon for VAT. It is currently still unclear how the State aid logic and the VAT logic interact. As is the case for the conceptualization of the reference system of taxation, these principles would then derive from European law instead of the domestic legal order.[691] It is, for example, conceivable that the neutrality of an exemption would be required to justify a derogation in the third step or inversely that a justification is possible, as long as an exemption is in line with the principle of neutrality.[692]

[C] Justification of Distinctions Within Special Purpose Levies

For special purpose levies, the normal approach to the justification of derogations from the reference system of taxation applies, albeit often with different results. Considerations that would be external to broad-based fiscal levies could, for example, play a role in the third step of the selectivity test of an environmental tax because they are inherent to this type of tax system.[693] For example, a justification of distinctions on grounds of the polluter pays principle is conceivable.

Conversely, not all justifications that can be relied on in the third step for fiscal levies necessarily apply to special-purpose levies. For example, one may wonder whether distinctions based on an undertaking's ability to pay could be justified. This may not be the case where this would contravene the objective of the levy itself.

Beyond this, it is unclear what other distinctions could be upheld in the third step, particularly because the CJEU appears to favour an approach identifying the formal inconsistencies of special purpose levies rather than naming exact grounds for justification and carrying out a strict proportionality test. It also does not survey the ability to achieve the stated goals of a levy relying on an *ex ante* or *ex post* (economic) assessment. This may be because it is hard to distinguish what the basic and guiding principles of special purpose levies – as opposed to the special purpose of the levy itself – are. This particularly holds true where such levies are not standardized. An analysis of the inconsistencies of such measures then suffices to reject a justification.

691. *See* Ch. §3.02[B] *supra*.
692. In a similar vein: Pfeiffer, *supra* n. 160, at 161. According to Englisch, *Indirect Tax Measures, supra* n. 160, at 16f., the principle of neutrality would come into play on the level of a distortion of competition. Since indirect taxes are often based on the destination principle and the destination is presumed to be relatively immobile, exemptions may not cause distortions, where the principle of neutrality is adhered to.
693. Ellenrieder, *Die materielle Selektivität steuerlicher Beihilfen, supra* n. 57, at 379ff.; Loewenthal, *supra* n. 136, at 51.

For example, in *Adria Wien Pipeline*, the CJEU rejected a justification for the restriction of energy tax rebates to undertakings whose activity consisted primarily in the production of goods based on the internal logic of the reference system. The CJEU argued that energy consumption is equally damaging whether it takes place in the services industry or the production of goods.[694] It furthermore indicated that it tended to agree with the Commission that the rebates were aimed at preserving the competitiveness of the manufacturing sector. This, however, is never a ground for justification.[695]

[D] Proportionality Test in State Aid Law

In *Paint Graphos*, the CJEU for the first time stated that an internal justification of a derogation from the reference system of taxation requires that the proportionality requirement is met. It stated that:

> In any event, in order for tax exemptions such as those at issue in the main proceedings to be justified by the nature or general scheme of the tax system of the Member State concerned, it is also necessary to ensure that those exemptions *are consistent with the principle of proportionality and do not go beyond what is necessary, in that the legitimate objective being pursued could not be attained by less far-reaching measures.*[696]

According to the CJEU, it was up to the Italian Corte Suprema di Cassazione to determine whether the exemptions for cooperatives were in line with the principle of proportionality. As the selectivity test amounts to a discrimination test, it was only logical that the proportionality test would be relied on by the CJEU sooner or later.

Yet while there is a large body of literature on the principle of proportionality under European law in general or in specific areas of European law,[697] its role in the

694. Case C-143/99 *Adria-Wien Pipeline*, para. 48.
695. *Ibid.*, para. 54.
696. Joined Cases C-78 to 80/08 *Paint Graphos*, para. 75; emphasis added by the author.
697. *See, e.g.*, Gráinne de Búrca, *The Principle of Proportionality and its Application in EC Law* 13 YEL 105ff. (1993) https://doi.org/10.1093/yel/13.1.105; Ivan Draganic, *State Aid or Compensation for Extra Costs: Tuning the Test of Proportionality in EC Competition Law* 5 EStAL 683ff. (2006) https://doi.org/10.21552/estal/2006/4/87; Eric Engle, *The History of the General Principle of Proportionality: An Overview* 10 Dartmouth Law Journal 1, 8ff. (2012); Dominik Freyer, *The Proportionality Principle under EU Tax Law: General and Practical Problems Caused by Its Extensive Application – Part 1* 57 European Taxation 384ff. (2017) https://doi.org/10.59403/34q3dsb; Tor-Inge Harbo, *The Function of the Proportionality Principle in EU Law* 1 European Law Journal 158ff. (2010) https://doi.org/10.1111/j.1468-0386.2009.00502.x; Francis G. Jacobs, *Recent Developments in the Principle of Proportionality in European Community Law*, in Ellis (ed.), The Principle of Proportionality in the Laws of Europe, 1ff. (1999); Jan H. Jans, *Proportionality Revisited* 27 Legal Issues of Economic Integration 239ff. (2000) https://doi.org/10.54648/281297; Artur Mudrecki, *Impact of the Principle of Proportionality in Tax Law on the Jurisprudence of the Court of Justice of the European Union and the Supreme Administrative Court in Poland* 3 Public Governance, Administration and Finances L. Rev. 46ff. (2018) https://doi.org/10.53116/pgaflr.2018.1.5; Aurelien Portuese, *Principle of Proportionality as Principle of Economic Efficiency* 19 European Law Journal 612ff. (2013) https://doi.org/10.1111/j.1468-0386.2012.00611.x; Margherita Poto, *The Principle of Proportionality in Comparative Perspective* 8 German Law Journal 835ff. (2007) https://doi.org/10.1017/s2071832200006003;

context of selectivity remains underexplored.[698] Thus, the potential impact of the proportionality test regarding fiscal aid is not altogether clear yet.

The principle of proportionality may in practice have been part of the selectivity analysis for quite some time. Szudoczky notes that the CJEU had already sometimes implicitly rejected a justification of tax measures in the third step because they were disproportionate before the requirement of proportionality was even expressly pointed out in the case law.[699] Yet beyond that, as far as can be seen, the CJEU has never clarified the exact role of the principle of proportionality in the third step of the selectivity test after it was first established in the judgment in *Paint Graphos*.[700] It has presumably not had a chance to do so, since the recent dynamic of State aid law primarily focuses on the first two steps of the selectivity test.

Therefore, many questions remain open. The case law on the principle of proportionality that was, for example, developed in the context of the fundamental freedoms may very well not be transferrable. The principle of proportionality as applicable in fiscal State aid law may be a new standard altogether that has little in common with its long-established function in other areas of EU law. An argument can be made that a low standard of control would be applicable, particularly for aid schemes.

The principle of proportionality is a general principle of EU law.[701] It is commonly held to promote rationality in decision-making.[702] By contrast, others challenge the assumption that the principle of proportionality can promote rationality since a balancing of interests can be goal-oriented depending on the institution by whom it is carried out.[703]

The scholarly literature is divided on the exact interpretation of the principle of proportionality under EU law and the applicable standard of control. Some have noted that there would be no such thing as a single principle of proportionality under EU law. A multitude of different versions would be applicable.[704] Others have sought to identify different indicators or areas that typically imply a high or inversely low standard of control.[705] Perhaps most commonly, two different standards of control are identified that would be applicable for Union measures (horizontal dimension) and Member States' measures (vertical dimension) respectively. For the former, a rather lenient

Wolf Sauter, *Proportionality in EU Law: A Balancing Act?* 15 Camb. Yearb. Eur. Leg. Stud. 439ff. (2013) https://doi.org/10.1017/s152887000003128; Tridimas, *supra* n. 121, at 136ff.

698. *See* however: Ismer & Piotrowski, *Selectivity in Corporate Tax Matters, supra* n. 77, at 162f.; Szudoczky, *Convergence of the Analysis of National Tax Measures, supra* n. 131, at 377f.
699. Szudoczky, *Convergence of the Analysis of National Tax Measures, supra* n. 131, at 377f.
700. According to Buendía Sierra, *Finding Selectivity, supra* n. 131, at 91 the reason for this might be that the principle of proportionality is difficult to apply in practice in this context.
701. Harbo, *supra* n. 697, at 159.
702. Freyer, *supra* n. 697, at 385.
703. Harbo, *supra* n. 697, at 169ff. with further references.
704. Eirik Bjorge & Jack R. Williams, *The Protean Principle of Proportionality: How Different is Proportionality in EU Contexts?* 75 CLJ 186, 188 (2016) https://doi.org/10.1017/s0008197316000386.
705. de Búrca, *supra* n. 697, at 147 identifies a number of indicators that would result in a low standard of control. Fiscal sovereignty as laid out below may well warrant being included in this list.

standard of control would be applicable. A mere monitoring for 'manifest appropriateness' would thus be carried out for EU measures. By contrast, for Member States' measures, a more stringent approach appears to be applicable which tests for suitability, necessity and proportionality *strictu sensu*.[706] As Tridimas notes, the proportionality test under EU law (also) serves to promote market integration rather than only balancing private vis-à-vis public interest. Consequently, due to this substantive bias towards the promotion of European integration, the standard of control would be more stringent for the measures of Member States than for Union measures.[707]

Transferring this to State aid law, this would at first glance appear to suggest that a high standard of control is applicable, since only the measures of Member States can amount to State aid under Article 107 TFEU. However, the opposite may be true: The function of the proportionality test is most often to strike a balance between public and private interests, between rights claims or between a rights provision and the public interest.[708] It has thus been described as a conflict rule.[709] The proportionality test as applicable in the law of the fundamental freedoms is a classic example of individual rights being weighed against public interest - in this case of the Member State restricting the freedom in question.[710] This simultaneously results in the above-mentioned bias towards market integration, since the fundamental freedoms are an essential element of the internal market. The literature on the principle of proportionality puts different degrees of emphasis on the rights of individuals in this context. While some hold that individual rights can be balanced against public policy goals, others argue that individual rights will generally trump any public policy goals.[711]

By contrast, the interests and rights of individuals only indirectly play a role in fiscal State aid law. Instead, the objective of the Member State granting a selective advantage is weighed against the objectives of State aid control. The exact significance of the proportionality test then comes back to the core conflict between fiscal sovereignty on the one hand and the internal market logic of State aid law on the other hand.[712] While it would at first glance appear as though the rights and interests of the beneficiaries of the advantage in question should play a role in State aid law, this is not the case because they receive an advantage. The individual rights of the beneficiaries

706. Sauter, *supra* n. 697, at 445ff.; Freyer, *supra* n. 697, at 385, 391f. Sceptical as to this distinction Harbo, *supra* n. 697, at 173. Harbo furthermore argues that the CJEU would in many cases in fact apply a reasonableness test rather than the principle of proportionality, at 184.
707. Tridimas, *supra* n. 121, at 138. Similarly: Freyer, *supra* n. 697, at 392.
708. de Búrca, *supra* n. 697, at 109.
709. Harbo, *supra* n. 697, at 164.
710. Freyer, *supra* n. 697, at 385.
711. *See* for an overview of the different approaches: Harbo, *supra* n. 697, at 166ff. On the one hand, Alexy based on the approach under German constitutional law argues that such balancing is possible (Robert Alexy, *A Theory of Constitutional Rights*, 66ff. (2010, Reprint)), whereas Dworkin, on the other hand, finds that there are absolute rights that cannot be trumped. *See also*: Sauter, *supra* n. 697, at 441. Stressing the individual rights dimension: Portuese, *supra* n. 697, at 619.
712. *See* on this conflict for the principle of proportionality in general: de Búrca, *supra* n. 697, at 112. Of course, the protection of competition within the internal market has an individual dimension in that competitors are protected. Similarly, the Member State introduces the aid in favour of individual beneficiaries of aid.

are not affected negatively as is the case for the fundamental freedoms, where it is precisely the restriction of the individual rights that has to be weighed against a public interest. Interestingly, the principle of proportionality under Article 5(3) TEU, which concerns the competences of the EU, embodies a comparable conflict between EU interests and the interests of Member States, albeit from the opposite perspective.[713] In this context, a low standard of control is applicable.[714]

What does this mean for the standard of control that should be applied to test for proportionality? While there are different views on the emphasis on individual rights in the context of proportionality, the consequences of individual rights not playing any role in the necessary balancing process are unclear. In any case, the individual rights that are embodied by the fundamental freedoms presumably act as an enhancement to the market integration dimension they represent that is absent in State aid law.

Moreover, one may argue that tax sovereignty as the backdrop to the objectives the Member State pursues with a State measure is a particularly significant dimension of sovereignty as a whole.[715] In light of tax sovereignty, the level of precision demanded from Member States cannot be overly high, since any other reading could again amount to positive integration through the backdoor. The proportionality of a State measure can only be assessed in broad strokes.

This holds all the more true since the analysis of aid schemes is necessarily more abstract than it is for singular infringements of the fundamental freedoms. First, this is because State aid control is conceptually meant to be carried out prior to the introduction of a State measure, i.e., upon notification. Of course, the vast majority of the case law on fiscal State aid law deals with cases, where there was no notification. Yet it cannot matter whether a State measure is assessed before its introduction or only after doubts as to its State aid compatibility arise. The resulting potential for error has to be considered in assessing the measure from an ex post perspective. Second, aid schemes are abstract in the sense that the analysis cannot consider the interests of every beneficiary of aid.

All this results in a low standard of control. Singular cases of overly privileged treatment have to be accepted since the alternative would be that the entire aid scheme falls foul of State aid law. Rather than a real balancing of interests – which in any case is rare in the case law of the CJEU on the principle of proportionality in other areas of EU law[716] – measures could only be disproportionate where they contain manifest (formal) inconsistencies. This would presumably amount to the standard of control that is ordinarily applicable to Union measures. Such a low standard of control in turn results in a bias towards the interests of the Member State concerned.

713. *See* on this, e.g., Poto, *supra* n. 697.
714. Tridimas, *supra* n. 121, at 138.
715. Sauter, *supra* n. 697, at 453ff. argues that the standard of control for the measures of Member States varies depending on the degree of harmonization which would appear to support our understanding. Jans, *supra* n. 697, at 242 points out that under EU law the division of powers between the EU and the Member States is impacted depending on how strict a standard of control is applied.
716. Sauter, *supra* n. 697, at 461.

Indications for such a low standard of control can be found in the case law, an example of which is the CJEU's judgment in *A-Brauerei*.[717] Beyond the prevention of double taxation, the CJEU also addressed the justifiability of the minimum holding period of five years before and after the transaction. The CJEU stated that this requirement was justified by the intention to prevent abuse and to exclude undesirable windfall effects as it prevents the acquisition of such shareholdings for a short period and for the sole purpose of benefitting from the tax exemption. In this, the CJEU referred to its judgment in *GIL Insurance* by analogy.[718]

However, in our view, what the CJEU is testing in this context is strictly speaking not a ground for justification in the third step. Instead, the CJEU is implicitly testing for proportionality, i.e., it is assessing whether the derogation goes too far. This is because, in the context of State aid law, it is conceptually always necessary to justify the existence of an *advantageous* derogation. By contrast, the principle of prevention of abuse can only ever be relied on to justify disadvantages. With the minimum holding period, the German legislator aims to prevent that the tax advantage goes further than strictly necessary. Yet the CJEU did in no way question the length of the minimum holding period. In fact, while this does not emerge clearly, it would presumably not have considered the tax exemption selective, had the German legislator not introduced such a minimum holding period at all.

This judgment shows that in many cases, an application of the principle of proportionality can come down to the question of whether a Member State would have been obliged to introduce an anti-abuse rule to limit the scope of application of a tax benefit, which would otherwise be justified. However, this question is hard to answer from an abstract perspective. There could be many different ways to make sure that a tax benefit does not go too far. The decision in this respect lies with the national legislator. In other words, Member States have to be awarded a certain degree of leeway in the third step, since there are different ways to ascertain proportionality or prevent abuse more generally.[719]

[E] Limited Potential of the Third Step to Restrict the Notion of Selectivity

In light of all this, one may wonder whether the third step of the selectivity test can significantly restrict the ambit of fiscal State aid control where its ambit is presumed to be too wide.[720] This would have a role model in the law of the fundamental freedoms where a counter-balance for the fact that even mere restrictions (as opposed to only direct and indirect discriminations) fell within the ambit of the fundamental freedoms was required. In its case law, the CJEU early on accepted certain unwritten grounds for

717. *See* already Ch. §3.04[B], [2] *supra*.
718. Case C-374/17 *A-Brauerei*, para. 51 with reference to Case C-308/01 *GIL Insurance*, para. 74.
719. In favour of such approach that only monitors for manifestly arbitrary or unreasonable distinctions for the sake of legal certainty Smit, *State Aid and Domestic Anti-tax Avoidance Rules*, *supra* n. 161, at 93.
720. In this vein: Wattel, *Comparing Criteria*, *supra* n. 164, at 68.

justifications where this is necessary to satisfy mandatory requirements derived from public interest.[721] The CJEU has even accepted some tax-specific grounds for a justification in its case law, such as the cohesion of the tax system[722] or the balanced allocation of taxing rights.[723]

A similar need for a counter-balance has become apparent in fiscal State aid law due to the broad notion of prima facie selectivity.[724] While the recent rollback of the CJEU has meant that there are already more restrictions in place, there is nevertheless arguably a need for a balancing process because the administrative structures of State aid law are not designed to handle a high caseload and surveying all types of distinctions for their compatibility under Article 107(2), (3) TFEU is not satisfying due to the discretion of the Commission.

Despite the emerging more lenient approach in *A-Brauerei,* the case law is currently restrictive as it precludes the legislator from pursuing tax policy objectives that cannot be derived from the levy itself. It therefore seems as though the third step can only have limited significance since a tax can only be based on very few underlying principles.[725]

It is theoretically conceivable that external objectives derived from EU law could be recognized in future case law. According to Szudoczky, in some judgments, the CJEU would already have tacitly acknowledged the relevance of social, environmental or other policy goals. A justification would have been rejected for lack of proportionality in implementation. While internal justifications would be per se permissible, the legitimacy of external objectives would be a question of appraisal.[726] To define permissible legitimate objectives, she refers to the case law of the CJEU on the fundamental freedoms. A justification should be excluded where it would be contrary to the very idea of the internal market. Examples would be the promotion of exports and international trade or measures that seek to increase the competitiveness of certain sectors. By contrast, a justification should be possible based on environmental objectives, the promotion of R&D or the maintenance of employment, training and education of employees or other educational, cultural or social objectives.[727]

Bartosch argues that State aid law would not truly distinguish between internal and external objectives. Instead, the judgment in *Adria-Wien Pipeline* would imply that there are some 'good' or 'bad' objectives. Building on this, a rule of reason approach would be warranted that builds on the objectives behind a given State measure. According to the case law, ecological objectives would be permissible. Other social, cultural or educative objectives may be conceivable. By contrast, objectives that go

721. Case 120/78 *Rewe-Zentral AG v. Bundesmonopolverwaltung für Branntwein* EU:C:1979:42, para. 8.
722. *See, e.g.,* Case C-204/90 *Bachmann v. Belgium* EU:C:1992:35.
723. *See, e.g.,* Case C-446/03 *Marks & Spencer* EU:C:2005:763, paras 44-46.
724. Szudoczky, *Convergence of the Analysis of National Tax Measures, supra* n. 131, at 370.
725. Loewenthal, *supra* n. 136, at 52. Juan Jorge Piernas López, *The Concept of State Aid Under EU Law,* 137 (2015), however, pointing to the logic of State aid law as a justification for this narrow reading.
726. Szudoczky, *Convergence of the Analysis of National Tax Measures, supra* n. 131, at 374.
727. *Ibid.,* at 375ff.

against the objectives of State aid law, such as attracting (foreign) investors to a Member State or a part thereof, would not be permissible.[728]

However, in our view, the currently existing case law does not support the permissibility of external objectives. The CJEU has indeed in its past case law not always rejected grounds of justification outright. Yet it seems to us as though the presumed external policy objectives referred to by Szudoczky and Bartosch can be explained by the fact that the levies in question were primarily special purpose levies, and in particular instruments of environmental policy. In the context of such levies, objectives based on environmental policies are not necessarily external but can be directly derived from the steering objectives of the levy itself.[729] Moreover, the mere fact that the CJEU did not outright reject certain grounds for justification and instead limited itself to identifying formal or logical inconsistencies in rejecting a justification, does not mean it implicitly condoned a justification based on these grounds.

728. Bartosch, *Rule of Reason*, *supra* n. 140, at 746f.
729. *See* on this Ch. §3.03[C] *supra*.

CHAPTER 4

The Notion of De Facto-Selectivity

De facto-selectivity has by now been firmly established as an alternative to de jure-selectivity, even though it is entirely unclear whether it will ever again be successfully invoked. A tax measure is de facto selective, where a levy is internally consistent, but where the boundaries of the levy are designed in an arbitrary manner, i.e., where the levy in question is externally inconsistent. For a tax measure to be de facto selective, a group of beneficiaries that are selectively favoured over others has to be identified. As such, de facto-selectivity is merely another emanation of the prohibition of discrimination. Since the assumption that tax measures can be de facto selective disregards the legislator's fundamental charging decision, tax sovereignty prescribes a restrictive application of de facto-selectivity. One possible area of application is progressive turnover-based taxes. Whether or not State aid law applies, very much depends on the exact design of the tax in question. The mere fact that turnover is not a perfect indicator of an undertaking's ability to pay, cannot lead to the finding of State aid. Instead, additional factors, such as the effects of the tax or the intent of the legislator would have to be identified. The CJEU has taken a restrictive stance in this respect. Therefore, one may perhaps have to concede that the notion of de facto-selectivity is as of now largely theoretical.

The three-step test for de jure-selectivity respects Member States' tax sovereignty and takes the general legislative charging decision of the national lawmaker as the point of departure. Only where legislation is not internally inconsistent, is there a need for a justification. As a result, however, there is room for reverse engineering. Member States can circumvent State aid law by simply designing internally consistent rules that factually grant generous tax advantages to certain groups of undertakings. This is not so much a problem for special purpose levies where the objective defines the scope of the reference system of taxation. It is then not relevant whether a tax contains explicit exemptions or whether certain constellations are not covered by the tax in the first place. Both can lead to de jure-selectivity. By contrast, fiscal taxes do not have a specific objective that can be translated into a necessary scope.[730]

The CJEU has seen the perils of reverse engineering. In its landmark judgment in *Gibraltar*, it clarified that even where there is no formal derogation from the reference system of taxation, a measure may nevertheless be de facto selective.[731] The judgment addressed an arbitrary design of the reference system.[732] While it has been extensively criticized in the literature, the CJEU has repeatedly reaffirmed the notion of de facto-selectivity as a complement to de jure-selectivity. There is thus a prohibition to design the reference system of taxation in an arbitrary manner.

In the following, we will show that such an approach disregards the legislator's initial charging decisions. Due to fiscal sovereignty, the notion of de facto-selectivity therefore has to be applied restrictively (§4.01). De facto-selectivity has recently become practically relevant in the context of progressive turnover-based taxes. Yet both for the narrow scope of these taxes and their progressivity, State aid law can only apply in exceptional cases (§4.02).

§4.01 THE NOTION OF DE FACTO-SELECTIVITY AS DEVELOPED IN THE CASE LAW

The notion of de facto-selectivity had first been developed in the CJEU's judgment in *Gibraltar*. The Government of Gibraltar after having had its previous tax regime struck down as incompatible State aid,[733] sought to reform its corporate tax system. The tax was to be made up of three elements, namely a payroll tax of GBP 3,000 per employee each year; a business property occupation tax (BPOT) at a rate equivalent to a percentage of their liability to the general rates charged on property in Gibraltar; and finally an annual registration fee. The sum of payroll tax and BPOT was capped at 15% of profits. A top-up tax applied to companies in the financial services sector and to utilities. The rates for the financial services sector ranged between 4% and 6% of profits. For this sector, the top-up tax with the payroll tax and the BPOT were capped at a total of 15%. The top-up tax for the utility sector was charged at a rate of 35% of profits. Such companies could deduct their annual payroll tax and BPOT from their top-up tax.[734]

In its judgment, the CJEU held that the Commission had not demonstrated the existence of selective advantages concerning the requirement to make a profit for there to be a tax burden at all, and to the capping of payroll tax and BPOT.[735] However, it rejected the reasoning of the General Court on selective advantages accruing to offshore companies.[736] In this, it referred to the effects doctrine, according to which

730. *See* Ch. §3.03[D] *supra*.
731. Joined Cases C-106 and 107/09 P *Gibraltar*.
732. Aalbers, *supra* n. 146, at 498.
733. *See* for details: Joined Cases C-106 and 109/09 P *Gibraltar*, paras 3ff.
734. *Ibid.*, para. 11.
735. *Ibid.*, paras 77ff.
736. *Ibid.*, paras 85ff.

State aid law does not distinguish between measures by reference to their causes or aims, but defines them in relation to their effects, and independently of the techniques used.[737] The General Court would have solely relied on the regulatory technique of the measures in question rather than assessing their actual effects. The case law on State aid law would not make the finding of selectivity contingent on the existence of a derogation from the reference system of taxation.[738]

It subsequently argued that contrary to what the General Court had held, the Commission had indeed succeeded in identifying a reference system of taxation.[739] It then stated:

> In view of the features of that regime, outlined in the preceding paragraph, it is apparent that the regime at issue, by combining those bases, even though they are founded on criteria that are in themselves of a general nature, *in practice discriminates between companies which are in a comparable situation with regard to the objective of the proposed tax reform, namely to introduce a general system of taxation for all companies established in Gibraltar.* Combining those bases of assessment not only results in taxation according to the number of employees and the size of the business premises occupied, but also, due to the absence of other bases of assessment, excludes from the outset any taxation of offshore companies, since they have no employees and also do not occupy business property.[740]

The mere fact that a different tax burden results from an (allegedly) general tax system, however, would not suffice.[741] It must also be possible to identify the beneficiaries of the selective tax advantages 'by virtue of the properties which are specific to them, as a privileged category, thus permitting such a regime to be described as favouring 'certain' undertakings or the production of '"certain" goods within the meaning of Article 87(1) EC'.[742] The fact that offshore companies are not taxed would not be a random consequence of the regime, but the inevitable consequence of the design of the tax, since offshore companies have neither employees nor do they occupy business premises.[743] In its judgment, the CJEU worked with the terminology of the three-step test for selectivity. It relied on the (alleged) objective of the tax system itself, which was to establish a general system of corporate taxation.[744] Yet in fact, it carried out a comparison test determining the actual effects of the tax.[745] This requirement of concrete selectivity instead of mere abstract selectivity presumably aims to ensure that not any facially neutral rule can come under State aid review.

737. *Ibid.*, para. 87.
738. *Ibid.*, para. 91.
739. *Ibid.*, paras 94f.
740. *Ibid.*, paras 101f.; emphasis added by the author.
741. *Ibid.*, para. 103.
742. *Ibid.*, para. 104.
743. *Ibid.*, paras 106f.
744. Quigley, *Direct Taxation and State Aid*, *supra* n. 146, at 115. Critical of this: Temple Lang, *The Gibraltar State Aid and Taxation Judgment*, *supra* n. 98, at 808.
745. Ismer & Piotrowski, *Selectivity in Corporate Tax Matters*, *supra* n. 77, at 163. Juan Jorge Piernas López, *The Concept of State Aid under EU Law*, 143 (2015) argues that the Court's conclusion recalls the real purpose test under which it is possible to ascertain the real object or purpose of a measure with reference to the Opinion of AG Lagrange in Case C-30/59 *Steenkolenmijnen v. High Authority* EU:C:1961:2, p. 43.

Initially, one could have understood the CJEU's reasoning as a rejection of a rule-exception approach to assessing selectivity. Thus, Lang took the view that the selectivity test would generally amount to a comparability analysis. While in *Paint Graphos,* the CJEU would have hesitated between both approaches, ultimately, the comparability analysis would have turned out to be decisive. A rule-exception approach would produce unsatisfactory results since the distinction between rules and exceptions would be problematic.[746]

However, later case law repeatedly reiterated the status of de facto-selectivity as a complement to de jure-selectivity.[747] As laid out above, the CJEU in its judgment in *World Duty Free Group* had clarified that abstract selectivity suffices in the context of the assessment of de jure-selectivity.[748] The CJEU clarified that the passage in its judgment in *Gibraltar* relating to the identification of a privileged category of undertakings had to be understood in the context of the particular constellation at issue:[749]

> It follows from a reading of all those grounds that the measure at issue in that judgment did not take the form of a tax advantage that derogated from an ordinary tax system, but rather involved the application of a 'general' tax scheme based on criteria that were, in themselves, also general. The Court held that the nature of that scheme did not preclude a finding that the measure concerned was selective, contrary to the ruling of the General Court, since the condition relating to selectivity has a broader scope that extends to measures which, by their effects, favour certain undertakings, in that case 'offshore' companies, on account of the specific features characteristic of those undertakings. *That measure accordingly operated de facto discrimination against undertakings that were in a comparable situation in the light of the objective pursued by that regime, in that case the objective of putting in place generalised taxation of all resident companies.* [...] While it therefore follows from the judgment [in Gibraltar] that the selectivity of a tax measure can be established even if that measure does not constitute a derogation from an ordinary tax system, but is an integral part of that system, the fact remains that that judgment is consistent with the Court's settled case-law [...].[750]

The CJEU thus went beyond merely rejecting that concrete selectivity was necessary in the context of de jure-selectivity but confirmed the notion of two separate forms of selectivity, with de facto-selectivity becoming relevant, where a tax system contains no formal derogation from the reference system.[751]

Yet this seemingly clear position by the CJEU still did not settle the matter: In his Opinion in *A-Brauerei,* AG Saugmandsgaard Øe interpreted the judgment in *Gibraltar* as an application of what he deemed the traditional method of analysis, which would be based on a general availability test. It would suffice that all operators may benefit from an advantage, for there to be no infringement of State aid law.[752] Interestingly, he

746. Lang, *Recent Trends in the Case Law of the ECJ, supra* n. 146, at 418f.
747. *See, e.g.,* Aalbers, *supra* n. 146, at 499; Drabbe, *supra* n. 79, at 101.
748. *See* Ch. §3.03[A] *supra.*
749. Joined Cases C-20 and 21/15 P *World Duty Free Group,* para. 73.
750. *Ibid.,* paras 74-76; emphasis added by the author.
751. *See* Ismer & Piotrowski, *Selectivity in Corporate Tax Matters, supra* n. 77, at 163.
752. Opinion of AG Saugmandsgaard Øe in Case C-374/17 *A-Brauerei,* para. 5.

thus interpreted the selectivity test deriving from the judgment in *Gibraltar* as a means to preserve tax sovereignty. Based on this, the exemption laid down in section 6a *Grunderwerbsteuergesetz* would not have been selective, since it is hypothetically open to all undertakings and does not irrevocably exclude certain undertakings or the production of certain goods.[753] The 'reference framework' method, by contrast, would be based on a discrimination test.[754] He proposed to apply the traditional method of analysis due to concerns as to the practical consequences of the use of the reference framework method in substantive and formal terms.[755]

The CJEU, however, stood its ground and swiftly rejected this notion of de facto-selectivity as the traditional (and preferable) method of analysis in its corresponding judgment. It held that the judgment in *Gibraltar* means that even a measure that does not derogate from the reference system can lead to selectivity if it discriminates between companies that are in a comparable situation in light of the objective of the tax system in practice. Nevertheless, a derogation is relevant where the effect of that technique is that operators are distinguished and are subject to a different treatment, even though they are in a comparable situation in the light of the objective pursued by that system.[756]

The judgment in *Gibraltar* has been subject to intense scrutiny in the scholarly literature.[757] Some have hailed it as additional guidance on selectivity that could herald a new age in State aid control.[758] Others have been more sceptical and have described the judgment as an infringement of tax sovereignty.[759] Temple Lang criticized that the CJEU considered all companies established in Gibraltar to be comparable. The CJEU would thereby compare the tax regime at issue with a hypothetical, comprehensive company tax. A more realistic reading would be that the CJEU held that Gibraltar had initially planned a comprehensive tax, but had deliberately chosen a narrow base, so as to exempt some situations.[760] Since the levy had no regulatory purpose, the only basis for arguing that offshore undertakings and other undertakings are comparable would be that the former were established or had assets or activities in Gibraltar, but were not taxed. The CJEU would thereby apply its own logic or rationale of what companies should be taxed, and override the discretion or policy choice by national authorities.[761] 'Revenue raising' would not be a sufficiently precise rationale to rely on as a

753. *Ibid.*, para. 69.
754. *Ibid.*, para. 6.
755. *Ibid.*, paras 8f.
756. Case C-374/17 *A-Brauerei*, paras 32f.
757. *See, e.g.*, Aalbers, *supra* n. 146; Ismer & Piotrowski, *The Selectivity of Tax Measures*, *supra* n. 77, at 566ff.; Ismer & Piotrowski, *Selectivity in Corporate Tax Matters*, *supra* n. 77, at 163ff.; Lang, *Recent Trends in the Case Law of the ECJ*, *supra* n. 146, at 414ff.; Luja, *(Re)shaping Fiscal State Aid*, *supra* n. 98, at 129ff.; Pistone, *supra* n. 146; Quigley, *Direct Taxation and State Aid*, *supra* n. 146, at 117ff.; Rossi-Maccanico, *Gibraltar*, *supra* n. 146; Staviczky, *supra* n. 146 who distinguishes it from the methodology applied in *Gibraltar;* Temple Lang, *The Gibraltar State Aid and Taxation Judgment*, *supra* n. 98.
758. Rossi-Maccanico, *Gibraltar*, *supra* n. 146, at 443.
759. Luja, *(Re)shaping Fiscal State Aid*, *supra* n. 98, at 131; Temple Lang, *The Gibraltar State Aid and Taxation Judgment*, *supra* n. 98, at 809ff.
760. Temple Lang, *The Gibraltar State Aid and Taxation Judgment*, *supra* n. 98, at 808.
761. *Ibid.*, at 810.

benchmark where there is no normal tax rule.[762] It has also been pointed out that, had the tax ever entered into force, it would have been impossible to recover the aid.[763]

The judgment in *Gibraltar* indeed touches upon the question of whether it is for EU law to conceive of an ideal tax system.[764] Yet it also becomes apparent that the CJEU in fact only outwardly relied on the idea of an (ideal) general corporate tax system to arrive at its conclusion. Admittedly, had Gibraltar not labelled the tax as a general corporate tax system, it would also have been harder to discern aid since the CJEU would have had to explain the external benchmark. Yet the alleged objective of the tax – to introduce a general corporate tax – cannot be decisive since it comes along with the potential for a circumvention of State aid law. For example, the result would arguably have been identical, had Gibraltar introduced a territorial tax system.[765] As argued elsewhere, there appear to be certain external consistency standards that Member States have to adhere to in addition to the requirement of internal consistency.[766] In this case, there was the problem that offshore undertakings were factually favoured. Beyond that, it has been pointed out that the CJEU appears to rely on legislative intent as a factor in the assessment of selectivity.[767] The system at issue was reverse-engineered, which seemed to play an important role in the assessment.[768] In this context, one may also wonder whether the specific environment in Gibraltar played a role. It is not clear whether there would also have been State aid if this case had taken place in another jurisdiction without such an important offshore sector.

The judgment in *Gibraltar* furthermore has to be delimitated from the methodology that was applied in the context of special purpose levies, namely in the judgment in *British Aggregates Association.*[769] Some have interpreted the judgment in *Gibraltar*

762. *Ibid.*, at 810f.
763. Daniël S. Smit, *International Income Allocation under EU Tax Law: Tinker, Tailor, Soldier, Sailor* 26 EC Tax Rev. 67, 72 (2017) https://doi.org/10.54648/ecta2017008; Temple Lang, *The Gibraltar State Aid and Taxation Judgment, supra* n. 98, at 811.
764. Such approach is not valid due to fiscal sovereignty, Schön, *Taxation and State Aid Law, supra* n. 7, at 923.
765. Ismer & Piotrowski, *The Selectivity of Tax Measures, supra* n. 77, at 568f.
766. *Ibid.*; Smit, *State Aid and Domestic Anti-tax Avoidance Rules, supra* n. 161, at 100 describes the benchmark as 'higher European (unwritten) norms'. Buriak & Lazarov, *supra* n. 127, at 5 refer to the Commission's discretion to evaluate selectivity as compared to hypothetical rules. According to Rossi-Maccanico, *Fiscal State Aids, Tax Base Erosion and Profit Shifting, supra* n. 56, at 65, this would be very far-reaching. Generally accepted principles would be the single-tax principle, the benefit principle and the non-discrimination principle. Even international mismatches could be covered by State aid law.
767. Temple Lang, *The Gibraltar State Aid and Taxation Judgment, supra* n. 98, at 810. *See also* Bacon, *State Aids and General Measures, supra* n. 359, at 302 prior to the judgment in *Gibraltar* for what she dubs indirect discriminations. The validity of such argument is disputed in the literature. *See* for further references Szudoczky & Károlyi, *The CJEU's Approach to the Objectives of Progressive Turnover-Based Taxes, supra* n. 95. According to Ruth Mason & Leopoldo Parada, *Company Size Matters* BTR 610, 631 (2019), the case law has resorted to both legislative intent and conclusions about the actual impact of a facially neutral rule as indications for de facto-selectivity.
768. Ismer & Piotrowski, *Selectivity in Corporate Tax Matters, supra* n. 77, at 164.
769. Also pointing out the similarities: Panci, *supra* n. 59, at 359; Ellenrieder, *Die materielle Selektivität steuerlicher Beihilfen, supra* n. 57, at 282ff.

as the establishment of an effect-based approach.[770] This would mean that the methodology that the CJEU relies on in the two judgments can essentially be equated. However, the levy at issue in *British Aggregates Association* had a regulatory objective, the implementation of which could be monitored in the framework of the assessment of de jure-selectivity.[771] De facto-selectivity is arguably primarily applicable for fiscal taxes since they have no specific regulatory purpose that would define the (necessary) scope of the reference system of taxation. The selectivity in the *Gibraltar* judgment could not solely be derived from the principle of effects being more relevant than the regulatory technique.[772] Instead, additional circumstances have to be present to arrive at the finding of selectivity.

The wider implications of the judgment in *Gibraltar* are still not altogether clear. Some have wondered whether the judgment may have been a singular occurrence due to the exceptional circumstances in the case or whether it could give rise to differential tax burdens deriving from non-differential rules being challenged as aid.[773]

Up until recently, the notion of de facto-selectivity had appeared to become highly relevant, in particular for the tax ruling cases. In several of its decisions on Member States' tax rulings, the Commission had postulated the existence of an EU arm's length standard. This had been highly controversial in the literature.[774] This arm's length standard would diverge from the applicable OECD standard.[775] An approach that does not take the national law as a point of departure would put into question the division of competences between the EU and the Member States.[776] A further common reproach against the Commission's approach was that stand-alone and group companies are considered comparable thereunder.[777] In assuming comparability, the Commission would ignore phenomena that would be the very reason to set up a group company, such as economies of scale.[778] It had therefore been suggested that the reference system should instead have been identified as the rules on cross-border transfer pricing instead of the corporate tax system.[779]

770. Rossi-Maccanico, *Gibraltar, supra* n. 146; Aalbers, *supra* n. 146, at 497.
771. Similarly Temple Lang, *The Gibraltar State Aid and Taxation Judgment, supra* n. 98, at 808ff. A different view is held by Lang, *Recent Trends in the Case Law of the ECJ, supra* n. 146, at 419f.
772. Ismer & Piotrowski, *Selectivity in Corporate Tax Matters, supra* n. 77, at 164.
773. Quigley, *Direct Taxation and State Aid, supra* n. 146, at 119. Also pointing to the difficulties of drawing a line and citing tax sovereignty concerns: Chesaites, *supra* n. 501, at 264; Prek & Lefèvre, *supra* n. 127, at 345 who advocate administrative clarifications by the Commission.
774. *See* only Allevato, *supra* n. 126, at 88ff.; Baker, *supra* n. 126, at 602f.; Cachia, *supra* n. 126, at 33f.; Daly, *The Constitutional Implications, supra* n. 126, at 72; Galendi Júnior, *supra* n. 96; Joris & De Cock, *supra* n. 126, at 613ff.; Kyriazis, *From Soft Law to Soft Law to Hard Law: The Commission's Approach to the State Aid Assessment of Tax Rulings, supra* n. 96, at 434; Mason, *Tax Rulings as State Aid, supra* n. 46; Mason, *Ding-Dong!, supra* n. 126, at 1253.
775. Castagna, *supra* n. 126, at 496.
776. Andreas Bartosch, *Nationale Steuersysteme im Fadenkreuz des Beihilferechts: wer bestimmt künftig den Maßstab?* 72 BB 2199, 2202 (2017) who in his contribution also refers to the danger that such external standards could also be relied on in areas other than taxation.
777. Baker, *supra* n. 126, at 603; Lovdahl Gormsen, *supra* n. 126, at 377; Nicolaides, *State Aid Rules and Tax Rulings, supra* n. 126, at 421ff.; Verhagen, *supra* n. 126, at 282f.
778. E.g., Verhagen, *supra* n. 126, at 282f.
779. Giraud & Petit, *Tax Rulings and State Aid Qualification, supra* n. 126, at 238; Lovdahl Gormsen, *supra* n. 126, at 377. Somewhat similarly: Nicolaides, *State Aid Rules and Tax Rulings, supra*

Specifically on the arm's length standard, the CJEU has, however, recently clarified that the Commission could not refer to an autonomous EU arm's length standard, where a Member State's tax law contains an arm's length standard itself.[780] The Commission had consequently not correctly identified the reference system of taxation.[781] The CJEU added that in the absence of harmonizing legislation under Article 114(2) and Article 115 TFEU, the examination carried out under Article 107(1) TFEU may solely rely on the normal tax rules laid down by the legislature of the Member State concerned.[782] It linked this assessment to the principle of legality of taxation as a general principle of EU law.[783]

Nevertheless, in its judgment, the CJEU did not reject the notion that tax rulings can confer State aid altogether. The CJEU merely underlined the importance of relying on the Member State's own fundamental charging decision as a point of reference. It even provided for a caveat related to the notion of de facto-selectivity:

> In particular, after having observed that a Member State has chosen to apply the arm's length principle in order to establish the transfer prices of integrated companies, the Commission must [...] be able to establish that the parameters laid down by national law are *manifestly inconsistent* with the objective of non-discriminatory taxation of all resident companies, whether integrated or not, pursued by the national tax system, by systematically leading to an undervaluation of the transfer prices applicable to integrated companies or to certain of them, such as finance companies, as compared to market prices for comparable transactions carried out by non-integrated companies.[784]

It held that the Commission in its decision had not carried out such examination.[785] The notion of de facto-selectivity may thus not be completely ruled out for tax rulings. Perhaps the Commission should not have postulated the existence of an autonomous arm's length standard but should have rooted its approach in the discrimination aspect of the selectivity test. As *Wattel* points out, the Commission might have avoided a lot of trouble had it simply called the EU arm's length principle the principle of equality. The arm's length principle as derived from the principle of equality might not be a principle of tax law but of competition law. As such, it may diverge from tax law.[786] It would then have been warranted to test for manifest inconsistency. Indeed, a complete lack of an arm's length standard or a comparable method for approximating the tax treatment of stand-alone and group companies or a

---

n. 126, at 425: the reference system for group companies would be a combination of the ordinary tax system and tax rulings.

780. de la Feria, *supra* n. 96, at 7 argues that the formal endorsement of the judgment in *Gibraltar* in the judgment in *Fiat* could be in line with the EU rule of precedent with the Court merely formally reinstating previous case law, while departing from it by means of a distinguishing on a factual basis.
781. Joined Cases C-885 and 898/19 P *Fiat*, para. 92.
782. *Ibid.*, para. 94.
783. *Ibid.*, para. 97.
784. *Ibid.*, para. 112; emphasis added by the author.
785. *Ibid.*, para. 113.
786. Wattel, *Stateless Income*, *supra* n. 126, at 792, 801. Sceptical: Buriak & Lazarov, *supra* n. 127, at 43.

standard that is otherwise manifestly inconsistent might still conceivably lead to the finding of State aid. The objectives of State aid law may thus require the existence of at least some kind of proxy to ensure equal treatment of group companies vis-à-vis stand-alone companies that is not manifestly inappropriate.[787]

Beyond this, it has been pointed out that the *Gibraltar* judgment could potentially have an impact in the area of environmental taxation. Temple Lang cites the example of a tax on emissions of a particular kind of pollutant. He contends that based on the *Gibraltar* judgment, there may be State aid if other pollutants that have comparable effects are not taxed at the same rate, even if they are not in competition, provided the tax could be applied without significant modifications and for similar environmental reasons. This would, in his view, amount to a substitution of the Court's views of what a tax base should be.[788] This does not appear convincing, since for special-purpose levies, it is not necessary to refer to the notion of de facto-selectivity as laid out above.[789] Luja convincingly argues that the full or partial exclusion of certain sources of income or profit from a corporate income tax may amount to State aid based on *Gibraltar* if it particularly benefits a certain sector of industry.[790]

In any case, de facto-selectivity will most likely have to be handled on a case-by-case basis. Since this leads to a lack of legal certainty, it has to be limited to exceptional cases, in which the factual discrimination is obvious and perhaps even intended. This holds all the more true since the methodology developed in the judgment in *Gibraltar* disregards the fundamental charging decision of the Member State.[791] This is also pointed out by the Commission in its Notice on the Notion of State aid when it lays out that such verification is only appropriate in 'certain exceptional cases' and where the reference system has been designed 'in a clearly arbitrary or biased way'.[792]

Finally, one may wonder whether a justification is conceivable for de facto-selectivity. In our view, a justification should theoretically be possible, since de facto-selectivity only covers what is dubbed prima facie selectivity for de jure-selectivity. However, in practice, the constellations leading to de facto-selectivity will always be extraordinary in that the levies in question have been designed in a manifestly arbitrary manner. Any legitimate reasons impacting the design of the levy will already have been considered on the level of the assessment of prima facie selectivity. The possibility for an (additional) justification is then merely theoretical.

787. Similarly: Theodoros Iliopoulos, *The State Aid Cases of Starbucks and Fiat: New Routes for the Concept of Selectivity* 16 EStAL 263, 270 (2017) https://doi.org/10.21552/estal/2017/2/11; Wattel, *Stateless Income, supra* n. 126, at 792. In a similar vein: Mason, *Ding-Dong!, supra* n. 126, at 1255 who, however, argues that allocation rules may constitute aid, but analysing transfer pricing rules would prove to be challenging, since they are 'structural rules' under tax expenditure theory.
788. Temple Lang, *The Gibraltar State Aid and Taxation Judgment, supra* n. 98, at 812.
789. *See* Ch. §3.03[C] *supra*.
790. Luja, *(Re)shaping Fiscal State Aid, supra* n. 98, at 130.
791. Ismer & Piotrowski, *Selectivity in Corporate Tax Matters, supra* n. 77, at 165; Daniël S. Smit, *International Juridical Double Non-taxation and State Aid* 25 EC Tax Rev. 109, 112 (2016) https://doi.org/10.54648/ecta2016011.
792. Commission Notice on the notion of State aid, *supra* n. 26, at para. 129.

§4.02 DE FACTO-SELECTIVITY IN PROGRESSIVE TURNOVER-BASED TAXES

One potential area of application of the notion of de facto-selectivity is progressive turnover-based taxes. As laid out above, progressivity generally does not lead to de jure-selectivity, since the progressive rate structure is understood to form part of the reference system.[793] Such taxes may still be de facto selective, however, if their design is manifestly (externally) inconsistent. This may be the case if the design of the reference system itself is arbitrary and inconsistent with the result that certain undertakings are factually discriminated against. Two types of argument could be made regarding progressivity. Turnover as such could be inappropriate to implement progressivity since it is an unsuitable measure for ability to pay. Alternatively, the problem could be the specific implementation of progressivity in some of these cases. It has now emerged from the case law that only the latter can conceivably lead to de facto-selectivity.

It has sometimes been argued that progressive turnover-based taxes would indeed be inconsistent in the scholarly literature. Szudoczky & Ka̋rolyi contend that turnover-based taxes would only be permissible with a single rate, unless the exemption of amounts below a certain threshold serves a different purpose, such as administrative simplification or efficiency.[794] Related to this, the idea that turnover is a neutral proxy for ability to pay has been questioned. It is widely accepted that profit taxes are a better indicator of ability to pay. Turnover taxes - by definition - do not allow for a deduction of costs. A high turnover is therefore not necessarily indicative of high profits. In sectors with high costs, turnover can be a meaningless indicator of an undertaking's ability to pay.[795] Turnover taxes may have a discriminatory effect for companies that - for whatever reason - have lower profit margins even with equal turnover.[796] Moreover, the economies of scale that companies experience with increasing size may vary between companies.[797]

Sinnig adds that a distinction between companies based on turnover would generally not be permissible for narrow-based fiscal taxes, since companies do not face differing subjective capabilities the way that individuals do. While the CJEU in its judgment in *ANGED* granted Member States wide discretion in adopting progressive brackets or thresholds - this reasoning would not apply to fiscal taxes. In particular, CJEU would not have endorsed the criterion 'sales area of a business' as an indicator of ability to pay.[798]

793. *See* Ch. §3.02[C], [2] *supra*.

794. Similarly Szudoczky & Ka̋rolyi, *The Troubled Story of the Hungarian Advertisement Tax*, *supra* n. 157, at 53.

795. *Ibid.* Similarly Bernatt & Grzejdziak, *supra* n. 149, at 195; Parada, *Vodafone Magyarorszа̋g Opinion*, *supra* n. 157, at 405f. Fichera, *supra* n. 149, at 490 argues that the finding that turnover is an indicator for ability for pay cannot be generalized for digital service taxes. This would depend on the economic sector.

796. Nicolaides, *Multi-rate Turnover Taxes and State Aid*, *supra* n. 157, at 233.

797. *Ibid.*

798. Sinnig, *supra* n. 157, at 111.

While there is merit to all these considerations, this does not necessarily mean that progressive turnover-based levies are selective. As to the first set of arguments – turnover as an indicator of ability to pay – it has to be seen that in the context of de facto-selectivity the fundamental charging decision of the legislator is disregarded and replaced by external benchmarks. In light of tax sovereignty, de facto-selectivity therefore has to be applied restrictively, and only in exceptional cases.[799] Turnover may indeed not necessarily be a good indicator of the ability to pay. However, for other types of narrow-based fiscal levies taxes, imperfect indicators for ability to pay would also be considered permissible even if these choices are (now) outdated or implausible.[800]

Even distinctions within such levies would not always be considered problematic. For example, assuming a real property tax contained distinctions based on size and the value of the property in question. Could such distinctions lead to selectivity? Of course, neither of the two is necessarily a perfect indicator of ability to pay. Yet it would also be far-fetched to consider the design of the boundaries of such levy State aid. Narrow-based fiscal levies may thus indeed fall through the cracks of State aid control. The reason the turnover-based levies in question are subject to State aid scrutiny is presumably first the fact that they are simultaneously under suspicion of infringing the fundamental freedoms. Second, they are perceived as being closely related to profit taxes. They are often promoted as a means to address profit shifting – which was one of the justifications brought forward by the Hungarian and Polish governments.

However, if such taxes are simply assessed in isolation, it becomes apparent that not all of these levies are necessarily problematic from a State aid law point of view. It has even been pointed out that a flatrate turnover tax that is meant to tax presumptive income would be regressive since the actual tax rate would gradually decline with increasing profits.[801]

The CJEU assessed the potential de facto-selectivity aspect in depth in its judgments on the Hungarian and Polish taxes and rejected the notion that the taxes were designed in a manifestly inappropriate manner. It held that the amount of turnover constitutes a neutral differentiation criterion and that turnover would be a relevant indicator of a taxable person's ability to pay.[802] Progressivity would not solely be permissible for taxes on profits from an EU law perspective. State aid law would only seek to remove selective advantages. To this end, it would be irrelevant that turnover may not be an ideal indicator of ability to pay or that the simultaneous levying of profit and turnover taxes may lead to economic double taxation.[803] The design of the tax would not be manifestly discriminatory, thus not leading to the finding of de facto-selectivity.[804]

799. *See* already Ch. §4.01 *supra*.
800. *See* Ch. §3.03[D] *supra*.
801. Stevanato, *supra* n. 157, at 544.
802. Critical: Bernatt & Grzejdziak, *supra* n. 149, at 194.
803. Case C-596/19 P *Commission v. Hungary*, para. 47.
804. *Ibid.*, para. 49 with reference to the Opinion of AG Kokott in Case C-596/19 P *Commission v. Hungary* EU:C:2020:835, paras 47 to 52.

This is in principle convincing. While indeed not a perfect proxy or ability to pay, turnover as a basis for progressivity does not appear manifestly inappropriate either. State aid law does not prescribe an ideal tax system. Member States are free to design their tax systems and their fundamental charging decision, including the rate structure, is only subject to limited review.[805] The assessment may only be different, where the rate structure is manifestly inconsistent. This amounts to a case-by-case approach, which will admittedly be hard to administer. Nicolaides describes the dilemma that Member States would face in designing such taxes as such: 'The closer the bands and the rates, the more likely that companies with similar turnover will in fact be quite different companies. The wider the bands and the more distant the rates, the more likely that the system favours small companies or, conversely, discriminates against large companies.'[806] He also points out that a flatrate turnover tax could then conceivably also be struck down with the argument that it discriminates against companies whose business model involves a high turnover with very low margins.[807]

Perhaps, the Hungarian Advertisement Tax with an overall tax burden of 80% for one single actor in 2014 and tax bands ranging from 0% to 50% should have been considered de facto selective by the CJEU.[808] Not only was the rate structure extremely steep but also the actual effects of the tax were primarily borne by one single operator. It appears far-fetched that such a rate structure truly implements the operators' ability to pay.[809] A similar objection could be made wherever the turnover thresholds are clearly designed in an arbitrary manner. The tax may then be externally inconsistent and thus selective. Interestingly, the reasoning on selectivity is essentially identical in both judgments (i.e., on the Hungarian Advertisement Tax and the Polish retail sector tax). This was despite the fact that the rate structures differed substantially, with the Hungarian tax displaying an excessively steep structure, which was not acknowledged by the CJEU.

The fact that the CJEU found no indications of manifest inconsistencies and thus applied an extremely limited standard of control in combination with the fact that there are clear tendencies to strengthen the first step of the selectivity test and to inversely limit the significance of the three-step test for selectivity may then lead to the question of whether this does not create too much room for Member States to reverse engineer

805. Schlücke, *supra* n. 113, at 441.
806. Nicolaides, *Multi-rate Turnover Taxes and State Aid*, *supra* n. 157, at 238.
807. *Ibid.*
808. Similarly as to the particularities of the Hungarian tax Károlyi, *supra* n. 157, at 276. According to Deák, *supra* n. 157, at 115f., progressive turnover taxes would be an indication of populist states' abuse of power and a decline of political democracy and the rule of law that could not necessarily be targeted with State aid law.
809. Strongly critical particularly as to the potential political motivations of the tax Szudoczky & Károlyi, *The Troubled Story of the Hungarian Advertisement Tax*, *supra* n. 157, at 54. The tax also contained rules according to which losses were deductible. Lang, *Recent Case Law on Progressive Turnover Taxes*, *supra* n. 157, at 520 argues that particularly this possibility to deduct losses from turnover would be evidently inconsistent. The judgment on the Hungarian Advertisement could therefore render the prohibition of State aid almost meaningless. Similarly Bernatt & Grzejdziak, *supra* n. 149, at 198ff.

their tax systems.[810] Should the applicable threshold truly be that only tax measures that are designed in a clearly abusive fashion could conceivably be caught by State aid control?[811]

In any case, even if some of these taxes were found to be selective, two conceptual problems remain. First, there is the question of whether there is, in fact, an advantage rather than a disadvantage for high turnover undertakings. While the two concepts can amount to two sides of the same coin, this is not always the case.[812] Especially in constellations, such as the one at issue in the Hungarian Advertisement tax case, one may wonder, whether they should not primarily be assessed as a potential infringement of the fundamental freedoms, an infringement of which had also been denied by the CJEU. This is because the vast majority of actors paying a lower amount of tax were subject to a lower overall tax burden. It then appears far-fetched to consider these actors the beneficiaries of aid. It therefore is likely that there would be no advantage, but a disadvantage.

Related to this issue is the second problem, namely recovery. Just as would have been the case for the tax at issue in *Gibraltar*, recovery would be close to impossible in such cases because of the problem of defining a standard rate or even identifying all the actors that the tax has to be recovered from.

The wider significance of these judgments could lie in the question of how to assess Member States' unilaterally imposed digital service taxes under State aid law.[813] From a policy point of view, it is unlikely that these taxes would be challenged by the European Commission since this would put into doubt efforts to introduce such tax through secondary law.[814] From a legal point of view, a State aid challenge has become even less likely following the judgments on the Hungarian and Polish taxes as the legal issues these taxes entail are very similar.[815]

---

810. In this vein: Bernatt & Grzejdziak, *supra* n. 149, at 197f. A different view is held by David Hummel, *Ertragsbesteuerung im Zeitalter der Digitalisierung: umsatzbasierte Steuern als Alternative zur herkömmlichen Gewinnbesteuerung?* 10 ISR 216, 220 (2021).
811. AG Kokott in her Opinion brought forward that the threshold should be that the *primary* objective of the measure is to disadvantage foreign companies, Opinion of AG Kokott in Case C-75/18 *Vodafone Magyarország* EU:C:2019:492, para. 92. This has been criticized as too high a threshold, albeit with reference to the problem of a potential indirect discrimination, Parada, *Vodafone Magyarország Opinion, supra* n. 157, at 402f. Similarly Károlyi, *supra* n. 157, at 277; Szudoczky & Károlyi, *The CJEU's Approach to the Objectives of Progressive Turnover-Based Taxes, supra* n. 95, at 93. They propose an application of the proportionality test in lieu of the standard of manifest inconsistency.
812. *See* Ch. §2.01 *supra*.
813. On the State aid compatibility of such taxes, e.g.,: Carro Pitarch, *supra* n. 158; Fichera, *supra* n. 149; Arguing that there is aid – albeit before the judgments on the Polish and Hungarian taxes, e.g., Mason & Parada, *Digital Battlefront in the Tax Wars, supra* n. 158. By contrast, a digital services tax based on secondary legislation could not lead to the finding of State aid, since it would not be imputable to the Member States, Georg Kofler & Julia Sinnig, *Equalization Taxes and the EU's 'Digital Services Tax'* 47 Intertax 176, 198 (2019) https://doi.org/10.54648/taxi2019017.
814. Mason & Parada, *supra* n. 158, at 1196f.
815. Carro Pitarch, *supra* n. 158, at 328f.; Georg Kofler, *The Future of Digital Services Taxes* 30 EC Tax Rev. 50, 52 (2021) https://doi.org/10.54648/ecta2021006.

Part II
Enforcement of State Aid Law and Its Limits

Even more than the perceived broad scope of material selectivity in fiscal aid schemes, it is the strict enforcement, and in particular the legal consequence of recovery that makes European State aid law so controversial. Of course, the Commission ordering recovery from the beneficiaries of aid is by no means the entirety of the State aid procedure,[816] but merely the result of a breach of the procedural obligations that Article 108 TFEU imposes on Member States. The core logic of State aid law is that it is based on a system of prior control by the Commission.[817] In this, the Commission is supported by the Member States, which have to notify any aid they plan to grant. Moreover, Article 108(3), (3) TFEU provides for a stand-still obligation. Thus, ideally, and if all actors respected their legal obligations, only aid that has been assessed by the Commission and found to be compatible with the internal market would be implemented in the first place.

The State aid procedure in principle is the same for positive and negative aid measures. Individuals are only involved in a limited capacity in so far as it pertains to preventing recovery: As an 'interested party' pursuant to Article 1(h) of Procedural Regulation 2015/1589, the beneficiary and third parties (e.g., competitors or trade associations) may submit a complaint to inform the Commission of any alleged unlawful or misused aid. Under Article 12(1) of Procedural Regulation 2015/1589, the Commission shall examine without undue delay any such complaint under Article 24(2). The decision opening the formal investigation procedure shall call upon

816. For an overview of the State aid procedure: Krumm, *supra* n. 173, at 564ff.; Pošćić, *supra* n. 114; Jesko Thiede, *Das Beihilfeverfahren und die Rechte und Pflichten der Beteiligten* 26 IStR 51ff. (2017).
817. Case 120/73 *Lorenz v. Germany* EU:C:1973:152, para. 2; Case C-199/06 *CELF and Ministre de la Culture et de la Communication (CELF I)* EU:C:2008:79, paras 36f.; Case C-284/12 *Deutsche Lufthansa AG* EU:C:2013:755, paras 25f.; Case C-75/18 *Vodafone Magyarország*, para. 19; Case C-323/18 *Tesco-Global Áruházak*, para. 31.

interested parties to submit comments.[818] Where an interested party has submitted such comments, they will be sent a copy of the decision according to Article 9.[819] Interested parties can also obtain copies of decisions pursuant to Articles 4, 9, 12(3) and 13.[820] While both beneficiaries' and competitors' judicial protection and options for private enforcement have been strengthened, their possibilities to influence the administrative procedure are thus still limited.[821] Most notably, notification as the only way to effectively prevent recovery is solely incumbent on the Member State.

There are some particularities of fiscal aid schemes on this level as well. For example, due to the bilateral relationship between tax authorities and taxpayers and issues of tax confidentiality, it has sometimes been suggested that the role of competitors in the enforcement of fiscal State aid law would necessarily be less significant than for positive subsidies.[822]

Specifically regarding the legal consequence of recovery of fiscal aid, several arguments against strict enforcement have been brought forward. For example, it has been noted that the recovery of positive subsidies is more straightforward than for negative subsidies. European State aid law would have originally been designed for positive subsidies, which means that the problems arising in the context of fiscal aid had not been envisaged.[823] Moreover, aid in the form of tax measures often comes in the form of an aid scheme that is embedded into highly complex tax laws. Therefore, special treatment would be warranted for the protection of legitimate expectations by the beneficiaries of aid.[824] Some have even argued that due to the high degree of complexity of tax laws, all types of undertakings could potentially become subject to State aid procedures even if they do not suspect being granted State aid at all, which would be too far-reaching.[825]

All this leads to significant concerns as to the protection of taxpayer rights in relation to recovery. To the extent that there has recently been a rollback in the CJEU's interpretation of selectivity, the issues discussed in this Part have certainly become less pressing. First, this is because many types of measures appear to be shielded from State aid control after all. Second, if it is true that the standard of control for a large number of tax measures is now moving towards a monitoring for 'manifest inappropriateness', beneficiaries profiting from such evidently selective aid measures would presumably not harbour *legitimate* expectations in their legality.

818. Articles 6(1) and 24(1), (1) of Procedural Regulation 2015/1589.
819. Article 24(1) & (2) of Procedural Regulation 2015/1589.
820. Article 24(3) of Procedural Regulation 2015/1589.
821. *See, e.g.*, Buendía Sierra, *The Role of Competitors*, *supra* n. 167, at 451f.
822. Lisa Paterno, *State Aid and Fiscal Protectionism in the European Union from the Perspective of Competitors* 65 BIT 343, 344f. (2011) https://doi.org/10.59403/jvwyze.
823. Maitrot de la Motte, *supra* n. 171, at 77.
824. *See, e.g.*, Hey, *EU-Beihilfen und Steuervergünstigungen*, *supra* n. 119, at 336.
825. Georgios Matsos, *Systematic Misconceptions of State Aid Law in the Area of Taxation* 13 EStAL 491 (2014). In poorer Member States there might be resource constraints for the administration that has to implement recovery. Therefore, a future two-speed system of State aid control would be likely, Hancher, *State Aid Recovery*, *supra* n. 114, at 4. Critical of a two-speed system: José Luis Buendía Sierra, *'Small on Small': Towards a Two-Speed State Aid Control?* 15 EStAL 501ff. (2016) https://doi.org/10.21552/estal/2016/4/2, albeit with reference to the distinction between the level of distortion caused.

Nevertheless, even in areas where the CJEU's line on material selectivity is now clear, the problem remains that taxpayers cannot necessarily avoid benefitting from undue tax advantages in the form of fiscal aid schemes and would then potentially face recovery. Therefore, taxpayers should have tools at their disposal to achieve legal certainty before making use of a tax measure that may amount to State aid. Alternatively, recovery could be excluded in cases that are problematic from a taxpayer rights perspective.

Our starting point is the recovery of fiscal aid and a potential modification to this legal consequence. According to the long-standing case law of the CJEU, recovery is the 'logical consequence' of the finding of unlawful aid. A general modification of the legal consequences of State aid law is not warranted despite intense criticism in the literature. Yet in exceptional cases, there may be a case – and room – for a reversal of the legal consequences of State aid law both after a negative Commission decision and in front of national courts (Chapter 5).

We will then turn to the case-by-case limits to recovery. We examine the principle of protection of legitimate expectation, which is interpreted narrowly under EU State aid law. Where aid has not been notified, legitimate expectations can only exclude recovery in exceptional cases. This requires precise, unconditional and consistent assurances given to the beneficiary of aid by an EU institution, body or agency. In exceptional cases, recovery could, however, be excluded if the CJEU acknowledged a notion of evolving case law, which can perhaps be derived from the principle of legal certainty. These case-by-case limits to recovery are similarly applicable in front of national courts in the assessment stage (Chapter 6).

Such a narrow reading of the principles of protection of legitimate expectation and legal certainty only appears justified to the extent that the beneficiary has the procedural means to achieve legal certainty, where they are or should have been aware of the State aid issues of a tax measure. Therefore, we propose to strengthen the procedural rights of taxpayers throughout the procedure and to enhance transparency. We address two selected issues. The (potential) beneficiary of aid should have a means to secure notification. Furthermore, the practice of issuing comfort letters instead of formal Commission decisions is detrimental to legal certainty and transparency. Comfort letters should be published but cannot be grounds for a protection of legitimate expectation (Chapter 7).

Chapter 5

Recovery of Unlawfully Granted Aid and Modification of Legal Consequences

This chapter discusses the legal consequence of recovery, which is often perceived to be problematic for fiscal aid schemes. We distinguish between enforcement by the Commission on the one hand and by national courts on the other. The case law requires an elimination of the advantage through recovery. Absolute impossibility will only rarely exclude recovery. The perceived structural and legal objections do not convince as a general solution for fiscal aid schemes and should instead be considered on a case-by-case basis. Yet there are very specific constellations where the discrimination underlying the infringement of State aid law can be remedied through a reimbursement of tax instead of recovery. This would eliminate the selective advantage. Following a Commission decision, this may be the case where it is possible for the Member State to retroactively abolish a levy from a domestic law perspective. Next to the role of the Commission, the objective and subjective enforcement function of national courts in the assessment stage, which is derived from Article 108(3), (3) TFEU, should not be neglected. At the same time, Article 108(3), (3) TFEU restricts the national court's room for manoeuvre. This significantly limits private enforcement. Competitors should at least be able to tackle the non-taxation of the beneficiaries of aid. Achieving an extension of the advantage rather than recovery is nevertheless conceivable if there is a simultaneous infringement of the fundamental freedoms, where the Laboratoires Boiron case law is applicable, or where a reimbursement otherwise does not lead to an infringement of Article 108(3), (3) TFEU.

Where a Member State implements State aid in infringement of the stand-still provision of Article 108(3), (3) TFEU, the advantage generally has to be recovered from the beneficiaries of the aid measure.[826]

In this chapter, we will discuss the legal consequences of the finding that new aid is either unlawful or incompatible with the internal market. The term *new aid* refers to all aid which is not existing aid and includes alterations to existing aid.[827] According to Article 108(3) TFEU, the Member State shall inform the Commission in sufficient time to enable it to submit its comments of any plans to grant or alter aid. Member States thus have to notify the Commission of planned State aid. The Commission shall then initiate the procedure provided for in Article 108(2), where it considers the aid to be incompatible with the internal market. According to Article 108(3), (3) TFEU, the Member State shall not put the proposed measure into effect until the procedure has resulted in a final decision.

Procedural Regulation 2015/1589 reiterates Member States' obligation to notify the aid before its introduction in sufficient time to allow the Commission to evaluate the aid.[828] There are two exceptions to the obligation to notify aid. First, where the conditions laid down in the *De minimis*-Regulation are fulfilled, such aid shall be deemed not to meet all the criteria in Article 107(1) TFEU and is consequently exempt from the notification requirement.[829] Second, aid schemes, individual aid granted under aid schemes, and ad hoc aid that fulfil the conditions laid down in Chapters I and III of the GBER shall be compatible with the internal market within the meaning of Article 107(2) or (3) and is thus exempted from the notification requirement under Article 108(3) TFEU.[830]

Unlawful aid is new aid that has been put into effect by the Member State in breach of the stand-still provision of Article 108(3), (3) TFEU.[831] The State aid procedure regarding unlawful aid is covered in Chapter III of Procedural Regulation 2015/1589. The Commission may on its own initiative examine information regarding alleged unlawful aid from whatever source.[832] Until it has decided on the compatibility

826. *See* on the recovery of aid, for example, Aalbers & Adriaanse, *supra* n. 170, at paras 30-001ff.; Margarida Afonso, *Recovery of Fiscal Aid,* in Rust & Micheau (eds), State Aid and Tax Law, 57ff. (2013); Micheau, *Récupération des aides d'État, supra* n. 170; Martini, *supra* n. 119, at 102f.; Papi Rossi, *supra* n. 168; Giuseppe Pizzonia, *Recovery in the Case of Aid Schemes in Tax Matters,* in Santa Maria (ed.), Competition and State Aid: An Analysis of EU Practice, 179ff. (2nd edn 2015).
827. Article 1(c) of Procedural Regulation 2015/1589.
828. Article 2(1) of Procedural Regulation 2015/1589. On the notification procedure: Janina Brandau, *Notifizierungsfragen* 8 HFSt 243ff. (2018).
829. Article 3(1) of Commission Regulation (EU) No. 1407/2013 of 18 December 2013 on the application of Arts 107 and 108 of the Treaty on the Functioning of the European Union to *de minimis* aid [2013] OJ L 352/1, last amended by Commission Regulation (EU) 2020/972 of 2 July 2020 [2020] OJ L 215/3.
830. Article 3 of Commission Regulation (EU) No. 651/2014 of 17 June 2014 declaring certain categories of aid compatible with the internal market in application of Articles 107 and 108 of the Treaty [2014] OJ L 187/1, last amended by Commission Regulation (EU) 2023/1315 of 23 June 2023 [2023] OJ L 167/1.
831. Article 1(f) of Procedural Regulation 2015/1589.
832. Article 12(1) of Procedural Regulation 2015/1589.

of aid, the Commission may adopt a suspension injunction[833] or, where the conditions of Article 13(2) are met, a recovery injunction, according to which the unlawful aid has to be recovered. Where the Commission issues a negative decision, it shall order the Member State concerned to recover the aid including interest,[834] unless this would be contrary to a general principle of EU law.[835] Recovery is effected under the pertinent procedures under national law, provided they allow for immediate and effective execution of the Commission decision.[836] Recovery is limited to a period of 10 years, which starts on the day on which the aid is awarded to the beneficiary.[837]

While it is always the Member States that need to recover aid, the decision that there is such obligation may originate either from a pertinent Commission decision or from the Member State itself, and in particular the judgment of a national court. This chapter is set against the background that some contributions in the literature have called for a modification of the legal consequences of State aid law. At least for fiscal aid schemes, an infringement of the stand-still obligation of Article 108(3), (3) TFEU should, according to these contributions, not (always) result in recovery.[838]

We argue that the Commission is obliged to order recovery de lege lata. Difficulties in recovery are only in exceptional circumstances accepted as precluding recovery. The arguments for a modification of the legal consequences of infringements of State aid law fail to convince, which means that excluding recovery de lege ferenda is not desirable. Instead, the arguments brought forward in the literature should only play a role in the context of the case-by-case limits to recovery under Article 16(1) of Procedural Regulation 2015/1589. There may exceptionally be room for a reversal of the legal consequences of infringements of State aid law, since particularly for narrow-based levies, the competitive advantage could sometimes equally be eliminated by retroactively abolishing the tax in question as a whole (§5.01).

The same issue will be examined for national courts, which are similarly obliged to at least provisionally recover aid.[839] This aspect is rarely addressed in the literature. This is perhaps because the most high-profile cases, and in particular the tax ruling cases, are currently based on Commission investigations. Moreover, the power to decide whether aid is compatible with the internal market lies with the Commission.[840] The Commission does not comprehensively monitor Member States' tax laws for infringements of State aid law, but will only tackle a limited number of cases. This in

833. Article 13(1) of Procedural Regulation 2015/1589.
834. Article 16(2) of Procedural Regulation 2015/1589.
835. Article 16(1) of Procedural Regulation 2015/1589.
836. Article 16(3) of Procedural Regulation 2015/1589.
837. Article 17(1) & (2) of Procedural Regulation 2015/1589.
838. *See* Ch. §5.01[B] and [C] *infra*.
839. *See* Ch. §5.02[A], [1] *infra*.
840. *See* in particular Case 74/76 *Ianelli and Volpi* EU:C:1977:51, paras 11f.; Case 78/76 *Steinike und Weinlig v. Germany* EU:C:1977:52, para. 9; Case C-354/90 *Fédération Nationale du Commerce Extérieur des Produits Alimentaires and Others v. France* EU:C:1991:440, para. 14; Case C-39/94 *SFEI and Others* EU:C:1996:285, para. 42; Case C-143/99 *Adria-Wien Pipeline*, para. 29; Case C-234/99 *Niels Nygard* EU:C:2002:244, para. 59; Case C-110/02 *Commission v. Council* EU:C:2004:395, para. 29; Case C-199/06 *CELF I*, para. 38; Case C-284/12 *Deutsche Lufthansa AG*, para. 29; as well as the reiteration in Case C-598/17 *A-Fonds* EU:C:2019:352, paras 47f.

turn means that there is a danger of asymmetric enforcement, or not purely legal considerations coming into play. The Commission is thus perceived as a somewhat political actor.[841]

Nevertheless, the role of national courts should not be underestimated. It has even been argued that the enforcement of State aid law by actors other than the Commission is more practically relevant than the role of the latter.[842] We make a distinction between two stages of the State aid procedure which we will dub the assessment stage and the recovery stage respectively.[843] The former extends to the entire period until there is a final Commission decision ordering recovery, whereas the latter refers to the period after such decision. We are primarily concerned with the role of national courts in the assessment stage of the State aid procedure.

National courts are obliged to remedy infringements of Article 108(3), (3) TFEU ex officio as well as upon application by certain third parties. This even extends to provisional recovery. While third parties cannot rely on the fact that a levy contains a tax exemption in order to avoid payment of that tax, they should have the possibility to tackle the non-taxation of the beneficiaries of aid in front of national courts. A refund of tax instead of recovery is conceivable in three constellations: First, this may be possible where there is simultaneously an infringement of the fundamental freedoms and the application of the fundamental freedoms does not lead to additional distortions. Second, the *Laboratoires Boiron* case law defines constellations where there is no infringement of Article 108(3), (3) TFEU despite a widening of recourse to the aid measure. Third, where a reimbursement of tax does not lead to an infringement of Article 108(3), (3) TFEU – for example, because the entire tax is eliminated – it is for the national court to decide which legal consequence applies. Whether this is conceivable is a matter of national law (§5.02).

§5.01 MODIFICATION OF THE LEGAL CONSEQUENCE OF RECOVERY FOLLOWING A COMMISSION DECISION

The Commission is obliged to order recovery unless this would be contrary to a general principle of Union law [A]. The threshold for a Member State to claim absolute impossibility is very high and will generally not be met [B]. The arguments that have been brought forward against recovery fail to convince as a general conclusion [C]. There may, however, be exceptional cases, in which a Member State can implement recovery through a retroactive elimination of the tax as a whole [D].

841. *See, e.g.*, Koenig, *supra* n. 49, at 611: '*State aid law has become an all-purpose tool to camouflage policy-making*'. Alberto Santa Maria, *Introduction*, in Santa Maria (ed.), Competition and State Aid: An Analysis of EU Practice, 1 (2nd edn 2015); Stephan Wernicke, *Vertrauensverluste: Deutschland versus Europäische Kommission?* 26 EuZW 649 (2015).

842. Krumm, *supra* n. 173, at 565. Also stressing the significance of decentralized enforcement by national courts Leo Flynn, '*Taking Flight, Not Taking Fright?*': *The National Court as a Full Partner in the Enforcement of the State Aid Discipline* 16 EStAL 335ff. (2017) https://doi.org/10.21552/estal/2017/3/2.

843. Ghazarian, *supra* n. 166, at 228 distinguishes three stages and further divides the first stage depending on whether there is already an opening decision by the Commission.

[A] Recovery as the Logical Consequence of the Finding of State Aid

The recovery of incompatible State aid is not laid down in Articles 107ff. TFEU. There is, however, an explicit legal basis for the recovery of aid in Article 16(1) of Procedural Regulation 2015/1589. The provision contains an obligation for the Commission to order recovery unless this would be contrary to a general principle of EU law.

The possibility of ordering recovery was first recognized by the CJEU in a tax case. The judgment in *Commission v. Germany* dealt with an investment grant for constructing or enlarging industrial establishments in mining areas in the form of a deduction from income tax or corporate tax.[844] In its decision, the Commission had ordered recovery which was disregarded by Germany. In the context of the admissibility of the action of the Commission tackling the non-compliance, Germany argued that the Commission's plea based on the obligation of recovery was inadmissible.[845] The CJEU rejected this:

> Such a request is admissible since the Commission is competent, when it has found that aid is incompatible with the Common Market, to decide that the State concerned must abolish or alter it. To be of *practical effect*, this abolition or modification *may* include an *obligation to require repayment of aid granted in breach of the Treaty*, so that in the absence of measures for recovery, the Commission may bring the matter before the Court. Moreover an application from the Commission, within the scope of the procedure under Articles 169 to 171, for a declaration that in omitting to take specific measures, a Member State has failed to fulfil an obligation under the Treaty, is equally admissible. Since the *aim of the Treaty is to achieve the practical elimination of infringements and the consequences thereof, past and future*, it is a matter for the Community authorities whose task it is to ensure that the requirements of the Treaty are observed to determine the extent to which the obligation of the Member State concerned may be specified in the reasoned opinions or decisions delivered under Articles 169 and 93 (2) respectively and in applications addressed to the Court. This plea must therefore be rejected.[846]

The Commission's action was ultimately dismissed as the Commission decision lacked a clarification of the geographical scope and applicable time limits for recovery, which were necessary for Germany to comply with the decision.[847] Nevertheless, the decision can be considered seminal as the CJEU thereby in principle accepted that the Commission may order recovery of aid in tax cases, but also in general.

Two aspects emerge from this judgment. First, the CJEU did not establish an obligation for the Commission to order the Member State to carry out recovery. Instead, recovery was deemed to be but one option next to ordering a modification or an abolition of the aid. The CJEU also did not lay down conditions for ordering recovery. Instead, it appeared as though it was up to the Commission to determine whether recovery was appropriate in a specific case at hand. The case law of the CJEU thus at

844. Case 70/72 *Commission v. Germany* EU:C:1973:87. On the history of the case law on recovery Aalbers & Adriaanse, *supra* n. 170, at paras 30-020ff.
845. Case 70/72 *Commission v. Germany*, para. 10.
846. *Ibid.*, para. 13; emphasis added by the author.
847. *Ibid.*, paras 21ff.

first focused on the fact that it is within the power of the Commission to opt for recovery in stating that it *may* do so.[848]

Second, the CJEU did not refer to the aims of State aid control in defining the objective of recovery. Instead, it merely referred to the aim of the Treaty, which would be the practical elimination of infringements of the Treaty and the consequences of such infringements for both the past and the future. It also stressed that the obligation of recovery was relevant in the context of the practical effect of the finding that aid is incompatible with the internal market. By contrast, the judgment contained no reference to any objectives of recovery beyond this, such as the elimination of the distortion of competition.

In later case law, the reference to the Commission being able to ('may') order recovery was often supplemented by the following:

> Removing unlawful aid by means of recovery is the *logical consequence* of a finding that it is unlawful and seeks to re-establish the previous situation.[849]

Eventually, the reference to the Commission being able to ('may') order recovery was omitted. Only the reference to recovery as the logical consequence of a finding of unlawful aid remains in current standing case law.[850] Yet even based on this wording, there would not necessarily be an obligation for the Commission to order recovery based on European primary law.

The obligation of recovery was then codified in Procedural Regulation No. 659/1999.[851] Recently, moreover, the CJEU has made it clear that such an obligation indeed also exists under primary law. This particularly emerged in the judgment of the CJEU in *Scuola Elementare Maria Montessori*.[852] In its underlying decision, the Commission had not ordered recovery. On this, the CJEU in its judgment first points to Article 14(1) of Procedural Regulation No. 659/1999 – the predecessor of Procedural Regulation 2015/1589 – as well as the settled case law that recovery is the logical and normal consequence of the finding of State aid that is incompatible with the internal market. The objective of recovery would be an elimination of the distortion of

848. *Ibid.*, para. 13; *see also* Case 310/85 *Deufil v. Commission*, para. 24; Joined Cases C-278 to 280/92 *Spain v. Commission* EU:C:1994:325, para. 78; Case C-24/95 *Alcan Deutschland*, para. 22; Joined Cases C-328/99 and C-399/00 *Italy and SIM 2 Multimedia SpA v. Commission* EU:C:2003:252, para. 65; Case C-277/00 *Germany v. Commission* EU:C:2004:238, para. 73.

849. *See* Joined Cases C-328/99 and C-399/00 *Italy and SIM 2 Multimedia SpA*, para. 66; Case C-277/00 *Germany v. Commission*, para. 74; emphasis added by the author.

850. *See, e.g.*, Case C-142/87 *Belgium v. Commission*, para. 66; Case C-183/91 *Commission v. Greece* EU:C:1993:233, para. 16; Case C-169/95 *Spain v. Commission* EU:C:1997:10, para. 47; Case C-372/97 *Italy v. Commission* EU:C:2004:234, para. 103; Case C-404/97 *Commission v. Portugal* EU:C:2000:345, para. 38; Case C-148/04 *Unicredito Italiano*, para. 113; Joined Cases C-71, 73 and 76/09 P *Comitato 'Venezia vuole vivere'*, para. 181; Case C-672/13 *OTP Bank* EU:C:2015:185, para. 70; Joined Cases C-164 and 165/15 P *Aer Lingus and Ryanair*, para. 116; Joined Cases C-622 to 624/16 P *Scuola Elementare Maria Montessori v. Commission* EU:C:2018:873, para. 77.

851. Council Regulation (EC) No. 659/1999 of 22 March 1999 laying down detailed rules for the application of Art. 93 of the EC Treaty [1999] OJ L 83/1, last amended by Council Regulation (EU) No. 734/2013 of 22 July 2013 [2013] OJ L 204/15. Papi Rossi, *supra* n. 168, at 142.

852. Joined Cases C-622 to 624/16 P *Scuola Elementare Maria Montessori*. *See* on this judgment, e.g., Gambaro & Mazzocchi, *supra* n. 167.

competition caused by the competitive advantage.[853] It further stated that the absolute impossibility to recover aid is the only defence that Member States can bring forward against recovery.[854] Ordering recovery where this is impossible from the outset would be contrary to general principles of EU law – which is the only exception to Article 14(1) of Procedural Regulation No. 659/1999.[855]

In the *Scuola Elementare Maria Montessori* case, the CJEU held that the conditions for a finding of impossibility of recovery were ultimately not fulfilled.[856] It has thus become clear beyond doubt that the Commission is obliged to order recovery unless this would be contrary to a general principle of EU law.

[B] Difficulties and Uncertainties in Recovery in Tax Cases Only Rarely Lead to Absolute Impossibility of Recovery

Some authors have discussed difficulties that Member States face in recovering fiscal aid. They hold that recovery will often be impossible or at least face substantial difficulties.[857] According to long-standing case law of the CJEU, the absolute impossibility of the implementation of a recovery order is the only admissible defence for Member States when faced with a recovery order.[858] Yet in light of the principle of effectiveness, the threshold for such impossibility is very high. As such, the absolute impossibility of recovery appears to be more of a theoretical limit.[859] Two cumulative conditions have to be met: First, the difficulties relied on by the Member State must be real, and second, there can be no alternative methods of recovery.[860] The Member State has to inform the Commission of these difficulties and must cooperate in order to overcome them.[861] To this end, it has to take real steps to recover the aid and propose

853. Joined Cases C-622 to 624/16 P *Scuola Elementare Maria Montessori*, paras 76f.
854. *Ibid.*, para. 80 with reference to Case 52/84 *Commission v. Belgium* EU:C:1986:3, para. 14; Case C-207/05 *Commission v. Italy* EU:C:2006:366, para. 45; Case C-481/16 *Commission v. Greece* EU:C:2017:845, para. 28.
855. Joined Cases C-622 to 624/16 P *Scuola Elementare Maria Montessori.*, paras 79, 81.
856. *Ibid.*, para. 96.
857. *See* in particular Maitrot de la Motte, *supra* n. 171, at 75ff., Micheau, *Récupération des aides d'État, supra* n. 170, at 349ff.; Moreno González, *Recovery of Tax-Related State Aid in Spain, supra* n. 169, at 392. *See also* the example in Aalbers & Adriaanse, *supra* n. 170, at para. 30-004.
858. E.g., Case 52/84 *Commission v. Belgium*, para. 14; Case C-94/87 *Commission v. Germany*, para. 8; Case C-348/93 *Commission v. Italy* EU:C:1995:95, para. 16; Case C-349/93 *Commission v. Italy* EU:C:1995:53, para. 12; Case C-404/97 *Commission v. Portugal*, para. 39; Case C-261/99 *Commission v. France* EU:C:2001:179, para. 23; Case C-499/99 *Commission v. Spain* EU:C:2002:408, para. 21; Case C-214/07 *Commission v. France* EU:C:2008:619, para. 44.
859. Alexander Birnstiel, *Recovery of Unlawful State Aid: The Role of Member State Courts in State Aid Recovery Scenarios* 11 EStAL 645, 650 (2012) https://doi.org/10.21552/estal/2012/3/309.
860. *See* only Joined Cases C-622 to 624/16 P *Scuola Elementare Maria Montessori*, para. 96.
861. Case 52/84 *Commission v. Belgium*, para. 16; Case C-94/87 *Commission v. Germany*, para. 9; Case C-349/93 *Commission v. Italy*, para. 13; Case C-378/98 *Commission v. Belgium* EU:C:2011:370, para. 31; Case C-261/99 *Commission v. France*, para. 24; Case C-499/99 *Commission v. Spain*, para. 24; Case C-404/97 *Commission v. Portugal*, para. 40; Case C-214/07 *Commission v. France*, para. 45; Case C-304/09 *Commission v. Italy* EU:C:2010:812, para. 37; Case C-37/14 *Commission v. France* EU:C:2015:90, para. 67; Joined Cases C-622 to 624/16 P *Scuola Elementare Maria Montessori*, para. 90.

alternative means of recovery.[862] Internal difficulties that are due to the Member State's authorities' own acts or omissions do not suffice to claim impossibility.[863] For example, the CJEU in a case that concerned a tax measure rejected absolute impossibility where Italy claimed that it was not possible to obtain the necessary information on the beneficiaries of aid from the Italian land registry and tax databases.[864] Even the principle of res iudicata is not necessarily sufficient to claim impossibility where there are still means to reverse a national judgment.[865]

The scholarly literature, however, does not condone this narrow stance. Numerous difficulties in implementing recovery have been named: Maitrot de la Motte cites procedural difficulties that relate to the parallel enforcement of State aid law by national authorities and the Commission as well as temporal aspects of recovery.[866] Specifically for tax cases, it would often be impossible to identify the beneficiaries of aid as they have never (had to) notify the tax administration of their existence.[867] He cites a French case, where the Commission held that recovery was impossible for some tax periods due to difficulties relating to the identification of the beneficiaries of aid and the calculation of the amount of aid. This was due to a French rule according to which financial records only had to be retained for ten years, which meant that no tax records were available for the periods in question.[868]

In some Member States, difficulties may furthermore arise from the discrepancy between national procedural laws and the requirements deriving from State aid law. For example, there may be a lack of procedural rules for the recovery of State aid.[869] Recovery can prove to be highly complex. The resulting issues warrant further comparative law research. Problems may arise with respect to the applicable legal provisions (e.g., tax law, administrative law, and civil law), the branches of government involved, vertical divisions within a Member State, or the legal basis for recovery. Moreover, provisions that do not technically bear relation to recovery can prove to be problematic.[870] For example, in Spain, it has been considered problematic that recovery proceedings are conducted through dialogue with the Commission, but

862. Joined Cases C-485 to 490/03 *Commission v. Spain* EU:C:2006:777, para. 74 with further references; Case C-214/07 *Commission v. France*, para. 46; Case C-37/14 *Commission v. France*, para. 66; Joined Cases C-622 to 624/16 P *Scuola Elementare Maria Montessori*, para. 91.
863. Case C-214/07 *Commission v. France*, para. 50; Joined Cases C-622 to 624/16 P *Scuola Elementare Maria Montessori*, para. 91.
864. Joined Cases C-622 to 624/16 P *Scuola Elementare Maria Montessori*, para. 95.
865. *See, e.g.*, Massimo Merola & Luigi Cappelletti, *The Obligation to Recover Unlawful Aid* 2 JECLAP 465ff. (2011) https://doi.org/10.1093/jeclap/lpr045; Birnstiel, *supra* n. 859.
866. Maitrot de la Motte, *supra* n. 171, at 81f.
867. *Ibid.*, at 82.
868. Case C-214/07 *Commission v. France*, paras 13, 21f.
869. On the problem in Spain and the updated legislation: Hugo López López, *Recent Developments in Spanish Legislation on State Aid Recovery of a Tax Nature* 14 EStAL 382ff. (2015); Moreno González, *Recovery of Tax-Related State Aid in Spain*, *supra* n. 169, at 393ff. For the Netherlands after the 2018 State aid Recovery Act: Leroy, *supra* n. 169.
870. *See, e.g.*, Leroy, *supra* n. 169, at 165 for the example of national rules on the obligation of taxpayers to store information that are shorter than the EU limitation period for recovery.

without hearing the beneficiary.[871] Furthermore, it is not in all cases altogether clear what the normally applicable tax treatment should be.[872]

Beyond that, it has been argued that it would presently be unclear whether alternative deductions or other types of reductions of the tax burden that hadn't been applied beforehand due to the application of the tax benefit could be taken into account.[873] The CJEU's judgment in *Unicredito Italiano* appears to contain some guidance in this respect. While the business decisions that are underlying a certain tax treatment have to be treated as a given, an alternative tax treatment that is more favourable for the beneficiary appears to be a valid reason for a reduction of the sum to be recovered:

> Re-establishing the status quo ante merely enables account to be taken, at the stage of recovery of the aid by the national authorities, of tax treatment which may be more favourable than the ordinary treatment which, in the absence of unlawful aid and in accordance with domestic rules which are compatible with Community law, would have been granted on the basis of the operation actually carried out.[874]

In its 2019 Recovery Notice, the Commission specifies that automatically applicable deductions provided for by national and international law or by the recovery decision can be taken into account to decrease the amount of recovery.[875] This appears convincing and has now been confirmed by the case law.[876] Beyond this, one may wonder whether such deductions necessarily have to be automatic to decrease the amount to be recovered. Where the criteria for such deductions are objective and are not contingent on a discretionary decision, a need for an application should not exclude a reduction. Taking such deductions and even alternative compatible aid schemes into account, recovery can become highly complex. This holds all the more true since the appropriate tax treatment has to be determined independently for every single beneficiary of a fiscal aid scheme.[877]

Other issues that had been identified in the literature have meanwhile turned out to be less complex than previously thought. For example, this concerns the determination of the amount to be recovered[878] and the identification of the effective beneficiary of aid.[879] The General Court's judgments on the ATT discussed above had created confusion in this respect.[880] In this case, the General Court had held that it was necessary to examine whether the tax advantage enjoyed by the airlines had been fully or at least partly passed on to the customers of the airlines to determine the correct

871. Miguel Sampol Pucurull, *Economic Penalties and Recovery of State Aid: Some Lessons from the Spanish Experience* 16 EStAL 431, 438 (2017) https://doi.org/10.21552/estal/2017/3/11.
872. *Ibid.*, at 436.
873. Moreno González, *Recovery of Tax-Related State Aid in Spain*, *supra* n. 169, at 392.
874. Case C-148/04 *Unicredito Italiano*, para. 119.
875. Commission Notice on the recovery of unlawful and incompatible State aid [2019] OJ C 247/1, paras 106f.
876. This has now been confirmed in Case 705/20 *Fossil (Gibraltar)*, para. 43.
877. Sampol Pucurull, *supra* n. 871, at 436.
878. Maitrot de la Motte, *supra* n. 171, at 83.
879. Moreno González, *Recovery of Tax-Related State Aid in Spain*, *supra* n. 169, at 392.
880. *See, e.g.*, Maitrot de la Motte, *supra* n. 171, at 83. *See* on this judgment Ch. §2.02[B], [1] *supra*.

amount to be recovered. Only the actual benefit received by the beneficiary of aid would have to be recovered.[881] This notion of the passing on of the tax advantage was set aside by the CJEU.[882] Instead, the exact difference between the higher and the lower tax rate had to be recovered. This is because recovery is not aimed at eliminating any (and only) the benefit derived from aid, but merely seeks to remove the immediate advantage from the beneficiary.[883]

In any case, only if recovery systematically posed a significant problem in fiscal aid cases, could recovery as a legal consequence of the finding of incompatible aid as such be put into question. This does not seem to be the case. In particular, the issues arising from the inadequacy of national procedural law have to be addressed by adjustments to the legal framework of the Member State in question. If at all, the requirements for absolute impossibility may be too strict, which means that recovery should be excluded more easily on a case-by-case basis.

[C] Potential Counter-Arguments Not Convincing

The contributions discussed in this section criticize recovery in tax cases as such and propose modifications to the applicable legal regime of fiscal State aid law. However, arguments that are derived from national constitutional law standards [1] or that are based on alleged conceptual shortcomings of State aid law do not put into question recovery as such [2].

[1] Retroactive Recovery of Fiscal Aid Schemes in Light of the Principle of Legality?

Several authors have brought forward arguments against recovery derived from the principle of legality of taxation – as well as related principles, such as the principle of legal certainty and the principle of protection of legitimate expectation.[884] The latter two principles will be discussed in more detail as case-by-case limits to recovery deriving from general principles of EU law.[885] By contrast, the criticism related to the principle of legality and retroactivity concerns an assumed structural issue. It is mainly rooted in a national constitutional law understanding of the principle. Ultimately, however, the principle of legality does not appear to pose an obstacle to recovery in the majority of cases.

---

881. E.g., Case T-500/12 *Ryanair v. Commission* EU:T:2015:73, paras 114ff.
882. *See* on the question of whether it can play a role in private enforcement Bruc, *supra* n. 242, at 54.
883. Joined Cases C-164 and 165/15 P *Aer Lingus and Ryanair*, paras 89ff. *See* Grith Skovgaard Olykke, *The Passing-on Defence Catapulted out of State Aid Law* 16 EStAL 93, 96 (2017) for the advantages of such approach. Critical as the amount of aid may exceed the benefit to the beneficiary Lever, *supra* n. 116, at 7.
884. Maitrot de la Motte, *supra* n. 171, at 75ff.; Matsos, *supra* n. 825, at 491ff.
885. *See* Ch. 6 *infra*.

The principle of legality is a general principle of EU law.[886] In the area of taxation, the principle requires that taxation take place on the basis of law. The principle is a fundamental democratic principle.[887] It was only recently acknowledged as a general principle of EU law in the area of taxation.[888] The judgment of the CJEU in *Fiat* shows that the principle might be gaining significance for fiscal State aid law. In its judgment, the CJEU stated the following in the context of its assessment of the existence of aid:

> This finding is an expression of the *principle of legality of taxation*, which forms part of the legal order of the European Union as a general principle of law, requiring that *any obligation to pay a tax and all the essential elements defining the substantive features thereof must be provided for by law, the taxable person having to be in a position to foresee and calculate the amount of tax due and determine the point at which it becomes payable* (see, to that effect, judgment of 8 May 2019, Związek Gmin Zagłębia Miedziowego, C-566/17, EU:C:2019:390, paragraph 39).[889]

This would appear to preclude retroactive tax legislation. Limits on retroactivity are also derived from the principle of legal certainty under EU law.[890]

Yet as far as can be seen, the CJEU has thus far not shown any willingness to invoke the principle of legality or its link with retroactivity as a limit to recovery under Article 16 of Procedural Regulation 2015/1589. It is presumably unlikely to do so as this would put recovery as a whole into question, which by its very nature is retroactive.[891]

In fact, in an older judgment and in an attempt to address concerns on retroactivity, the CJEU held that recovery in fiscal aid matters does not necessarily have to take the form of a retroactive tax, which would be absolutely impossible to enforce in light of the principles of EU law. The Member State would merely have to make sure that the beneficiary of aid pays an amount that corresponds to the advantage that had been granted by the Member State.[892] The determination of whether the recovered amount is a tax or whether it has a character of its own thus appears to be left to the implementing Member State.[893] However, the clarification that the CJEU made in this case appears to be based on a formality and is not necessarily sufficient to address the concerns that have been brought forward in the scholarly literature.

For example, AG Kokott argues that for abstract tax measures, recovery through subsequent retroactive taxation would be problematic in light of the constitutional law requirement of a legal basis for taxation.[894] In particular, she contends that Article 16 of Procedural Regulation 2015/1589 would not be sufficiently precise to serve as a basis

886. Case C-566/17 *Związek Gmin Zagłębia Miedziowego* EU:C:2019:390, para. 39.
887. Kokott & Pistone, *supra* n. 111, at 83f.
888. Case C-566/17 *Związek Gmin Zagłębia Miedziowego*, para. 39. Outside of tax law, e.g., Case C-46/87 *Hoechst v. Commission* EU:C:1989:337, para. 19.
889. Joined Cases C-885 and 898/19 P *Fiat*, para. 97; emphasis added by the author.
890. *See* Kokott, *Steuerrecht*, *supra* n. 20, at §2, paras 49ff.
891. *See* Ch. §5.01[A] *supra* on the purpose of recovery.
892. Case C-183/91 *Commission v. Greece*, para. 17.
893. Pizzonia, *supra* n. 826, at 187f. on the implications of either of these options with further references for the Italian situation.
894. Juliane Kokott, *Der EuGH als Garant fairen Steuerwettbewerbs* 6 ISR 395, 400f. (2017); Kokott, *Steuerrecht und unionsrechtlicher Beihilfebegriff*, *supra* n. 164, at 555ff.

for such retroactive taxation.[895] *Krumm* contends that the retroactive recovery of fiscal aid schemes would generally be justified, since the risk of a misapplication of a norm also lies with the taxpayer in other situations. Yet this would require that the taxpayer could detect the necessity of a notification. Otherwise, (abstract) legitimate expectations would have to be protected on grounds of the legislative provisions in question.[896]

Matsos makes out several constitutional law particularities of taxation. Articles 107f. TFEU would not contain a sufficient legal basis to impose taxes, which would lead to an infringement of the principle of legality of tax. He also points to the fact that neither the Commission nor the CJEU qualify as legislative bodies. There would also be an infringement of the prohibition of retroactive taxation.[897] Maitrot de la Motte holds that recovery would be problematic in light of the principle of 'no taxation without representation'. The legislator as the democratic representative of the taxpayer never meant to levy the recovered tax. Instead, this taxation would be imposed upon the Member State by the Commission or a Court through the recovery order.[898]

Two different groups of arguments against the retroactive recovery of fiscal aid schemes can be identified from this. While some commentators focus on the objective dimension of the principle of legality, others criticize the retroactivity of recovery in light of the expectations of individuals. The transferability of these arguments from national constitutional law to European law has to be examined in turn.

First, the arguments derived from the objective dimension of the principle of legality are not necessarily convincing. The case law of the CJEU shows that recovery is instituted under national law. This means that while the obligation of recovery derives directly from the Treaties, the basis for the levying of the recovered tax is nevertheless national law. It is true that the wording of the national law granting the tax benefit in question has to be disregarded to institute recovery. However, this does not necessarily mean that there is an infringement of the principle of legality. This is because the point of departure in the assessment of selectivity is always the reference system of taxation, i.e., the initial decision of the Member State, as to what (or who) it wants to tax. The State aid problem in cases of de jure-selectivity arises from the fact that the Member State failed to implement its own fundamental charging decision in an internally consistent manner.[899] It could then be argued that State aid law does not impose retroactive taxation that was never intended by the Member State, but merely holds the legislator to its own standards. This would mean that the democratic principle of 'no taxation without representation' is not necessarily infringed upon.

Admittedly, this argument only applies for de jure-selectivity, which tests for internal consistency. In cases of de facto-selectivity, the applicable benchmark does not derive from domestic law. However, in any case, as laid out above, the notion of de facto-selectivity is problematic from a tax sovereignty perspective and should only be

895. Kokott, *Tax Harmonisation*, *supra* n. 102, at 467.
896. Krumm, *supra* n. 173, at 582ff.
897. Matsos, *supra* n. 825, at 493ff.
898. Maitrot de la Motte, *supra* n. 171, at 77.
899. *See* Ch. 3 *supra*.

applied in exceptional cases.[900] Even when it is applicable, there may be a rare case of an absolute impossibility of recovery, since the beneficiaries of aid may not be identifiable.[901]

Second, it also appears doubtful whether the link with the principle of protection legitimate expectation as a subjective dimension of the principle of legality would be plausible under European law. To demonstrate the differences, we first have to briefly lay out the German approach. Under German constitutional law, the prohibition of retroactive legislation is derived from the principle of protection of legitimate expectation as well as the principle of legal certainty.[902] The German case law acknowledges a protection of the legitimate expectation in the reliability and predictability of the legal order. In particular, this comprises a protection of the expectation that laws will remain valid.[903] The German *Bundesverfassungsgericht* has established a link with the separation of powers. As soon as a law has left the 'sphere' of the legislator, it is for the judiciary to interpret and the legislator can only intervene in exceptional cases or for the present or future.[904] 'True retroactivity' (*echte Rückwirkung* (as opposed to retroactivity, which attaches a legal consequence to constellations that have begun in the past but have not yet ended)) is generally prohibited. There are, however, some narrow exceptions. This is the case, where there are imperative overriding reasons of public interest that are essentially typologies of an exceptional lack of legitimate expectation in the status quo of the legal order.[905] Examples are constellations, where the legal situation was unclear and confusing and the situation is cleared up through the change[906] or where the individual had to anticipate the rule at a point in time, for which the retroactive provision changes the legal situation.[907]

The German understanding amounts to a very wide notion of the protection of legitimate expectations since legal provisions are understood as a source thereof. Even under German constitutional law, however, it is questionable whether retroactivity would be precluded. It has been pointed out that the Federal Financial Court has in the past held that the necessity to remedy an infringement of State aid law constitutes an overriding reason, which may justify true retroactivity under German constitutional law.[908] Related to this, one may wonder whether the expectation in the continuity of internally inconsistent laws is truly *legitimate*. As laid out above, the *Bundesverfassungsgericht* has accepted that retroactivity may be permissible, where the legal

900. *See* Ch. §4.01 *supra*.
901. *See* Ch. §5.01[B] *supra*.
902. BVerfG, Cases 2 BvR 499/74 and 1073/75, BVerfGE 45, 142, para. 64; Decision of 18 July 2012, of 17 December 2013, Case 1 BvL 5/08, BVerfGE 135, 1, para. 63.
903. BVerfG, Case 1 BvF 1/94, BVerfGE 101, 239, para. 105; Hans Dieter Jarass, *GG Art. 20*, in Jarass & Pieroth (eds), Grundgesetz für die Bundesrepublik Deutschland, para. 94 (17th edn 2022).
904. BVerfG, Case 1 BvL 5/08. BVerfGE 135, 1, para. 54.
905. *See, e.g.*, Jarass, *Art. 20*, *supra* n. 903, at paras 100ff. for further examples from the case law of the *BVerfG*.
906. BVerfG, Cases 1 BvR 2530/05, 1 BvL 11/06, 1 BvL 12/06, 1 BVL 13/06, BVerfGE 126, 369, para. 71; Case 2 BvL 5/10, BVerfGE 131, 20, para. 77; Case 1 BvL 5/08. BVerfGE 135, 1, para. 62.
907. BVerfG, Cases 1 BvR 1314/12, 1 BvR 1630/12, 1 BvR 1694/13, 1 BvR 1874/13, BVerfGE 145, 20, para. 199.
908. Schnitger, *supra* n. 41, at 428 with reference to *Bundesfinanzhof*, Case III R 35/95, BFHE 193, 204.

situation is unclear. A similar argument could potentially be made for internally inconsistent laws.

Admittedly, European law also only considers retroactivity permissible under strict conditions, one of which is that the legitimate expectations of the affected persons are respected.[909] However, it has to be seen that the principle of protection of legitimate expectation under European law has a significantly more restricted ambit than under German constitutional law. For one, the principle can only be invoked for acts of EU institutions. Legitimate expectations may, for example, derive from EU legislative acts.[910] By contrast, a mere abstract protection of expectations in the continuity of the legal order of Member States does not appear to exist under European law.[911] As far as can be seen, European law also does not recognize an increased standard of protection for legislative acts as opposed to administrative acts. The 'technique' of granting aid, i.e., the question of whether the aid derives from an administrative act or an underlying legislative provision is and should not be relevant. This holds all the more true since such techniques can vary significantly among Member States.

Therefore, while it is true that retroactive recovery may lead to frictions under national constitutional law, these concerns are not necessarily transferrable to European law and thus do not warrant a modification of the legal consequence of taxation from a legal point of view.

[2] Conceptual Shortcomings in the Concept of Recovery?

Others have criticized perceived shortcomings in the structure of State aid law and in particular recovery as applied to tax measures. The arguments and suggestions laid out in this section appear to aim at a general modification of the legal consequences of State aid law or at least for the area of taxation. In our view, a modification of the legal consequence of recovery for structural reasons is not warranted. We will address the three main points of criticism, namely that recovery could not achieve its purpose of eliminating the distortion of competition in fiscal aid cases [a], that recovery would not lead to a realistic *status quo ante* [b], and that the taxpayer would be the only 'victim' of State aid law, even though they are not the ones to commit the infringement, and that the Member States receives the revenue from recovery [c].

[a] Prevention of Distortive Effects Through Recovery Only for Positive Aid

It has been questioned whether the recovery of fiscal aid schemes for a period of ten years can achieve its purpose and remedy the distortion of competition. The tax assessment regularly takes place after the underlying business decisions have been made. Recovery would then primarily serve to penalize Member States' fiscal policy at

909. Tridimas, *supra* n. 121, at 254.
910. *Ibid.*, at 273ff.
911. Kokott, *Steuerrecht*, *supra* n. 20, at §2, para. 52.

the expense of taxpayers. By contrast, for direct subsidies, swift recovery might still forestall the effect on trade as such subsidies are generally approved before the incentivized action takes place.[912] Consequently, tax measures that infringe upon State aid law should only have to be repealed for the future.[913]

In our view, however, such understanding is not compatible with the purpose of recovery. While this purpose was initially laid down as the elimination of the infringement of the Treaties,[914] it is now clear that the purpose of recovery is to restore the previous situation and thereby eliminate the distortion of competition caused by the advantage that was granted to the beneficiary undertaking by the Member State in question.[915]

For example, in the judgment in *Germany v. Commission*, the CJEU held:

> Removing unlawful aid by means of recovery is the *logical consequence* of a finding that it is unlawful and seeks to re-establish the previous situation [...]. By repaying the aid, the recipient forfeits the advantage which it had enjoyed over its competitors on the market, and the situation prior to payment of the aid is restored [...]. Consequently, the main purpose of the repayment of unlawfully paid State aid is to eliminate the distortion of competition caused by the competitive advantage afforded by the unlawful aid.[916]

The argument brought forward in the literature is based on a different understanding of the purpose of recovery. It assumes that the effects of State aid can never be reversed and thus the assumed purpose of recovery could never be achieved, where the underlying transactions or business decisions are no longer reversible. In fact, if this argument was valid, one could also reject an application of the fundamental freedoms or other iterations of the general principle of equality for the same reason. In all these cases, the unequal treatment is removed retroactively. This does not appear convincing. Instead, it is merely necessary to retroactively eliminate the selective advantage and as a result treat every economic actor equally, where the unequal treatment was distortive.

There is furthermore no reason to privilege the recipient of fiscal aid as compared to beneficiaries of positive subsidies. If at all, the particularities of fiscal aid should play a role in the context of the protection of legitimate expectations.

---

912. Report of the Advisory Board to the Federal Ministry of Finance, 'Tax benefits and EU state aid control: The problem of and approaches to resolving the conflict of jurisdiction with fiscal autonomy' (2017) https://www.bundesfinanzministerium.de/Content/EN/Standardartikel/Ministry/Advisory_Board/2018-02-07-tax-benefits-and-eu-state-aid-control-download.pdf;jsessionid=EFE3C2242E5EF90FE729347D727DA3D3?__blob=publicationFile&v=2, p. 35.
913. *Ibid.*, at 37.
914. Case 70/72 *Commission v. Germany*, para. 13. In this judgment, the CJEU held that the purpose of the treaties was (also) to avoid infringements of the treaties, justifying recovery.
915. Case C-142/87 *Belgium v. Commission*, para. 66; Joined Cases C-278 to 280/92 *Spain v. Commission*, para. 75; Case C-348/93 *Commission v. Italy*, para. 23; Case C-24/95 *Alcan Deutschland*, para. 23; Joined Cases C-164 and 165-715 P *Aer Lingus and Ryanair*, para. 89f.
916. Case C-277/00 *Germany v. Commission*, paras 74ff.; emphasis added by the author.

[b] Recovery Does Not Recreate Realistic Status Quo Ante

The scholarly literature has furthermore criticized the result of recovery for tax measures since it would not amount to the *status quo ante.* Undertakings would often only take certain business decisions due to the availability of the measure at issue. The result of recovery would thus amount to a purely hypothetical situation. This would particularly hold true since State aid law has to be seen in the context of tax competition between Member States. Tax revenue may never have accrued in the Member State that granted the aid in the absence of the aid measure.[917]

Indeed, this observation may have some merit for MNEs that are relatively mobile in their choice of investment location. Yet this does not put into question the notion of recovery. The CJEU had early on addressed this point of contention in its judgment in *Unicredito Italiano.*[918] The case dealt with income tax reductions granted to banks which merged or engaged in similar restructuring for five years for profits that were placed in a special reserve that could not be distributed for three years. These profits could not exceed 1.2% of the difference between credits and debits of the post-merger bank and the sum of credits and debits of the largest pre-merger bank. The CJEU delivered the judgment in response to a reference for a preliminary ruling in the course of proceedings between Unicredito Italiano as the beneficiary of aid and the Revenue Agency Genoa 1 Office. Unicredito Italiano had initially transferred the alleged aid but then requested reimbursement.[919] In the context of the question of whether the recovery order infringed upon the principle of proportionality, the CJEU addressed whether recovery would merely lead to an approximation of a purely hypothetical situation:

> It would not be right to determine the amounts to be repaid in the light of various operations which could have been implemented by the undertakings if they had not opted for the type of operation which was coupled with the aid. That choice was made in the knowledge of the risk of recovery of aid granted contrary to the procedure laid down in Article 88(3) EC. Those undertakings could have avoided that risk by opting immediately for operations structured in other ways. *In addition, in circumstances such as those in the case in the main proceedings, reestablishing the status quo ante means returning, as far as possible, to the situation which would have prevailed if the operations at issue had been carried out without the tax reduction. That does not imply reconstructing past events differently on the basis of hypothetical elements such as the choices, often numerous, which could have been made by the operators concerned, since the choices actually made with the aid might prove to be irreversible.*[920]

917. In this vein: Giraud & Petit, *Tax Rulings and State Aid Qualification, supra* n. 126, at 236ff. albeit in the context of the assessment of whether the criterion of state resources pursuant to Art. 107(1) TFEU is met.
918. Case C-148/04 *Unicredito Italiano.*
919. *Ibid.*, paras 3ff. for a description of the facts of the case.
920. *Ibid.*, paras 114ff.; emphasis added by the author.

This aspect was again raised in the CJEU's judgment in *Aer Lingus and Ryanair*, where the statement from *Unicredito Italiano* that recovery does not imply reconstructing past events differently on the basis of hypothetical events was taken up.[921] In its judgment, the CJEU linked the question of recovery to the quantification of the advantage and thus declared irrelevant any alternative business decisions or the benefits received from the aid:

> It follows, as the Advocate General observed, in essence, in point 62 of his Opinion, that recovery of such aid entails the restitution of the advantage procured by the aid for the recipient, not the restitution of any economic benefit the recipient may have enjoyed as a result of exploiting the advantage. That benefit may not be the same as the advantage constituting the aid and there may indeed be no such benefit, but that cannot justify any failure to recover that aid or the recovery of a different sum from that constituting the advantage procured by the unlawful aid in question.[922]

The CJEU's arguments in these judgments very much resemble those made in the context of the identification of the advantage, where it has become clear that State aid law only aims at the elimination of the immediate monetary advantage. Whether the undertaking has derived any further benefit therefrom or whether it has inversely passed on the advantage to a third person is irrelevant.[923]

Of course, the result after recovery is not a reliable approximation of a market-based outcome. Such reconstruction will most often be impossible. However, this does not imply that there should be no recovery. Disregarding substitution effects and other types of counterfactuals is well in line with the basic logic of State aid law since it only seeks to retroactively eliminate the immediate unequal treatment that leads to distortions. The business decisions underlying the tax treatment have to be treated as a given.

[c] Taxpayer as the Only Victim and Member State Profits from Recovery

Others have criticized a perceived structural shortcoming of recovery in State aid law. The taxpayer would be the only 'victim' of the enforcement, while the Member State profits from recovery, even though it infringes upon State aid law. Both points ultimately fail to convince.

As to the first aspect, Maitrot de la Motte criticizes that it is solely the taxpayer who bears the consequences of the granting of the advantage, who, however, often acts in good faith.[924] Yet imposing the financial burden on the taxpayer is warranted as there would otherwise be a risk of an enforcement deficit for structural reasons. Member States have a double role of granting the aid and being involved in enforcement. They thus often have no interest in enforcement. By contrast, the Commission cannot comprehensively monitor Member States' tax laws for infringements of State

921. Joined Cases C-164 and 165/15 P *Aer Lingus and Ryanair*, para. 91.
922. *Ibid.*, para. 92.
923. *See* Ch. §2.02 *supra*.
924. Maitrot de la Motte, *supra* n. 171, at 85f. Similarly Lever, *supra* n. 116, at 6.

aid law. If it were not for recovery, the issues of collusion and aggressive tax competition between Member States through State aid would be exacerbated. From the perspective of competitors and competition as a whole, eliminating the distortion only for the future as a rule does not seem convincing either. The advantage has to be withdrawn for the past. Furthermore, the purpose of recovery is not only an elimination of the distortion for the past but also deterrence. This speaks for a retroactive effect of State aid law through recovery as an efficient deterrent, provided there is a sufficient degree of legal certainty as to the ambit of State aid law.[925]

One may, however, indeed wonder whether the amount to be recovered should be allocated to the Member State or whether the Member State should somehow be penalized. In this context, some contributions have highlighted the incentives for Member States. Under the current system, Member States would not have to fear negative consequences for infringements of State aid law. A modification of the legal consequences would be warranted de lege ferenda.[926]

Others have emphasized the problem of moral hazard: Where a Member State grants aid without prior notification, one of two outcomes that are both beneficial for the Member State would arise: Either the Commission does not tackle a measure or the Member State receives the recovered amounts. Thus, recovery should be implemented only in the relationship between the Member State and the EU. To prevent problematic incentives, the Member State should de lege ferenda be subject to an obligation to pay, be it as a sanction, be it in the form of recovery.[927]

It has also been pointed out that recovery may promote hypocrisy as State aid could be granted for political purposes before elections, which would later on be recovered based on European law. Member States should therefore have to pay a lump sum each time they violate Article 108 TFEU.[928]

These concerns may indeed be valid where the Member State knowingly accepts the risk of an infringement of State aid law. However, a more realistic perspective might be that Member States often actively seek to prevent enforcement of State aid law by the Commission. Recovery not only frustrates the original purposes of the aid but it can also be highly detrimental to the investment climate in a Member State. This is evidenced by the vehement resistance of Luxembourg and Ireland against the Commission decisions in the tax ruling cases.

If at all, and so as not to hinder the effectiveness of State aid control, the Member State should bear a financial burden in addition to the taxpayer, as this would not be problematic in light of the objective of recovery.[929] Infringement proceedings do not

925. Similarly Krumm, *supra* n. 173, at 611, who, however, contends that this distribution of risks would not be justified, where the Member State could not have foreseen the necessity for notification.
926. Reich, *supra* n. 174, at, 232ff.
927. Martini, *supra* n. 119, at 107, 110f. Similarly as to the problem of moral hazard: Brandau et al., *supra* n. 163, at 1187; Lever, *supra* n. 116, at 7 dubs this a 'win-win position' for the Member State; Raymond Luja, *Will the EU's State Aid Regime Survive BEPS?* BTR 379, 383 (2015).
928. Maitrot de la Motte, *supra* n. 171, at 88.
929. *See* Ch. §5.01[A] *supra*.

seem a viable approach to achieve this result. Once recovery has been implemented, no more infringement can be tackled.[930]

In light of the argument that taxpayers often act in good faith, awarding the beneficiaries of aid damages for infringements of State aid law could be considered. They would effectively shift the financial burden from the taxpayer to the Member State. Beneficiaries of aid may, for example, envisage an action for damages on grounds of an infringement of the principle of protection of legitimate expectation. There is some case law on this. Yet it has been found that such actions rarely succeed.[931] The CJEU has in principle recognized that although damages for the beneficiary of aid and aid itself differ fundamentally,[932] damages cannot be awarded, where they would substitute the unlawful aid. The effet utile of Article 108(3), (3) TFEU as well as the obligation to recover aid as laid out above would otherwise be undermined.[933] Moreover, the relevant European law standard for the protection of legitimate expectations would be applicable.[934] Thus, if there was no infringement of this standard, such action on grounds of EU law cannot be successful.[935] However, where there was indeed such infringement, recovery would be excluded in any case. The same has to hold true for actions under national law. Only where the beneficiary's claim – if successful – would not lead to a substitution of the aid itself, could a national court award damages.[936] This shows that the question of whether the taxpayer acted in good faith should only be considered on a case-by-case basis under Article 16(1) of Procedural Regulation 2015/1589.

Finally, others have suggested that the recovered amounts could be assigned to the EU or in cases of unfair tax competition to the budget of the State from which investment, jobs and/or consumption were distracted.[937] This could be implemented through DTCs, the Multilateral Instrument or a Regulation on the duty to forward recovered aid on grounds of Article 109 TFEU.[938]

Such an approach is not convincing. First, investment decisions are highly complex. It would be close to impossible to exactly determine which other Member State investment was diverted from – and to which extent – by means of a tax benefit.[939] Investment decisions can depend on a variety of factors that are not purely tax-related. The proposed solution appears to presume that there is exactly one location where the entire investment would have been located in the absence of the tax benefit.

930. Reich, *supra* n. 174, at 235f.
931. Joanna Goyder & Margot Dons, *Damages Claims Based on State Aid Law Infringements* 16 EStAL 418, 419 (2017) https://doi.org/10.21552/estal/2017/3/10.
932. Joined Cases C-106 to 120/87 *Asteris and Others v. Greece* EU:C:1988:457.
933. Bacon, *European Union Law of State Aid, supra* n. 20, at para. 20.34.
934. *See* on the relationship between damages and the principle of protection of legitimate expectation also European Commission, 'Study on the enforcement of State aid rules and decisions be national courts' [2019] https://ec.europa.eu/competition/publications/reports/kd0219428enn.pdf, p. 73.
935. *See* Case C-672/13 *OTP Bank*, paras 77f.
936. *See* Goyder & Dons, *supra* n. 931, at 429 for some examples in national case law.
937. Kube et al., *supra* n. 171, at 247, 257; Reich, *supra* n. 174, at 234; Brandau et al., *supra* n. 163, at 1187.
938. Kube et al., *supra* n. 171, at 257.
939. Also sceptical: Reich, *supra* n. 174, at 235.

This does not appear plausible. Where would this location be? Who would have to prove this and how could the entity in question do so? An attempt at retracing alternative investment locations would moreover require comprehensive cooperation from the beneficiaries, which does not appear plausible. There is often no 'natural' location of income in an increasingly globalized economy. Finally, tax benefits may not change investment decisions at all.

Second, it is unclear which tax treatment should be applied to the recovered tax. Assuming the level of tax in this alternative location was lower than in the Member State that had granted the aid, it does not appear justified to have the former profit from the higher tax level in the other Member State. If the level of tax in the location from where the revenue had been diverted was relevant, it would be necessary to calculate a tax level based on hypothetical events.

Third, where the investment would have been allocated to a third country instead of another Member State, it is barely conceivable that the recovered tax would be allocated to this country. Inversely, however, the resulting different treatment of the two constellations (investment diverted from another Member State versus from a third country) also does not appear plausible.

The suggestion that the recovered tax could be allocated to the EU budget or all other Member States employing an allocation formula does not appear convincing either. It goes against the purpose of recovery, which is meant to restore the situation which would have existed had the aid not been granted. State aid law is an instrument of competition law. Recovery should not be understood as a means to penalize Member States or beneficiaries.[940]

Admittedly, this purpose of recovery is in contrast to other areas of EU competition law, where the revenue of fines imposed on undertakings in the context of public enforcement is allocated to the budget of the EU. Fines in areas aside from State aid law are linked to aspects, such as the severity and the duration of the infringement.[941] However, it has to be seen that Member States play a different role in competition law aside from State aid law. Allocating the revenue from fines or penalties to a Member State is not convincing as the money would never have accrued to the Member State in the first place. Fines thus have a completely different function than recovery. They do not seek to re-establish competition but aim at punishment and deterrence.[942] The function of re-establishing competition is assigned to private enforcement, which plays a more prominent role than in State aid law. Competitors or other private actors that have been harmed by the breach can claim the damages they have suffered in front of national courts, which will then (conceptually) lead to an approximation to the outcome had there been no infringement of competition law.

940. Case C-75/97 *Belgium v. Commission*, para. 65; Commission Notice on the recovery, *supra* n. 875, at para. 26.
941. *See* Art. 24(2) & (3) of Council Regulation (EC) No. 1/2003 of 16 December 2002 on the implementation of the rules on competition laid down in Articles 81 and 82 of the treaty [2003] OJ L 1/1, last amended by Council Regulation (EC) No. 487/2009 of 25 May 2009 [2009] OJ L 148/1.
942. Carsten Nowak, *VerfVO Art. 23 Geldbußen*, in Loewenheim et al. (eds), Kartellrecht, paras 2ff. (4th edn 2020).

If the Member State is to bear a financial burden from an infringement of State aid law, an imposition of additional sanctions should be considered instead.[943] This could be the case where the Member State knowingly accepts the risk of subsequent recovery to be able to engage in tax competition in the short run. The advantage is that the sanctions could be tailored to the severity of the infringement of State aid law.

[D] Modification of the Legal Consequences of Recovery

The above considerations have shown that a general modification of the legal consequences of State aid law is not convincing or desirable. Nevertheless, recovery may in some cases not be appropriate or necessary. Article 16(1) of Procedural Regulation 2015/1589 leads to an exclusion of recovery on a case-by-case basis, where there would otherwise be an infringement of a general principle of EU law.[944] By contrast, the approaches discussed in this chapter would set in at an earlier stage. The following section will discuss two approaches. A procedural solution based on the temporal limitation of judgments of the CJEU, which would effectively prevent recovery for the past does not appear to be viable [1]. By contrast, the legal consequence of the finding of aid may in very specific constellations not be recovery, but a reimbursement of tax. Where the Commission decides that a tax exemption is incompatible with the internal market, there appear to be recent tendencies to allow the Member State to eliminate the infringement by retroactively abolishing the tax as a whole or at least the unequal treatment therein through reimbursement as an alternative to recovery [2].

[1] Procedural Solution Not Necessary

AG Kokott discusses the case law according to which the temporal effects of a judgment of the CJEU can be limited in exceptional cases, where a certain interpretation of EU law was not foreseeable, but ultimately convincingly rejects this approach in the constellations discussed here.[945] This approach would mean that while recovery is still the 'logical consequence' of an infringement of State aid law, it could not be implemented for the past. She points out that there would be no obligation to levy tax due to Member States' tax sovereignty for the future.[946] In its judgment in *Meilicke and others*, the CJEU had held the following:

> It is only *exceptionally* that, in application of a *general principle of legal certainty* which is inherent in the Community legal order, the Court may decide to *restrict*

943. Similarly Maitrot de la Motte, *supra* n. 171, at 88, Temple Lang, *EU State Aid Rules*, *supra* n. 139, at 441.
944. *See* Ch. 6 *infra*.
945. Kokott, *Steuerrecht und unionsrechtlicher Beihilfebegriff*, *supra* n. 164, at 558f. and Kokott, *Steuerrecht*, *supra* n. 20, at §3, paras 235f., 241 with reference to Case C-292/04 *Meilicke and others* EU:C:2007:132, paras 38ff.
946. Kokott, *Steuerrecht und unionsrechtlicher Beihilfebegriff*, *supra* n. 164, at 558f.

> *the right to rely upon a provision,* which it has interpreted, with a view to calling in question legal relations established in good faith [...] In addition, as the Court has consistently held, such a restriction may be allowed *only in the actual judgment ruling upon the interpretation sought* [...] Indeed, there must necessarily be a *single occasion* when a decision is made on the temporal effects of the requested interpretation, which the Court gives of a provision of Community law. In that regard, the principle that a restriction may be allowed only in the actual judgment ruling upon that interpretation guarantees the *equal treatment* of the Member States and of other persons subject to Community law, under that law, fulfilling, at the same time, the requirements arising from the principle of legal certainty.[947]

Transferring this approach to State aid law would imply that when the CJEU first interprets a provision in a certain manner, the principle of legal certainty may require a temporal limitation of the legal consequences of the judgment.

A number of objections can be raised against transferring this case law to fiscal State aid law. AG Kokott points to the incompatibility with the considerations underlying State aid law. The case law was developed for the reverse constellation. It was meant to protect the Member State from the ramifications of a judgment of the CJEU.[948] While mere substantial financial ramifications do not suffice,[949] they can in exceptional cases lead to an exclusion of the retroactive effect of a judgment where a certain interpretation of EU law was not foreseeable for the Member State.[950] By contrast, in State aid law, it is the beneficiary of aid that may have to be protected against unforeseeable developments of State aid law. The Member State on the other hand receives the recovered sums and thus at least does not suffer financial ramifications.[951]

Moreover, according to Article 16(1) of Procedural Regulation 2015/1589, the Commission shall not order recovery, where this would be contrary to a general principle of EU law, of which the principle of legal certainty is an example. Thus, where a Commission decision does not take into account the general principles of EU law, it is void in any case. The procedural solution similarly seeks to foster legal certainty. If both solutions aim at preventing breaches of the principle of legal certainty, there would appear to be no room for a procedural solution.

947. Case C-292/04 *Meilicke and others*, paras 35ff.; emphasis added by the author.
948. *See, e.g.*, Joined Cases C-197 and 252/94 *Bautiaa and Société française maritime v. Directeurs des services fiscaux des Landes and du Finistère* EU:C:1996:47, para. 55, where the Court referred to the protection of taxpayer rights under EU law as a reason to rule out such limitation.
949. E.g., Joined Cases C-367 to 377/93 *Roder and Others v. Inspecteur der Invorrechten en Accijnzen* EU:C:1995:261, para. 48; Joined Cases C-197 and 252/94 *Bautiaa and Société française maritime*, para. 55; Case C-137/94, *The Queen v. Secretary of State for Health, ex parte Richardson* EU:C:1995:342, para. 37.
950. *See* in particular Case C-200/90 *Dansk Denkavit and Poulsen Trading v. Skatteministeriet* EU:C:1992:152, paras 20ff.
951. Kokott, *Steuerrecht, supra* n. 20, at §3, para. 241.

[2] *Remedying the Breach of State Aid Law through a Redefinition of Recovery Based on a Commission Decision*

In its decision on the Hungarian advertising tax, the Commission ordered recovery.[952] However, in the elaborations on recovery – to which Article 4 of the Decision explicitly refers – the Commission allowed for two different ways of eliminating the distortion. Hungary could either recover the aid by retroactively subjecting all undertakings to a single tax rate or it could retroactively abolish the advertising tax as of the date of its entry into force.[953] These two options were confirmed in an Order of the President of the General Court, which concerned Hungary's application for the suspension of operation of the Commission decision.[954] The Commission decision was later annulled by the General Court, which held that there was no selective advantage.[955] The judgment was confirmed by the CJEU.[956] Nevertheless, the elaborations on recovery were not touched upon by the judgments and may very well continue to stand.

The retroactive abolishment of such tax amounts to an extension of the advantage to all economic actors and thus eliminates the aid. The same result could in some cases be achieved by extending the tax benefit to only the extent that is required to eliminate selectivity, for example, because the derogation from the reference system would then be justified in the third step. The result would be a partial refund of tax to only some undertakings.[957] The question is then whether this is permissible from an EU law point of view. Otherwise, such modification of the legal consequences of European State aid law could only be considered de lege ferenda.

AG Kokott objects that according to the case law of the CJEU, the illegality of State aid has no impact on the legality of the tax itself.[958] Doing away with the tax itself through a refund to all actors would contradict this case law. It would go against the considerations underlying Article 108(3), (3) TFEU[959] as well as the standing case law, which calls for recovery, i.e., a removal of the advantage.[960] Indeed, CJEU has so far not explicitly condoned an approach, under which recovery can be implemented through a refund of tax following a negative Commission decision.

In our view, these concerns do not pose a major obstacle, however. This is because the choice of the recovery method would be up to the Member State. The decision to implement recovery through a refund of the tax would not be an emanation

952. *See* Art. 4(1) of Commission Decision (EU) 2017/329 of 4 November 2016 on the measure SA.39235 implemented by Hungary on the taxation of advertisement turnover [2017] OJ L 49/36. *See* on this case already Chs §3.02[C], [2]; [D] and §4.02 *supra*.
953. *Ibid.*, paras 91, 96.
954. Order of the President of the General Court, Case T-20/17 R *Hungary v. Commission* EU:T:2017:203, para. 15.
955. Case T-20/17 *Hungary v. Commission*.
956. Case C-596/19 P *Commission v. Hungary*.
957. *See* on the parallel constellation for the relationship between the fundamental freedoms and fiscal State aid law: Ismer & Piotrowski, *Relationship of Fiscal State Aid and the Fundamental Freedoms*, *supra* n. 164.
958. Kokott, *Steuerrecht und unionsrechtlicher Beihilfebegriff*, *supra* n. 164, at 558.
959. Kokott, *Steuerrecht*, *supra* n. 20, at §3 para. 234.
960. Kokott, *Steuerrecht und unionsrechtlicher Beihilfebegriff*, *supra* n. 164, at 557.

of the illegality of the tax from an EU law point of view. Instead, the Member State could choose to refund the tax if its domestic law allows for such approach. The legislator would likely have to be involved in such retroactive change or abolition of the law. Since this change is not detrimental to any taxpayer, there are no issues related to the retroactivity of the change or the protection of legitimate expectation. Alternatively, the Member State may decide to implement the decision through recovery in the way it is conventionally understood if for whatever reason doing away with the aid through retroactive abolition is not an option.

The case law that those liable to pay a charge cannot rely on the argument that the exemption enjoyed by others constitutes State aid in order to avoid payment of that charge or obtain reimbursement is not an obstacle either. This case law is based on the reasoning that the fact that a tax contains an aid element does not invalidate the entire tax and limits the scope of action of national courts in the assessment stage. In practice, it limits the options for competitors to seek an elimination of the infringement of State aid law. Yet the considerations underlying Article 108(3), (3) TFEU do not appear to pose a problem here. While the decision of the CJEU in *Laboratoires Boiron* concerned the role of the national court in the assessment stage, this case shows that a refund of tax on grounds following a breach of State aid law is not excluded per se. In this judgment, the CJEU had held that a refund on grounds of State aid law claimed by an undertaking in front of a national court was possible for parafiscal levies. In this specific constellation, there would have been no danger that a refund could be in circumvention of Article 108(3), (3) TFEU.[961]

At least a retroactive elimination of a tax as a whole would never be problematic with a view to Article 108(3), (3) TFEU as non-taxation of all actors cannot constitute State aid. The principle of equality does not appear to pose an obstacle either since the elimination of the tax as a whole would eliminate any unequal treatment. Where the extension of the advantage through a refund of tax would still involve an unequal treatment, this approach would be ruled out in any case, since there would otherwise (likely)[962] be an infringement of Article 108(3), (3) TFEU.

A refund of the tax would also be compatible with the CJEU's case law on the purpose of recovery. Admittedly, the CJEU in its current jurisprudence states that recovery is the logical consequence of an infringement of State aid law. Redefining recovery - as the Commission has done in its decision on the Hungarian tax - in allowing for a refund of the tax as a whole would at first glance appear to be a mere terminological trick. Yet this does not necessarily mean that such an approach would not be permissible. For positive subsidies, a refund to another undertaking is not possible. Defining recovery as a removal of the advantage was therefore only logical. This does not appear to be a decisive argument against the implementation of the Commission's recovery order through a refund of the tax as a whole, where this would be possible. The purpose of recovery can also be achieved through a retroactive

961. Case C-526/04 *Laboratoires Boiron* EU:C:2006:528. *See* in detail Ch. §5.02[C] *infra*.
962. *See* Ismer & Piotrowski, *Relationship of Fiscal State Aid and the Fundamental Freedoms*, *supra* n. 164, at 466.

abolition of the tax. While the result would not be identical to the situation before the payment of the aid, such a dynamic view is not necessarily warranted.

Where EU law does not preclude recovery through a refund of the tax, a retroactive elimination of the tax as a whole or a partial refund may even be required from a national constitutional law point of view to avoid an infringement of the rule of law and as an emanation of the principle of proportionality.

Of course, this approach would only be viable in rare constellations. In addition to the condition that there must be no infringement of Article 108(3), (3) TFEU, the retroactive abolishment of an entire tax would in practice only be possible for narrow-based levies.[963] By contrast, a retroactive abolition of broad-based taxes, such as corporate tax, is not conceivable. The main advantage of such an approach is that it does not go to the detriment of competition and competitors. In this respect, it appears preferable to the approaches that exclude the retroactive effect of State aid law and thus condone the distortion of competition for the past.

§5.02 EXTENSION OF THE ADVANTAGE IN FRONT OF NATIONAL COURTS

National courts can play a significant part in the enforcement of fiscal State aid law as they have an objective and subjective enforcement function derived from Article 108(3)(3) TFEU. In this function, national courts are also obliged to recover unlawful aid [A]. At the same time, Article 108(3)(3) TFEU is the main limit to a potentially reversal of the legal consequence of recovery because condoning an expansion of the advantage runs the risk of the national court expanding the circle of beneficiaries of aid. Where there is a simultaneous infringement of the fundamental freedoms and State aid law and the application of the fundamental freedoms can completely eliminate the unequal treatment, the correct legal consequence should nevertheless be a refund instead of recovery [B]. The *Laboratoires Boiron* case law[964] moreover defines constellations where the extension of the advantage would not be in infringement of Article 108(3)(3) TFEU [C]. Further constellations may be conceivable, where a refund poses no danger to Article 108(3)(3) TFEU. The decision on whether the legal consequence should then be a refund depends on national law [D].

[A] National Courts and Private Actors in the Assessment Stage and Article 108(3), (3) TFEU

National courts have an enforcement function that is derived from the stand-still provision of Article 108(3)(3) TFEU [1]. For this enforcement function to fully contribute to a thorough implementation of State aid law, competitors have to have procedural rights that allow them to initiate proceedings. While the enforcement

963. Similarly Afonso, *supra* n. 826, at 66: '*where the State aid has been granted in the form of an exemption from a tax imposed on a narrow sector of the economy (exceptional tax burden)*'.
964. Case C-526/04 *Laboratoires Boiron*.

function prevents a widening of the recourse to aid measures upon application by competitors, they should be able to tackle the non-taxation of competitors without benefitting therefrom directly [2].

[1] The Enforcement Function of National Courts

National courts play an increasingly significant, but often overlooked role in the enforcement of State aid law.[965] The latter may be partly because there is only very limited explicit legal guidance on the role of national courts.[966]

The obligations of the national court in the assessment stage are mainly derived from the stand-still provision of Article 108(3), (3) TFEU, which has a direct effect.[967] The immediate significance of the stand-still provision is as follows: The Commission is meant to be notified of plans to grant new aid according to Article 108(1) TFEU. Where there is, indeed, aid, the Commission decides on the compatibility of aid. Article 108(3), (3) TFEU provides that a Member State shall not put its proposed aid measures into effect until the procedure before the Commission has resulted in a final decision.

Beyond that, however, the stand-still provision of Article 108(3), (3) TFEU entails an enforcement function for national courts. It appears as though there is an *ex-officio* obligation for national courts to enforce State aid law based on Article 108(3), (3) TFEU as well as a subjective dimension, i.e., the obligation to act on actions by competitors.[968]

To this end, the national court may have to interpret the material State aid provision of Article 107(1) TFEU. This was first laid down in the CJEU's judgment in *Steinike & Weinlig*.[969] To ensure that State aid law is applied in a coordinated fashion, national courts may be obliged to refer a case to the CJEU under the procedure provided for in Article 267 TFEU.[970] The national court may also seek clarification from the Commission, where it entertains doubts as to whether a measure constitutes State aid.[971] Yet a possible justification of derogations from the reference system of taxation is ultimately for the national court to assess. In light of the growing importance of the

965. On the role of national courts *see, e.g.*, José Luis Buendía Sierra & Miguel Ángel Bolsa Ferruz, *State Aid Assessment: What National Courts Can Do and What They Must Do* 16 EStAL 408ff. (2017) https://doi.org/10.21552/estal/2017/3/9; De Pietro, *supra* n. 173; Denis Jouve, *Recovering Unlawful and Incompatible Aids by National Courts: CELF and Scott/Kimberly Clark Cases* 16 EStAL 367ff. (2017) https://doi.org/10.21552/estal/2017/3/6; Flynn, *supra* n. 842; Alke Metselaar, *Who Can Invoke State Aid Law before National Judges: That Floating Question of Legal Interest in the Case Law of Dutch Courts* 13 EStAL 250ff. (2014); Sampol Pucurull, *supra* n. 871; Schnitger, *supra* n. 41, at 433ff.; Van de Vijver, *supra* n. 114; Adam Scott, *Co-Operation and Good Faith: State Aid Rules and National Courts: Procedural and Interpretive Consequences* 16 EStAL 354ff. (2017) https://doi.org/10.21552/estal/2017/3/5.
966. This would be a weakness of the Procedural Regulation, Jouve, *supra* n. 965, at 368.
967. Bacon, *European Union Law of State Aid*, *supra* n. 20, at para. 20.05.
968. Krumm, *supra* n. 173, at 567.
969. E.g., Case 78/76 *Steinike & Weinlig*, para. 14; Case C-39/94 *SFEI*, para. 49; Case C-296/97 *Piaggio* EU:C:1999:313, para. 31; Case C-368/04 *Transalpine Ölleitung in Österreich* EU:C:2006:644, para. 39.
970. *See, e.g.*, Case C-39/94 *SFEI*, para. 39.
971. *Ibid.*, para. 50.

third step of the selectivity test in tax matters, this may afford national courts with some leeway, which is not subject to review by EU institutions.[972]

The Commission and national courts have complementary but separate roles in the enforcement of State aid law.[973] The relationship between the Member States and the Commission throughout the entirety of the procedure should be governed by respect for the principle of sincere cooperation under Article 4(3) TFEU.[974] In its judgment in *Adria-Wien Pipeline*, the CJEU defined the division of competences in the enforcement of State aid law as follows:

> In order to ensure the effectiveness of that prohibition, Article 93 of the EC Treaty (now Article 88 EC) [now Article 108 TFEU] places on the Commission a specific duty to monitor aid and imposes on the Member States specific obligations to facilitate the Commission's task and to prevent faits accomplis for that institution.[975]

In this context, the CJEU has referred to the stand-still provision of Article 108(3), (3) TFEU as 'the safeguard of the review machinery established by that article which, in turn, is essential for protecting the proper functioning of the common market'.[976]

National courts thus safeguard the rights of individuals faced with a possible breach of the stand-still obligation until there is a final Commission decision on an aid measure.[977] The role of national courts is thus first and foremost designed to be of an interim nature,[978] even though in practice this may not be the case. The national court does not have jurisdiction on the compatibility of aid and instead only gives effect to the stand-still provision until there is a Commission decision of any kind.[979]

This enforcement role of national courts may not only require a suspension or disapplication[980] of the measures in question but may also include an obligation to recover aid for the entire period before the implementation of a final Commission decision and also an assessment of the validity of measures through which aid is granted as well as the implementation of possible interim measures. The national

972. Problematic in this respect: Case C-374/17 *A-Brauerei*. *See* Ch. §3.04[B], [2] *supra*.
973. Case C-39/94 *SFEI*, para. 41; Joined Cases C-261 and 262/01 *van Calster and Others* EU:C:2003:571, para. 74; Case C-368/04 *Transalpine Ölleitung*, paras 36f.; Case C-284/12 *Deutsche Lufthansa AG*, para. 27; Case C-574/14 *PGE* EU:C:2016:686, para. 30; Case C-598/17 *A-Fonds*, para. 45; Case C-75/18 *Vodafone Magyarország*, para. 20; Case C-323/18 *Tesco-Global Áruházak*, para. 32.
974. *See* Scott, *supra* n. 965 for a detailed account of the dimensions of cooperation.
975. Case C-143/99 *Adria-Wien Pipeline*, para. 23, [current legal provision added by the author].
976. *Ibid.*, para. 24. Similarly Case C-199/06 *CELF I*, para. 36 with further references.
977. *See, e.g.*, Case 120/73 *Lorenz v. Germany*, para. 8; Case C-39/94 *SFEI*, para. 40; Case C-296/97 *Piaggio*, para. 31; Joined Cases C-261 and 262/01 *van Calster*, para. 75; Case C-368/04 *Transalpine Ölleitung*, para. 38; Case C-1/09 *CELF and ministre de la Culture and de la Communication (CELF II)* EU:C:2010:136, para. 26; Case C-284/12 *Deutsche Lufthansa AG*, para. 27; Case C-75/18 *Vodafone Magyarország*, para. 21; Case C-323/18 *Tesco-Global Áruházak*, para. 33.
978. In a similar vein, De Pietro, *supra* n. 173, at 108 speaks of the powers of national judge being conceived as functional in that they aim at guaranteeing the effectiveness of Art. 108(3), (3) TFEU, and thereby also the assessment of the Commission.
979. *See, e.g.*, Case C-354/90 *FNCE*, para. 14; Case C-199/06 *CELF I*, para. 38.
980. E.g., Joined Cases C-78 to 79/08 *Paint Graphos*, even though the final assessment of the measures was left to the referring court.

courts must in this context ensure that in the interest of individuals all appropriate conclusions are drawn from the infringement of the stand-still obligation.[981] The choice of which remedy is warranted appears to be a matter of the definition of 'appropriate conclusions'.[982] While the case law is not entirely clear, it appears as though the national court is in principle obliged to recover unlawful aid, where this is the only means to remedy the infringement of the stand-still provision.[983] For example, in *Residex Capital*, the CJEU held that EU law does not impose a specific consequence that must necessarily be drawn from an infringement of Article 108(3), (3) TFEU. However, the objective of the enforcement function of national courts is a restoration of the competitive situation prior to the aid being granted. The steps taken by the national court must lead to this objective being fulfilled.[984] In *Eesti Pagar*, the CJEU confirmed an obligation for national authorities to recover unlawful aid for cases of a misapplication of the GBER.[985] This goes beyond the obligations of the Commission which has to order the recovery of only incompatible aid.[986] The national court even appears to be precluded from staying the proceedings to await the final decision of the Commission on the aid.[987]

981. E.g., Case C-354/90 *FNCE*, para. 12; Case C-39/94 *SFEI*, para. 40; Case C-143/99 *Adria-Wien Pipeline*, para. 27; Case C-234/99 *Niels Nygard*, para. 59; Joined Cases C-393/04 and 41/05 *Air Liquide Industries Belgium* EU:C:2006:403, para. 42; Case C-71/04 *Xunta de Galicia* EU:C:2005:493, para. 49; Case C-284/12 *Deutsche Lufthansa AG*, para. 30; Case C-75/18 *Vodafone Magyarország*, para. 23; Case C-323/18 *Tesco-Global Áruházak*, para. 35. *See also* Joined Cases C-261 and 262/01 *van Calster*, para. 64; Case C-368/04 *Transalpine Ölleitung*, para. 47; Case C-199/06 *CELF I* EU:C:2008:79, para. 41.
982. Ghazarian, *supra* n. 166, at 229.
983. *See, e.g.*, Case C-672/13 *OTP Bank*, para. 69 with reference to further case law. In the literature *see* Bacon, *European Union Law of State Aid, supra* n. 20, at para. 20.16; Schnitger, *supra* n. 41, at 433; Scott, *supra* n. 965, at 358 with reference to Case C-354/90 *FNCE*, para. 12. Sceptical in this respect Buendía Sierra & Bolsa Ferruz, *supra* n. 965, at 415 with reference to the judgments in Case C-39/94 *SFEI* and Case C-505/14 *Klausner Holz* EU:C:2015:742. Thomas Jaeger, *CELF II: Settling into a Weak effet utile Standard for Private State Aid Enforcement* 1 JECLAP 319, 323f. (2010) https://doi.org/10.1093/jeclap/lpq022 contends that the judgment of the CJEU in *CELF II* would have reinforced a weak effet utile standard to Art. 108(3), (3) TFEU that had already been established in *CELF I*, which does not include deterrence (recovery only of the advantage of the aid being granted early). This may speak against full recovery regardless of the compatibility of aid.
984. Case C-275/10 *Residex Capital IV* EU:C:2011:814, paras 44f.
985. Case C-349/17 *Eesti Pagar AS* EU:C:2019:172, paras 89ff.
986. Case C-301/87 *France v. Commission* EU:C:1990:67, paras 19 to 22; Case C-354/90 *FNCE*, para. 13; Case C-39/94 *SFEI*, para. 43.
987. The Commission's final decision cannot regularize *ex post facto* the implementation of measures which were invalid because the Member State had infringed upon the stand-still provision with a view to ensuring the provision's effet utile, Case C-354/90 *FNCE*, para. 16; Case C-368/04 *Transalpine Ölleitung*, para. 41; Joined Cases C-261 and 262/01 *van Calster*, para. 63; Case C-199/06 *CELF I*, para. 39. This then also means that the national court as an emanation of Art. 108(3), (3) TFEU is still under an obligation to order recovery where a claim in that respect has been brought by a third party, *see* para. 45. *See* on this case law, e.g., Jouve, *supra* n. 965, at 369ff. Critical since the CJEU would not acknowledge that this constitutes a departure from the case law in *Transalpine Ölleitung*, since the effect would nevertheless be a regularization *ex post facto*, Benjamin Cheynel & Adrien Giraud, *New Paradigm for Recovery of Unlawful Aid in the EU: National Judges and the 'Exception of Compatibility'* 31 W. Comp. 557, 563f. (2008) https://doi.org/10.54648/woco2008045.The relevant advantage to be recovered then only extends to the unlawfulness of the aid, i.e., the fact that it was granted prematurely.

There are two dimensions to the enforcement function of national courts, namely a subjective and an objective function. As to the subjective enforcement function, competitors – and potentially other private actors[988] – can at least in principle rely on the direct effect of Article 108(3), (3) TFEU and request an elimination of the distortion of competition, e.g., through recovery from the beneficiary of aid.[989]

As to the objective enforcement function, the national court cannot apply national law, where this would lead to an infringement of Article 108(3), (3) TFEU.[990] This represents the most important limit to a reversal of the legal consequence of recovery for national courts. This even extends to cases, where the legal dispute does not concern State aid law at all, but a completely unrelated question. For example, in *A-Brauerei,* the core issue of the national court proceedings concerned the interpretation of the group privilege under the German Real Estate Transfer Tax and not State aid law. In this, it has to be stressed that the CJEU has recently clarified that the establishment of State aid can never directly result from a judicial decision, since judicial decisions merely clarify the law. The existence of State aid follows directly from the applicable legal provision.[991]

Nevertheless, the full significance of Article 108(3), (3) TFEU in fiscal State aid matters is not altogether clear yet. In this context, it has been argued that the role of national courts in fiscal State aid control would be limited. The judgment in *Finanzamt Linz* would rule out both an ex-officio application of Article 108(3), (3) TFEU in the interest of one of the parties of the main proceedings and in general.[992] The facts of the case were as such: Austrian corporate tax law allowed for a depreciation of goodwill in the context of the taxation of a group of companies upon acquisition of a holding in a company. The taxpayer claimed the depreciation of goodwill for the acquisition of a holding in a company established in Slovakia, arguing that the restriction of the depreciation to domestic holdings in resident companies was at odds with the freedom of establishment. The referring court questioned the compatibility of the provisions at issue with both State aid law and the fundamental freedoms.[993] In its judgment, the CJEU considered the question pertaining to State aid law inadmissible based on the standing case law that those liable to pay a tax cannot rely on the argument that a fiscal measure enjoyed by other businesses constitutes State aid in order to avoid payment of that tax.[994]

This means it consists in the non-payment of interest it would have had to pay if the beneficiary had to borrow that amount on the market on the one hand and the improvement of its competitive position while the unlawfulness lasts on the other hand, Case C-199/06 *CELF I*, para. 51. By contrast, it is not obliged to recover the aid itself. It may, however, still do so within the framework of domestic law, paras 53f. Critical: Cheynel & Giraud, *supra* n. 987, at 561f.

988. For example, it has been argued that other third parties beyond competitors should be considered to have sufficient legal interest on grounds of a direct effect on their relative tax burden, Scott, *supra* n. 965, at 355.
989. *See* Ch. §5.02[A], [2] *infra*.
990. *See, e.g.*, the procedural constellation in Joined Cases C-78 to 79/08 *Paint Graphos*.
991. *See* Joined Cases C-702/20 and 17/21 *Dobeles HES* EU:C:2023:1, para. 76.
992. Fierstra, *supra* n. 169, at 126.
993. *See* Case C-66/14 *Finanzamt Linz* EU:C:2015:661, paras 3ff. for the facts of the case.
994. *Ibid.*, para. 21. For details *see* Ch. §5.02[A], [2], [a] *infra*.

However, instead of reading the judgment as a limitation of the obligations of the national court, the CJEU's conclusion appears to derive from the procedural limitations of European law, which do not bear relation to the obligations of the national court. AG Kokott in her Opinion convincingly pointed out that the question on State aid law was nevertheless relevant to the case despite the case law on admissibility, albeit not in favour of the taxpayer.[995] Where the fundamental freedoms would lead to an extension of the circle of recipients of an unlawful aid measure, this could constitute an infringement of Article 108(3), (3) TFEU. Consequently, in such a constellation, the legal consequence of the fundamental freedoms (elimination of the discrimination through an extension of the advantage) could be granted.[996] She thus explicitly alluded to the objective enforcement function of the national court. Despite the CJEU's stance on admissibility, Article 108(3), (3) TFEU would still prohibit the national court from widening the circle of beneficiaries of unlawful aid as a result of an application of the fundamental freedoms. Regardless of whether this fact was raised by one of the parties, it would do so if it delivered a judgment that allows for the application of a provision that amounts to aid.[997]

In the judgment in *Aer Lingus and Ryanair*, which only concerned State aid law, the beneficiaries of aid had brought forward that airlines subject to the higher tax rate could be entitled to a reimbursement of tax. This could be either on grounds of the fundamental freedoms or of the judgment of the CJEU in *Laboratoires Boiron*, which concerned the exceptional case of an extension of the advantage following an infringement of State aid law.[998] As a result, the original beneficiaries of aid could conceivably be discriminated against.[999] Regardless of whether this would be possible, the CJEU held that it was for the Member State concerned to ensure that any national measure with the effect of reimbursement for certain actors would not give rise to new aid to the benefit of the undertakings receiving such reimbursement.[1000] In this judgment, the CJEU thus acknowledged the significance of Article 108(3), (3) TFEU, which can restrict the scope of action for national courts in giving effect to the fundamental freedoms.

In its judgment in *A-Fonds*, the CJEU then clarified that a national court is precluded from assessing a residence condition, which may be in infringement of the

995. In detail: Ismer & Piotrowski, *Relationship of Fiscal State Aid and the Fundamental Freedoms*, *supra* n. 164, at 462f.
996. Opinion of AG Kokott in Case C-66/14 *Finanzamt Linz* EU:C:2015:242, para. 30.
997. Fierstra, *supra* n. 169, at 128 separates this from the obligation from ex officio application. He further cites the limited role of the principle of res iudicata and the Commission's competence to examine existing aid as reasons why there would be no obligation of an ex officio application of Art. 108(3), (3) TFEU. While it is true that an ex officio-obligation should be exceptional, the judgment of the CJEU in *Sytraval* does not necessarily appear to support such conclusion as the Commission's role is not comparable with the national court's role as the former is not bound by Art. 108(3), (3) TFEU, *see* Case C-367/95 P *Sytraval* EU:C:1998:154, para. 60.
998. *See* Ch. §5.02[C] *infra*.
999. Joined Cases C-164 and 165/15 P *Aer Lingus and Ryanair*, para. 119.
1000. *Ibid.*, para. 123.

free movement of capital, where the refund of tax would constitute an aid scheme and thus lead to an infringement of Article 108(3), (3) TFEU.[1001]

The seemingly different stances in the judgments appear to come down to the question of whether the particular role of Article 108(3), (3) TFEU as a limiting factor for the taxpayer's claim (as opposed to in favour of it) – i.e., the objective enforcement function of the national court – was raised by the national court in its referral or not. Yet the ex officio-obligation to apply Article 108(3), (3) TFEU exists nevertheless.

[2] *Article 108(3), (3) TFEU as a Limit to Private Enforcement*

The subjective enforcement function of national courts is inextricably linked with the procedural rights of competitors in front of national courts. The case law of the CJEU indicates a wide understanding of competitors in fiscal aid matters.[1002] Nevertheless, the scholarly literature has contended that the role of national courts would be limited due to a lack of procedural lights of competitors in fiscal aid matters.[1003] We argue that this is not necessarily the case. There are indeed limits where competitors seek an extension of the scope of unnotified aid to themselves that are derived from Article 108(3), (3) TFEU [a]. Yet there is not always a danger of an infringement of the stand-still provision for private enforcement. The objective of Article 108(3), (3) TFEU as well as the principle of effectiveness even require that a competitor has the procedural means to tackle the non-taxation of the beneficiaries of aid in front of national courts [b].

[a] *No Widening of Recourse to Unnotified Aid Measures*

Competitors may have an interest in avoiding the payment of a tax that the beneficiaries of aid do not have to pay as they profit from a tax measure within that tax. According to the standing case law of the CJEU, questions on State aid in this context are regularly inadmissible, unless the narrow requirements laid down in the *Laboratoires Boiron* case law are met.[1004]

For example, in the aftermath of its judgment in *Adria-Wien Pipeline*, the CJEU again had to deal with the energy tax rebates in question (before the amendment of the law). After the Commission decision had declared the aid compatible with the internal market, the tax authorities again issued refusal decisions to undertakings based on the sector they were operating in. In *Transalpine Ölleitung in Österreich*, the CJEU held that the applications for grant of the unlawful aid measure may be likened to an application for a partial exemption. This, however, would be contrary to the case law that

1001. Case C-598/17 *A-Fonds*, para. 52.
1002. Paterno, *supra* n. 822, at 344f. with respect to aid schemes.
1003. *Ibid.*, at 345ff.
1004. *See* Ch. §5.02[C] *infra*.

'*businesses liable to pay an obligatory contribution cannot rely on the argument that the exemption enjoyed by other businesses constitutes State aid in order to avoid payment of that contribution*'.[1005] In more recent case law, the CJEU has stated that '*those liable to pay a tax cannot rely on the argument that a fiscal measure enjoyed by other businesses constitutes State aid in order to avoid payment of that tax [...]*'.[1006] It is sometimes specified that this case law is based on the fact that a tax exemption that constitutes illegal State aid does not affect the legality of the levy itself.[1007]

The CJEU's judgment in *Air Liquide Industries Belgium* then brought an important clarification on this case law. The case concerned exemptions from municipal and provincial taxes on motive force, which Air Liquide could not profit from. The CJEU found that the exemption in question could indeed constitute State aid, but left this determination to the referring court.[1008] In its judgment, the CJEU crucially linked the denial of the tax exemption to the stand-still provision of Article 108(3), (3) TFEU. An extension of the circle of recipients through reimbursement or non-payment of the tax would lead to an increase instead of an elimination of the effects of the aid and infringe upon Article 108(3), (3) TFEU.[1009]

According to the CJEU, this case law would not apply where a tax and an exemption form an integral part of an aid measure so that the tax itself is hypothecated to the aid measure under the relevant national rules, i.e., where the revenue from the tax is necessarily allocated for the financing of the aid and has a direct impact on the amount thereof.[1010]

In our view, the link with Article 108(3), (3) TFEU that was established in *Air Liquide Industries Belgium* is essential to explaining cases, such as the constellation underlying the judgment in *ANGED*:[1011] The procedural limitation of Article 108(3), (3) TFEU does not apply in constellations where taxpayers do not seek to achieve an exemption from a tax that contains tax benefits for other undertakings, but where they challenge the tax as a whole on grounds of an infringement of EU law – as opposed to only an implementing act, such as a tax bill. From an EU law perspective, this could not be successful due to the case law discussed above. Yet the illegality of the tax as a

1005. Case C-368/04 *Transalpine Ölleitung*, para. 16.
1006. Case C-66/14 *Finanzamt Linz*, para. 21. *See also* Case C-390/98 *Banks* EU:C:2001:456, para. 80; Joined Cases C-430 and 431/99 *Sea-Land Service and Nedlloyd Lijnen* EU:C:2002:364, para. 47; Joined Cases C-266 to 270, 276 and 321 to 325/04 *Casino France and Others* EU:C:2005:657, paras 42f.; Joined Cases C-393/04 and 41/05 *Air Liquide*, para. 43; Case C-75/18 *Vodafone Magyarország*, para. 24; Case C-323/18 *Tesco-Global Áruházak*, para. 36.
1007. Joined Cases C-393/04 and 41/05 *Air Liquide*, para. 43, Case C-233/16 *ANGED*, para. 26; Case C-75/18 *Vodafone Magyarország* para. 24; Case C-323/18 *Tesco-Global Áruházak*, para. 36.
1008. Joined Cases C-393/04 and 41/05 *Air Liquide*, para. 38.
1009. *Ibid.*, para. 45.
1010. *Ibid.*, para. 46 with reference to Case C-174/02 *Streekgewest* EU:C:2005:10, paras 25f.; Joined Cases C-266 to 270, 276 and 321 to 325/04 *Casino France*, para. 40.
1011. On this case *see* José Manuel Almudí Cid, *Spain: Regional Taxes on Large Retail Establishments Justified for Environmental Reasons*, in Lang et al. (eds), CJEU: Recent Developments in Direct Taxation, 2018, 145ff. (2019).

whole might derive from national law. The CJEU thus stated the following in *ANGED*, which concerned a challenge to a tax as a whole:

> the dispute in the main proceedings does not concern an application to be exempted from the contested tax, but the legality of the rules relating to that tax as a matter of EU law. It is therefore by no means obvious that the second and third questions are not of genuine interest for the purpose of ruling on the dispute before the referring court (see, by analogy, judgment of 15 June 2006, Air Liquide Industries Belgium, C-393/04 and C-41/05, EU:C:2006:403, paragraph 25).[1012]

The legal consequence could then in some cases be reimbursement of the tax if the entire tax was found to be in infringement of EU law. Since the tax is eliminated as a whole, there is no danger that the circle of beneficiaries of aid is widened, which may result in an infringement of Article 108(3), (3) TFEU.[1013]

At the same time, it has to be seen the *ANGED* case very much hinged on the particularities of Spanish domestic law. It is not possible in all Member States to challenge a tax as a whole on grounds of an infringement of EU law. In fact, in *ANGED* the challenge against the tax did not concern the law, which introduced the tax on large retail establishments. Instead, ANGED brought an action against a decree, which implemented the regulations on this tax before the *Tribunal Superior de Justicia de Cataluña*.[1014] Another jurisdiction, where such constellations could emerge is Italy. Due to Article 117 of the Italian constitution, the EU law compatibility of a tax is part of the constitutional review. Thus, in Italy, an infringement of State aid law due to a tax exemption leads to the unconstitutionality of the tax as a whole.[1015] This was the reason why the questions on State aid law in *Regione Sardegna* were not inadmissible.[1016] The legal consequence of such infringement of constitutional law would then be for national law to determine. By contrast, for example, German law knows no such provision.

On a more abstract level, this case law demonstrates the pivotal role of Article 108(3), (3) TFEU, which precludes national courts from widening the recourse to unlawful aid. Where there is no danger of an infringement of Article 108(3), (3) TFEU, however, the assumption that competitors necessarily have a weak position in front of national courts appears flawed. Moreover, from the perspective of legal consequences, this case law indicates that the legal consequence of an infringement of State aid law could conceivably be reimbursement instead of recovery.

1012. Case C-233/16 *ANGED*, para. 26.
1013. Hummel, *Das nationale Steuergesetz*, *supra* n. 519, at 393 explains this with the erga omnes effect of the judgment of the Spanish court.
1014. Case C-233/16 *ANGED*, para. 14.
1015. Szudoczky, *The Sources of EU Law*, *supra* n. 172, at 695; Peter J. Wattel, *Some Fringe Areas of EU State Aid Law in Direct Tax Matters*, in Weber (ed.), EU Income Tax Law: Issues for the Years Ahead, 139, 142 (2013).
1016. Case C-169/08 *Regione Sardegna*, paras 51ff., which, however, did not concern the action brought by an individual taxpayer. On this, e.g., Ismer & Piotrowski, *Relationship of Fiscal State Aid and the Fundamental Freedoms*, *supra* n. 164 at 461 with further references.

[b] *Tackling the Non-taxation of the Beneficiaries of Aid*

The situation is even less clear for competitors[1017] intending to achieve recovery from the beneficiary of aid (as opposed to their own non-taxation). While this is not the focus of our analysis, the constellation touched upon in this chapter demonstrates the two dimensions of the stand-still provision. As discussed above, Article 108(3), (3) TFEU limits an extension of the circle of beneficiaries of unlawful aid. At the same time, the subjective enforcement function of State aid law is also derived from the very same provision. The purpose of Article 108(3), (3) TFEU in this dimension is to protect competitors from the distortions of competition that arise from unlawful aid.[1018] This then also has to go along with procedural options to eliminate the distortion by bringing an action in front of a national court.[1019] In our view, such procedural options should exist regardless of the type of aid, since the necessary subjective dimension can be derived from Article 108(3), (3) TFEU.

A right of competitors to rely on directly applicable provisions in the area of taxation has a role model in VAT law.[1020] In the case underlying the judgment in *Feuerbestattungsverein Halle,* a charitable association operating a crematorium competed with a local authority that also offered such services. The German Federal Financial Court referred the question to the CJEU whether a taxable person can rely on Article 4(5) of Sixth Council Directive 77/388/EEC[1021] (VAT Directive), where they are in competition with a body governed by public law and assert that the non-taxation or under-taxation of that body is unlawful. According to this provision, local government authorities shall be considered taxable persons in respect of activities or transactions where treatment as non-taxable persons would lead to significant distortions of competition. The judgment itself dealt with the refusal of the tax authorities to disclose

1017. Since European law does not define the concept of a competitor with standing, heterogenous national procedural law definitions continue to apply in practice. For example, in some jurisdictions, competitors do not have standing before tax courts, Metselaar, *supra* n. 965, at 254f. The principle of procedural autonomy provides for an applicability of domestic procedural law in actions aimed at ensuring the protection of rights derived from the direct effect of Union law, unless EU law explicitly provides otherwise. This general rule is, however, very often overridden by the principle of effectiveness, *see* only Case 33/76 *Rewe v. Landwirtschaftskammer Saarland* EU:C:1976:188, para. 5; Case 45/76 *Comet* EU:C:1976:191, paras 13ff.; Case 68/79 *Just* EU:C:1980:57, para. 25; Joined Cases 331, 376 and 378/85 *Bianco and Girard* EU:C:1988:97, para. 12; Case C-312/93 *Peterbroeck, Van Campenhout & Cie* EU:C:1995:437, paras 12f.; Case C-231/96 *Edis* EU:C:1998:401, paras 19, 34; C-343/96 *Dilexport* EU:C:1999:59, para. 25; Case C-62/00 *Marks & Spencer* EU:C:2002:435, paras 34ff.; Case C-446/04 *Test Claimants in the FII Group Litigation* EU:C:2006:774, para. 9; Metselaar, *supra* n. 965, at 259.

1018. *See* Ch. §5.02[A], [1] *supra*.

1019. Similarly albeit with respect to the definition of private actors that derive rights from Art. 108(3), (3) TFEU under Dutch case law Metselaar, *supra* n. 965, at 255. *See also* Goyder & Dons, *supra* n. 931, at 421 and Clélia Jadot, *Damages Actions and State Aid: Time for Action at EU Level?* 6 Market and Competition L. Rev. 89, 92ff. (2022) with respect to claims for damages under the *Francovich* doctrine.

1020. *See* Case C-430/04 *Feuerbestattungsverein Halle* EU:C:2006:347.

1021. Sixth Council Directive 77/388/EC of 17 May 1977 on the harmonization of the laws of the Member States relating to turnover taxes – Common system of value added tax: uniform basis of assessment [1977] OJ L 145/1.

to the competitor information subject to confidentiality in tax matters relating to that local authority[1022] yet the judgment may have wider implications. This is because the information required by the taxpayer was intended to enable private enforcement as described above.

The CJEU held that the provision in question sought to ensure compliance with the principle of neutrality.[1023] If the economic activity in question were to give rise to distortions of competition, the operation of the crematorium by the local authority would be taxable under Article 4(5).[1024] The CJEU further stated that Article 4(5) of the Sixth Directive had direct effect.[1025] The reply to the question referred by the Federal Financial Court was thus that the competitor could rely on Article 4(5) of the Sixth Directive in proceedings between the private person and the national tax authorities outside the bilateral relationship of tax authorities and taxpayers.[1026] This was despite the fact that domestic procedural law did not provide for such a possibility.

This case is comparable to the constellations discussed in the context of fiscal State aid law.[1027] Article 108(3), (3) TFEU is directly applicable and in its subjective dimension is meant to provide the competitor of aid with an avenue to eliminate the distortion of competition. In the constellations discussed here, the competitor would not claim damages or seek to improve their own tax treatment. Their objective would be to achieve taxation of the beneficiary of aid by attacking the infringement of Article 108(3), (3) TFEU. This might be derived directly from European law, i.e., from Article 108(3), (3) TFEU. With the judgment in *Scuola Elementare Maria Montessori*, the CJEU recognized a right for competitors under Article 263(4) TFEU to attack positive Commission decisions and thus secure recovery – at least for aid schemes.[1028] It should be possible for the competitor to achieve the same result in front of national courts since the two avenues of enforcement should be aligned admittedly, even where such procedural rights are acknowledged, the problem remains that the relationship between the tax authorities and the taxpayer is bilateral in nature and subject to confidentiality. Even where procedural rights exist, the competitor does not necessarily have access to the information required to launch such proceedings.[1029] Yet it could conceivably even be possible to obtain such information on grounds of Article 108(3), (3) TFEU.

1022. Case C-430/04 *Feuerbestattungsverein Halle*, para. 22.
1023. *Ibid.*, para. 24 with further references.
1024. *Ibid.*, para. 26.
1025. *Ibid.*, para. 30 with reference to Case C-4/89 *Comune di Carpaneto Piacentino and Others* EU:C:1990:204, paras 31, 33.
1026. Case C-430/04 *Feuerbestattungsverein Halle*, para. 32.
1027. Similarly Thiede, *supra* n. 816, at 55. Michael Lang, *Die Auswirkungen des gemeinschaftlichen Beihilferechts auf das Steuerrecht*, 96f. (2009) contends that this could potentially be derived from Art. 108(3), (3) TFEU. The judgment in *Feuerbestattungsverein Halle* would not have brought anything new. Paterno, *supra* n. 822 at 344 holds that this case law would be limited to Art. 4(5) of the VAT Directive.
1028. On this, e.g., Valérie Noël & Sébastien Thomas, *Locus Standi in State Aid Litigation after Montessori* 20 EStAL 512ff. (2021). *See* on this judgment in relation to the obligation to order recovery, Ch. §5.01[A] *supra*.
1029. Paterno, *supra* n. 822, at 346.

Interestingly, the judgments in *Air Liquide Industries Belgium* and *Feuerbestattungsverein Halle* were both issued by the Second Chamber of the CJEU within one week of each other. The difference between the two judgments is that in the former, there was the danger of an infringement of Article 108(3), (3) TFEU, had the competitor been granted such procedural right, whereas no comparable provision exists under VAT. In any case, this type of subjective enforcement is likely to be more relevant for individual aid than it could be for aid schemes.

[B] Extension of the Advantage in Cases of Overlap with the Fundamental Freedoms

Where a measure comes in front of a national court and is found to be in infringement of both the fundamental freedoms and European State aid law, the question of which legal consequence is applicable arises. The fundamental freedoms will generally require an extension of the advantage to the operator that was discriminated against, whereas State aid law requires recovery.[1030] We are not concerned with a detailed examination of the relationship between the fundamental freedoms and State aid law here. Instead, we argue that the legal consequence of a simultaneous infringement of the two sets of rules can in some cases be an extension of the advantage despite the constraints of Article 108(3), (3) TFEU. In this context, some contributions in the literature have pointed to the case law of the CJEU in *Ianelli & Volpi* and thus argued that State aid law has to take precedence over the fundamental freedoms.[1031] Others have in our view convincingly pointed out that the key to solving an overlap of the two sets of rules is Article 108(3), (3) TFEU. This is where the enforcement function of national courts comes into play. While Article 108(3), (3) TFEU does not positively prescribe a solution for the conflict of law, it prevents the national court from giving precedence to the fundamental freedoms, where this would lead to an infringement of Article 108(3), (3) TFEU. Conversely, where the advantage can be extended without an infringement of the stand-still provision, the solution is less clear, since neither result appears inherently preferable.[1032]

1030. On the relationship between the fundamental freedoms and fiscal State aid law *see, e.g.*, Engelen, *supra* n. 164; Englisch, *Das Beihilfenverbot im Steuerrecht, supra* n. 67, at paras 9.53ff.; Ismer & Piotrowski, *Relationship of Fiscal State Aid and the Fundamental Freedoms, supra* n. 164; Kokott, *Steuerrecht und unionsrechtlicher Beihilfebegriff, supra* n. 164, at 550ff.; Lang, *Seminar J, supra* n. 164; Micheau, *Fundamental Freedoms and State Aid Rules under EU Law, supra* n. 164; O'Brien, *supra* n. 164; Rossi-Maccanico, *EU Review of Direct Tax Measures, supra* n. 164; Staes, *supra* n. 164; Szudoczky, *The Sources of EU Law, supra* n. 172; Peter J. Wattel, *Forum: Interaction of State Aid, Free Movement, Policy Competition and Abuse Control in Direct Tax Matters* 5 WTJ 128ff. (2013) https://doi.org/10.59403/1rxxhrw; Wattel, *Comparing Criteria, supra* n. 164.

1031. Engelen, *supra* n. 164, at 207ff.; Micheau, *Fundamental Freedoms and State Aid Rules under EU Law, supra* n. 164, at 211; Szudoczky, *The Sources of EU Law, supra* n. 172, at 663; Leigh Hancher, *The General Framework*, in Hancher et al. (eds), EU State Aids, para. 3.235 (5th edn 2016).

1032. Englisch, *Das Beihilfenverbot im Steuerrecht, supra* n. 67, at paras 9.56; Ismer & Piotrowski, *Relationship of Fiscal State Aid and the Fundamental Freedoms, supra* n. 164, at 465; Lang,

Szudoczky identifies certain constellations, where Article 108(3), (3) TFEU would be infringed upon if the advantage were expanded, namely particularly regional tax benefits.[1033] We have argued elsewhere that this will also generally be the case for indirect discriminations, since an application of the fundamental freedoms can only eliminate the cross-border discrimination – purely domestic cases would still not profit from the measure, which means that the circle of beneficiaries of aid could potentially be expanded by applying the fundamental freedoms.[1034] This, in turn, means that State aid law would have to take precedence. The national court thus cannot eliminate the discrimination on grounds of the fundamental freedoms and the taxpayer loses the case.[1035]

By contrast, where an application of the fundamental freedoms can eliminate the unequal treatment altogether, there is no danger of an infringement of Article 108(3), (3) TFEU. This may, for example, be the case where a tax measure is applicable in the entire territory of a Member State and contains a direct discrimination.[1036] This result can in our view be derived from substantive law. Unlike State aid law, the fundamental freedoms are directly applicable. This means that they have a direct impact on the reading of national law. While the fundamental freedoms only ever concern one particular case, one could nevertheless argue that a 'correct reading' of national law that takes into account the infringement of the fundamental freedoms would eliminate all unequal treatment. Where the fundamental freedoms can then fully eliminate the State aid problem, they should take precedence.[1037]

[C] Extension of the Advantage under the *Laboratoires Boiron* Case Law

There may furthermore be cases where there is no simultaneous infringement of the fundamental freedoms, but where the extension of the advantage is nevertheless the correct legal remedy in fiscal State aid cases. Szudoczky derives this result from the case law of the CJEU in *Laboratoires Boiron*, which concerned a tax on direct sales of medicines by pharmaceutical laboratories, which was levied for the National Sickness Insurance Fund for Employees and was meant to even out competition between the different distribution channels for medicines. The tax was not levied on sales from wholesale distributors. The latter were subject to certain duties of public service, namely a duty to keep a permanent stock of certain medicines and to guarantee delivery of medicines within 24 hours of receipt of an order. Laboratoires Boiron, a

Seminar J, supra n. 164, at 579, however also pointing to the potential impact of the *Laboratoires Boiron* case law. *See* Ch. §5.02[C] *infra*.

1033. Szudoczky, *The Sources of EU Law, supra* n. 172, at 697ff.

1034. *See* already Ismer & Piotrowski, *Relationship of Fiscal State Aid and the Fundamental Freedoms, supra* n. 164, at 465f.

1035. *Ibid.* and Szudoczky, *The Sources of EU Law, supra* n. 172, at 707f. according to whom the legal consequence may nevertheless be an extension of the advantage on grounds of *Laboratoires Boiron, see* Ch. §5.02[C] *infra*.

1036. Ismer & Piotrowski, *Relationship of Fiscal State Aid and the Fundamental Freedoms, supra* n. 164, at 465; Szudoczky, *The Sources of EU Law, supra* n. 172, at 707f.

1037. Ismer & Piotrowski, *Relationship of Fiscal State Aid and the Fundamental Freedoms, supra* n. 164, at 465.

pharmaceutical laboratory, sought reimbursement of the tax it had paid on grounds of State aid law.[1038]

In its judgment, the CJEU made a distinction between the case law that those liable to pay a tax cannot rely on the argument that an exemption enjoyed by others constitutes State aid in order to avoid payment themselves[1039] on the one hand and the constellation in *Laboratoires Boiron* on the other hand.[1040] The former concerned exemptions from a tax of general application, which led to the finding of State aid.[1041] By contrast, the latter concerned '*a charge for which only one of the two categories of competing operators, namely pharmaceutical laboratories, is liable*'. The aid would then derive from the fact that another category of undertakings, with which the taxpayer is in direct competition, is not liable to the tax.[1042] The CJEU went on to state the following:

> In such a case, it should be accepted that an economic operator such as Boiron may plead that the charge on direct sales is unlawful, for the purposes of applying for reimbursement, on the ground that it amounts to an aid measure. The result of this would not, in any case, be to allow the national court to increase the number of recipients of the aid. On the contrary, such reimbursement, to the extent that it is payable, is a very appropriate way of reducing the number of economic operators harmed by the measure deemed to constitute aid, and thus, of limiting the anti-competitive effects of that measure.[1043]

All this means that in such a constellation reimbursement of the aid that is based on a decision of a national court would not be in breach of Article 108(3), (3) TFEU. The CJEU to a certain extent defines the problem away and contends that instead of widening recourse to the aid, reimbursement would limit the anti-competitive effects of the measure.

According to Szudoczky, this case law could be transferred to constellations, where the aid is granted through the selective imposition of a tax on only certain categories of taxpayers, as was the case in the judgment in *Regione Sardegna*.[1044] The CJEU did not have to determine the applicable legal remedy, since the question of the EU law compatibility of the levy arose in the context of the constitutional law review of the tax.[1045] If the *Laboratoires Boiron* case law was transferrable, an extension of the advantage could be achieved on grounds of State aid law. Szudoczky concedes that it

1038. Case C-526/04 *Laboratoires Boiron*, paras 3ff. for a description of the measure.
1039. *See* Ch. §5.02[A], [2], [a] *supra*. Case C-526/04 *Laboratoires Boiron*, para. 30 with reference to Case C-390/98 *Banks*, para. 80; Joined Cases C-266 to 270, 276 and 321 to 325/04 *Casino France*, paras 42, 44; Joined Cases C-393/04 and 41/05 *Air Liquide*, para. 43.
1040. Case C-526/04 *Laboratoires Boiron*, para. 31.
1041. *Ibid.*
1042. *Ibid.*, paras 32f.
1043. *Ibid.*, paras 40f.
1044. Case C-169/08 *Regione Sardegna*. Szudoczky, *The Sources of EU Law*, *supra* n. 172, at 703f. Unclear as to the potential impact of the *Laboratoires Boiron* case law: Lang, *Seminar J*, *supra* n. 164, at 579.
1045. *See* Ch. §5.02[A], [2], [a] *supra*.

would be difficult to distinguish whether the aid is derived from the imposition of the stopover tax on non-residents or from an exemption from the tax for residents.[1046]

Jaeger appears to be rather lenient in this respect and contends that based on the judgment in *Laboratoires Boiron,* reimbursement could be claimed whenever the general legal basis and the exemption form two parts of the same fiscal measure and where there is a close competitive relationship. The *Laboratoires Boiron* case law would thus not only apply to parafiscal charges but also to exemptions from taxes as long as these conditions are met.[1047]

By contrast in our view, a narrow reading of the judgment is warranted.[1048] Just as the proposed solution according to which recovery could be carried out by retroactively abolishing a tax,[1049] the case law can only conceivably be applied to narrow-based taxes. Beyond this, there are considerable doubts as to the applicability of the case law to tax measures, such as the one at issue in the *Regione Sardegna* case based on the criteria brought forward in the judgment of the CJEU in *Laboratoires Boiron.*

The CJEU contends that a distinction has to be drawn between exemptions from a tax of general application and a charge for which only one of two categories of competing operators is liable.[1050] Yet according to the long-standing case law of the CJEU, 'Article 107(1) does not distinguish between measures of State intervention by reference to their causes or their aims but defines them in relation to their effects' (effects doctrine).[1051] Another phrasing of this effects doctrine states that the State aid provision defines State interventions on the basis of their effects, and thus independently of the techniques used.[1052] As a result, the approach to State aid law should not be overly formalistic. In fact, the judgment in *Laboratoires Boiron* derives the distinction between the two types of measures from differences between the two types of material law provisions. In light of the effects doctrine, however, the difference in regulatory technique does not appear to allow for a clear delimitation of the two types of aid.

Second, and perhaps somewhat more plausibly, the CJEU bases its distinction on the aspect of competition between the economic operators subject to and exempt from the tax liability.[1053] This aspect again does not necessarily allow for a delimitation of the two types of aid as there is no clear guidance on the criterion of 'competition between operators' thus far. In his opinion in the *Ferring* case, which dealt with the

1046. Szudoczky, *The Sources of EU Law, supra* n. 172, at 704. *See also* Micheau, *Récupération des aides d'État, supra* n. 170, at 354.
1047. Jaeger, *Tax Measures, supra* n. 73, at para. 105.
1048. Similarly Micheau, *Récupération des aides d'État, supra* n. 170, at 354.
1049. *See* Ch. §5.01[D], [2] *supra.*
1050. Case C-526/04 *Laboratoires Boiron,* paras 30ff.
1051. *See, e.g.,* Case 173/73 *Italy v. Commission,* para. 13; Case C-241/94 *France v. Commission* EU:C:1996:353, para. 20; Case C-382/99 *Netherlands v. Commission,* para. 61; Case C-126/01 *GEMO* EU:C:2003:622, para. 34; Case C-172/03 *Heiser,* para. 46; Case C-487/06 P *British Aggregates Association,* paras 87 and 89.
1052. Case C-487/06 P *British Aggregates Association,* paras 89 and Joined Cases C-106 and 107/09 P *Gibraltar,* para. 87.
1053. Case C-526/04 *Laboratoires Boiron,* paras 33f.

same levy, *AG Tizzano* suggested a case-by-case approach to determine whether there was a sufficient link.[1054] *Jaeger* proposes that activities within the same branch or the introduction of a parafiscal charge, which allows exempted undertakings to gain market shares, should be considered sufficient to qualify as a competitive relationship.[1055]

Third, the CJEU refers to its case law on parafiscal charges, namely its judgment in *Van Calster*, which dealt with a Belgian parafiscal levy.[1056] This is because the question had been raised whether reimbursement would be consistent with the principles underlying the *Van Calster* case law. In this judgment, the CJEU had held that where an aid measure has been implemented in breach of Article 108(3), (3) TFEU and where the method of financing (through a levy) is an integral part of that aid, national courts must order reimbursement of these charges or contributions that were levied specifically for financing purposes.[1057] The CJEU states that the tax at issue in *Laboratoires Boiron* did not solely constitute an integral part of the aid measure. Instead, the charge itself and the alleged measure constituted inseparable elements of one and the same fiscal measure.[1058] Granting reimbursement would therefore be in line with the *Van Calster* case law. The case law on parafiscal charges, which are not dealt with in detail in the context of this book, is particular in that the aid in such cases generally (if not necessarily) derives from the use of the revenue derived from such levy.[1059] By contrast, the revenue from taxes is generally not allocated for specific purposes. Instead, State aid will regularly derive from distinctions within a levy or the design thereof. Admittedly, the tax at issue in *Laboratoires Boiron* was somewhat of a borderline case as the revenue of the tax was allocated to the National Sickness Insurance Fund for Employees. Yet the aid nevertheless derived from a different treatment of competing actors on the level of the levy.

Fourth, a rather narrow understanding emerges from the CJEU's judgment in *Aer Lingus and Ryanair*. The airlines had submitted that there may be a danger of operators that were subject to the higher tax rate of ATT could claim reimbursement of the difference between the two tax rates based on the *Laboratoires Boiron* case law, which would then disadvantage the original beneficiaries of aid.[1060] The CJEU clarified that the ATT was in no way comparable with the measure at issue in *Laboratoires Boiron* since the ATT was a tax of general application. The State aid was granted through a partial exemption from the tax. In such constellations, the *Laboratoires Boiron* case law would be inapplicable.[1061]

1054. Opinion of AG Tizzano in Case C-53/00 *Ferring* EU:C:2001:253, paras 35ff.
1055. Jaeger, *Tax Measures, supra* n. 73, at para. 106 with reference to Case C-53/00 *Ferring*, para. 19.
1056. Case C-526/04 *Laboratoires Boiron*, paras 42ff. with reference to Joined Cases C-261 and 262/01 *van Calster*.
1057. Joined Cases C-261 and 262/01 *van Calster*, para. 54.
1058. Case C-526/04 *Laboratoires Boiron*, para. 45.
1059. On parafiscal charges in the system of State aid law: Jaeger, *Tax Measures, supra* n. 73, at paras 82ff.
1060. Joined Cases C-164 and 165/15 P *Aer Lingus and Ryanair*, para. 119.
1061. *Ibid.*, paras 120f.

Finally, what appears to speak for a narrow understanding of the case law is the CJEU's focus on the very objective of the tax. In its judgment in *Laboratoires Boiron*, the CJEU states that the absence of liability for the wholesale distributors of pharmaceuticals was '*a deliberate objective, if not the principal objective of the tax on direct sales*'.[1062] By this, the CJEU refers to the objective of the tax to compensate for the imposition of certain public service obligations on wholesale distributors and thereby balance competition.[1063] It therefore appears as though the applicability of the case law may be limited to very specific special purpose levies, which seek to compensate certain operators for public service obligations. Taxes, such as the one at issue in the CJEU's *Regione Sardegna* case do not appear to fall within the ambit of this case law.

All this means that the potential transferral of the *Laboratoires Boiron* case law to other types of levies is limited. Beyond that, doubts remain as to whether the compensatory effect of a tax is the only objective that can lead to a reversal of the legal consequences of State aid (reimbursement instead of recovery). Moreover, clarifications as to the nature of the competitive relationship between the beneficiaries of the aid and those liable to a tax are required. In fact, the distinction between the two types of aid measures, which leads to reimbursement in some cases and recovery in others, appears to be somewhat arbitrary and not entirely convincing.

[D] Constellations Where Article 108(3), (3) TFEU Poses No Obstacle

Beyond the issues surrounding the boundaries of the *Laboratoires Boiron* case law, further constellations, where a national court may reimburse tax on grounds of an infringement of State aid law, are conceivable. At first glance, the standing case law of the CJEU on the procedural position of competitors in State aid law, which was established in the judgment in *Air Liquide Industries Belgium* would appear to prevent such a result. According to this case law, the fact that a levy contains an exemption which amounts to State aid does not invalidate the tax as a whole. Consequently, such actions are generally inadmissible.[1064] However, as has been laid out above, the CJEU linked this stance to the risk of an infringement of Article 108(3), (3) TFEU. Therefore, where there is no risk of an infringement of the stand-still provision – for example, where the reimbursement leads to the elimination of the tax as a whole[1065] – the national court could nevertheless extend the advantage. Where selectivity can be eliminated in two different directions, the choice would be left to the national court.

Whether those two options even exist would be a matter of national law. Reimbursing tax as a result of an infringement of State aid law may infringe upon the decision of the legislator to tax certain situations. Yet there may be a case for extending the advantage for other reasons, in particular national constitutional law reasons.

1062. Case C-526/04 *Laboratoires Boiron*, para. 35.
1063. *Ibid.*, para. 36 with reference to the judgment in Case C-53/00 *Ferring*.
1064. *See* Ch. §5.02[A], [2], [a] *supra*.
1065. Similarly Bacon, *European Union Law of State Aid*, *supra* n. 20, at para. 20.29 albeit contending that this approach would be limited to exceptional cases.

Examples may be the principle of protection of legitimate expectation or the principle of proportionality under national constitutional law.

Examples that a reimbursement on grounds of an infringement of State aid law is in principle possible can be found in the case law, namely in the *Regione Sardegna* and *ANGED* judgments. The judgments did not address the legal consequences of the infringements of the rules in question. Nevertheless, it is noteworthy that the CJEU answered the questions on State aid law instead of referring to the case law in *Air Liquide Industries Belgium* and considering them inadmissible. Under Spanish national law, the infringement of State aid law constituted a reason for the invalidation of the tax. Whether the legal consequence would then actually be reimbursement is a matter of national constitutional law.[1066] The solution advocated here would not contradict the case law in *Air Liquide Industries Belgium*, according to which the fact that a tax contains an exemption does not invalidate the tax as a whole because it would not be derived from EU law, but from national law. In national law, there may be reasons for the invalidation of the tax as a whole, even where EU law does not require this legal consequence.

The judgment in *Aer Lingus and Ryanair* also does not speak against such a solution: It is true that in paragraph 119, the CJEU directly contrasted the *Laboratoires Boiron* and the *Air Liquide Industries Belgium* case law.[1067] Yet this does not appear to be a convincing argument against the solution advocated here. The *Laboratoires Boiron* case law merely identifies constellations, where the CJEU holds that exceptionally there is no infringement of Article 108(3), (3) TFEU, i.e., the infringement is 'defined away'. *Air Liquide Industries Belgium* concerns constellations, where there is a (potential) infringement of Article 108(3), (3) TFEU. In our view, the case law simply does not cover constellations, where Article 108(3), (3) TFEU is not touched upon in the first place.

This result would be aligned with the Member State's scope for action following a negative Commission decision discussed above.[1068] Moreover, the tax sovereignty of Member States would speak for such a solution. Admittedly, constellations where this could become relevant will be rare. Just like for Commission decisions, it is only conceivable for narrow-based levies.

1066. *See* already Ch. §5.02[A], [2], [a] *supra*.
1067. Joined Cases C-164 and 165/15 P *Aer Lingus and Ryanair*, para. 119.
1068. *See* Ch. §5.01[D], [2] *supra*.

CHAPTER 6

Case-by-Case Limits to Recovery Derived from the General Principles of EU Law

This chapter explores the case-by-case limits to recovery. The principle of protection of legitimate expectation can only rarely be relied upon to exclude recovery in tax cases due to its narrow reading by the European courts. In particular, it is linked with the requirement of notification. The case law makes no special case for tax measures. While this is unsatisfactory, the main problem stems from the fact that material State aid law is still not completely fleshed out. Ongoing legal uncertainty can also not serve to exclude recovery. In exceptional constellations, the principle of legal certainty in its dimension that precludes retroactive legislation may apply. These solutions are limited to constellations, where a beneficiary of aid did not have to be aware of the fact that a measure constitutes aid that has to be notified. Such a narrow reading of the general principles of EU law is only justified to the extent that taxpayers have appropriate procedural options at their disposal to minimize the risk of recovery. The case-by-case limits should apply both for national courts in the assessment stage and where there is a negative Commission decision.

Article 16(1) of Procedural Regulation 2015/1589, which implements the general obligation for the Commission to order recovery, is subject to the caveat that recovery is excluded where this would be contrary to a general principle of EU law.[1069] The wording 'shall not require recovery of the aid' must be understood as an ex officio-obligation to take into account such principles based on the information at the Commission's disposal. Where the Commission fails to do so, its decision would be

1069. *See* on the general principles of EU law in general particularly Tridimas, *supra* n. 121 as well as Rzotkiewicz, *supra* n. 168. For a more abstract analysis of principles of EU law, suggesting a distinction between Common Principles (comparative law approach) and general principles Stephanie Law, *The Rationales, Reasoning and Methodology Underpinning the Judicial Recognition of Principles of Union Law* 52 Cahiers de droit européen 11ff. (2016).

vitiated with error.[1070] At the same time, Article 16(1) is merely a codification and resolution of the primary law conflict between the obligation of recovery and the general principles of EU law. It opens the door for a case-by-case approach to mitigating unjust consequences of the enforcement of State aid law for the beneficiary of aid. In practice, however, the general principles of EU law are interpreted narrowly under the case law of the European courts. This is in line with the logic of EU law: Since they limit the effective implementation of European State aid law, the principles have to be interpreted restrictively.[1071]

The general principles of EU law are not explicitly codified in European primary law.[1072] In its Notice on Recovery, the Commission lists the principles that are most commonly invoked against recovery, namely the principle of legal certainty, the principle of protection of legitimate expectations, the principle of res judicata as well as absolute impossibility to recover.[1073]

Beyond that, it has been pointed out that ever since the Treaty of Lisbon, the ChFR has been of equal hierarchical status as European State aid law. Therefore, while up until now, State aid law had often been given precedence, the picture may have changed. Taking this into account, the fundamental rights enshrined in the ChFR, but also the other general principles of EU law may and should play a more significant role.[1074]

The reason why the general principles of EU law have recently become relevant is that the scholarly literature has criticized an alleged 'new approach' in fiscal State aid law. This supposed shift in the Commission's and the Courts' interpretation of State aid law would not have been foreseeable. If it were upheld by the Courts, recovery should be excluded based on the principles of protection of legitimate expectation and legal certainty. If at all, the 'new approach' should be applicable for future cases. This primarily concerned the transfer pricing cases, i.e., individual aid,[1075] but the question is relevant for fiscal aid schemes all the same.

A clarification is warranted concerning timing issues. An alleged 'new approach' in State aid control in tax matters cannot lead to an exclusion of recovery on grounds of Article 16(1) of Procedural Regulation 2015/1589 indefinitely. While the exact ambit of State aid law in the area of direct taxation may indeed not have been entirely clear in the past, the interpretation of State aid law as well as the inherent risks are now becoming increasingly clear. Moreover, a rollback can be observed in the case law of the European courts. Taxpayers have become more sensitive to potential State aid issues and Member States are notifying more tax measures to create legal certainty. All this will eventually make deliberations on the general principles of EU law as a limit to

1070. A different view is apparently held by Rzotkiewicz, *supra* n. 168, at 473.
1071. Joined Cases T-394, 408, 453 and 454/08 *Regione autonoma della Sardegna and Others v. Commission* EU:T:2011:493, para. 283; Commission Notice on the recovery, *supra* n. 875, at para. 33.
1072. Commission Notice on the recovery, *supra* n. 875, at para. 33.
1073. *Ibid.*, para. 34.
1074. Moreno González, *Recovery of Tax-Related State Aid in Spain*, *supra* n. 169, at 409; Rzotkiewicz, *supra* n. 168, at 474.
1075. *See, e.g.*, Allevato, *supra* n. 126, at 93; Lovdahl Gormsen & Mifsud-Bonnici, *supra* n. 126.

recovery less relevant. It is therefore necessary to address the structural weakness of State aid law that taxpayers who are faced with legal uncertainty are in no position to notify potential aid to the Commission.[1076]

This chapter will not comprehensively address all aspects of the case-by-case limits to the obligation of recovery. The literature on the significance of general principles of EU law in State aid law has, for example, also addressed the principle of national identity under Article 4(2) TEU, the principle of *ne bis in idem*, the principle of proportionality or the principle of equality.[1077] We will particularly focus on the principle of protection of legitimate expectation as it is most commonly brought forward in the literature on the recovery of fiscal aid schemes and because it most clearly embodies the perspective of individual taxpayers who are faced with a recovery order.

This chapter will therefore begin with a detailed survey of the role principle of protection of legitimate expectation in EU State aid law. The principle is construed narrowly due to the link to the obligation to notify new aid and thus has only rarely led to an exclusion of recovery. We will then shed light on selected dimensions of the principle of protection of legitimate expectation, namely objective and subjective aspects, the question of whether a balancing of interests is necessary, the competent courts and preclusion effects as well as actors that can bring forward legitimate expectations to fend off recovery. The focus will then turn to the protection of legitimate expectations in fiscal aid cases. While the CJEU makes no special case for fiscal aid schemes, the Commission regularly at least partly excludes recovery based on the principle of protection of legitimate expectation. In light of the strengthened position of competitors after the judgment in *Scuola Elementare Maria Montessori*, such constellations may very well come under scrutiny by the CJEU. It is not clear whether the Commission's more lenient approach would be endorsed in all cases. The principle of protection of legitimate expectation cannot be invoked due to the alleged nature of abstract tax benefits as aid that is 'imposed upon' the beneficiary ('aufgedrängte Beihilfe') or in light of other particularities of tax law (§6.01).

Ongoing legal uncertainty in principle cannot exclude recovery. The problem in such constellations is that taxpayers cannot notify new aid themselves, but depend on the Member State to do so. Where an interpretation of State aid law first emerges and was not foreseeable, we propose to exclude recovery in application of the principle of legal certainty (§6.02).

The national court's enforcement function derived from Article 108(3), (3) TFEU may involve an obligation to recover aid regardless of whether it is compatible with the internal market. Article 16(1) of Procedural Regulation 2015/1589, which restricts recovery where there would otherwise be an infringement of State aid law, is not applicable but the limits to recovery should coincide (§6.03).

1076. Similarly identifying the weak position of the taxpayer in light of legal uncertainty as the main issue Soltész, *supra* n. 174, at 24.
1077. Rzotkiewicz, *supra* n. 168.

§6.01 THE PRINCIPLE OF PROTECTION OF LEGITIMATE EXPECTATION AS A LIMIT WITH A NARROW SCOPE

The case law of the European courts indicates that the principle of protection of legitimate expectation as a limit to the enforcement of State aid law is construed narrowly [A]. We will examine the different dimensions of the principle in more detail [B]. No special case is made for tax measures in the case law of the CJEU, even though the Commission' practice on fiscal aid schemes appears to be more lenient [C]. There appears to be no room for a more taxpayer-friendly interpretation of the principle, which remains a shortcoming of fiscal State aid law [D].

[A] The Case Law on the Principle of Protection of Legitimate Expectation

The European courts have interpreted the principle of protection of legitimate expectation in the context of State aid law narrowly. It requires precise, unconditional, and consistent assurances by an EU institution or representatives thereof [1]. Specifications also emerge from the case law on the necessity for transitional measures, although this case law, just like the case law on recovery, lacks a theoretical foundation [2].

[1] The Case Law on Recovery

An infringement of the principle of protection of legitimate expectation as a general principle of EU law[1078] excludes recovery under Article 16(1) of Procedural Regulation 2015/1589.[1079] Most often, the plea alleging an infringement of the principle will not succeed.[1080] It has therefore been argued that the principle would be interpreted more narrowly in European State aid law than in other areas of EU law.[1081]

The right of an individual to rely on the principle of protection of legitimate expectation in EU law, in general, requires precise, unconditional and consistent assurances given to the beneficiary of aid by an EU institution, body or agency. These assurances have to originate from authorized, reliable sources and they have to be

1078. *See* only, e.g., Case 112/80 *Dürbeck v. Hauptzollamt Frankfurt a.M.* EU:C:1981:94, para. 48; Case C-369/09 P *ISD Polska and Others v. Commission* EU:C:2011:175, para. 122.
1079. On the principle of protection of legitimate expectation in State aid law, e.g., De Pietro, *supra* n. 173, at 108ff.; Fink, *supra* n. 168; Giraud, *supra* n. 168; Jaros & Ritter, *supra* n. 168; Krumm, *supra* n. 173, at 575ff.; Lovdahl Gormsen & Mifsud-Bonnici, *supra* n. 126, at 426ff.; Martini, *supra* n. 119; Papi Rossi, *supra* n. 168, at 155ff.; Mason, *State Aid Special Reports, supra* n. 173; Salvador Pastoriza, *supra* n. 173; Rzotkiewicz, *supra* n. 168, at 467ff.; Saavedra Pinto, *supra* n. 168.; Schönfeld & Ellenrieder, *supra* n. 173. On the principle of protection of legitimate expectation in State aid law in general: Sharpston, *Legitimate Expectations and Economic Reality, supra* n. 168; Sharpston, *European Community Law and the Doctrine of Legitimate Expectations, supra* n. 168; Weiß & Haberkamm, *supra* n. 168. *See also* Paul P. Craig, *Substantive Legitimate Expectations in Domestic and Community Law* 55 CLJ 289, 304ff. (1996); Kokott, *Steuerrecht, supra* n. 20, at §2 paras 37ff. on the principle in general.
1080. *See, e.g.,* Saavedra Pinto, *supra* n. 168, at 273; Schönfeld & Ellenrieder, *supra* n. 173, at 446.
1081. Saavedra Pinto, *supra* n. 168, at 273.

given to the person concerned by the competent authorities of the EU. From this, the private actor has to have derived well-founded expectations.[1082]

Crucially, undertakings can normally only entertain legitimate expectations as to the lawfulness of aid where the aid has been notified to the Commission.[1083] Since the lack of notification is the most common scenario in fiscal aid cases, legitimate expectations can only rarely exclude recovery.[1084] According to the CJEU, an economic operator exercising due care should normally be able to determine whether aid has been notified.[1085] This notion of a diligent businessman and the link with notification have significantly reduced the potential scope of the principle of protection of legitimate expectation.[1086] For example, in its judgment in *Italy v. Commission,* the CJEU stated that the fact that the beneficiaries of aid were small undertakings could not justify legitimate expectations as to the lawfulness of the aid.[1087] It thus outright rejected to introduce distinctions within the benchmark of 'diligent businessman'. Therefore, this benchmark does not appear to have much practical significance in itself.[1088] By contrast, where aid has not been notified, legitimate expectations can only be recognized under exceptional circumstances.[1089]

The principle of protection of legitimate expectation can also not be relied on against an unambiguous provision of EU law.[1090] This, for example, means that there

1082. E.g., Case C-537/08 P *Kahla Thüringen Porzellan v. Commission* EU:C:2010:769, para. 63; Joined Cases C-630 to 633/11 P *HGA and Others v. Commission* EU:C:2013:387, para. 132; Case C-349/17 *Eesti Pagar,* para. 97; Joined Cases C-649, 658 and 662/20 P *Spain and Others v. Commission*, para. 81; Case T-620/11 *GFKL,* para. 187. Different phrasing in Joined Cases C-182 and 217/03 *Belgium and Forum 187*, para. 147 and Case C-519/07 P *Commission v. Koninklijke FrieslandCampina* EU:C:2009:556, para. 84. *See also* Case C-369/09 P *ISD Polska,* para. 123.

1083. *See* only Case C-5/89 *Commission v. Germany;* para. 14; Case C-24/95 *Alcan Deutschland,* para. 25; Case C-169/95 *Spain v. Commission*, para. 51; Case C-91/01 *Italy v. Commission* EU:C:2004:244, para. 65; Joined Cases C-183 and 187/02 P *Demesa and Territorio Histórico de Álava v. Commission* EU:C:2004:701, para. 44; Case C-148/04 *Unicredito Italiano*, para. 104; Case C-81/10 P *France Télécom v. Commission* EU:C:2011:811, para. 59; Joined Cases C-630 to 633/11 P *HGA and Others v. Commission*, para. 134; Case C-672/13 *OTP Bank*, para. 77; Case C-349/17 *Eesti Pagar*, para. 98; Case T-620/11 *GFKL;* para. 188.

1084. *See* Fink, *supra* n. 168, at 136f.; Martini, *supra* n. 119, at 104f.; Schönfeld & Ellenrieder, *supra* n. 173, at 446f.

1085. Case C-5/89 *Commission v. Germany*, para. 14; Case C-24/95 *Alcan Deutschland*, para. 25; Case C-148/04 *Unicredito Italiano*, para. 104; Case C-81/10 P *France Télécom*, para. 59; Case C-672/13 *OTP Bank*, para. 77; Case C-349/17 *Eesti Pagar*, para. 98; Case T-620/11 *GFKL*, para. 188.

1086. De Pietro, *supra* n. 173, at 109; Jaros & Ritter, *supra* n. 168, at 573f.; Krumm, *supra* n. 173, at 580f.

1087. Case C-298/00 P *Italy v. Commission* EU:C:2004:240, para. 88.

1088. A different view appears to be held by Saavedra Pinto, *supra* n. 168, at 275f.

1089. Case C-5/89 *Commission v. Germany*, para. 16; Case C-148/04 *Unicredito Italiano*, para. 111; Case C-199/06 *CELF I*, para. 65; Similarly Giraud, *supra* n. 168, at 1427 as well as De Pietro, *supra* n. 173, at 109.

1090. Joined Cases C-31 to 44/91 *Lageder and Others v. Amministrazione delle finanze dello Stato* EU:C:1993:132, para. 35; Case C-568/11 *Agroferm* EU:C:2013:407 (on Union aid), para. 52; Case C-120/17 *Ministru kabinets* EU:C:2018:638, para. 52; Case C-349/17 *Eesti Pagar*, para. 104.

can be no legitimate expectations where a Member State misapplied the GBER and consequently failed to notify an aid measure.[1091]

This narrow interpretation of the principle of protection of legitimate expectation generally leads to the CJEU rejecting from the outset that there could be an infringement thereof.[1092] Consequently – except for transitional measures[1093] – the CJEU has not often had the opportunity to clarify the exact requirements for a protection of legitimate expectations in State aid law.[1094] As a consequence, the case law is somewhat blurred.[1095]

[2] The Case Law on the Necessity of Transitional Measures

The exact interpretation of the principle of the protection of legitimate expectation in State aid law perhaps emerges most clearly in the context of the necessity for transitional measures where rules have to be abolished. While the main issues dealt with in this case law are not directly related to recovery, the principles that emerge should be transferrable.

The CJEU's judgment in *Forum 187 and Belgium v. Commission* dealt with tax advantages awarded to Belgian coordination centres. The scheme in question constituted existing aid as the Commission had repeatedly found that the scheme did not involve State aid. This meant that the later finding of illegal State aid, which came about in the context of an examination of measures potentially constituting harmful tax competition, could not lead to recovery. Instead, the scheme only had to be abolished for the future.[1096]

The scheme involved an approval process. Approval was granted for a period of 10 years. In its decision, the Commission granted a transitional period for coordination centres that had already obtained approval to profit from the scheme This was because the Commission recognized that such approval would cause the expectation of continuity. According to the Commission, once the current approval period had run

---

1091. Case C-349/17 *Eesti Pagar*, para. 106.

1092. *See* however, e.g., Case 223/85 *RSV v. Commission* EU:C:1987:502, para. 17 due to the extraordinary length of the procedure as well as Case T-6/99 *ESF Elbe-Stahlwerke Feralpi v. Commission* EU:T:2001:145, paras 188ff. Critical, e.g., Papi Rossi, *supra* n. 168, at 160.

1093. *See* Ch. §6.01[A], [1] *infra.*

1094. Sharpston, *Legitimate Expectations and Economic Reality, supra* n. 168, at 158 contends that the case law on the principle of protection of legitimate expectation would pivot around the foreseeability of change. Where changes of view by the authorities would usually not be foreseeable, changes in the underlying circumstances and changes caused by increased problems of the same essential kind as earlier problems would generally be foreseeable. Where regulations linked to the latter then change, there can be no protection of legitimate expectation.

1095. Similarly Giraud, *supra* n. 168, at 1400; Jaros & Ritter, *supra* n. 168, at 573. Moreover, it has been noted that there is little theoretical foundation to the principle of protection of legitimate expectation as applied in European State aid law. Sharpston, *Legitimate Expectations and Economic Reality, supra* n. 168, at 160 holds that this comes down to the pragmatic attitudes of the European courts. It would apply general principles of EU law, where the result would otherwise be inequitable or economically unsound.

1096. Joined Cases C-182 and 217/03 *Belgium and Forum 187. See* paras 5ff. for the facts of the case.

out, it could not be renewed and the coordination centre ceased to profit from the scheme.[1097] This latter aspect was challenged in front of the European courts.

In its judgment, the CJEU indeed found a breach of the principle of protection of legitimate expectation for failure to allow for a renewal in cases where the ten-year period ran out shortly after the Commission had issued its decision. The CJEU applied a three-step approach. First, it verified whether there had been any 'expectation' on the side of the beneficiary undertakings.[1098] Second, it addressed the legitimacy of these expectations.[1099] Third, the CJEU ascertained whether there was an overriding public interest which may take precedence over the interest of the undertakings – a step which only appears to be necessary for transitional measures.[1100] Since there was a legitimate expectation and there was no overriding public interest, there was indeed an infringement of the principle of the protection of legitimate expectation.[1101]

As to the first aspect, the CJEU held that the Commission's prior decisions and a reply given to a written question of a Member of the European Parliament on the Commission's behalf by the Commissioner for Competition, according to which the scheme did not contain elements of State aid, indeed created relevant expectations.[1102] It added that there was neither a discretionary element to the renewal process nor a maximum number of renewals.[1103]

The CJEU then addressed the legitimacy of these expectations. The decision to initiate the formal investigation procedure dated from June 2002. The decision was published in February 2003. This period of time was too short for the undertakings as prudent economic operators to adjust their business decisions.[1104]

The CJEU then concluded that the Commission had not shown that there was an overriding public interest that would preclude the granting of a transitional period.[1105]

Another case that concerned the protection of legitimate expectations in the area of taxation and transitional measures was the CJEU's *Commission v. Koninklijke FrieslandCampina*, albeit with the opposite result.[1106] This case dealt with a tax scheme for international financing activities of undertakings. The scheme allowed entities that belonged to an international group and that carried out financing activities solely in the Netherlands and to the profit of group entities established in at least four States or on two continents to set aside 80% of its total taxable profit in a risk reserve, provided this had been authorized ('GFA scheme'). This authorization was granted for ten years. The entity could then use these amounts to acquire shares in or contribute capital to the Netherlands or a foreign company. Fifty per cent to a hundred per cent of the price of

1097. *Ibid.*, para. 32.
1098. *Ibid.*, paras 150ff.
1099. *Ibid.*, paras 159ff.
1100. *Ibid.*, paras 164ff.
1101. *Ibid.*, para. 167.
1102. *Ibid.*, para. 155.
1103. *Ibid.*, para. 156.
1104. *Ibid.*, para. 162.
1105. *Ibid.*, para. 165.
1106. Case C-519/07 P *Koninklijke FrieslandCampina*.

acquisition or the capital reserve could be taken from the risk reserve. These amounts were thus exempt from taxation.[1107]

The Commission did not order recovery as the beneficiaries of the scheme could rely on the principle of protection of legitimate expectation in light of prior decisions on the Belgian coordination centre regime. It allowed for a transitional period for entities that had already been granted GFA authorizations at the time when the Commission decision was taken until the 10-year period had run out or at the latest until 31 December 2019. Such actors could consequently both constitute new reserves and use existing reserves.[1108]

Koninklijke FrieslandCampina NV (KFC) had requested GFA authorization before the Commission's decision on the GFA scheme had been issued, but the request had not been approved yet. It was later rejected as the applicant did not fulfil the requirements to profit from the transitional period.[1109]

The CJEU denied the existence of legitimate expectations because the undertaking did not yet profit from the GFA scheme, but had merely submitted a request for first authorization, which could moreover be subject to conditions. This situation would not only be different from that of an operator that had already received approval but also from operators that request renewal of the authorization to profit from the scheme, for which the Commission recognized legitimate expectations in its decision on the Belgian coordination centres.[1110] It stated that:

> In that judgment, the Court took account of the significant investments which those undertakings, which were benefiting from authorisation under the BCC scheme and were requesting renewal, had made, and of the long-term commitments which they had undertaken. Those who have requested a first GFA authorisation are not, in principle, in the same situation as a taxpayer who is already a beneficiary of the GFA in relation to investments and commitments.[1111]

KFC would not have brought forward that it had made such investments or entered into commitments.[1112] The difference between the two situations would thus be that while KFC could merely have benefitted from the scheme in the future, the undertakings in the Belgian coordination centre case would have suffered losses due to investments that were undertaken when it was beyond doubt that the scheme was not problematic from a State aid point of view.[1113]

While a certain methodology appears to emerge, some points remain open. These cases are very similar. Yet the CJEU does not follow the approach to establishing whether there was a breach of the principle of protection of legitimate expectation it had relied upon in the Belgian coordination centre case in its later judgment. It also remains open whether it is always necessary to separate the aspects of expectation and

1107. *See* in detail *ibid.*, paras 2ff.
1108. *Ibid.*, paras 15f.
1109. *Ibid.*, paras 17ff.
1110. *Ibid.*, paras 88ff.
1111. *Ibid.*, para. 91.
1112. *Ibid.*, para. 92.
1113. *Ibid.*, paras 93f.

legitimacy[1114] or indeed what the exact steps to verify both aspects are. Finally, the nature of overriding public interest that could be brought forward by the Commission does not emerge, nor is it clear whether such reasons could also be relevant in the context of Article 16(1) of Procedural Regulation 2015/1589.

[B] Dimensions of the Principle of Protection of Legitimate Expectation

The following section will go into more detail about some of the dimensions of the principle of protection of legitimate expectation in State aid law. These dimensions often do not emerge clearly from the case law and sometimes the European courts will take contradictory positions.

Attempts at establishing a theoretical foundation have perhaps most notably been undertaken by Giraud and Sharpston.[1115] For example, Giraud distinguishes: the legitimate nature of the expectation (i), the object of the legitimate expectation (ii), the source of the legitimate expectation (iii) and the balance of interest (iv).[1116] The different aspects are closely intertwined and will be classified slightly differently here: In the following, we first examine the objective aspects of the protection of legitimate expectation, i.e. the sources of a protection of legitimate expectation [1], before addressing the subjective aspects, i.e. the nature and object of such protected expectations [2]. We argue that no balancing of interests is required [3]. Additionally, we examine in front of which court legitimate expectations can be brought forward [4] and which actors may do so [5].

[1] Objective Aspects: Definition of Exceptional Circumstances

In the absence of notification, the principle of protection of legitimate expectation can only lead to an exclusion of recovery under exceptional circumstances. From the case law laid out above it is clear that exceptional circumstances require some sort of act in the widest sense that can qualify as a precise and unconditional assurance. At first glance, this case law would appear to suggest that there has to be direct contact with

1114. Sharpston, *Legitimate Expectations and Economic Reality*, *supra* n. 168, at 105 contrasts reasonable expectation and legitimate expectation. The former would refer to a prediction that an operator arrives at through the logical analysis of a reasonable body of information. The latter would refer to expectations for which the operator can claim legal validity under EU law. *See*, for example, on a lack of legitimacy Craig, *supra* n. 1079, at 306, albeit not solely in the context of State aid law.

1115. Giraud, *supra* n. 168. Sharpston, *Legitimate Expectations and Economic Reality*, *supra* n. 168. According to *Giraud*, the determination of the legitimate nature of expectation would require an objective and a subjective test. The former aims at establishing whether there are exceptional circumstances, while the latter would allow the court to reject claims relating to the principle of protection of legitimate expectation, where the beneficiary entertained significant doubts as to the legality of the aid granted to it. Sharpston, *European Community Law and the Doctrine of Legitimate Expectations*, *supra* n. 168. *See also* Papi Rossi, *supra* n. 168, at 156: (i) legal basis of legitimate expectation, (ii) legitimacy of expectations, (iii) no overriding public-policy interest.

1116. Giraud, *supra* n. 168, at 1406ff.

the institution issuing such assurances and that the assurances have to be made concerning a specific case and beneficiary and for the aid measure in question. However, this does not appear to be the case.[1117] As Giraud notes, implicit assurances or even general assurances (e.g., a lack of clarity of previous decision practice) have sometimes been accepted as grounds for an exclusion of recovery.[1118] Moreover, in some cases, beneficiaries of aid have successfully invoked precise assurances that were not given to them, but to actors in a comparable situation.[1119]

The fact that both Member States and EU institutions are involved in the enforcement of State aid law implies that beneficiaries of aid could theoretically derive legitimate expectations from assurances by actors from both levels.

Actions by EU institutions may certainly be grounds for a protection of legitimate expectation,[1120] even though not every type of assurance suffices. For example, in its judgment in *Forum 187 and Belgium v. Commission*, the CJEU acknowledged that a Commission decision on the specific measure at issue can give rise to legitimate expectations.[1121] Such expectations are not recognized where decisions not to raise objections or positive decisions were successfully challenged in due time before the Court.[1122] The same holds true during the period for bringing an action or while such action is pending before the European courts.[1123] By contrast, where such decisions are not challenged, this would lead to existing aid, excluding recovery. The principle of protection of legitimate expectation could then warrant transitional measures.[1124] Member States' fiscal aid schemes often have similarities. Yet the CJEU has not taken a definite stance on Commission decisions on similar aid measures in other Member States.

The fact that many of the national tax practices now considered problematic under State aid law had long been public knowledge without being tackled by the Commission is irrelevant and cannot lead to the existence of legitimate expectations.[1125] Changes in the case law of the European courts that had not been foreseeable or otherwise contradictory or misleading case law of the CJEU would, however, suffice.[1126]

1117. Lovdahl Gormsen & Mifsud-Bonnici, *supra* n. 126, at 428f.
1118. Giraud, *supra* n. 168, at 1413ff. *See* Krumm, *supra* n. 173, at 577f. for another example of general assurances.
1119. Rzotkiewicz, *supra* n. 168, at 468.
1120. *See* only Joined Cases C-182 and 217/03 *Belgium and Forum 187*, para. 147; Case C-519/07 P *Koninklijke FrieslandCampina*, para. 84; Case C-194/09 *Alcoa Trasformazioni v. Commission* EU:C:2011:497, para. 71; Martini, *supra* n. 119, at 105f.
1121. Joined Cases C-182 and 217/03 *Belgium and Forum 187*, para. 155.
1122. Case C-169/95 *Spain v. Commission*, para. 53.
1123. Case C-199/06 *CELF I*, paras 66ff., albeit in the context of the national court's enforcement obligations that are derived from Art. 108(3), (3) TFEU. *See* the judgments in CELF I and Case C-1/09 *CELF II*, para. 52, according to which not even a succession of three positive decisions that were later on annulled could give rights to legitimate expectations. *See also* Case C-91/01 *Italy v. Commission*, paras 66f.
1124. *See* Ch. §6.01[A], [2] *supra*.
1125. Joined Cases C-183 and 187/02 P *Demesa and Territorio Histórico de Álava*, para. 52; Case C-81/10 P *France Télécom*, para. 60; Krumm, *supra* n. 173, at 579; Martini, *supra* n. 119, at 106.
1126. *See* Ch. §6.01[C] *infra* for an example.

In contrast to this, assurances or any other type of behaviour of national authorities will generally not qualify as an exceptional circumstance.[1127] This is only logical in light of the double role of Member States in State aid law.[1128] In particular, the Court has clarified that there can be no legitimate expectation of a beneficial treatment contrary to EU law where a national authority responsible for applying EU law acts in breach of that law.[1129] This would even be the case where recovery marks a breach of good faith as the authority is responsible for the illegality of the decision.[1130]

[2] Subjective Aspects: Object and Nature of Expectations

There can be no legitimate expectation as to the compatibility of an aid measure.[1131] Instead, a distinction has to be made between the questions of (i) whether aid is lawful, i.e., if it has been notified, and (ii) whether there is aid in the first place. The first aspect can theoretically lead to a protection of legitimate expectation and thus exclude recovery. However, in light of the case law on the necessity of notification and the notion of the 'diligent businessman', it can only very rarely be invoked successfully.[1132]

The second aspect – the qualification of a State measure as aid – is not only more relevant but also significantly blurrier. As far as can be seen, the case law of the CJEU does not explicitly acknowledge that the expectations of the beneficiaries of aid can also refer to this aspect. Yet the question of whether beneficiaries could realize that they were receiving aid that would have had to be notified is most often implicitly the core of the deliberations on the principle of protection of legitimate expectation and recovery may be excluded for this reason.[1133]

One may furthermore wonder whether abstract expectations in the lawfulness of a tax measure suffice. The latter approach (abstract expectations) seeks to identify the characteristics groups of beneficiaries or constellations, where legitimate expectations (could potentially) exist. The former approach (concrete expectations) examines the expectations of every single beneficiary of aid. In any case, it appears to be irrelevant whether the individual beneficiary has taken dispositions in light of the precise

1127. *See, e.g.*, Case C-148/04 *Unicredito Italiano*, para. 107; Englisch, *Das Beihilfenverbot im Steuerrecht*, *supra* n. 67, at para. 9.69; Giraud, *supra* n. 168, at 1418; Martini, *supra* n. 119, at 105; Mason, *State Aid Special Reports*, *supra* n. 173, at 619.
1128. Jaros & Ritter, *supra* n. 168, at 576.
1129. Joined Cases C-31 to 44/91 *Lageder and Others v. Amministrazione delle finanze dello Stato*, paras 34f.; Case C-568/11 *Agroferm*, para. 52 (on Union aid); Case C-349/17 *Eesti Pagar*, para. 104; Case C-120/17 *Ministru kabinets*, para. 52 (on Union aid); Case T-620/11 *GFKL*, para. 191.
1130. Case C-24/95 *Alcan Deutschland*, para. 39. It has been suggested that an exception should be made for national courts in the assessment stage as they are explicitly competent to interpret Art. 107(1) TFEU. Where a decision addresses the potential State aid problem, but denies that there is aid, this should lead to a protection of legitimate expectation, provided the national court did not infringe upon its obligation to refer questions to the CJEU, Schönfeld & Ellenrieder, *supra* n. 173, at 446.
1131. Giraud, *supra* n. 168, at 1411f.
1132. *Ibid.*, at 1408.
1133. Similarly *Ibid.*, at 1409 with reference to Case 310/85 *Deufil v. Commission*, para. 24. In favour such exclusion also Saavedra Pinto, *supra* n. 168, at 275.

assurances, i.e., whether their actions were influenced by the expectations that were created by the conduct of the relevant EU institution.[1134] It appears as though abstract legitimate expectations suffice for aid schemes. Yet the decisional practice is by no means clear.[1135] The confusion may partly stem from the fact that concrete legitimate expectations of individual beneficiaries of aid schemes will often be left for the national courts to assess, which means that the CJEU has no reason to take a definite stance. Moreover, as soon as the Commission indeed does accept that the principle of protection excludes recovery, it will be very rare that the CJEU has to deal with this aspect of the Commission decision.

[3] No Balancing of Interests

The fundamental conflict between the effectiveness of State aid control and the general principles of EU law is codified by Article 16(1) of Procedural Regulation 2015/1589, which generally requires recovery as the logical consequence of an infringement of State aid law. Recovery is excluded as soon as it would be contrary to a general principle of EU law. One may then wonder whether Article 16(1) correctly resolves the underlying conflict rooted in primary law. Alternatively, these considerations could play a role in the context of the assessment of the infringement of the principle of protection of legitimate expectation. The CJEU has explicitly rejected that the principle of proportionality – which generally implies a balancing of interests – limits recovery. According to this case law, recovery is the logical consequence of an infringement of State aid law and it is necessary to restore the *status quo ante* through recovery. Consequently, a recovery order cannot be disproportionate.[1136]

However, it has sometimes been argued that this case law of the CJEU would be misleading in that recovery would merely be a manifestation of the effet utile and the

1134. Schönfeld & Ellenrieder, *supra* n. 173, at 448 with reference to the Commission decisions underlying the judgment in *World Duty Free Group*, where recovery was even excluded for the period prior to the assurances that led to the protection of legitimate expectations. A different view for the principle of protection of legitimate expectation in general was held by Sharpston, *Legitimate Expectations and Economic Reality*, *supra* n. 168, at 158.

1135. The approach of the CJEU in the cases that do exist, does not appear to be consistent. For example, the procedural constellations in the two judgments on the necessity of transitional measures were comparable. In its judgment in *Belgium and Forum 187 v. Commission*, the CJEU relied not on the concrete applicant Forum 187, but on the entire group of coordination centres whose authorization was up for renewal and that could therefore not profit from the transitional period laid down in the Commission decision. It thus adopted an abstract approach to determining whether there were legitimate expectations. By contrast, in its judgment in *Commission v. Koninklijke FrieslandCampina*, the CJEU did not clearly distinguish whether it approaches the protection legitimate expectation from an abstract or a concrete perspective, apparently relying on both approaches at the same time to a certain extent.

1136. *See* only Case C-142/87 *Belgium v. Commission*, para. 66; Case C-169/95 *Spain v. Commission*, para. 47; Case C-75/97 *Belgium v. Commission*, para. 68; Case C-148/04 *Unicredito Italiano*, para. 113.

supremacy of EU law. These considerations would conflict with the general principles of EU law,[1137] presumably with the latter potentially taking precedence.

Consequently, the conflicting interests would have to be balanced. Recovery would thus need to be appropriate for attaining the underlying policy objective, necessary in the sense that it is the least restrictive means of achieving this objective, and not disproportionate to this aim.[1138] It is not clear if this would be a part of the assessment of the requirements for a protection of legitimate expectation or whether this would be a test in its own right.

However, in contrast to other areas of EU law, a balancing of interests nevertheless does not seem necessary.[1139] The CJEU has only relied on it for transitional measures which may not be necessary if there is an overriding public interest.[1140] There is a difference between the necessity for transitional measures and the exclusion of recovery. For the latter, the relevant issues of the case are in the past, which means that the public interest in remedying the infringement is perhaps less relevant than the interest of individuals. By contrast, transitional measures concern the current state of play. Providing for transitional measures effectively means that the infringement of State aid law is allowed to go on. The role of public policy interests may therefore have to be stronger. Moreover, where there is a failure to notify, the result of the balancing of interest is to a certain extent pre-empted in that it is only in exceptional circumstances that recovery will be excluded in any case.[1141]

[4] Competent Fora

Both national courts and European courts can potentially be in charge of deciding whether legitimate expectations exclude recovery in a specific case at hand.[1142] While the principles determining which court is competent are not entirely clear from the case law, national courts are precluded from directly assessing the validity of the Commission decision. Instead, only the national acts implementing the negative Commission decision can be assessed by the national court.

The determination of the correct forum is linked to the question of whether the Commission is obliged to examine a potential exclusion of recovery on grounds of the principle of protection of legitimate expectation in a specific case at hand. If the Commission fails to take into account the principle of protection of legitimate expectation even though it was obliged to do so, the Commission decision itself has to be (partly) annulled. It nevertheless becomes binding unless it is challenged in time. The

1137. Rzotkiewicz, *supra* n. 168, at 471f.; Saavedra Pinto, *supra* n. 168, at 281.
1138. Saavedra Pinto, *supra* n. 168, at 281. Similarly: Krumm, *supra* n. 173, at 577; Lovdahl Gormsen & Mifsud-Bonnici, *supra* n. 126, at 429.
1139. A different view is held by De Pietro, *supra* n. 173, at 110; Lovdahl Gormsen & Mifsud-Bonnici, *supra* n. 126, at 427; Rzotkiewicz, *supra* n. 168, at 470.
1140. *See* Ch. §6.01[A], [2] *supra*. Similarly for areas that do not concern State aid law, e.g., Case C-183/95 *Affish v. Rijksdienst voor de deuring van Vee en Vlees* EU:C:1997:373, para. 57 with further references.
1141. Similarly Giraud, *supra* n. 168, at 1419.
1142. *See* Giraud, *supra* n. 168, at 1423; Jaros & Ritter, *supra* n. 168, at 574f.

beneficiary of aid would then be precluded from bringing forward circumstances which may lead to a protection of legitimate expectation at a later stage.[1143]

At the same time, the CJEU has consistently held that the beneficiary of aid can rely on exceptional circumstances, which had led them to believe that the aid would be lawful. Where such a case is brought before a national court, it would be for the national court to assess the material circumstances.[1144] This case law appears contradictory. According to Englisch, it should be understood as a primary obligation to attack the Commission's decision, since the Commission is obliged by law to assess whether recovery has to be excluded due to the principle of protection of legitimate expectation. Only the concrete circumstances of a specific case could be dealt with by the national court.[1145]

In our view, the case law is simply not clear, since there are not enough decisions, for unambiguous principles to emerge. The judgments by the European Courts mainly concern actions that were brought against Commission decisions by individual beneficiaries or in the case of the judgment in *Spain v. Commission*[1146] by the Member State regarding individual aid. In such cases, the Commission will in its decision examine the individual circumstances of the beneficiary, who had the opportunity to submit comments in the course of the formal investigation procedure. Consequently, the concrete and abstract expectations of the individual beneficiary concern the legality of the Commission decision itself.

Yet where an individual beneficiary of an aid scheme is concerned, the dividing line is blurry.[1147] This is not so much problematic if the individual beneficiary had a choice of forum. By contrast, if they were precluded from bringing forward arguments in front of the national court because they failed to do so in front of the European courts, the dividing line has to be clear.

In our view, at least the aspects of an abstract protection of legitimate expectation already have to be dealt with by the Commission in its decision. The Commission is under an ex officio-obligation to determine whether legitimate expectations have to be taken into account, even where neither a Member State nor the beneficiaries of aid have brought forward arguments in this respect in the course of the formal investigation procedure.[1148] The Commission's decision per se is therefore vitiated by error, where it did not take into account legitimate expectations.[1149] Therefore, these aspects have to be brought forward in front of the European courts, where this is possible. Where beneficiaries are not aware of the fact that they are (potential) beneficiaries of

1143. Jaros & Ritter, *supra* n. 168, at 575.

1144. Case C-5/89 *Commission v. Germany*, para. 16; Case C-310/99 *Italy v. Commission*, para. 103; Case T-620/11 *GFKL*, para. 190 with reference to Case T-67/94 *Ladbroke Racing*, paras 182f.; Case T-109/01 *Fleuren Compost v. Commission* EU:T:2004:4, paras 136f.; Case T-309/12 *Zweckverband Tierkörperbeseitigung v. Commission* EU:T:2014:676, para. 237.

1145. Englisch, *Das Beihilfenverbot im Steuerrecht*, *supra* n. 67, at para. 9.71.

1146. Case C-169/95 *Spain v. Commission*.

1147. *See* on this conflict Jaros & Ritter, *supra* n. 168, at 574f.

1148. Aalbers & Adriaanse, *supra* n. 170, at para. 30-048. Similarly Krumm, *supra* n. 173, at 575f. and Rzotkiewicz, *supra* n. 168, at 472 with reference to the judgments in Case 223/85 *RSV v. Commission* and Case C-346 and 529/03 *Atzeni and Others* EU:C:2006:130.

1149. Similarly Jaros & Ritter, *supra* n. 168, at 576.

aid, they could nevertheless indirectly bring forward such considerations in front of the national court.[1150]

It is furthermore evident that neither the Commission nor the CJEU necessarily has the capacity to examine the individual circumstances relating to the principle of legitimate expectation for every beneficiary of an aid scheme. It, therefore, appears logical to leave the assessment for individual beneficiaries mainly up to the national courts. The validity of the Commission decision itself would then not necessarily be affected by a failure to take into account the concrete circumstances of individual beneficiaries.

[5] Actors That Can Bring Forward Legitimate Expectations

The relevant actor in the application of the principle of protection of legitimate expectation is the beneficiary of aid. The expectations of the Member State are irrelevant.[1151] This is underlined by the fact that according to the case law of the CJEU, the principle of protection of legitimate expectation is a general principle of EU law 'for the protection of the individual'.[1152] Yet one may wonder whether not only the beneficiary but also the Member State can bring forward the legitimate expectations of beneficiaries of aid to challenge the validity of the Commission decision.

In the context of infringement proceedings for failure to implement recovery orders, Member States have brought forward that they could not implement recovery as they had to protect the legitimate expectations of the beneficiaries of aid. In response to this, the CJEU has clarified that a Member State cannot rely on the legitimate expectations of the beneficiaries of aid to claim an impossibility of recovery due to its own failure to notify. Otherwise, the State aid provisions would be rendered ineffective.[1153]

The case law on the challenge of the validity of a Commission decision is not clear. The judgment of the CJEU in *Spain v. Commission* points towards a different stance than in the context of absolute impossibility. The CJEU stated that while this was indeed a different constellation to the Member State pleading impossibility of recovery, the plea based on the protection of legitimate expectation as grounds for

1150. According to Jaros & Ritter, *supra* n. 168, at 575, the beneficiary has to have a real possibility to rely on the principle for there to be a preclusion. An invitation to submit comments in the OJ would not necessarily suffice.

1151. Aalbers & Adriaanse, *supra* n. 170, at para. 30-047. Jaros & Ritter, *supra* n. 168, at 576 with reference to a number of Commission decisions, which created confusion in this respect. Similarly Micheau, *Récupération des aides d'État, supra* n. 170, at 348; Saavedra Pinto, *supra* n. 168, at 273. A different view appears to be held by Giraud, *supra* n. 168, at 1413, 1421f. Rzotkiewicz, *supra* n. 168, at 468 similarly appears to advocate such approach de lege ferenda.

1152. Joined Cases C-104/89 and 37/90 *Mulder and Other v. Council and Commission* EU:C:1992:217, para. 15.

1153. Case C-5/89 *Commission v. Germany*, para. 17; Case C-310/99 *Italy v. Commission*, para. 104. Aalbers & Adriaanse, *supra* n. 170, at para. 30-051.

annulment of the Commission decision could in any case not succeed because the requirements for a protection of legitimate expectations were not met.[1154]

This point was again addressed in the General Court's judgment in *Ladbroke Racing v. Commission*, where it was derived from the case law on absolute impossibility that the Member State cannot itself invoke the existence of legitimate expectations held by the beneficiary of the aid.[1155] Upon appeal, the CJEU confined itself to rejecting the existence of legitimate expectations and did not clarify whether the Member State was entitled to bring them forward.[1156] The judgment of the CJEU in *Italy v. Commission* concerned a challenge of the Member State against a Commission decision.[1157] While the CJEU again rejected that the substantive requirements for a protection of legitimate expectation were met, it did not exclude that the Member State could bring forward such arguments.[1158]

[C] The Protection of Legitimate Expectation in Fiscal Aid Cases

The case law of the European courts makes no special case for fiscal aid schemes. For example, in its judgment in *Unicredito Italiano,* the CJEU considered several aspects of the protection of legitimate expectation but ultimately rejected that the beneficiaries of the aid could rely on this principle to avoid recovery. First, this concerned a similar tax reduction, which had been in place before the tax measure in question. Since this measure had also not been notified, the CJEU denied that the similarity or the fact that it had been in place for a certain period of time without the Commission taking action could have led to legitimate expectations.[1159] Second, it denied that Commission decisions on aid granted to specified beneficiary banks could have created legitimate expectations as these measures differed from those at issue in the case at hand.[1160] Third, the Banca d'Italia had authorized each of the operations involving the tax reductions. The CJEU pointed out that only the Commission can examine the compatibility of aid so that no legitimate expectations could be derived from this authorization. The requirement of precise assurances by a competent institution was not fulfilled.[1161] In this case, the CJEU thus applied the general doctrine on the principle of protection of legitimate expectation and addressed no particularities of taxation.

1154. Case C-169/95 *Spain v. Commission,* para. 49.
1155. Case T-67/94 *Ladbroke Racing,* para. 183. Similarly: Joined Cases T-116 and 118/01 *P & O European Ferries (Vizcaya) v. Commission* EU:T:2003:217, para. 203.
1156. Case C-83/98 P *France v. Ladbroke Racing and Commission* EU:C:2000:248, para. 58.
1157. Case C-298/00 P *Italy v. Commission.*
1158. A different view is apparently held by Aalbers & Adriaanse, *supra* n. 170, at para. 30-051 and Bacon, *European Union Law of State Aid, supra* n. 20, at para. 18.131. Rzotkiewicz, *supra* n. 168, at 468 reads the case law as preventing Member States from bringing forward an infringement of the principle of protection of legitimate expectation. However, where the Member State itself received assurances from the Commission, it should (presumably de lege ferenda) be able to bring forward these expectations.
1159. Case C-148/04 *Unicredito Italiano,* para. 105.
1160. *Ibid.,* para. 106.
1161. *Ibid.,* para. 107.

In its decision in *France Télécom v. Commission*, the CJEU held that the mere fact that the tax regime at issue in the case was complex cannot give rise to legitimate expectations.[1162] The restrictive approach to the interpretation of the principle of protection of legitimate expectation in fiscal aid cases continued in the CJEU's judgment on the Spanish tax leasing system.[1163]

The General Court addressed several arguments that concerned the protection of legitimate expectation in its judgments on the German restructuring clause. The restructuring clause was ultimately deemed not selective by the CJEU.[1164] The elaborations on the protection of legitimate expectation therefore became redundant. Nevertheless, the judgments offer some insights into whether the particularities of taxation can play a role.

In *GFKL v. Commission*, the General Court rejected an infringement of the principle of protection of legitimate expectation in substance.[1165] The claims related to binding information by the national tax authorities, alleged difficulties in recognizing that the restructuring clause was selective and checking whether aid had been notified, as well as the existence of similar provisions in other Member States.[1166] In *Heitkamp BauHolding (HBH) v. Commission*, by contrast, the plea alleging an infringement of this principle was considered inadmissible because it was raised too late in the proceedings.[1167] However, the point that had been raised is nevertheless interesting. HBH had claimed that both the Commission's practice and its 1998 Notice on the notion of State aid had created a legitimate expectation that the restructuring clause would not be classified as a selective measure.[1168]

According to the General Court, doubts or difficulties on the interpretation of State aid law do not in themselves lead to a protection of legitimate expectation.[1169] This is because these doubts or difficulties could have been eliminated through a notification of the measures in question.

One of the other arguments that was brought forward by GFKL was that it was difficult, if not impossible for the beneficiary of aid to determine whether the aid had been notified or whether this would have been necessary.[1170] With these arguments, GFKL presumably referred to the particularities of taxation. Fiscal aid is often granted in an abstract manner and automatically. Such aid might therefore have to be assessed differently as there is no interaction with the Member State, which would suffice to even raise suspicions as to the State aid compatibility of the measure. This is to say that the beneficiary may not be aware of the preferential treatment. The argument was, however, also rejected by the General Court.[1171] While the beneficiaries of aid thus

1162. Case C-81/10 P *France Télécom*, para. 62.
1163. Joined Cases C-649, 658 and 662/20 P *Spain and Others v. Commission*, paras 81-106.
1164. *See* Ch. §3.02[D][1] *supra*.
1165. Case T-620/11 *GFKL*, paras 185ff.
1166. *Ibid.*, para. 185.
1167. Case T-287/11 *Heitkamp BauHolding v. Commission*, paras 146ff.
1168. *Ibid.*, para. 146.
1169. Case T-620/11 *GFKL*, para. 189.
1170. *Ibid.*, para. 185.
1171. *See* Ch. §6.01[D] *infra*.

raised points on the particularities of fiscal aid, the GC did not acknowledge their significance.

Nevertheless, in our view, the point that was raised in *Heitkamp BauHolding v. Commission* may have been valid, even if it was not considered in substance.[1172] The 1998 Notice contained the following passage:

> Tax measures which are *open to all economic agents* operating within a Member State are in principle *general measures*. They must be effectively open to all firms on an equal access basis, and they may not de facto be reduced in scope through, for example, the discretionary power of the State to grant them or through other factors that restrict their practical effect. [...] Provided that they apply without distinction to all firms and to the production of all goods, the following measures do not constitute State aid:
>
> - [...]
> - measures pursuing general economic policy objectives through a reduction of the tax burden related to certain production costs (research and development (R&D), the environment, training, employment).
>
> The fact that some firms or some sectors benefit more than others from some of these tax measures does not necessarily mean that they are caught by the competition rules governing State aid. Thus, measures designed to reduce the taxation of labour for all firms have a relatively greater effect on labour-intensive industries than on capital-intensive industries, without necessarily constituting State aid. Similarly, tax incentives for environmental, R&D or training investment favour only the firms which undertake such investment, but again do not necessarily constitute State aid.[1173]

It is particularly the passage in bold that does not appear to be in line with the current interpretation of selectivity. Where such reduction of tax only applies to certain production costs - even if applicable regardless of sector - it would presumably be selective. The fact that theoretically every undertaking could profit from a tax measure does not suffice to exclude selectivity.[1174] Based on this notice, which was in force until it was replaced by the 2016 Notice on the notion of State aid,[1175] a taxpayer may very well have concluded that tax measures are not selective as long as they are at least theoretically open to every undertaking and serve objectives of general economic policy.

At the same time, it has to be noted that the Commission appears to be more lenient in concluding that recovery has to be excluded due to legitimate expectations.[1176] Where the Commission indeed does not order recovery, this will naturally but rarely be subject to litigation, since the beneficiaries of aid have no interest in challenging this conclusion. This may conceivably change as the competitors of the

1172. Case T-287/11 *Heitkamp BauHolding v. Commission*, para. 146.
1173. Commission Notice on the application of the State aid rules to measures relating to direct business taxation [1998] OJ C 384/3, paras 13f.; emphasis added by the author.
1174. *See* Ch. §3.03[A] *supra*.
1175. Commission Notice on the notion of State aid, *supra* n. 26.
1176. Giraud, *supra* n. 168, at 1417. *See* Papi Rossi, *supra* n. 168, at 155ff. for further examples.

beneficiaries of aid have recently been afforded a stronger position in the case law.[1177] While the Commission's decision-making practice can thus serve as a valuable indicator, generalizations can be problematic since it is not clear whether such interpretation would be upheld by the European courts.

For example, a Commission decision can – according to the Commission – lead to the protection of legitimate expectation in other Member States, where similar schemes exist. In this constellation, which became relevant in the Commission decision underlying the CJEU's judgment in *Commission v. Koninklijke FrieslandCampina*, the protection of legitimate expectation can warrant both an exclusion of recovery for the past and the granting of a transitional period for the future.[1178]

Another constellation, which concerned the area of taxation, was the example of the CJEU's judgment in *Adria-Wien Pipeline* and the subsequent Commission decision on an amendment of the scheme in question. In its later decision, the Commission did not order recovery due to the potentially misleading wording in the CJEU's judgment in *Adria-Wien Pipeline.*[1179] In its subsequent judgment, the CJEU found that the scheme in question indeed constituted State aid, as it was restricted to undertakings whose activity was shown to consist primarily in the manufacture of goods.[1180] The Commission later found that while the aid was granted in breach of what is now Article 108(3), (3) TFEU, it was compatible with the internal market.[1181] However, by then, the scheme in question had been amended by the Austrian legislator so that undertakings could profit from the rebate regardless of sector. The condition that the total of the taxes due must exceed 0.35% of the net value of production was maintained.[1182] The Commission again investigated the scheme and found that the scheme constituted incompatible State aid.[1183] It did not order recovery as it held that a passage in the CJEU's judgment in *Adria-Wien Pipeline* was not clear.[1184] Beneficiaries of aid can therefore conceivably derive legitimate expectations from a potentially contradictory or misleading judgment of the CJEU.

[D] No Room for a Tax-Specific Approach

This narrow reading of the principle of protection of legitimate expectation under State aid law has provoked mixed reactions in the literature. Some have noted that a narrow interpretation of the principle would indeed be warranted. It would mirror the essence of State aid law itself in that the notion of compatible aid is exceptional per se. Any

1177. *See* Ch. §5.01[A] *supra.*
1178. Commission Decision 2003/515/EC of 17 February 2003 on the State aid implemented by the Netherlands for international financing activities [2003] OJ L 180/52.
1179. Commission Decision 2005/565/EC of 9 March 2004 on an aid scheme implemented by Austria for a refund from the energy taxes on natural gas and electricity in 2002 and 2003 [2005] OJ L 190/13, para. 66.
1180. Case C-143/99 *Adria-Wien Pipeline,* para. 55.
1181. Case C-368/04 *Transalpine Ölleitung,* para. 16.
1182. *Ibid.,* para. 17.
1183. *Ibid.,* para. 18.
1184. Commission Decision 2005/565/EC, para. 66.

more lenient approach would detrimentally affect competition within the internal market.[1185]

By contrast, some authors have based their case for a stronger protection of legitimate expectations on the persisting legal uncertainty regarding the State aid compatibility of tax measures: Englisch contends that the main problem lies in the fact that the case law of the CJEU on the existence of fiscal aid would be blurry and that it would not allow a clear identification of aid measures. Consequently, the bar for legitimate expectations should be much lower than the one set by the case law of the CJEU. Legitimate expectations should be protected as soon as the conclusion that a tax measure constitutes aid is not inevitable.[1186] In a similar vein, Hey points to the problems regarding the identification of the reference system of taxation, where there would be room for interpretation. In light of the harsh legal consequences of State aid law, the narrow interpretation of the principle of protection of legitimate expectation would be problematic.[1187]

As has been laid out above, changes in the case law – where they do exist – can certainly lead to an exclusion of recovery. However, where the legal situation is simply not clear, an application of the principle of protection of legitimate expectation is not warranted. The true potential impact of fiscal State aid law had indeed for a long time not been clear to both taxpayers and the Member States. However, awareness in this respect has certainly grown substantially. In a situation of legal uncertainty, the suspected aid could simply be notified to eliminate the risk of recovery. This link with the notification requirement is well-established in the case law of the European courts. The problem is then the weak procedural position of the taxpayer.[1188]

It has furthermore been argued that such a narrow reading of the principle of protection of legitimate expectation would fail to consider the particularities of taxation. A special case should therefore be made for tax measures, and in particular fiscal aid schemes.[1189]

Indeed, a number of particularities of taxation exist that could potentially warrant making a special case for fiscal aid schemes. For example, AG Kokott argues that some

1185. Fink, *supra* n. 168, at 141.

1186. Englisch, *Das Beihilfenverbot im Steuerrecht, supra* n. 67, at para. 9.70. Similarly Schönfeld & Ellenrieder, *supra* n. 173, at 445 contend that European law requires the beneficiary to infallibly interpret Art. 107(1) TFEU, which would be unreasonable. In a similar vein: Jaros & Ritter, *supra* n. 168, at 578.

1187. Hey, *EU-Beihilfen und Steuervergünstigungen, supra* n. 119, at 336.

1188. *See* on this Ch. §7.01[D] *infra*.

1189. Anzinger, *supra* n. 173, at 183; Dorenkamp, *supra* n. 173, at 641 for abstract benefits; Englisch, *Das Beihilfenverbot im Steuerrecht, supra* n. 67, at para. 9.70; Hey, *EU-Beihilfen und Steuervergünstigungen, supra* n. 119, at 336; Jaros & Ritter, *supra* n. 168, at 578 (in the context of the notion of 'diligent businessman'); Kühn, *supra* n. 173, at 366; Martini, *supra* n. 119, at 106ff.; Mellinghoff, *supra* n. 173, at 227 with reference to the potential State aid law incompatibility of parts of the German inheritance tax act; Schönfeld & Ellenrieder, *supra* n. 173, at 445. For a nuanced assessment Krumm, *supra* n. 173, at 580ff.; Reich, *supra* n. 174, at 231. For a limitation of the stand-still obligation leading to the non-application of national tax law by tax authorities (i.e., the executive branch) to clear cut cases: Malte Rosenberg, *Das beihilferechtliche Durchführungsverbot im Steuerverfahren*, 308 (2014) on grounds of the EU principle of legal certainty and the national principles of legal certainty and the rule of law as components of the core of the German constitution pursuant to Art. 79(3) *Grundgesetz*.

types of abstract tax measures would be imposed upon the taxpayer in the sense that they have no opportunity to deny being granted the aid (*aufgedrängte Beihilfe*). Moreover, for positive aid, there is an explicit transfer of funds, which will generally only be granted upon some sort of application and allow the beneficiary to consider the question of whether there is aid. The same holds true for fiscal aid that involves an explicit application or another right to choose, such as tax rulings. In such cases, the beneficiary of aid would have an occasion to consider the legality of the measure. By contrast for aid schemes, regardless of whether the tax due is determined through self-assessment or not, taxpayers may not be aware of the preferential tax treatment they are receiving. This may especially hold true where the law is complex.[1190] Others have argued that it would be problematic that the taxpayer will sometimes be in contact with the national tax authorities in the process of tax assessment and receive information from the tax authorities, which leads them to believe that a measure is not problematic.[1191]

Especially where the reference system of taxation of a narrow-based levy is wider than the scope of the tax, operators that benefit from the tax measure are in no way in touch with the tax authorities and will often not be aware of their identity as beneficiaries of aid.[1192]

Hey contends that the risk for collusion between the taxpayer and the Member State would be significantly lower for abstract tax measures. In weighing legal certainty and the danger of a circumvention of State aid law in the absence of recovery against each other, the latter would be less relevant.[1193]

As laid out above, these particularities have not been addressed in the case law. They may indeed warrant an exclusion of recovery on a case-by-case basis. Yet there appears to be no room for a less restrictive interpretation of the principle of protection of legitimate expectation. Indeed, this case law is in principle warranted, as the effective enforcement of State aid law would otherwise be put into question for the structural reasons explained above.

The result – recovery of aid from potentially unsuspecting taxpayers – is nevertheless unsatisfactory because there is still significant legal uncertainty in fiscal State aid law. However, it would appear to us as though the criticism would be more appropriately directed towards the current state of affairs of the case law on material selectivity rather than the requirements for the recognition of legitimate expectations. In any case, the problem becomes significantly less pressing to the extent that there are now clear tendencies of a rollback and the applicable standard appears to move

1190. Kokott, *Steuerrecht*, *supra* n. 20, at §3, para. 232; Similarly Martini, *supra* n. 119, at 107f. who also points to an asymmetry of information and competences that would be inherent to tax law. *See also* Kokott, *Tax Harmonisation*, *supra* n. 102, at 466f. Similarly on the complexity of tax measures Hey, *EU-Beihilfen und Steuervergünstigungen*, *supra* n. 119, at 336; Martini, *supra* n. 119, at 108.
1191. Schönfeld & Ellenrieder, *supra* n. 173, at 445. This would, however, be necessary, since otherwise the effectiveness of State aid law would be impeded.
1192. In this vein: Maitrot de la Motte, *supra* n. 171, at 82 albeit not in connection with the principle of protection of legitimate expectation.
1193. Hey, *EU-Beihilfen und Steuervergünstigungen*, *supra* n. 119, at 336.

towards manifest inconsistency for many types of tax measures. If, indeed, only manifestly inconsistent measures can lead to the finding of fiscal aid, there would rarely be room for legitimate expectations because it would then be far-fetched to assume that the beneficiaries of the aid could not have suspected that there was aid.

§6.02 THE PRINCIPLE OF LEGAL CERTAINTY AS A POTENTIAL LIMIT

While the principle of protection of legitimate expectation is construed narrowly, there may nevertheless be a case for an exclusion of recovery based on other legal principles. Ongoing legal uncertainty should not exclude recovery since the uncertainty could be rectified through a notification [A]. By contrast, in exceptional cases, recovery may be excluded due to the notion of emerging case law, which is an emanation of the principle of legal certainty [B].

[A] Ongoing Legal Uncertainty Not Sufficient

As an alternative to excluding recovery on grounds of the principle of protection of legitimate expectation, the principle of legal certainty may be considered, where the legal situation governing a constellation that is considered contrary to State aid law is objectively unclear.[1194]

According to the CJEU, rules of law must be clear and precise and their application must be foreseeable.[1195] The objective of the principle of legal certainty is to ensure that situations and legal relationships governed by EU law remain foreseeable for interested parties.[1196] Nevertheless, the underpinnings of the principle of legal certainty are still quite blurry. The case law of the CJEU has been dubbed 'sprawling, confused and contradictory'.[1197] Even though the principle of legal certainty is regularly brought forward by the beneficiaries of aid,[1198] it has only very rarely been

1194. Lovdahl Gormsen & Mifsud-Bonnici, *supra* n. 126, at 425f. hold that recovery should be excluded in tax ruling cases on grounds of the principle of legal certainty due to the 'novel interpretation of State aid law'.

1195. Case C-63/93 *Duff and Others* EU:C:1996:51, para. 20; C-143/93 *Gebroeders van ES Douane Agenten* EU:C:1996:45, para. 27; Case C-107/97 *Rombi and Arkopharma* EU:C:2000:253, para. 66; Case C-17/03 *VEMW and Others* EU:C:2005:362, para. 80; Case C-199/03 *Ireland v. Commission* EU:C:2005:548, para. 69; C-94/05 *Emsland-Starke* EU:C:2006:185, para. 43; Case C-76/06 P *Britannia Alloys & Chemicals v. Commission* EU:C:2007:326, para. 79; C-345/06 *Heinrich* EU:C:2009:140, para. 44; Case C-201/08 *Planatol* EU:C:2009:539, para. 46; Case C-29/08 *SKF* EU:C:2009:665, para. 77; Joined Cases C-649, 658 and 662/20 P *Spain and Others v. Commission*, para. 81. *See* on this principle, e.g., Kokott, *Steuerrecht, supra* n. 20, at §2, paras 27ff.; John Temple Lang, *Legal Certainty and Legitimate Expectations as General Principles of Law*, in Bernitz & Nergelius (eds), General Principles of European Community Law, 163ff. (2000).

1196. Case C-63/93 *Duff and Others*, para. 20; Case C-81/10 P *France Télécom*, para. 100.

1197. Jérémie van Meerbeeck, *The Principle of Legal Certainty in the Case law of the European Court of Justice: From Certainty to Trust* 41 European L. Rev. 275, 276 (2016) https://doi.org/10.1007/978-94-017-0353-6_6.

1198. *See, e.g.*, Joined Cases C-74 and 75/00 P *Falck and Acciaierie di Bolzano v. Commission*, EU:C:2002:524.

accepted as a limit to recovery. For example, in *Salzgitter v. Commission*, the General Court had held that there was indeed an infringement of the principle of legal certainty.[1199] Upon appeal, however, the CJEU annulled the judgment for precisely this reason.[1200]

The CJEU has sometimes dubbed the principle of protection of legitimate expectation as the corollary of the principle of legal certainty.[1201] Consequently, it does not always clearly separate the two principles. This raises questions as to their delimitation. For example, in *Unicredito Italiano*, the CJEU assessed the two principles together and denied a breach of the principle of legal certainty by simply stating that the risk of national proceedings was foreseeable from the moment the aid was implemented.[1202]

It is clear that the principle can only apply in situations where the EU legal provisions or other acts lead to an unclear legal situation, which then leads to a lack of foreseeability. This means that the particularities of taxation mentioned above cannot be addressed through reliance on the principle of legal uncertainty. By contrast, the constellations referred to by Englisch, i.e., the complexities of State aid law in its application to tax measures itself, might at first glance be covered.[1203]

The principle of legal certainty is an objective principle.[1204] This means that the perspective of the concrete beneficiary of aid or differences between beneficiaries should be irrelevant. Instead, one has to ask whether the necessity of a notification emerged clearly from the Commission practice and case law of the European courts. The analysis in Part I has shown that at the margin, uncertainties as to the exact scope of State aid law and the notion of selective advantage remain. The outcome of a Commission investigation is not always foreseeable for the beneficiaries of aid. This particularly concerns the issues of special purpose levies and the notion of de facto-selectivity. The case law on some of these issues is still very much dynamic.

Despite this, recovery should not be excluded on grounds of the principle of legal certainty. This is because as soon as the beneficiary of aid had to be aware of the fact or at least had to have doubts as to the State aid compatibility, the ongoing legal uncertainty surrounding such measures could easily be addressed through notification.[1205] The Commission then has an opportunity to investigate the measure in question. Notification may even be warranted where a measure has already been introduced to eliminate the legal certainty surrounding the measure in question for the future and thus mitigate recovery risks.

1199. Case T-308/00 *Salzgitter v. Commission* EU:T:2004:199, paras 182ff.
1200. Case C-408/04 P *Commission v. Salzgitter* EU:C:2008:236, paras 85ff. and 98ff.
1201. *See, e.g.*, Case C-63/93 *Duff and Others*, para. 20. In this vein, e.g., Temple Lang, *Legal Certainty and Legitimate Expectations as General Principles of Law*, *supra* n. 1195, at 164f. referring to a number of sub-principles, including the principle of protection of legitimate expectation.
1202. Case C-148/04 *Unicredito Italiano*, para. 104.
1203. *See* Ch. §6.01[D] *supra*.
1204. A different view is apparently held by Lovdahl Gormsen & Mifsud-Bonnici, *supra* n. 126, at 425.
1205. Similarly, albeit for the principle of protection of legitimate expectation: Rzotkiewicz, *supra* n. 168, at 470.

This holds all the more true since the principle of protection of legitimate expectation and the principle of legal certainty are closely related. A potential exclusion of recovery due to the principle of legal certainty will only ever become relevant where a measure has not been notified. A broad interpretation of the principle of legal certainty, which would not be linked to the requirement of notification at all would lead to a circumvention of the narrow reading of the principle of protection of legitimate expectation. A link between the principle of legal certainty and the obligation for Member States to notify aid has also emerged from the case law of the CJEU, albeit less clearly than in the context of the principle of protection of legitimate expectation.[1206]

Admittedly, the main weakness of such an approach lies in the feeble procedural position of the taxpayer. The latter should be remedied by the strengthening of such procedural rights.[1207] Taxpayers have to have tools at their disposal to ensure that the measure is (or has been) notified. Otherwise, such a narrow reading of both the principle of legal certainty and the principle of protection of legitimate expectation is problematic.[1208] Where the taxpayer then does not make use of these tools, they knowingly accept the risk of recovery – or at least this is the assumption underlying European law as can be seen in the context of the principle of protection of legitimate expectation.

[B] The Notion of Emerging Case Law as an Emanation of the Principle of Legal Certainty

The previous section focused on the issue of ongoing legal uncertainty, i.e., a situation where conflicting or unclear (case) law exists. One may furthermore wonder whether recovery can be excluded in constellations, where the Commission and the European courts first have to decide on a specific issue and where this stance cannot not be derived from previous case law, i.e., where there is neither a divergence from[1209] nor a mere concretization of the case law.

A new approach in State aid law will not qualify as a precise, unconditional and consistent assurance, where there was truly no earlier case law or any other basis for legitimate expectations. Mere inaction by the Commission also does not suffice. The principle of protection of legitimate expectation can therefore not apply.[1210]

A somewhat related dimension of the principle of legal certainty – which is, however, not directly pertinent – had emerged in the CJEU's *Racke* judgment. According to this judgment, the principle of legal certainty precludes the retroactive application of Union measures.[1211] It may only 'be otherwise where the purpose to be

1206. *See, e.g.*, Case C-408/04 P *Commission v. Salzgitter*, para. 104.
1207. *See* on this Ch. §6.01 *infra.*
1208. Similarly Jaros & Ritter, *supra* n. 168, at 579.
1209. As pointed out by Lars Dobratz, *Artikel 108 AEUV*, in Musil & Weber-Grellet (eds), Europäisches Steuerrecht, para. 83 (2022), the principle of protection of legitimate expectation applies where there is an explicit divergence from prior case law.
1210. *See* Ch. §6.01[A], [1] *supra.*
1211. Case 98/78 *Racke* EU:C:1979:14, para. 15; Case 99/78 *Decker v. Hauptzollamt Landau* EU:C:1979:15, para. 8; Case 84/81 *Staple Dairy Products* EU:C:1982:187, para. 12; Joined

achieved so demands and where the legitimate expectations of those concerned are duly respected'.[1212] The relevant point in time for the application of this case law is the publication of the measure in the Official Journal.[1213] This principle can certainly not be brought forward against the obligation of recovery itself – which is retroactive by definition. One may, however, wonder, whether a novel interpretation of State aid law in the case law, which was not foreseeable for the beneficiary of aid, may nevertheless be covered by this case law.[1214]

Of course, the era of big leaps in the case law of the European law may be over. Yet in principle, such constellations should exist in an area of law where the majority of the basic principles of assessment are established by case law and cannot be directly derived from Articles 107ff. TFEU. Where such emerging case law has no direct link to the existing substantive law provisions or previous case law, there should be no recovery. Such a principle should be construed objectively. Its application should not depend on the perspective of the individual beneficiaries of aid.

The CJEU's judgment in *Wächtler* – which amounts to primary law – shows that such an approach must in theory indeed be accepted: The judgment concerned the non-discrimination provisions contained in the EU-Swiss Agreement on the Free Movement of Persons (AFMP),[1215] and in particular the applicability of the case law of the CJEU on exit taxation to a German-Swiss cross-border case.[1216] German law had been amended in the past in order to create compatibility with European law. As a consequence, section 6(5) *Außensteuergesetz* (German External Tax Relations Act (AStG)) allows for a deferral of tax for nationals of a Member State or of another State to which the European Economic Area (EEA) agreement applies and where they are subject to tax in the host State comparable to German income tax liability. The judgment dealt with the question of whether exit taxation of a German national moving their residence to Switzerland was contrary to the non-discrimination provisions in the AFMP. According to Article 16(2) AFMP, the relevant case law of the CJEU, which had existed before the date of the signature of the AFMP, has to be taken into account in the application of the AFMP. Subsequent case law merely has to be brought to Switzerland's attention. The consequences have to be determined by a Joint Committee. The question was thus whether the CJEU's case law, which ultimately led to an amendment of the German law, was already in existence when the AFMP was signed.[1217]

Cases C-74 and 75/00 P *Falck and Acciaierie di Bolzano*, para. 119; Case C-369/09 P *ISD Polska*, para. 71. On the distinction between actual and apparent retroactivity Craig, *supra* n. 1079, at 304f.

1212. Case 98/78 *Racke*, para. 20.

1213. *Ibid.*, paras 15f.

1214. In this vein: Lovdahl Gormsen & Mifsud-Bonnici, *supra* n. 126, at 426; Van Cleynenbreugel, *supra* n. 168, at 46.

1215. Agreement between the European Community and its Member States, of the one part, and the Swiss Confederation, of the other, on the free movement of persons [2002] L 114/6, last amended by Decision No. 1/2020 of the Joint Committee established under the Agreement between the European Community and its Member States, of the one part, and the Swiss Confederation, of the other, on the free movement of persons of 15 December 2020 [2021] L 42/15.

1216. Case C-581/17 *Wächtler* EU:C:2019:138.

1217. *Ibid.*, paras 3ff. for the facts of the case.

According to the CJEU, not only past case law has to be taken into account but also subsequent case law must be considered insofar as it merely clarifies or confirms the principles of the case law up to that date concerning concepts of EU law.[1218] This confirms that EU law does not assume that all the principles laid down in the case law can be derived from the Treaties. Instead, the concept of emerging case law must indeed exist.

At the same time, as evidenced by the judgment, the CJEU's approach is bound to be rather strict. An exclusion of recovery on grounds of emerging case law is of a rather theoretical nature. In this context, the EU arm's length standard as a principle that is directly derived from State aid law by the Commission could have potentially been considered emerging case law. It had been suggested that there could be only partial recovery in tax ruling cases, namely only for the period of time starting from the date of publication of the decisions to initiate formal investigations.[1219] However, this appears to have become obsolete because the CJEU has recently firmly rejected the notion of an EU arm's length standard.[1220]

§6.03 GENERAL PRINCIPLES OF EU LAW IN THE ASSESSMENT STAGE IN FRONT OF NATIONAL COURTS

Derived from Article 108(3), (3) TFEU, a national court may be obliged to apply the substantive law provision of Article 107(1) TFEU and assess whether there is aid. The resulting obligation to eliminate the distortion of competition is not necessarily final in that it is contingent on the final decision of the Commission, which may eventually find that the aid is compatible with the internal market. One may then wonder whether the national court should be able to – or is even obliged to – consider the general principles of EU law as limits to recovery in the assessment stage.[1221] Article 16(1) of Procedural Regulation 2015/1589 is not applicable for national courts.

At first glance, the two situations (recovery due to a final negative Commission decision and recovery in the assessment stage on grounds of Article 108(3), (3) TFEU) do not seem comparable. Enforcement by the national court is meant to be provisional. This is underlined by the case law of the CJEU according to which the Commission and national courts have complementary, but separate roles in State aid control.[1222] The national court protects the rights of individuals faced with a possible breach of the stand-still provision of Article 108(3), (3) TFEU. Therefore, it would seem as though the focus should be on the immediate harmful effects of the aid. The bigger these distortions in the short term, the more urgent is the need to recover the aid before there is a final decision of the Commission. Inversely, the more likely a positive Commission decision, the less urgent is recovery.

1218. *Ibid.*, para. 39.
1219. Philip Lowe, *The Commission's Powers to Enforce the Law: And to Propose Changes to It* 42 European L. Rev. 909, 914 (2017).
1220. *See* Ch. §4.01 *supra*.
1221. In this vein: Bacon, *European Union Law of State Aid*, *supra* n. 20, at para. 20.22.
1222. *See* Ch. §5.02[A], [1] *supra*.

At the same time, this conflict is not necessarily pertinent since the decision of the national court may end up being the final decision on the aid in question. The Commission may never become involved.[1223] Moreover, the CJEU has held that even a positive Commission decision does not have the effect of regularizing ex post facto the unlawfulness of the aid.[1224] This then means that the likelihood of the Commission later on finding the aid compatible with the internal market has to be irrelevant in any case. The function of the national court thus often goes beyond a mere preliminary role. A case could thus be made that national courts are obliged to test for infringements of the general principles of EU law. In our view, Article 16(1) TFEU codifies the overarching principle that the distortion of competition that is created by unlawful or even incompatible State aid does not have to be removed at all costs.

In its judgment in *SFEI and Others,* which is one of the landmark judgments concerning the national court's obligation to enforce State aid law in the assessment stage, the CJEU indeed held that there could be 'exceptional circumstances' in which it would be inappropriate for the national court to order repayment of the aid. In its judgment, the court referred to the elaborations in the Opinion of AG Jacobs.[1225] The AG drew a parallel to the case law of the CJEU concerning the role of the national court in the recovery stage.[1226] According to this case law, a beneficiary of aid is in principle not precluded from relying on exceptional circumstances to fend off recovery in front of a national court.[1227] The same principle should apply to the role of the national court in the assessment stage. It would thus be for the national court to assess whether a case involves such exceptional circumstances. When in doubt, it could obtain a preliminary ruling from the CJEU.[1228] In its judgment, as well as in the subsequent case law, however, the CJEU did not take a clear stance on the question of what could constitute such exceptional circumstances. In our view, the term should at least be understood to comprise the general principles of EU law.

In its case law, the CJEU does not always clearly separate the role of the national court in the assessment stage and the recovery stage.[1229] Moreover, the purpose of recovery is similar in both constellations.[1230] Where no exceptional circumstances exist, the national court has to implement recovery.[1231] While one may argue that the limits have to go beyond the limits to recovery under Article 16(1) of Procedural

1223. A different view is apparently held by Tim Maxian Rusche, *Artikel 108 AEUV*, in Immenga & Joachim Mestmäcker (eds), Wettbewerbsrecht, para. 51 (5th edn 2016, vol. 3), according to whom the Commission would then be obliged to take up the case and come to a final decision.
1224. *See, e.g.,* Case C-354/90 *FNCE*, para. 67; Case C-672/13 *OTP Bank*, para. 76.
1225. Case C-39/94 *SFEI*, para. 70. *See also* Case C-199/06 *CELF I*, para. 42; Case C-1/09 *CELF II*, paras 42f.; Case C-275/10 *Residex Capital IV*, para. 35; Case C-672/13 *OTP Bank*, para. 72. On this Aalbers & Adriaanse, *supra* n. 170, at para. 30-062.
1226. Opinion of AG Jacobs in Case C-39/94 *SFEI and Others* EU:C:1995:445, paras 73ff.
1227. Case C-5/89 *Germany v. Commission*, para. 16.
1228. Opinion of AG Jacobs in Case C-39/94 *SFEI and Others*, paras 73ff.
1229. *See, e.g.,* Case C-199/06 *CELF I*, para. 43, referring to Case C-5/89 *Germany v. Commission*, para. 16 (recovery stage).
1230. Case C-390/98 *Banks*, para. 75; Case C-275/10 *Residex Capital IV*, para. 34; Bacon, *European Union Law of State Aid, supra* n. 20, at para. 20.15.
1231. *See* Bacon, *European Union Law of State Aid, supra* n. 20, at para. 20.16 for the exact conditions.

Regulation 2015/1589 since the decisions of the national court in the assessment stage are not subject to review by the European courts, such an approach ultimately fails to convince. This is because the application of the general principles of EU law is a matter of law and involves no discretionary elements. It therefore appears as though the limits to the obligation to recovery that national courts can and have to accept are similar regardless of the exact function of the national court. Regardless of whether Article 16(1) of Procedural Regulation 2015/1589 is thus applicable, the general principles of EU law as limits to recovery have to be interpreted identically.[1232]

1232. Similarly De Pietro, *supra* n. 173, at 105.

CHAPTER 7

Strengthening Taxpayer Rights in the State Aid Procedure

Where the taxpayer is aware that a tax measure could potentially amount to aid, the main problem is that they have limited procedural options throughout the State aid procedure. Legal certainty should be promoted through a higher degree of taxpayer protection, i.e., comprehensive rights throughout the procedure and access to judicial protection. In particular, we advocate a right to have unlawful aid notified to the Commission, which can already be derived from primary law, but should nevertheless be codified. Moreover, comfort letters and pre-notification letters should be published. They should, however, not have legal value or create legitimate expectations. Nevertheless, a publication can contribute to legal certainty for taxpayers.

The case-by-case limits we have discussed only apply where the beneficiaries of aid are not aware of the fact that a tax measure amounts to State aid. By contrast, where taxpayers are or should be aware that a tax measure could potentially amount to State aid, they have limited procedural options.[1233] In particular, taxpayers cannot notify aid to the Commission, which would eliminate the State aid risk.[1234] The Member State may somewhat understandably be reluctant to notify measures it does not consider aid.[1235]

In light of this, the scholarly literature has voiced concerns about the combination of a weak procedural position of taxpayers and strict recovery: *Santa Maria* has

1233. Similarly Lever, *supra* n. 116, at 8; Maria J. Segura Catalán et al., *Third Party Rights and the State Aid Procedures Revisited by the European Courts: An Ever-Sounder State Aid Control* 10 JECLAP 212 (2019) https://doi.org/10.1093/jeclap/lpz033 pointing to the Code of Best Practices, which suggests involving the beneficiaries of aid. Such provisions should be included in an updated Procedural Regulation; Christiana HJI Panayi, *Advanced Issues in International and European Tax Law*, 246f. (2015).

1234. Laprévote, *supra* n. 115, at 438.

1235. Keith O'Donnell & Anne Muller, *State Aid and Tax Law: Enter the Taxpayer*, in Rust & Micheau (eds), State Aid and Tax Law, 175, 200 (2013).

motivated his scepticism towards recovery with the lack of taxpayer rights throughout the procedure. He proposes two alternatives to the current approach: Either the undertaking concerned would be an active party throughout the State aid proceedings. Where this the case, their awareness of impending recovery may be presumed. Alternatively, if the taxpayer has no right to participate in the procedure, the right of defence would imply that there has to be a rebuttable presumption that the taxpayer was not aware of the risk of recovery.[1236] We have shown, however, that recovery is generally necessary to achieve the enforcement goals of European State aid law. A rebuttable presumption would make recovery the exception.

Thus, a procedural solution is preferable. It must be possible for taxpayers to achieve legal certainty before making use of a tax measure. Neither the option to lodge a complaint as an interested party, nor an extension of the categories of aid covered by the GBER, or the possibility for taxpayers to notify aid themselves are viable solutions. Instead, a right to have potential aid notified should be included in an updated Procedural Regulation, but can already be derived from European law (§7.01).

Second, instead of issuing formal decisions, the Commission will sometimes send comfort letters to Member States. We argue that these comfort letters should be published. However, they are no grounds for a protection of legitimate expectation. At best, recovery could be excluded on grounds of the principle that the administration is bound by its own acts (§7.02).

§7.01 ACHIEVING LEGAL CERTAINTY BY MEANS OF NOTIFICATION

The current legal framework considers the beneficiary of aid an 'interested party', which means that they can technically lodge complaints with the Commission [A]. An extension of the categories of aid covered by the GBER would do away with the requirement of notification for the categories of aid within its scope [B]. The legal framework could be amended to allow taxpayers to notify aid themselves [C]. Yet ultimately, the only viable solution would be to grant the beneficiary of aid a legally enforceable right that the Member State notifies potential aid [D].

[A] Option to Lodge Complaints as Interested Party

As an 'interested party' pursuant to Article 1(h) of Procedural Regulation 2015/1589, the beneficiary of aid (as well as their competitors)[1237] may submit a complaint to inform the Commission of any alleged unlawful aid or any alleged misused aid, Article 24(2) of Procedural Regulation 2015/1589.[1238] The case law of the European courts

1236. Santa Maria, *supra* n. 841, at 18f.

1237. Critical as their motive would most often not be a restoration of competition, Ulrich Soltész, *Nach der Reform ist vor der Reform: Herausforderungen für die künftige europäische Beihilfekontrolle* 26 EuZW 277, 278 (2015).

1238. According to Reich, *supra* n. 174, at 238, the Commission would then not be able to take decisions in a timely fashion, which means that the undertaking will ultimately make use of

ensures that such a complaint leads to the opening of the preliminary investigation procedure.[1239] This significantly promotes the position of competitors.

By contrast, this possibility does not offer a convincing avenue for the beneficiaries of aid. The fact that such a complaint can only be submitted for suspected unlawful or misused aid, shows that this is not a viable option for the beneficiary of aid, where they merely seek to obtain legal certainty in advance – as unlawful aid is aid that has been introduced without respecting the stand-still obligation of Article 108(3), (3) TFEU. The contents of the complaint form provided for by the Commission[1240] moreover demonstrate that it is assumed that the interested party believes that there is indeed aid. This is not necessarily in the interest of the (potential) beneficiary of the aid, for whom the best-case scenario would be that they receive a confirmation that there is no aid. The possibility to submit a complaint is therefore not comparable to notification of the aid and does not in all cases provide a satisfying avenue for taxpayers as potential beneficiaries of aid.

The General Court has confirmed this in its judgment in *Solar Electric and Others v. Commission* in a case where a beneficiary of aid lodged a complaint form intending to obtain a decision not to raise objections to the compatibility of the measure in question.[1241] In reaching its conclusion, the GC pointed out that an option for beneficiaries of aid to lodge a complaint would put into question the sole responsibility of the Member State to notify aid.[1242]

[B] Extension of the Categories of Aid Covered by the GBER

Furthermore, an extension of the categories of aid covered by the GBER could be considered. This would mean that such aid does not have to be notified. At least in theory, the risk of recovery for aid that is covered by the GBER would be eliminated. A strengthening of the procedural position of the taxpayer would be less pressing. To a certain extent, this has already happened in the Commission's State aid Modernization Initiative (SAM), which focused on a prioritization of cases that have the biggest impact on the internal market.[1243] Yet no significant progress was made for fiscal aid schemes.

This makes sense. Fiscal State aid will often be granted as operating aid as opposed to investment aid. Operating aid is considered to have a more substantial

---

the measure without knowing whether it constitutes State aid. The capacities of the Commission would thus have to be increased.

1239. Pastor-Merchante, *supra* n. 115, at 536 with reference to Case T-182/10 *AISCAT v. Commission* EU:T:2013:9, paras 25ff. and Case C-521/06 P *Athinaiki Techniki AE v. Commission* EU:C:2008:422, para. 40; Case C-516/11 P *Commission v. Ryanair* EU:C:2013:310, paras 30ff. On the *Commission v. Ryanair* judgment *see* Eduardo Cabrera Maquedo, *Commission v. Ryanair: In the Field of State Aid Complaints Are Not Subject to Formal Requirements (For Now)* 4 JECLAP 423ff. (2013) https://doi.org/10.1093/jeclap/lpt044. *See* on the improvements of the rights of complainants also Laprévote, *supra* n. 115, at 433.
1240. *See* http://ec.europa.eu/competition/forms/download_en.html.
1241. Case T-678/20 *Solar Electric and Others v. Commission* EU:T:2021:780, para. 24.
1242. *Ibid.*, para. 27.
1243. Laprévote, *supra* n. 115, at 434.

detrimental effect on the internal market.[1244] Therefore, an exemption from notification would not necessarily be appropriate. The GBER is also not necessarily a suitable instrument to address tax-specific issues. Luja cites the example of the cumulation of aid. Where the notification threshold is exceeded, the GBER is not applicable. For tax benefits, this is hard to determine from an *ex ante* perspective.[1245] Moreover, relying on the GBER will only be viable for certain 'standard' categories of aid. An expansion of the GBER would not help to address the truly problematic cases where considerable legal uncertainty prevails.

Furthermore, including certain categories of aid measures in the GBER can also be due to policy considerations and priorities, which do not necessarily (only) reflect the low potential for distortions of competition. For example, environmental aid is often highly distortive, but will nevertheless – even more so with the recent amendments due to the 'Green Deal' – often be exempted from the obligation to notify aid. Achieving a consensus in this respect for tax measures would presumably be complicated. Beyond that, the risk of a misapplication of the GBER does not lie with the Member State but with the beneficiary of aid.[1246]

Finally, there may be an issue of competence. The regulatory technique of the GBER, which contains detailed descriptions of the measures that are compatible with the internal market, means that it may come quite close to positive integration. Yet the GBER is a Commission Regulation, which is based on the enabling Council Regulation 2015/1588.[1247] The European Parliament and the Council are not involved in the process of drafting such a regulation. While it may be argued that the GBER merely minimizes the uncertainties Member States face in drafting rules that are compatible with State aid law, this could nevertheless lead to de facto harmonization. Member States will inevitably rely on aid measures covered by the GBER instead of running the risk of inadvertently granting illegal aid. This goes beyond mere negative integration and circumvents the ordinary legislative process.

[C] Granting the Beneficiary the Right to Notify Aid?

One may furthermore consider amending the State aid procedure and enabling the beneficiaries of aid to notify aid themselves.[1248] This would presumably require a change of the existing legal framework. Under Article 108(3), (3) TFEU, it is for the Member State that intends to grant the presumed aid to notify the Commission– even

1244. Bacon, *European Union Law of State Aid, supra* n. 20, at para. 3.23 and Leigh Hancher, *Article 107(2) and Article 107(3)*, in Hancher et al. (eds), EU State Aids, paras 4-131ff. (5th edn 2016) with further references.

1245. Raymond Luja, *Does the Modernisation of State Aid Control Put Legal Certainty and Simplicity at Risk* 13 EStAL 765f. (2014) https://doi.org/10.21552/estal/2012/4/311.

1246. *See* in particular Case C-349/17 *Eesti Pagar*.

1247. Council Regulation (EU) 2015/1588 of 13 July 2015 on the application of Articles 107 and 108 of the Treaty on the Functioning of the European Union to certain categories of horizontal State aid [2015] OJ L 248/1, last amended by Council Regulation (EU) 2018/1911 of 26 November 2018 [2018] OJ L 311/8.

1248. Trencsik & Thiede, *supra* n. 143, at 183, albeit pointing to capacity issues.

though the wording is not altogether clear in this respect. By contrast, Article 2 of Procedural Regulation 2015/1589 is clear in that the Member State has to notify the aid. This is also in line with the logic of State aid law as notification should normally take place before the introduction of the aid. Particularly for fiscal aid schemes, the beneficiary generally does not have sufficient information to notify the aid prior to its introduction. This solution is therefore not viable.

Somewhat related, Temple Lang suggests that a potential beneficiary of aid could bring an action in front of a national court to obtain a judgment on the lawfulness of the aid. The Commission could be indirectly involved in the procedure on grounds of the duty of cooperation. Such a solution does not appear practical since it does not result in a formal Commission decision. The national court cannot decide on the compatibility of aid. This means that the judgment can only concern the existence of aid and potentially the applicability of the GBER. Instead, such an approach should presumably force the Commission to act on grounds of the duty of cooperation. Yet it is not clear how the latter would be enforced.[1249]

[D] Granting the Beneficiary the Right to Have Aid Notified by the Member State

Against this background, the most promising solution appears to be a procedure that is based on a notification of the measure by the Member State. The beneficiary of aid should have a legal means to insist on notification by the Member State that intends to grant the potential aid. They would have to make their claim in front of national courts if a Member State fails to notify the aid. To this end, a registry of all notified measures on a national level would have to exist.

The question is then where such right could be derived from. While the stand-still provision of Article 108(3), (3) TFEU has direct effect, it is not a suitable legal basis for the beneficiary of aid. The direct effect of this provision can only be relied on to obtain relief from the anti-competitive effects of unlawfully granted aid.[1250]

Instead, legal sources outside of State aid law may have to be considered. For example, it has been brought forward that the German constitution would already provide the beneficiary of aid with a subjective right to notification, which could be claimed in front of German courts. Such right could be derived from the freedom to pursue a professional activity under Article 12 *Grundgesetz* (German Basic Law) in conjunction with the rule of law principle – and in particular the legality of administration.[1251]

Transferring this reasoning to the European legal order, such right may already be inherent to Article 16 ChFR, which covers the freedom to exercise an economic or

1249. This would be possible on grounds of the case law in Case C-432/05 *Unibet* EU:C:2007:163, Temple Lang, *EU State Aid Rules*, *supra* n. 139, at 452f.
1250. *See* on this dimension Ch. §5.02[A], [1] *supra*.
1251. Brandau et al., *supra* n. 163, at 1187; sceptical of the effectiveness: Krumm, *supra* n. 173, at 611.

commercial activity, the freedom of contract and free competition.[1252] Indeed, the uncertainty undertakings face in acting within a tax system without knowing whether fiscal benefits – that they cannot necessarily escape – amount to aid and may in the future be recovered can significantly impact an undertaking's business activities and decisions. Moreover, there is a clear obligation for Member States to notify aid prior to its introduction that is derived from EU law. The failure to notify is thus a relevant infringement of Article 16 ChFR de lege lata. Nevertheless, while we believe that the right to have aid notified can be directly derived from primary law, such right to notification should nevertheless be codified in order to promote legal certainty. It could be included in an updated Procedural Regulation.

Meanwhile, the obligation to notify new aid only extends to measures that fulfil all the criteria of Article 107(1) TFEU.[1253] The problem is thus how to deal with cases, where it is not altogether clear whether there is truly aid from an *ex ante* perspective. The case law is quite clear in this respect: Where it subsequently turns out that a measure does not amount to State aid, there was no obligation to notify it. By contrast, where the aid quality is subsequently confirmed, the stand-still clause and the obligation to notify apply.[1254]

In our view, the right to have aid notified should, however, go further than the obligation to notify aid under Article 108(3), (1) TFEU. In other words, it should not exclusively apply to what are certainly State aids since the main source of legal uncertainty regarding fiscal aid schemes is not their compatibility but the question of whether there is aid in the first place. Moreover, the State aid quality of tax measures is not necessarily clear from an *ex ante* perspective. This is because the arguments for a justification of a derogation from the reference system of taxation have to be brought forward by the Member State in the course of the administrative proceedings.[1255] From the taxpayer's perspective, there must thus be a possibility to achieve a notification of all unclear cases. Even where there is a certain degree of doubt, the taxpayer should have the possibility to demand notification.

Admittedly, granting the potential beneficiary a right to notification then entails the risk of over-notification: In a climate of legal uncertainty, Member States might tend to notify more measures than strictly necessary to be on the safe side. Such a flood of notifications could quickly lead to capacity issues for the Commission. This particularly holds true for standard types of individual State measures, which are granted to a large number of undertakings, such as tax rulings. According to Article 4(6) of Procedural Regulation 2015/1589, aid shall be deemed to have been authorized by the Commission if it does not decide within a period of two months after receipt of a complete notification.[1256] Even where the Commission does open the formal investigation procedure, the period of 18 months available to the Commission according to Article

1252. E.g., Case C-356/21 *TP (Monteur audiovisuel pour la télévision publique)* EU:C:2023:9, para. 74 with further references.
1253. *See* Rosenberg, *supra* n. 1189, at 191ff. with extensive references to case law and literature.
1254. *Ibid.*, at 221f.
1255. *Ibid.*, at 215.
1256. This does not mean the Commission can indefinitely delay the procedure. The notification is deemed to be complete, if within two months from its receipt, or from the receipt of additional

9(6) of Procedural Regulation 2015/1589 is relatively short. At worst, too much aid will be (deemed to be) authorized due to capacity issues. There is thus a risk of under-enforcement of State aid law. Such aid becomes existing aid and as such can later on still be examined by the Commission, but not recovered. While it has been argued that such an option would in practice only rarely be relied on as taxpayers would rarely have an interest in invoking it,[1257] this does not appear entirely plausible in a climate of legal uncertainty.

Therefore, there have to be limits. First, the beneficiaries would have to make it known that they want to make use of their right. Second, to avoid a flood of notifications, the beneficiary's claim that there may conceivably be aid has to be substantiated. This could, for example, be achieved by providing evidence of the decisional practice of the Commission in other Member States.[1258]

Finally, one may wonder whether this right to notification should also extend to the acts of national courts in the assessment stage. The case law of the CJEU appears to preclude an approach, where the national court itself triggers notification. The CJEU in its judgment in *CELF II* decided that the national court in its enforcement function may not stay the proceedings to await the Commission's decision on the compatibility of aid:

> A decision to stay proceedings would, de facto, have the same effect as a decision to refuse the application for safeguard measures. It would have the effect that no decision on the merits of that application would be taken before the Commission's decision. It would amount to maintaining the benefit of aid during the period in which implementation is prohibited, which would be inconsistent with the very purpose of Article 88(3) EC and would render that provision ineffective.[1259]

Where a court case in front of a national court is already pending, at least the existence of aid can be examined by the European courts due to the obligation to refer questions to the CJEU under Article 267 TFEU. Moreover, this is not convincing since it would lead to a shift in the role of national courts. The function of the national court in practice goes beyond a mere preliminary role. Where the presumed beneficiary then relies on their right to have aid notified, the enforcement function of the national court would become obsolete to a certain extent. The Commission would issue a decision with the final assessment on whether the aid has to be recovered. This decision would be subject to judicial review by the European courts. The envisaged decentralization of State aid control could not be achieved. Moreover, the beneficiary of aid would not necessarily be a party to the proceedings, which would make it nearly impossible to enforce their right to have aid notified.

In such cases, it, therefore, appears more workable for the beneficiary of aid to be able to launch independent proceedings to have the aid notified, even if the national

information requested, the Commission does not request further information, Art. 4(5), (3) of Procedural Regulation 2015/1589.

1257. Reich, *supra* n. 174, at 239f.

1258. Soltész, *supra* n. 174, at 25 calls for some sort of negative clearing procedure or the publication of comfort letters.

1259. Case C-1/09 *CELF II* EU:C:2010:136, paras 31f.

court has already given effect to its enforcement function by suspending or recovering the aid.[1260] Where the administrative proceedings later on result in the finding that there was no aid in the first place or that the aid was compatible with the internal market, the initial decision of the national court would have to be reversed.

§7.02 PUBLICATION OF BILATERAL COMMUNICATIONS

In some cases, the State aid procedure may be conducted outside the boundaries of the formal State aid procedure provided for by Procedural Regulation 2015/1589, which means that the beneficiaries of aid as well as their competitors may not be receiving the amount of information they would ordinarily be entitled to.

For example, a large number of notifications result in a so-called comfort letter, instead of a formal Commission decision. It is issued to the Member State in question. Comfort letters have thus far only received little attention in the scholarly literature on State aid law.[1261] However, this instrument is also often relied upon in other areas of European competition law, and in particular in the context of Article 101 TFEU.[1262] In particular before the introduction of the block exemption regulations on the application of Article 101(3) TFEU, the Commission was inundated with notifications seeking exemptions. Consequently, a large number of cases were closed relying on such comfort letters.

The Communication from the Commission on Best Practices for the conduct of State aid control procedures also contains elaborations on the so-called pre-notification procedure.[1263] It allows for informal interactions between the Member States and the Commission to discuss the information that is required for the notification of State aid measures, the legal and economic aspects of a proposed measure and potential necessary amendments, and the eligibility for the streamlined procedure.[1264] The procedure is voluntary and confidential.[1265] While the decision on this lies with the Member States, the Notice suggests that for individual measures that have major technical, financial and project-related implications, the beneficiaries should be involved in the pre-notification contacts.[1266] The outcome of the pre-notification procedure is, if possible, an informal preliminary assessment of the measure, which is not binding.[1267]

1260. *Ibid.*
1261. *See*, however, Reich, *supra* n. 174, at 237.
1262. *See, e.g.*, Mario Siragusa, *The Millenium Approaches: Rethinking Article 85 and the Problems and Challenges in the Design and Enforcement of the EC Competition Rules* 21 Fordham Int. Law J. 650, 661ff. (1998); Temple Lang, *Legal Certainty and Legitimate Expectations as General Principles of Law*, *supra* n. 1195, at 175.
1263. Code of Best Practices for the conduct of State aid control procedures [2018] OJ C 253/14, paras 9ff.
1264. *Ibid.*, paras 10ff.
1265. *Ibid.*, para. 22.
1266. *Ibid.*, para. 18. Segura Catalán et al., *supra* n. 1233, at 214 call for an introduction of such right for the beneficiaries of aid in the Procedural Regulation.
1267. Code of Best Practices, *supra* n. 1263, at para. 20.

As there is no publication requirement for both of these contacts, they not only cannot serve to create legal certainty for the beneficiaries of aid but they can also not promote an overall understanding of the decision-making practice of the Commission. The perception of the decisional practice of the Commission is distorted as only measures that are considered problematic are dealt with in publicly available decisions. Moreover, the lack of publication contributes to intransparent structures. It has therefore convincingly been suggested that comfort letters as well as pre-notification letters could be published in a central registry.[1268] Such publication requirement has a role model in Article 18 of the Dispute Resolution Directive (DRD).[1269] Under this provision, final decisions under Article 15 of the Directive are published in full or – in the absence of consent of the competent authorities or affected persons – as an abstract. According to Article 19(3) DRD, the Commission shall maintain a central repository in which the published decisions are archived and made available online.

Finally, the question is what the legal consequence of such a publication would be. This primarily depends on the legal status of such instruments. At least in other areas of competition law, they appear to have no legal value.[1270] This was clarified by the CJEU for comfort letters issued in the context of what is now Article 101 TFEU. The CJEU held that the letters were neither decisions granting negative clearance nor decisions in application of what is now Article 101(3) TFEU, but were instead 'merely administrative letters informing the undertaking concerned of the Commission's opinion that there is no need to take action [...] and that the file on the case may therefore be closed.'[1271] In its decision on the status of comfort letters in the context of Article 101 TFEU, the CJEU also emphasized that formal decisions under the pertinent regulations require publication.[1272] As a consequence, the letters are not binding for national courts in their assessment of the agreements in question. They merely constitute a factor which the national court may take into account in its assessment.[1273] The judgment does not contain elaborations on the legal value of such letters for the Commission itself as this was not relevant to the case.

In light of the comparable function of comfort letters in State aid law, a similar assessment appears warranted.[1274] This holds all the more true since there is no structured procedure for the beneficiary of aid to be made aware of the existence of such a comfort letter. This is in contrast to Article 101 TFEU where the comfort letter will be addressed to the private actors involved in the agreement in question. Therefore, they can presently have no legal effect.

1268. Brandau et al., *supra* n. 163, at 1187; Reich, *supra* n. 174, at 237. According to Schnitger, *supra* n. 41, at 436, pre-notifications by the German government could be published in the German *Bundessteuerblatt*.
1269. Council Directive (EU) 2017/1852 of 10 October 2017 on tax dispute resolution mechanisms in the European Union [2017] L 265/1.
1270. Siragusa, *supra* n. 1262, at 662f.
1271. Joined Cases 253/78 and 1 to 3/79 *Procureur de la République v. Giry and Guerlain* EU:C:1980:188, para. 12.
1272. *Ibid.*
1273. *Ibid.*, para. 13.
1274. Hinz, *supra* n. 163, at 1029 points to the lack of legal value.

De lege ferenda it does not appear warranted to assign legal value to such comfort letters either, even with a publication requirement. In particular, they should not serve to create legitimate expectations since they are not issued in the context of a formal decision-making procedure.[1275] They are not based on an in-depth assessment of the measure in question. In particular, such an approach would be problematic since they could then be relied upon to exclude recovery not only for the measure at issue but also in comparable constellations. Assigning legal value to such letters would do away with their function. They are meant to enable the Commission to focus on problematic cases and carry out more targeted State aid control by assuring the Member State that – based on the limited information the Commission has – it does not intend to take action on a measure. At best, comfort letters could lead to an exclusion of recovery on grounds of the principle that the administration is bound by its own acts.

Such publication requirement without legal value again has a precedent in the EU's DRD, where precedential value is explicitly excluded according to Article 15(4). Nevertheless, a publication can in the long run lead to emerging international tax law standards[1276] and promote accountability and transparency in the decision-making of the Commission and legal certainty for taxpayers.

1275. Temple Lang, *Legal Certainty and Legitimate Expectations as General Principles of Law*, *supra* n. 1195, at 175 goes further and contends that they lead to a protection of legitimate expectation. However, in other areas of competition law, such comfort letters only ever concern a specific case.

1276. Sophia Piotrowski et al., *Towards A Standing Committee Pursuant to Article 10 of the EU Tax Dispute Resolution Directive: A Proposal for Implementation* 47 Intertax 678, 685 (2019) https://doi.org/10.54648/taxi2019068.

CHAPTER 8
Conclusion and Outlook

In this book, we have analysed the balance between the objectives of State aid control on the one hand and two core concepts limiting any excessive application of fiscal State aid law on the other, namely Member States' tax sovereignty and taxpayer rights. It has been structured in two parts. Part I has dealt with the existence of aid under Article 107(1) TFEU, and in particular the criterion of 'selective advantage'. In Part II, we have addressed the legal consequences of an infringement of State aid law, dealing both with the role of public and private enforcement in the State aid procedure and the recovery of unlawfully granted aid to identify shortcomings in the protection of taxpayers and potential improvements.

In Part I, we have surveyed the notion of selective advantage in light of one of the two main limits to fiscal State aid law, fiscal sovereignty. We have demonstrated the stand-alone significance of the notion of advantage. State aid control only applies to advantages as opposed to disadvantages (§2.01).

Moreover, we have examined the link between the notion of advantage and the identification of the beneficiary of aid. The beneficiary of aid has to be identified on a case-by-case basis for each type of tax and every tax measure at issue. This may particularly be problematic for indirect taxes. To this end, neither the actual economic incidence nor the legally presumed incidence can be relied on. We have developed some criteria that allow for a determination of the beneficiary of the aid, namely the question of legislative intent, whether there is a tax-inherent mechanism to pass on the tax or the method of granting the advantage (i.e., automatic or through a rebate). We have demonstrated that the beneficiary of aid in the area of VAT will generally be the final consumer as long as the passing-on mechanism of VAT is not hindered. Beyond this, additional indirect advantages may be relevant. However, unless they can be easily identified and quantified, they will most likely fall through the cracks of State aid control. Mere secondary effects that would require an in-depth economic analysis are not subject to State aid control (§2.02).

We have then turned our focus to material selectivity, arguing that there are two different selectivity tests in the case law, namely the test for de jure-selectivity on the one hand and the test for de facto-selectivity on the other hand.

We first briefly traced the evolution of the case law of the European courts, finding that the case law has long followed a consistent discrimination approach. An initial phase of expansion has now been replaced by a stronger emphasis on fiscal sovereignty (§3.01).

The test for de jure-selectivity is the standard test. It is applicable where a tax measure formally derogates from the reference system of taxation. The three-step selectivity test amounts to a discrimination test which relies on the reference system of taxation as a benchmark. This benchmark serves to determine the tax that – according to the fundamental charging decision of the Member State – is the amount of tax that would ordinarily be due in the absence of the tax measure in question.

For the first step of the selectivity test, this implies that there has to be a reference system of taxation in the first place. Otherwise, there can be no aid. Moreover, there has to be a different treatment of undertakings that are in a comparable factual and legal position in light of the objective of this reference system of taxation. This underlines that the selectivity test is a discrimination test and that fiscal sovereignty plays a pivotal role in the analysis since the national legislator is held to its original fundamental charging decision when the internal consistency of tax measures is tested. Taxes that are internally inconsistent are prima facie selective. The reference system of taxation again becomes relevant in the third step of the selectivity test since only internal grounds for justification are permissible.

It has now become clear that the reference system is generally the entire levy in which a potential aid measure is embedded. The exact elements as well as the objective of the reference system are determined normatively, i.e., relying on an interpretation of the levy itself. Alternatively, it may sometimes be possible to apply an empirical approach to determine what is the general rule. Particular problems arise in the distinction between technical rules that form an integral part of the reference system itself and rules that can potentially lead to a derogation. Presumably in an effort to safeguard fiscal sovereignty, there appears to be a trend to consider more and more rules inherent to the tax system itself. Yet it is not yet possible to clearly distinguish between the two. Similar problems arise in the context of tax expenditure theory. However, the general approach to assessing de jure-selectivity nevertheless has to be maintained because taking the fundamental charging decision of the Member State as a point of departure is warranted from a tax sovereignty point of view. For example, the progressivity of tax systems does not even lead to a derogation from the reference system of taxation and may only be de facto selective.

Depending on how far the CJEU is willing to go in strengthening tax sovereignty by deeming measures an integral part of the reference system of taxation, this may result in a greatly diminished significance of the three-step test for de jure-selectivity.

The case law on measures that are structured in several steps has also restricted State aid law. Despite the effects doctrine, tax benefits which constitute a return to a general beneficial rule may fall through the cracks of State aid law altogether. Where, by contrast, the general rule is detrimental to the taxpayer, there can be State aid. This case law is bound to have wider implications for the design of anti-abuse legislation. It entails the danger of an arbitrary design of tax measures. This does not appear convincing. Instead, it should also be possible to monitor the internal consistency of sub-systems of the reference system of taxation (§3.02).

In the second step, there has to be a derogation from the reference system of taxation. Such derogation exists where there is an unequal treatment of undertakings that are in a comparable legal and factual situation. The correct yardstick in this respect is the objective of the reference system of taxation instead of the tax measure. Tax measures may be selective even where they are theoretically open to all undertakings. Concrete selectivity is only required in the context of de facto-selectivity.

The case law on the three-step selectivity test, which may at first glance appear unsystematic, can be made sense of by distinguishing three different types of taxes, namely first broad-based fiscal levies, second narrow-based fiscal levies, and third special purpose levies. For broad-based fiscal levies, the problem is that in light of the objective to levy funds, each and every undertaking that is subject to the tax is in principle comparable. The same holds true for narrow-based fiscal levies to the extent that a situation is covered by the scope of the levy in the first place.

For special-purpose levies, the analysis of selectivity has an additional dimension. Selectivity may not only stem from a derogation from the reference system of taxation but also from an inconsistent design of the boundaries of the levy. This is to say that Member States have to design such levies in accordance with their stated objective. At the same time, we have shown that beyond the monitoring of formal inconsistencies, Member States have a high degree of autonomy in choosing the objectives they wish to pursue and how they implement them. This is because strict scrutiny would encroach upon Member States' tax sovereignty. State aid control thus can only strike down obvious ways to grant aid. This makes special purpose levies perhaps the most State aid proof of the three types of levies. We have also examined some dimensions of the identification of the objective of special purpose levies.

Finally, the choice of proxies for the ability to pay that informs the scope of narrow-based fiscal levies is generally not subject to State aid control because there is simply no special purpose whose consistent implementation could be monitored (§3.03).

The exact significance of the third step of the selectivity test is not altogether clear yet since the CJEU has mainly confined itself to rejecting justifications based on formal inconsistencies or because Member States relied on grounds for justification that could not be derived from the tax system itself. Nevertheless, the third step does have stand-alone significance as the relevant yardstick in this respect is the objective of the tax measure. The distinction between the different types of levies is also relevant in the third step since the types of internal grounds for justification necessarily depend on the type of tax. We, for example, explored the avoidance of international double taxation as potential grounds for a justification. The specifics of the proportionality test in State aid law are also not entirely fleshed out yet. The CJEU appears to apply a low standard of control. In light of this narrow interpretation, the third step has only limited potential to significantly restrict fiscal State aid law. At best, justifications that can be derived from EU law (as opposed to national law) could be accepted in the future (§3.04).

The second test for selectivity monitors tax laws for de facto-selectivity. It is applicable where a measure does not formally derogate from the reference system of taxation, but nevertheless entails an advantage for an identifiable group of undertakings. Since the test disregards the fundamental charging decision of the Member State, a measure can only be de facto selective, where it contains clearly arbitrary distinctions. It is unclear where the applicable standards are derived from. In any case, they appear to be standards of what can be dubbed external consistency. The test for de facto-selectivity can only apply under exceptional circumstances since it is problematic from a tax sovereignty perspective (§4.01). The case law on progressive turnover-based taxation has shown that the notion of de facto-selectivity currently appears to be a rather theoretical limit to Member States' tax sovereignty since the CJEU appears to be unwilling to arrive at the finding of de facto-selectivity (§4.02).

In Part I, we have therefore shown that tax sovereignty concerns regarding the notion of material selectivity indeed do exist, particularly for broad-based levies. However, they are by now not as significant as had initially been feared. The aspect of fiscal sovereignty informs several aspects of the three-step test for selectivity. This particularly concerns the first and the third step of the selectivity test as well as the applicable standard of control. Overall, fiscal state aid has through the concept of the selective advantage arrived at striking a sensible balance between rationality control on the one hand and Member States' sovereignty concerns on the other hand. Nevertheless, it cannot be denied that some problematic aspects remain that lead to legal uncertainty, namely in particular the exact identification of the reference system of taxation for complex regulatory techniques and the question of which elements of a tax system could constitute derogations in the first place and which elements are deemed to form part of the reference system of taxation. There are also still uncertainties as to the exact role of the third step.

In Part II, we have addressed the second main limit to fiscal State aid law, taxpayer rights, in light of the findings from Part I. We have discussed two main issues, namely first the legal consequence of recovery and potential modifications thereto both in abstract and for individual beneficiaries. Second, we have examined avenues for a stronger position of taxpayers in light of the shortcomings of the State aid procedure.

We have distinguished between enforcement by the Commission and by national courts. The case law requires an elimination of the advantage through recovery. The perceived structural and legal objections against the recovery of fiscal aid schemes fail to convince and inversely, recovery is very much necessary to ensure the effectiveness of State aid control. We therefore reject approaches that would do away with the retroactive effect of fiscal State aid law altogether. Yet there are very specific constellations where the discrimination underlying the infringement of State aid law can be remedied through a reimbursement of tax instead of recovery. Following a Commission decision, this may be the case where it is possible for the Member State to retroactively abolish a levy from a domestic law perspective (§5.01).

Next to the role of the Commission, the enforcement function of national courts in the assessment stage, which is derived from Article 108(3), (3) TFEU, cannot be neglected. There is a subjective and an objective aspect to the enforcement function of national courts. Competitors could conceivably rely on Article 108(3), (3) TFEU to achieve enforcement of State aid law that results in recovery from their competitors. By contrast, they cannot achieve an extension of an unlawful aid measure to themselves as this would amount to an infringement of Article 108(3), (3) TFEU. In front of national courts, resorting to an extension of the advantage rather than recovery is nevertheless conceivable, where this would not infringe upon the stand-still provision. This may exceptionally be possible where there is a simultaneous infringement of the fundamental freedoms, where the *Laboratoires Boiron* case law is applicable, or where a reimbursement otherwise does not infringe upon Article 108(3), (3) TFEU (§5.02).

We have then turned to the case-by-case limits to recovery and have found that the principle of protection of legitimate expectation can only rarely be invoked in tax cases. This is because it is linked with the requirement of notification. In particular, the case law does not recognize any particularities of fiscal aid schemes, even though the Commission is somewhat more lenient in this respect (§6.01).

Yet in very rare constellations, the principle of legal certainty in its dimension that precludes retroactive legislation may apply to emerging case law. These solutions can only apply, where a beneficiary of aid does not have to be aware of the fact that a measure constitutes aid that has to be notified. Therefore, ongoing legal uncertainty does not suffice since the aid should then have been notified (§6.02).

There is also a limited potential to exclude recovery in the assessment stage since the national court can take into account 'exceptional circumstances'. The case-by-case limits to recovery should be identical regardless of the institution enforcing State aid law (§6.03).

By contrast, where the taxpayer was aware that a tax measure could potentially amount to aid, the main problem is that they have limited procedural options. This is a significant structural failure of fiscal State aid law. Legal certainty should be promoted through better taxpayer protection. In particular, we advocate a right to have unlawful aid notified to the Commission, which can in our view already be derived from primary law but should nevertheless be codified to promote legal certainty (§7.01).

Furthermore, bilateral communications with the Commission, which substitute formal Commission decisions, should be published. They do not have legal value but can contribute to transparency, accountability and a more thorough understanding of the decision-making practice of the Commission (§7.02).

The main conclusion of Part II is therefore that the position of taxpayers in the State aid procedure has to be strengthened significantly. However, this holds true regardless of the type of aid. There is no room for a tax-specific approach since the main problem in the area of taxation is legal uncertainty regarding the notion of material selectivity which has to be solved on this level. In other words, the mere fact that material State aid law in the area of taxation comes with a number of particularities and complexities does not mean that procedural law should be adapted.

The question is then what the future will bring for State aid law as applied to fiscal aid schemes. The case law indicates quite clearly that State aid law is not an adequate tool to tackle the inadequacies of the international tax system and the problem of a lack of full harmonization in the area of direct taxation. The more restrictive approach of the CJEU on material selectivity was certainly pressing from a tax sovereignty and taxpayer rights point of view. It also has to be acknowledged that European State aid law is not designed to comprehensively monitor Member States' tax laws for elements of aid from a mere capacity perspective.[1277] Therefore, more focused State aid control, preferably on the level of the existence of aid, was clearly warranted.

However, in our view, the current approach has its weaknesses that may lead to under-enforcement. There now appears to be a tendency to consider many elements of a tax system an integral part of the reference system of taxation itself. This became apparent in the CJEU's judgments on progressive turnover-based taxes and we consider this to be convincing. The judgment in *Andres* has shown that even where there are clear distinctions within technical rules, as was the case for the restructuring clause, Member States could avoid an application of State aid law through intelligent tax design. All this means that many kinds of technical rules could only conceivably be de facto selective. The applicable standard of control would then be a control for manifest inconsistencies. However, the judgment in *Gibraltar* is interpreted very restrictively to the extent that the CJEU has never again found de facto-selectivity.[1278] Depending on how far the CJEU goes in the acknowledgement of technical elements of the reference system of taxation, this extremely high threshold may well curtail the Commission's room for manoeuvre too much.[1279]

It appears as though instead of clearly addressing the ambiguities in identifying the reference system of taxation, the CJEU is relying on a lowered standard of control altogether.[1280] In other words, the test for de facto-selectivity may become the new normal. But if it effectively never applies, what room is there for effective State aid control? This may create the potential for reverse engineering and loopholes.[1281]

Should the standard of control that is applicable in the context of de facto-selectivity therefore be modified? This does not appear desirable since the very reason that the test for de facto-selectivity is only used sparingly is the fact that there is, in fact, no formal derogation from the reference system of taxation which is problematic from a tax sovereignty point of view. A lower standard control could lead to all kinds of

1277. Stephen Daly, *The Power to Get It Wrong* 137 Law Quarterly Rev. 280, 286 (2021) for individual aid.

1278. Szudoczky, *The Future of Fiscal State Aid, supra* n. 461, at 280 holds that de facto-selectivity will gain significance.

1279. Bernatt & Grzejdziak, *supra* n. 149, at 198.

1280. In favour of a stronger role for the particularities of tax law: Jaeger, *Fehlstellungen im Verhältnis von Steuer- und Beihilferecht, supra* n. 29. For such lower standard, e.g., Hummel, *Das nationale Steuergesetz, supra* n. 519, at 396.

1281. Bernatt & Grzejdziak, *supra* n. 149, at 197; Fichera, *supra* n. 149, at 490; Szudoczky, *The Future of Fiscal State Aid, supra* n. 461, at 283. Szudoczky & Károlyi, *The CJEU's Approach to the Objectives of Progressive Turnover-Based Taxes, supra* n. 95 also criticize the move towards a monitoring for manifest inconsistencies for this very reason and propose an application of the principle of proportionality.

facially neutral rules being subject to State aid control, which clearly goes too far. The approach relied on for de facto-selectivity can perhaps best be described as 'I know it when I see it.' Where exactly the applicable standards in this respect derive from, is presently still unclear.

At the same time, one may wonder what is the remaining significance of the three-step test for de jure-selectivity. Its advantage over the test for de facto-selectivity is that it is in theory neutral in that it merely puts the Member State's fundamental charging decision to the test. As the case law stands, however, it would only be applicable, where State aid derives from explicit limitations based on aspects, such as size, sector or activity. One may of course argue that this is all State aid law was ever intended to cover. However, this would in our view disregard the fact that State aid could also be awarded by use of facially neutral rules and there should be a way to tackle such differentiations without having to meet the high threshold of manifest inconsistency.

In any case, the current state of play is not necessarily the end of the road. Nothing prevents the CJEU from further differentiating its case law and thereby restricting the ambit of its case law in *Andres*. Room for manoeuvre particularly exists for the identification of the inherent elements of the reference system of taxation. Moreover, the CJEU has consistently stressed that the case law in *Gibraltar* can still constitute a limit to State aid control. This had last emerged in its judgment in *Fiat*:

> In particular, after having observed that a Member State has chosen to apply the arm's length principle in order to establish the transfer prices of integrated companies, the Commission must, in accordance with the case-law cited in paragraph 70 of the present judgment, be able to establish that the parameters laid down by national law are manifestly inconsistent with the objective of non-discriminatory taxation of all resident companies, whether integrated or not, pursued by the national tax system, by systematically leading to an undervaluation of the transfer prices applicable to integrated companies or to certain of them, such as finance companies, as compared to market prices for comparable transactions carried out by non-integrated companies.[1282]

With this statement, the CJEU perhaps is issuing a warning to Member States and taxpayers alike not to go too far. The CJEU is apparently not willing to relinquish all control.

This, in turn, means that despite the recent trend towards a more restricted ambit for State aid control of fiscal aid schemes, the promotion of taxpayers' rights in the State aid procedure continues to be of utmost importance. In this context, the current status quo is still somewhat unsatisfactory since the case law on State aid law tends to sacrifice the general principles of EU law on the altar of the effectiveness of State aid control.[1283]

A modification of the legal consequences of State aid law as well as a reliance on the general principles of EU law can only address to a very limited extent the problem of taxpayers simply not realizing that a tax measure may amount to State aid. As laid

1282. Joined Cases C-885 and 889/19 P *Fiat*, para. 122.
1283. In this vein: Stefan, *supra* n. 116, at 441f.

out above, changes to this framework de lege ferenda are not necessarily desirable. As to the way forward, the recent developments of the case law should certainly be laid down in a new Commission Notice because the 2016 Notice no longer fully reflects the current status quo. Beyond that, perhaps the only hope – however unsatisfactory – is the further clarifications in the case law of the European courts yet to come. By contrast, the problem that taxpayers are not in a position to notify aid could be addressed without putting into question the general framework of State aid law. An updated Procedural Regulation should therefore contain a right to notification.

In any event, beyond the loss of the Commission's momentum and the more restrictive tendencies of the case law, the period of increased reliance on State aid law in tax matters may be over for now due to external circumstances. The worldwide crises triggered by the COVID-19 pandemic and by a changed geopolitical climate have had a profound impact on economies across the globe. The high degree of globalization of value chains has meant that such disturbances are felt all over the world. Most recently, energy prices and inflation are still causing concern. This unprecedented situation has triggered support actions by governments. Within the EU, tackling the economic slump with subsidies is of course subject to the constraints of State aid law. Yet the crises have shown that these constraints have often been theoretical. From the very start of the pandemic, Member States quickly pledged impressive aid volumes. In this, the very rationales of State aid control had at times appeared to become irrelevant, when Member States proceeded to save national champions.[1284] In other words, it has become apparent that even though State aid law provides a legal framework, both the enforcement and the State aid procedure can be purely pragmatic. Perhaps one has to acknowledge that State aid law becomes less relevant in a crisis.

Nevertheless, we do not believe that fiscal State aid law has thereby become redundant. Indeed, it was in the wake of the previous financial crisis that State aid law had tremendously gained in relevance. State aid law might thus well become more relevant than ever. There will presumably be a need for financial consolidation. The aids that have been granted in recent years – while often clearly warranted – were arguably highly distortive and depended on the financial capabilities of the respective Member States.[1285] In other words, while State aid control may have been temporarily stalled, the need for rationality control will be all the more urgent in the aftermath of the crises. Therefore, State aid law – with all its complexities – still has to be taken seriously and merits continued attention by scholars and practitioners alike.

1284. On this: Luja, *EU Fiscal State Aid Rules and COVID-19, supra* n. 165. For an economic perspective: Chiara Fumagalli et al., *Which Role for State Aid and Merger Control During and After the Covid Crisis?* 11 JECLAP 294ff. (2020).

1285. Maczkovics, *supra* n. 165, at 279.

Bibliography

Maarten Aalbers, *Gibraltar: A Rock Solid Interpretation of the Selectivity Criterion* 16 EStAL 495 (2017).

Maarten Aalbers & Paul Adriaanse, *Recovery of Unlawful Aid*, in Hancher et al. (eds), EU State Aids, 1097 (5th edn 2016).

Stuart Adam et al., *Tax by Design* (2011).

Advisory Board to the Federal Ministry of Finance, 'Tax Benefits and EU State Aid Control: The Problem of and Approaches to Resolving the Conflict of Jurisdiction with Fiscal Autonomy' (2017) https://www.bundesfinanzministerium.de/Content/EN/Standardartikel/Ministry/Advisory_Board/2018-02-07-tax-benefits-and-eu-state-aid-control-download.pdf; jsessionid = EFE3C2242E5EF90FE729347D727DA3D3?__blob = publicationFile&v = 2.

Margarida Afonso, *Recovery of Fiscal Aid*, in Rust & Micheau (eds), State Aid and Tax Law, 57 (2013).

Irene Agnolucci, *Turnover-Based Taxes in EU State Aid Control: The 'Hypothecation Test' and Its Relationship with Free Movement* 19 EStAL 193 (2020).

Robert Alexy, *A Theory of Constitutional Rights* (2010, Reprint).

Giulio Allevato, *Judicial Review of the State Aid Decisions on Advance Tax Rulings: A Last Resort to Safeguard the Rule of Law* 62 European Taxation 86 (2022).

José Manuel Almudí Cid, *Spain: Regional Taxes on Large Retail Establishments Justified for Environmental Reasons*, in Lang et al. (eds), CJEU: Recent Developments in Direct Taxation 2018, 145 (2019).

William D. Andres, *Personal Deductions in an Ideal Income Tax* 86 Harvard L. Rev. 309 (1972).

Heribert Anzinger, *Stand und Perspektiven der positiven und negativen Integration des materiellen Steuerrechts in der EU* 6 HFSt 123 (2017).

Christoph Arhold, *The German Scheme on the Fiscal Carry-Forward of Losses: A Selected Case* 10 EStAL 71 (2011).

Anthony B. Atkinson, *Optimal Taxation and the Direct Versus Indirect Tax Controversy* 4 Canadian Journal of Economics 590 (1977).

Alan J. Auerbach, *Who Bears the Corporate Tax? A Review of What We Know*, in Poterba (ed.), Tax Policy and the Economy 1 (2006).

Reuven S. Avi-Yonah, *Taxation as Regulation: Carbon Tax, Health Care Tax, Bank Tax and Other Regulatory Taxes* Accounting, Economics, and Law 1 (2011).

Josef Azizi, *The Tension Between Member States' Autonomy and Commission Control in State Aid Matters: Selected Aspects*, in Kanninen et al. (eds), EU Competition Law in Context, 307 (2009).

Kelyn Bacon, *State Aids and General Measure* 17 YEL 269 (1997).

Kelyn Bacon, *European Union Law of State Aid* (3rd edn 2017).

Philip Baker & Pasquale Pistone, *General Report* 100B IFA Cahiers 17 (2015).

Philip Baker, *The Week of the 10 May 2021: A Week of State Aid, Transfer Pricing and Tax Rulings* 49 Intertax 602 (2021).

Chiara Balbinot, *Europäisches Beihilfeverbot vs. Mitgliedstaatliche Steuersouveränität: eine kritische Untersuchung der Anwendung des Art. 107 Abs. 1 AEUV im Steuerrecht* 100 FR 729 (2018).

Chiara Balbinot, *§ 8c Abs. 1a KStG (Sanierungsklausel) doch keine unionsrechtswidrige Beihilfe? Schlussanträge des Generalanwalts Wahl in der Rs. Heitkamp (C-203/16 P)* 56 DStR 334 (2018).

Marc Barennes, *The Standing of the Competitors of the Aid Recipient in State Aid Cases*, in Kanninen et al. (eds), EU Competition Law in Context 321 (2009).

René Barents, *The Single Market and National Tax Sovereignty*, in Jansen (ed.), Fiscal Sovereignty of the Member States in an Internal Market: Past and Future 51 (2011).

María Cruz Barreiro Carril, *National Tax Sovereignty and EC Fundamental Freedoms: The Impact of Tax Obstacles on the Internal Market* 38 Intertax 105 (2010).

Bruce Bartlett, *The End of Tax Expenditures as We Know Them?* 84 IRET policy Bulletin (2001).

Andreas Bartosch, *Is There a Need for a Rule of Reason in European State Aid Law? Or How to Arrive at a Coherent Concept of Material Selectivity?* 47 CMLR 729 (2010).

Andreas Bartosch, *Procedural Rights Denied for Too Long: Is Legal Conservativism Finally Heading for Its "Götterdämmerung"?* 10 EStAL 579 (2011).

Andreas Bartosch, *Nationale Steuersysteme im Fadenkreuz des Beihilferechts: wer bestimmt künftig den Maßstab?* 72 BB 2199 (2017).

Andreas Bartosch, *Differenzierungen im nationalen Steuerrecht und das Selektivitätsmerkmal des EU-Beihilfeverbots: Sind die Steuerregelungen betreffend den deutschen Mittelstand in Gefahr* 73 BB 2199 (2018).

Andreas Bartosch, *Spanish Goodwill: A Textbook on Material Selectivity Awaiting a Second Edition* 21 EStAL 65 (2022).

Nieves Bayón Fernández, *The Selective Advantage Criterion in Tax Rulings: The Path Towards a More Coherent and Thorough Analysis of Selectivity* 12 JECLAP 200 (2021).

Anna Beckers, *The Creeping Juridification of the Code of Conduct for Business Taxation: How EU Codes of Conduct Become Hard Law* 37 YEL 569 (2018).

Maciej Bernatt & Łukasz Grzejdziak, *Selectivity of State Aid and Progressive Turnover Taxes – Leaving the Door (Too) Wide Open?: Commission v Poland* 59 CMLR 187 (2022).

Andrea Biondi, *The Rationale of State Aid Control: A Return to Orthodoxy* 12 Camb. Yearb. Eur. Leg. Stud. 35 (2010).

Andrea Biondi, *State Aid Is Falling Down, Falling Down: An Analysis of the Case Law on the Notion of Aid* 50 CMLR 1719 (2013).

Alexander Birnstiel, *Recovery of Unlawful State Aid: The Role of Member State Courts in State Aid Recovery Scenarios* 11 EStAL 645 (2012).

Boris I. Bittker, *Accounting for Federal 'Tax Subsidies' in the National Budget* 22 NTJ 244 (1969).

Boris L. Bittker, *The Tax Expenditure Budget – A Reply to Professors Surrey & Hellmuth* 22 NTJ 538 (1969).

Gianluigi Bizioli, *Balancing the Fundamental Freedoms and Tax Sovereignty: Some Thoughts on Recent ECJ Case Law on Direct Taxation* 48 European Taxation 133 (2008).

Gianluigi Bizioli, *Building the EU Tax Sovereignty: Lessons from Federalism* 14 WTJ 407 (2022).

Eirik Bjorge & Jack R. Williams, *The Protean Principle of Proportionality: How Different Is Proportionality in EU Contexts?* 75 CLJ 186 (2016).

Janina Brandau, *Notifizierungsfragen* 8 HFSt 243 (2018).

Janina Brandau et al., *Brennpunkt Beihilferecht: Das deutsche Steuerrecht auf dem Prüfstand* 72 BB 1175 (2017).

Yariv Brauner, *An Essay on BEPS, Sovereignty, and Taxation,* in Rocha & Christians (eds), Tax Sovereignty in the BEPS Era, 73 (2017).

Christian Brodersen & Norbert Mückl, *The German Restructuring Privilege (Section 8c(1a) of the Corporate Income Tax Act) and the EU State Aid Rules (Article 107(1) of the TFEU)* 54 European Taxation 56 (2014).

Cécile Brokelind *Intellectual Property, Taxation and State Aid Law,* in Richelle et al. (eds), State Aid Law and Business Taxation 221 (2016).

Edouard Louis Jean-Baptiste Bruc, *Passing-on and Recoverable Unlawful State Aid under European Union Law*17 EStAL 54 (2018).

José Luis Buendía Sierra, *The Role of Competitors in State Aid Procedures* 14 EStAL 451 (2015).

José Luis Buendía Sierra, *'Small on Small': Towards a Two-Speed State Aid Control?* 15 EStAL 501 (2016).

José Luis Buendía Sierra, *Judicial Control and the Recovery Phase* 17 EStAL 173 (2018).

José Luis Buendía Sierra, *Finding Selectivity or the Art of Comparison* 17 EStAL 85 (2018).

José Luis Buendía Sierra & Miguel Ángel Bolsa Ferruz, *State Aid Assessment: What National Courts Can Do and What They Must Do* 16 EStAL 408 (2017).

José Luis Buendía Sierra & Ben Smulders, *The Limited Role of the 'Refined Economic Approach' in Achieving the Objectives of State Aid Control: Time for Some*

Realism, in EC State Aid Law: Liber Amicorum Francisco Santoalalla Gadea 1 (2008).

Svitlana Buriak & Ivan Lazarov, *Between State Aid and the Fundamental Freedoms: The Arm's Length Principle and EU Law* 56 CMLR 1 (2019).

Caroline Buts et al., *Determinants of the European Commission's State Aid Decisions* 11 J Ind Compet Trade 399 (2011).

Eduardo Cabrera Maquedo, *Commission v Ryanair: in the Field of State Aid Complaints are not Subject to Formal Requirements (for Now)* 4 JECLAP 423 (2013).

Franklin Cachia, *Analysing the European Commission's Final Decisions on Apple, Starbucks, Amazon and Fiat Finance & Trade* 26 EC Tax Rev. 23 (2017).

Luis Calderon Gomez, *Transcending 'Tax' Sovereignty and Tax Standardization: Three Questions* 45 The Yale Journal of International Law 191 (2020).

Maria Carro Pitarch, *Analysis of the (In)compatibility of Digital Services Taxes with State Aid Rules* 31 EC Tax Rev. 326 (2022).

Stefano Castagna, *On the European Commission's Understanding of the Arm's Length Principle in International Taxation Versus State Aid Matters: Treaty Violations and High Stakes in Play* 13 WTJ 481 (2021).

Luzius U. Cavelti, *Automatic Exchange Versus the Withholding Tax Regime Globalization and Increasing Sovereignty Conflicts in International Taxation* 5 WTJ 172 (2013).

Nicola Chesaites, *Tax Incentives as State Aid*, in Tomljenović et al. (eds), EU Competition and State Aid Rules 253(2017).

Benjamin Cheynel & Adrien Giraud, *New Paradigm for Recovery of Unlawful Aid in the EU: National Judges and the 'Exception of Compatibility'* 31 W. Comp. 557 (2008).

Allison Christians, *Sovereignty, Taxation and Social Contract* 18 Minnesota Journal of International Law 99 (2009).

Commission, 'Study on the Enforcement of State Aid Rules and Decisions Be National Courts' [2019] https://ec.europa.eu/competition/publications/reports/kd0219428enn.pdf.

Kimberly A. Clausing, *Who Pays the Corporate Tax in a Global Economy* 66 NTJ 151 (2013).

Axel Cordewener, *Asymmetrical Tax Burdens and EU State Aid Control* 21 EC Tax Rev. 288 (2012).

Paul P. Craig, *Substantive Legitimate Expectations in Domestic and Community Law* 55 CLJ 289 (1996).

José Luís da Cruz Vilaça, *Material and Geographic Selectivity in State aid: Recent Developments* 8 EStAL 443 (2009).

Tsilly Dagan, *Klaus Vogel Lecture 2021: Unbundled Tax Sovereignty – Refining the Challenges* 76 BIT 318 (2022).

Stephen Daly, *The Constitutional Implications of an EU Arm's Length Principle* 60 European Taxation 70 (2020).

Stephen Daly, *The Power to Get It Wrong* 137 Law Quarterly Rev. 280 (2021).

Daniel Deák, *Cloaking Member State Objectives Through Legislative Instruments* 30 EC Tax Rev. 111 (2021).

Luc De Broe, *The State Aid Review Against Aggressive Tax Planning: 'Always Look a Gift Horse in the Mouth'* 24 EC Tax Rev. 290 (2015).

Luc De Broe, *Can Tax Treaties Confer State Aid* 26 EC Tax Rev. 228 (2017).

Luc De Broe, *The State Aid Selectivity-Test in Corporate Tax Matters: CJEU Applies Common Sense in Its Judgments on the German 'Sanierungs'-clause, but Do We Have All Pieces of the Puzzle Now?* 27 EC Tax Rev. 285 (2018).

Luc De Broe & Mélanie Massant, *The General Court's Judgment in Engie: The Non-application of a National GAAR Confers State Aid* 31 EC Tax Rev. 6 (2022).

Gráinne de Búrca, *The Principle of Proportionality and its Application in EC Law* 13 YEL 105 (1993).

Francesco de Cecco, *State Aid and the European Economic Constitution* (2013).

Francesco de Cecco, *A Constitutional View of State Aid*, in Piernas López et al. (eds), The Future of EU State Aid Law: Consolidation and Expansion 25 (2023).

Rita de la Feria, *Pillar 2, Fiat, and the EU Unanimity Rule on Tax Matters* 32 EC Tax Rev. 1 (2023).

Carla De Pietro, *The EU Notion of Legitimate Expectations in the Context of State Aid Law: What Role for National Judges*, in De Pietro (ed.), New Perspectives on Fiscal State Aid: Legitimacy and Effectiveness of Fiscal State Aid Control 103 (2019).

Jacques Derenne, *Commission v World Duty Free Group a.o.: Selectivity in (Fiscal) State Aid, Quo Vadis Curia?* 8 JECLAP 311 (2017).

Nicolas de Sadeleer, *Preliminary Ruling on the Compatibility of Taxation of Superstores with the Right to Freedom of Establishment and State Aid Law: Case C-233/16, ANGED* 27 RECIEL 341 (2018).

Marc Desens, *Die neue Besteuerung von Sanierungserträgen* 99 FR 981 (2017).

Michael Devereux & Simon Loretz, *What Do We Know about Corporate Tax Competition* 66 NTJ 745 (2013).

Jan de Weerth, *Sanierungsklausel, Sanierungserlass und andere Steuererleichterungen im Fokus des EU-Beihilferechts* 52 DStR, 2485 (2014).

Martin F. de Wilde, *Some Thoughts on a Fair Allocation of Corporate Tax in a Globalizing Economy* 38 Intertax 281 (2010).

Peter Dietsch & Thomas Rixen, *Tax Competition and Global Background Justice* 22 The Journal of Political Philosophy 150 (2014).

Lars Dobratz, *Artikel 107 AEUV*, in Musil & Weber-Grellet (eds), Europäisches Steuerrecht (2022).

Lars Dobratz, *Artikel 108 AEUV*, in Musil & Weber-Grellet (eds), Europäisches Steuerrecht (2022).

Christian Dorenkamp, *Seminar G: EU-Vorschläge zur Besteuerung der Digitalwirtschaft sowie EU-Beihilfenrecht und Verrechnungspreise* 27 IStR 640 (2018).

António Carlos dos Santos & Cidália Mota Lopez, *Tax Sovereignty, Tax Competition and the Base Erosion and Profit Shifting Concept of Permanent Establishment* 25 EC Tax Rev. 296 (2016).

Humbert Drabbe, *The Test of Selectivity in State Aid Litigation: The Relevance of Drawing Internal and External Comparisons to Identify the Reference Framework*, in Rust & Micheau (eds), State Aid and Tax Law 87 (2013).

Ivan Draganic, *State Aid or Compensation for Extra Costs: Tuning the Test of Proportionality in EC Competition Law* 5 EStAL 683 (2006).

Stephan Eilers & Stefan Schmitz, *Indirekte Steuern und EU-Beihilfenrecht: Europäische Kommission verbietet (teilweise) den Vollzug der ungarischen Werbesteuer/Krisensteuer* 4 ISR 211 (2015).

Jens Ekkenga & Javid Safaei, *Bedroht die EU-Beihilfenaufsicht die Steuerautonomie der EU-Mitgliedstaaten: Zweifel sind angebracht: Ein Gegenplädoyer am Beispiel von Steuererleichterungen in Krisen- und Insolvenzfällen* 56 DStR 1993 (2018).

David C. Elkins, *The Merits of Tax Competition in a Globalized Economy* 91 Indiana Law Journal 905 (2016).

Benedikt Ellenrieder, *Verhandlung der Grundsätze der beihilferechtlichen Selektivität: Grundlegende Gedanken im Nachgang zur mündlichen Verhandlung des EuG in den Rechtssachen World Duty Free und Banco Santander und Santusa* 27 IStR 480 (2018).

Benedikt Ellenrieder, *Die materielle Selektivität steuerlicher Beihilfen* (2020).

Sylvia Elwes, *The Internal Market Versus the Right of Member States to Levy Direct Tax: A Clash of Fundamental Principles* 41 Intertax 15 (2013).

Frank Engelen, *State Aid and Restrictions on Free Movement: Two Sides of the Same Coin?* 52 European Taxation 204 (2012).

Eric Engle, *The History of the General Principle of Proportionality: An Overview* 10 Dartmouth Law Journal 1 (2012).

Joachim Englisch, *EU State Aid Rules Applied to Indirect Tax Measures* 22 EC Tax Rev. 9 (2013).

Joachim Englisch, *Das Beihilfenverbot im Steuerrecht*, in Schaumburg & Englisch (eds), Europäisches Steuerrecht (2nd edn 2020).

Joachim Englisch, *Umsatzsteuer*, in Tipke & Lang (eds), Steuerrecht (24th edn 2020).

Joachim Englisch, *Spezielle Verkehr- und Verbrauchsteuern*, in Tipke & Lang (eds), Steuerrecht (24th edn 2020).

Joachim Englisch, *State Aid Prohibition: The New GAAR in Town* 30 EC Tax Rev. 144 (2021).

Lilian V. Faulhaber, *The Trouble with Tax Competition: From Practice to Theory* 71 Tax L. Rev. 311 (2018).

Martin Feldstein, *Incidence of a Capital Income Tax in a Growing Economy with Variable Saving Rates* 41 Review of Economic Studies 505 (1974).

Delia Ferri & Juan Jorge Piernas López, *The Social Dimension of EU State Aid Law and Policy* 21 Camb. Yearb. Eur. Leg. Stud. 75 (2019).

Marc Fierstra, *Ex-Officio Application of EU State Aid Rules by National Courts*, in De Pietro (ed.), New Perspectives on Fiscal State Aid: Legitimacy and Effectiveness of Fiscal State Aid Control 117 (2019).

Federico Fichera, *Digital Service Taxes under State Aid Scrutiny* 20 EStAL 479 (2021).

Eve Fink, *The Possibility of Protection of Legitimate Expectations in Recovery of Unlawful State Aid* 20 Juridica International 133 (2013).

Leo Flynn, *'Taking Flight, Not Taking Fright?': The National Court As a Full Partner in the Enforcement of the State Aid Discipline* 16 EStAL 335 (2017).

Emily Forrester, *Is the State Aid Regime a Suitable Instrument to Be Used in the Fight Against Harmful Tax Competition?* 27 EC Tax Rev. 19 (2018).

Edouard Fort, *EU State Aid and Tax: An Evolutionary Approach* 57 European Taxation 370 (2017).

Benedikt Freund & Moritz Seiler, *Magnetrol v Commission: When Do Advance Tax Rulings Become an Aid Scheme under Article 1(d) Regulation (EU) 2015/1589 – Case C-337/19 P Magnetrol v Commission* 21 EStAL 302 (2022).

Dominik Freyer, *The Proportionality Principle under EU Tax Law: General and Practical Problems Caused by Its Extensive Application – Part 1* 57 European Taxation 384 (2017).

Don Fullerton & Gilbert E. Metcalf, *Tax Incidence,* in Auerbach & Feldstein (eds), 4 Handbook of Public Economics 1788 (2002).

Chiara Fumagalli et al., *Which Role for State Aid and Merger Control During and After the Covid Crisis?* 11 JECLAP 294 (2020).

Sissie Fung, *The Questionable Legitimacy of the OECD/G20 BEPS Project* 11 Erasmus L. Rev. 76 (2017).

Stjepan Gadžo, *The Principle of 'Nexus' or 'Genuine Link' as a Keystone of International Income Tax Law: A Reappraisal* 46 Intertax 194 (2018).

Klaus Gärditz, *§ 11 Verfassungsidentität und Schutz der Verfassung,* in Stern et al. (eds), Das Staatsrecht der Bundesrepublik Deutschland im europäischen Staatenverbund (2nd edn 2022, Vol. 1).

Guilherme Galdino, *Special Charges, Free Movement and State Aid* 18 EStAL 510 (2019).

Ricardo André Galendi Júnior, *State Aid and Transfer Pricing: The Inherent Flaw under a Supranational Reference System* 46 Intertax 994 (2018).

Edoardo Gambaro & Francesco Mazzocchi, *Montessori v Commission: A New Frontier for Competitors of Beneficiaries to Bring Action Against a Commission Decision on Aid Schemes?* 10 JECLAP 91 (2019).

Ioannis Ganoulis & Reiner Martin, *State Aid Control in the European Union: Rationale, Stylised Facts and Determining Factors* 36 Intereconomics 289 (2001).

Lucyne Ghazarian, *Recovery of State Aid: The Obligations of Member States, National Courts and National Authorities in State Aid Recovery and Recent Developments in the Case-Law of the Court of Justice of the European Union* 15 EStAL 228 (2016).

Adrien Giraud, *A Study of the Notion of Legitimate Expectations in State Aid Recovery Proceedings: "Abandon All Hope Ye Who Enter Here"?* 45 CMLR 1399 (2008).

Adrien Giraud and Sylvain Petit, *Tax Rulings and State Aid Qualification: Should Reality Matter* 16 EStAL 233 (2017).

Adrien Giraud & Sylvain Petit, *Bury Them Deep: The Court of Justice Annuls the Autogrill and Banco Santander Judgments of the General Court* 16 EStAL 310 (2017).

Joanna Goyder & Margot Dons, *Damages Claims Based on State Aid Law Infringements* 16 EStAL 418 (2017).

Tim Hackemann & Sabine Sydow, *Richtungsentscheidung des EuGH in der Rs. C-6/12, P Oy für die Voraussetzungen der Einstufung einer Sanierungsklausel als staatliche Beihilfe; Auswirkungen auf die suspendierte deutsche Sanierungsklausel des § 8c Abs. 1a KStG* 22 IStR 786 (2013).

Leigh Hancher, *State Aid Recovery: A New Public Order?* 12 EStAL 1 (2013).

Leigh Hancher, *The General Framework,* in Hancher et al. (eds), EU State Aids 49 (5th edn 2016).

Leigh Hancher, *Article 107(2) and Article 107(3),* in Hancher et al. (eds), EU State Aids 123 (5th edn 2016).

Leigh Hancher, *The Role of Presumptions and the Burden of Proof in Recent State Aid Cases: Some Reflections* 18 EStAL 470 (2019).

Arnold C. Harberger, *The Incidence of the Corporation Income Tax* 70 Journal of Political Economy 215 (1962).

Tor-Inge Harbo, *The Function of the Proportionality Principle in EU Law* 1 European Law Journal 158 (2010).

Werner Haslehner, *Double Taxation Relief, Transfer Pricing Adjustments and State Aid Law,* in Richelle et al. (eds), State Aid Law and Business Taxation 133 (2016).

Kevin A. Hassett & Aparna Mathur, *A Spatial Model of Corporate Tax Incidence* 47 Applied Economics 1350 (2015).

Johanna Hey, *EU-Beihilfen und Steuervergünstigungen: Gemeinsamkeiten und Unterschiede* 92 StuW 331 (2015).

Johanna Hey, *Steuerbefreiung für Sanierungsgewinne und EU-Beihilferecht: Zum Notifizierungsverfahren* 99 FR 453 (2017).

Johanna Hey, *Steuersystem und Steuerverfassungsrecht,* in Tipke & Lang (eds), Steuerrecht, (24th edn 2020).

Chris Hilson, *Rights and Principles in EU Law: A Distinction without Foundation?* 15 Maastricht Journal of Comparative Law 193 (2008).

Robert Hinz, *Sanierungserträge: § 3a EStG – eine zulässige Beihilfe?* 104 FR 1021 (2022).

Michael Honoré, *Selectivity and Taxation: Reflections in Light of Case C-487/06 P, British Aggregates Association* 8 EStAL 527 (2009).

Michael Honoré, *State Aid and Taxation: All Clear* 14 EStAL 306 (2015).

Michael Honoré, *Selectivity,* in Werner & Verouden (eds), EU State Aid Control: Law and Economics 119 (2017).

David Hummel, *Das nationale Steuergesetz unter der umfassenden Kontrolle des unionsrechtlichen Beihilferechts?* 110 GmbH-Rundschau 390 (2019).

David Hummel, *Ertragsbesteuerung im Zeitalter der Digitalisierung: umsatzbasierte Steuern als Alternative zur herkömmlichen Gewinnbesteuerung?* 10 ISR 216 (2021).

Theodoros Iliopoulos, *The State Aid Cases of Starbucks and Fiat: New Routes for the Concept of Selectivity* 16 EStAL 263 (2017).

Mathieu Isenbaert, *EC Law and the Sovereignty of the Member States in Direct Taxation* (2010).

Roland Ismer, *Grundlagen,* in Vogel/Lehner (eds), DBA (7th edn 2021).

Roland Ismer, *Judicial Review of Tax Laws: The Coherence Requirement (Folgerichtigkeitsgebot),* in Meßerschmidt & Lalana (eds), Rational Lawmaking under Review 209 (2016).

Roland Ismer & Christoph Jescheck, *Taxes on Digital Services and the Substantive Scope of Application of Tax Treaties: Pushing the Boundaries of Article 2 of the OECD Model?* 46 Intertax 573 (2018).

Roland Ismer & Sophia Piotrowski, *Selektivität von Beihilfen: Dogmatische Grundfragen am Beispiel von IP-Boxen* 24 IStR 257 (2015).

Roland Ismer & Sophia Piotrowski, *Falsche Begründung: richtiges Ergebnis? – Zur beihilferechtlichen Argumentation im Vorlagebeschluss zum Sanierungserlass* 53 DStR 1993 (2015).

Roland Ismer & Sophia Piotrowski, *The Selectivity of Tax Measures: A Tale of Two Consistencies* 43 Intertax 559 (2015).

Roland Ismer & Sophia Piotrowski, *Selectivity in Corporate Tax Matters After World Duty Free: A Tale of Two Consistencies Revisited* 46 Intertax 156 (2018).

Roland Ismer & Sophia Piotrowski, *Relationship of Fiscal State Aid and the Fundamental Freedoms,* in Panayi et al. (eds), Research Handbook on European Union Taxation Law 450 (2020).

Francis G. Jacobs, *Recent Developments in the Principle of Proportionality in European Community Law,* in Ellis (ed.), The Principle of Proportionality in the Laws of Europe 1 (1999).

Clélia Jadot, *Damages Actions and State Aid: Time for Action at EU Level?* 6 Market and Competition L. Rev. 89 (2022).

Thomas Jaeger, *CELF II: Settling into a Weak Effet Utile Standard for Private State Aid Enforcement* 1 JECLAP 319(2010).

Thomas Jaeger, *Fehlstellungen im Verhältnis von Steuer- und Beihilferecht: Ein Plädoyer für mehr Ausgewogenheit* 23 EuZW 92 (2012).

Thomas Jaeger, *From Santander to LuxLeaks: And Back* 14 EStAL 345 (2015).

Thomas Jaeger, *Tax Incentives under State Aid Law: A Competition Law Perspective,* in Richelle et al. (eds), State Aid Law and Business Taxation 39 (2016).

Thomas Jaeger, *Tax Measures,* in Säcker & Montag (eds), European State Aid Law 1109 (2016).

Thomas Jaeger, *Schwächen der Prüfung von Steuerbeihilfen am Beispiel der Urteile Fiat und Starbucks* 31 EuZW 18 (2020).

Jan H. Jans, *Proportionality Revisited* 27 Legal Issues of Economic Integration 239 (2000).

Hans Dieter Jarass, *Schutz durch rechtsstaatliche Grundsätze des Unionsrechts* 133 Deutsches Verwaltungsblatt 1249 (2018).

Hans Dieter Jarass, *Einleitung: Grundlagen und Bedeutung der Grundrechte,* in Jarass (ed.), Charta der Grundrechte der EU (4th edn 2021).

Hans Dieter Jarass, *GG Art. 20,* in Jarass & Pieroth (eds), Grundgesetz für die Bundesrepublik Deutschland (17th edn 2022).

Krzysztof Jaros & Nicolai Ritter, *Pleading Legitimate Expectations in the Procedure for the Recovery of State Aid* 3 EStAL 573 (2004).

Tony Joris & Wout De Cock, *Is Belgium and Forum 187 v Commission a Suitable Legal Source for an EU "At Arm's Length Principle"?* 16 EStAL 607 (2017).

Denis Jouve, *Recovering Unlawful and Incompatible Aids by National Courts: CELF and Scott/Kimberly Clark Cases* 16 EStAL 367 (2017).

Šime Jozipović, *Die Anwendung des EU-Beihilferechts auf das internationale Steuerrecht* (2018).

Jeffery M. Kadet, *Thoughts on Treasury's White Paper on EU State Aid* TNI 877 (2016).

Douglas A. Kahn & Jeffery S. Lehman, *Tax Expenditures: A Critical View* 54 Tax Notes 1661 (1992).

Balázs Károlyi, *Progressive Turnover-Based Taxes and Their Legal Repercussions Under EU Law* 29 EC Tax Rev. 271 (2020).

James Kavanaugh & Nicole Robins, *Corporate Tax Arrangements Under EU State Aid Scrutiny* 14 EStAL 358 (2015).

Wolfgang Kessler & Christoph Spengel, *Checkliste potenziell EU-rechtswidriger Normen des deutschen direkten Steuerrechts* 73 Beilage 02 Der Betrieb 1 (2020).

Paul Kirchhof, *§ 181 Der allgemeine Gleichheitssatz*, in Isensee & Kirchhof (eds), Handbuch des Staatsrechts für die Bundesrepublik Deutschland 609 (3rd edn 2010, vol. 8).

Paul Kirchhof, *Art. 3 Abs. 1 Gleichheit vor dem Gesetz*, in Dürig et al. (eds), Grundgesetz-Kommentar (100th edn 2023).

Felix Klemt, *Richtungsentscheidung für Kompetenzen in Europa: lässt das Beihilferecht die Sanierungsklauseln in § 8c Abs. 1a KStG zu?* 51 DStR 1057 (2013).

Martin Köhler, *Private Enforcement of State Aid Law: Problems of Guaranteeing EU Rights by means of National (Procedural) Law* 11 EStAL 369 (2012).

Christian Koenig, *Where Is State Aid Law Heading To?* 13 EStAL 611 (2014).

Georg Kofler, *EU Power to Tax: Competences in the Area of Direct Taxation*, in Panayi et al. (eds), Research Handbook on European Union Taxation Law 11 (2020).

Georg Kofler, *The Future of Digital Services Taxes* 30 EC Tax Rev. 50 (2021).

Georg Kofler & Julia Sinnig, *Equalization Taxes and the EU's 'Digital Services Tax'* 47 Intertax 176 (2019).

Juliane Kokott, *Der EuGH als Garant fairen Steuerwettbewerbs* 6 ISR 395 (2017).

Juliane Kokott, *Steuerrecht und unionsrechtlicher Beihilfebegriff*, in Lang (ed.), Europäisches Steuerrecht 535 (2018).

Juliane Kokott, *Das Steuerrecht der Europäischen Union* (2018).

Juliane Kokott, *Tax Harmonisation Through the Prohibition of State Aid?* 21 EStAL 462 (2022).

Juliane Kokott & Pasquale Pistone, *Taxpayers in International Law* (2022).

Marcel Krumm, *Verfahrensrechtliche Aspekte steuerlicher Beihilfen*, in Lang (ed.), Europäisches Steuerrecht 561 (2018).

Dimitrios Kyriazis, *From Soft Law to Soft Law to Hard Law: The Commission's Approach to the State Aid Assessment of Tax Rulings* 15 EStAL 428 (2016).

Dimitrios Kyriazis, *Fiscal State Aid Law as a Tool Against Harmful Tax Competition in the EU: déjà vu?* 42 YEL 1 (2022).

Hanno Kube et al., *Tax Policy: Trends in the Allocation of Powers Between the Union and Its Member States* 25 EC Tax Rev. 247 (2016).

Julia Kühn, *Die Rückforderung unionsrechtswidrig gewährter Steuerbeihilfen nach deutschem Recht* 7 ISR 360 (2018).

Bartłomiej Kurcz & Dimitri Vallindas, *Can General Measures Be … Selective? Some Thoughts on the Interpretation of a State Aid Definition* 45 CMLR 159 (2008).

Patricia Lampraeve, *Harmful Tax Competition and Fiscal State Aid: Two Sides of the Same Coin?* 59 European Taxation 197 (2019).

Johannes Laitenberger & Thomas Lieflaender, *Beihilfeaufsicht: die Versöhnung von unabhängiger Rechtsdurchsetzung mit direkter Wirkung und demokratiegesteuerter Ermessensausübung* 38 EuZW 281 (2017).

Michael Lang, *Die Auswirkungen des gemeinschaftlichen Beihilferechts auf das Steuerrecht* (2009).

Michael Lang, *Seminar J: Steuerrecht, Grundfreiheiten und Beihilfeverbot* 19 IStR 570 (2010).

Michael Lang, *State Aid and Taxation: Recent Trends in the Case Law of the ECJ* 11 EStAL 411 (2012).

Michael Lang, *State Aid and Taxation: Selectivity and Comparability Analysis*, in Richelle et al. (eds), State Aid Law and Business Taxation 27 (2016).

Michael Lang, *Taxation and State Aid: Recent Case Law on Progressive Turnover Taxes* 61 European Taxation 516 (2021).

François-Charles Laprévote, *A Missed Opportunity? State Aid Modernization and Effective Third Parties Rights in State aid Proceedings* 13 EStAL 426 (2014).

Stephanie Law, *The Rationales, Reasoning and Methodology Underpinning the Judicial Recognition of Principles of Union Law* 52 Cahiers de droit européen 11 (2016).

Moris Lehner, *Limitation of the National Power of Taxation by the Fundamental Freedoms and Non-discrimination Clauses of the EC Treaty* 9 EC Tax Rev. 5 (2000).

Oliver Lepsius, *Zur Neubegründung des Rückwirkungsverbots aus der Gewaltenteilung* 69 Juristenzeitung 488 (2014).

Julie Leroy, *Recovery of Fiscal State Aid in the Netherlands and the Role of the National Judge*, in De Pietro (ed.), New Perspectives on Fiscal State Aid 159 (2019).

Jeremy Lever, *EU State Aid Law – Not a Pretty Sight* 12 EStAL 5 (2013).

Li Liu & Rosanne Altshuler, *Measuring the Burden of the Corporate Income Tax under Imperfect Competition* 66 NTJ 215 (2013).

Paul-John Loewenthal, *Fiscal Selectivity: A Notion in Need of Clarity*, in De Pietro (ed.), New Perspectives on Fiscal State Aid 31 (2019).

Hugo López López, *General Thought on Selectivity and Consequences of a Broad Concept of State Aid in Tax Matters* 9 EStAL 807 (2010).

Hugo López López, *Recent Developments in Spanish Legislation on State Aid Recovery of a Tax Nature* 14 EStAL 382 (2015).

Liza Lovdahl Gormsen, *EU State Aid Law and Transfer Pricing: A Critical Introduction to a New Saga* 7 JECLAP 369 (2016).

Liza Lovdahl Gormsen & Clement Mifsud-Bonnici, *Legitimate Expectation of Consistent Interpretation of EU State Aid Law: Recovery in State Aid Cases Involving Advanced Pricing Agreements on Tax* 8 JECLAP 423 (2017).

Philip Lowe, *The Commission's Powers to Enforce the Law: And to Propose Changes to it* 42 European L. Rev. 909 (2017).

Markus Ludwigs, *Demokratieferne Gestaltung der europäischen Beihilfeaufsicht* 28 EuZW 41 (2017).

Raymond Luja, *Tax Treaties and State Aid: Some Thoughts* 44 European Taxation 234 (2004).

Raymond Luja, *Revisiting the Balance Between Aid, Selectivity and Selective Aid in Respect of Taxes and Special Levies* 9 EStAL 161 (2010).

Raymond Luja, *(Re)shaping Fiscal State Aid: Selected Recent Cases and Their Impact* 40 Intertax 120 (2012).

Raymond Luja, *Does the Modernisation of State Aid Control Put Legal Certainty and Simplicity at Risk* 13 EStAL 765 (2014).

Raymond Luja, *Will the EU's State Aid Regime Survive BEPS?* BTR 379 (2015).

Raymond Luja, *Do State Aid Rules Still Allow European Union Member States to Claim Fiscal Sovereignty* 25 EC Tax Rev. 312 (2016).

Raymond Luja, *Tax Incentives, Harmful Tax Competition and State Aid Considerations in the EU*, in Richelle et al. (eds), State Aid Law and Business Taxation 65 (2016).

Raymond Luja, *State Aid Benchmarking and Tax Ruling: Can We Keep It Simple?*, in Richelle et al. (eds), State Aid and Business Taxation 111 (2016).

Raymond Luja, *EU Fiscal State Aid Rules and COVID-19: Will One Survive the Other?* 29 EC Tax Rev. 147 (2020).

Raymond Luja, *Andres: The Unfinished Business of a Seemingly Selective Non-advantage* 20 EStAL 578 (2021).

Joris Luts, *Compatibility of IP Box Regimes with EU State Aid Rules and Code of Conduct* 23 EC Tax Rev. 258 (2014).

Richard Lyal, *Transfer Pricing Rules and State Aid* 38 Fordham Int. Law J. 1017 (2015).

Richard Lyal, *State Aid, Tax Integration and State Sovereignty*, in Panayi et al. (eds), Research Handbook on European Union Taxation Law 410 (2020).

Timothy Lyons, *Luxembourg v European Commission; Amazon EU Sarl and Amazon.com Inc v European Commission: The Issue of Competence Again* BTR 470 (2021).

Carole Maczkovics, *How Flexible Should State Aid Control Be in Times of Crisis?* 19 EStAL 271 (2020).

Alexandre Maitrot de la Motte, *The Recovery of the Illegal Fiscal State Aids: Tax Less to Tax More* 26 EC Tax Rev. 75 (2017).

Spyridon E. Malamis, *The Future of OECD Tax Arbitration: The Relevance of Investment Treaty and WTO Dispute Settlement Practice in Promoting a Gradual Evolution of the International Tax Dispute Resolution System* 48 Intertax 966 (2020).

Fabian Mang, *The (In)Compatibility of IP Box Regimes with EU Law, the Code of Conduct and the BEPS Initiatives* 55 European Taxation 78 (2015).

Sandra Marco Colino, *The Long Arm of State Aid Law: Crushing Corporate Tax Avoidance* 44 Fordham Int. Law J. 397 (2020).

Ruben Martini, *Rechtsfolgen unionsrechtswidriger Beihilfen im Steuerrecht* 94 StuW 101 (2017).

Ruth Mason, *State Aid Special Reports – Part 2: Legitimate Expectations* TNI 615 (2017).

Ruth Mason, *Tax Rulings as State Aid – Part 4: Whose Arm's-Length Standard?* TNI 947 (2017).

Ruth Mason, *What the CJEU's Hungarian Cases Mean for Digital Taxes* TNI 161 (2020).

Ruth Mason, *Identifying Illegal Subsidies* 69 American University L. Rev. 479 (2020).

Ruth Mason, *Ding-Dong! The EU Arm's Length Standard Is Dead* TNI 1249 (2022).

Ruth Mason, *Tax Competition and State Aid* 43 YEL 1 (2023).

Ruth Mason & Leopoldo Parada, *Digital Battlefront in the Tax Wars* TNI 1183 (2018).

Ruth Mason & Leopoldo Parada, *Company Size Matters,* BTR 610 (2019).

Georgios Matsos, *Systematic Misconceptions of State Aid Law in the Area of Taxation* 13 EStAL 491 (2014).

Charles E. McLure, *Globalization, Tax Rules and National Sovereignty* 55 BIT 328 (2001).

Danish Mehboob, *Turnover Taxes Do Not Violate EU State Aid Law, Finds CJEU* 32 International Tax Review 69 (2021).

Rudolf Mellinghoff, *Europäisches Steuerrecht und grenzüberschreitender Rechtsschutz* 6 HFSt 221 (2017).

Massimo Merola & Luigi Cappelletti, *The Obligation to Recover Unlawful Aid* 2 JECLAP 465 (2011).

Alke Metselaar, *Who Can Invoke State Aid Law Before National Judges: That Floating Question of Legal Interest in the Case Law of Dutch Courts* 13 EStAL 250 (2014).

Claire Micheau, *Fundamental Freedoms and State Aid Rules under EU Law: The Example of Taxation* 52 European Taxation 210 (2012).

Claire Micheau, *State Aid, Subsidy and Tax Incentives under EU and WTO Law* (2014).

Claire Micheau, *Récupération des aides d'État illegals et incompatibles sous forme fiscale* 50 Revue trimestrielle de droit européen 343 (2014).

Claire Micheau & Gauthier Charles de la Brousse, *Case Studies of Tax Issues on Selectivity: Analysis of the Patent Box Scheme and the Reduced Taxation of Foreign-Source Interest Income,* in Rust & Micheau (eds), State Aid and Tax Law 153 (2013).

Bob Michel, *ECJ Determines "Only in Belgium" Excess Profit Ruling Practice Constitutes Aid Scheme, but Did It Provide Illegal Aid?* 62 European Taxation 95 (2022).

Andreas Möhlenkamp, *Steuerfreie Sanierungsgewinne, EU-Beihilfenverbot und Wettbewerb* 39 ZIP 1907 (2018).

Jörg Manfred Mössner, *Umsatzbasierte direkte Steuern* 9 ISR 162 (2020).

Mario Monti, *How State Aid Affects Tax Competition* 8 EC Tax Rev. 208 (1999).

Saturnina Moreno González, *Recovery of Tax-Related State Aid in Spain: Current Scenario and Legislative Initiatives for Immediate and Effective Recovery* 14 EStAL 391 (2015).

Saturnina Moreno González, *State Aid and Tax Competition: Comments on the European Commission's Decisions on Transfer Pricing Rulings* 15 EStAL 556 (2016).

Andrew P. Morriss & Lotta Moberg, *Cartelizing Taxes: Understanding the OECD's Campaign Against "Harmful Tax Competition"* 4 Columbia Journal of Tax Law 1 (2012).

Luis Moscoso del Prado & Tomás Arranz, *A New Step in Material Selectivity in Tax Measures* 12 EStAL 401 (2013).

Artur Mudrecki, *Impact of the Principle of Proportionality in Tax Law on the Jurisprudence of the Court of Justice of the European Union and the Supreme Administrative Court in Poland* 3 Public Governance, Administration and Finances L. Rev. 46 (2018).

Francesco Nanetti & Giovanni Mameli, *The Creeping Normative Role of the EC Commission in the Twin-Track Struggle Against State Aids and Harmful Tax Competition* 11 EC Tax Rev. 185 (2002).

Phedon Nicolaides, *Fiscal State Aid in the EU: The Limits of Tax Autonomy* 27 W. Comp. 365 (2004).

Phedon Nicolaides, *New Limits to the Concept of Selectivity: The Birth of a 'General Exception' to the Prohibition of State Aid in EU Competition Law* 6 JECLAP 315 (2015).

Phedon Nicolaides, *The Economics of State Aid,* in Hancher et al. (eds), EU State Aids (5th edn 2016).

Phedon Nicolaides, *State Aid Rules and Tax Rulings* 15 EStAL 416 (2016).

Phedon Nicolaides, *Excessive Widening of the Concept of Selectivity* 16 EStAL 62 (2016).

Phedon Nicolaides, *The Definition of the Reference Tax System Is Still a Puzzle* 17 EStAL 419 (2018).

Phedon Nicolaides, *Multi-rate Turnover Taxes and State Aid: A Prelude to Taxes on Company Size?* 18 EStAL 226 (2019).

Phedon Nicolaides, *Can Selectivity Result from the Application of Non-Selective Rules?* 18 EStAL 15 (2019).

Phedon Nicolaides & Ioana Eleonora Rusu, *The Concept of Selectivity: An Ever Wider Scope* 11 EStAL 791 (2012).

Phedon Nicolaides & Antonis Metaxas, *Asymmetric Tax Measures and EU State Aid Law* 13 EStAL 51 (2014).

Valérie Noël & Sébastien Thomas, *Locus Standi in State Aid Litigation after Montessori* 20 EStAL 512 (2021).

Kristina Nordlander & David Went, *Checks and Balances in EU State Aid Procedures: Should More Be Done to Protect the Rights of Aid Recipients and Third Parties?* 11 ERA Forum 367 (2010).

Carsten Nowak, *VerfVO Art. 23 Geldbußen,* in Loewenheim et al. (eds), Kartellrecht, (4th edn 2020).

Martha O'Brien, *Company Taxation, State Aid and Fundamental Freedoms: Is the Next Step Enhanced Cooperation* 30 European L. Rev. 209 (2005).

Keith O'Donnell & Anne Muller, *State Aid and Tax Law: Enter the Taxpayer*, in Rust & Micheau (eds), State Aid and Tax Law 175 (2013).

Shu-Yi Oei & Diane Ring, *Leak-Driven Law* 65 UCLA L. Rev. 532 (2018).

Christiana HJI Panayi, *Limitation on Benefits and State Aid* 44 European Taxation 83 (2004).

Christiana HJI Panayi, *State Aid and Tax: The Third Way?* 32 Intertax 283 (2004).

Christiana HJI Panayi, *Advanced Issues in International and European Tax Law* (2015).

Lorenzo Panci, *Latest Developments on the Interpretation of the Concept of Selectivity in the Field of Corporate Taxation* 17 EStAL 353 (2018).

Antonio Papi Rossi, *Recovery of Unlawful and Incompatible Aid*, in Santa Maria (ed.), Competition and State Aid: An Analysis of EU Practice 141 (2nd edn 2015).

Leopoldo Parada, *How the Vodafone Magyarország Opinion Affects EU Debate on Turnover-Based Digital Taxes* TNI 399 (2019).

Leopoldo Parada, *Between Apples and Oranges: The EU General Court's Decision in the 'Apple Case'* 30 EC Tax Rev. 55 (2021).

Fernando Pastor-Merchante, *The Protection of Competitors under State Aid Law* 15 EStAL 527 (2016).

Juan Salvador Pastoriza, *The Recovery Obligation and the Protection of Legitimate Expectations: The Spanish Experience*, in Richelle et al. (eds), State Aid Law and Business Taxation 247 (2016).

Lisa Paterno, *State Aid and Fiscal Protectionism in the European Union from the Perspective of Competitors* 65 BIT 343 (2011).

Mehrdad Payandeh, *Das Gebot der Folgerichtigkeit: Rationalitätsgewinn oder Irrweg der Grundrechtsdogmatik* 136 AöR 578 (2011).

Bruno Peeters, *Recovery Procedures and National Issues: The Belgian 'Excess Profit Exemption' Scheme*, in De Pietro (ed.), New Perspectives on Fiscal State Aid 143 (2019).

Dionysios Pelekis, *The Burden and Standard of Proof in the Tax Ruling Cases: A Practical Limit to the EU's Arm's Length Principle?* 12 JECLAP 669 (2021).

Begoña Pérez-Bernabeu, *Refining the Derogation Test on Material Tax Selectivity: The Equality Test* 16 EStAL 582 (2017).

Begoña Pérez-Bernabeu, *The Spanish Hydroelectric Tax: Asymmetrical Taxation with Environmental Flavour* 19 EStAL 352 (2020).

Christian Pérez Merino, *The Commission's Burden of Proof in Respect of Fiscal State Aid Following the ECJ Decision in the Spanish Sports Clubs Case* 61 European Taxation 485 (2021).

Gabriella Perotto, *How to Cope with Harmful Tax Competition in the EU Legal Order: Beyond the Elusive Quest for a Definition and the Misplaced Reliance on State Aid Law* 13 EJLS 309 (2021).

Katerina Perrou, *Fundamental Rights in EU Tax Law*, in Panayi et al. (eds), Research Handbook on European Union Taxation Law 511 (2020).

Cees Peters, *The Legitimacy of EU Fiscal State Aid Control: What Is Your Legitimation Narrative*, in De Pietro (ed.), New Perspectives on Fiscal State Aid 5 (2019).

Cees Peters, *Tax Policy Convergence and EU Fiscal State Aid Control: In Search of Rationality* 28 EC Tax Rev. 6 (2019).

Henrik Petyz & Thomas Mygind, *Direct Action in State Aid Cases: Tightropes and Legal Protection* 9 EStAL 617 (2010).

Sebastian Pfeiffer, *Asymmetrically Relying on the EU VAT Directive: Is VAT a Picnic?* 24 Int. VAT Monitor 158 (2015).

Juan Jorge Piernas López, *The Concept of State Aid Under EU Law* (2015).

Juan Jorge Piernas López, *Revisiting Some Fundamentals of Fiscal Selectivity* 17 EStAL 274 (2018).

Carlo Pinto, *Tax Competition and EU Law* (2003).

Sophia Piotrowski et al., *Towards a Standing Committee Pursuant to Article 10 of the EU Tax Dispute Resolution Directive: A Proposal for Implementation* 47 Intertax 678 (2019).

Alice Pirlot, *Exploring the Impact of EU Law on Energy an Environmental Taxation,* in Panayi et al. (eds), Research Handbook on European Union Taxation Law 359 (2020).

Pasquale Pistone, *Smart Tax Competition and the Geographical Boundaries of Taxing Jurisdictions: Countering Selective Advantages Amidst Disparities* 40 Intertax 85 (2012).

Giuseppe Pizzonia, *Recovery in the Case of Aid Schemes in Tax Matters,* in Santa Maria (ed.), Competition and State Aid: An Analysis of EU Practice 179 (2nd edn 2015).

Aurelien Portuese, *Principle of Proportionality as Principle of Economic Efficiency* 19 European Law Journal 612 (2013).

Ana Pošćić, *Procedural Aspects of EU State Aid Law* 1 EU and Comparative Law Issues and Challenges 490 (2017).

Margherita Poto, *The Principle of Proportionality in Comparative Perspective* 8 German Law Journal 835 (2007).

Miro Prek & Silvère Lefèvre, *The Requirement of Selectivity in the Recent Case-Law of the Court of Justice* 11 EStAL 335 (2012).

Conor Quigley, *Direct Taxation and State Aid: Recent Developments Concerning the Notion of Selectivity* 40 Intertax 112 (2012).

Conor Quigley, *European State Aid Law and Policy* (3rd edn 2015).

Marc Rasch & Pawel Wroblewski, *Fiat State Aid Coming to a Positive End?* 29 ITPJ 216 (2022).

Daniel Reich, *Rechtsfolgen steuerlicher Verstöße gegen das Beihilferecht* 8 HFSt 219 (2018).

Brigitta Renner-Loquenz, *State Aid in Energy Taxation Measures: First Experiences from Applying the Environmental Aid Guidelines 2001* 2 EStAL 21 (2003).

Diane Ring, *One Nation Among Many: Policy Implications of Cross-Border Tax Arbitrage* 44 Boston College L. Rev. 79 (2002).

Diane Ring, *Democracy, Sovereignty and Tax Competition: The Role of Tax Sovereignty in Shaping Tax Cooperation* 9 Florida Tax Review 555 (2009).

Stefan Rode, *Steuervergünstigungen, Beihilfen und Steuerwettbewerb: Zur Relevanz des europäischen Beihilfenrechts für das nationale Steuerrecht der Mitgliedstaaten* (2006).

Julie Roin, *Competition and Evasion: Another Perspective on International Tax Competition* 89 Georgetown Law Journal 543 (2001).

Cristina Romariz, *Revisiting Material Selectivity in EU State Aid Law: Or the Ghost of Yet-to-Come* 13 EStAL 39 (2014).

Malte Rosenberg, *Das beihilferechtliche Durchführungsverbot im Steuerverfahren* (2014).

Pierpaolo Rossi-Maccanico, *Gibraltar: Beyond the Pillars of Hercules of Selectivity* 11 EStAL 443 (2012).

Pierpaolo Rossi-Maccanico, *EU Review of Direct Tax Measures: Interplay Between Fundamental Freedoms and State Aid Control* 22 EC Tax Rev. 19 (2013).

Pierpaolo Rossi-Maccanico, *Fiscal State Aids, Tax Base Erosion and Profit Shifting,* 24 EC Tax Rev. 63 (2015).

Pierpaolo Rossi-Maccanico, *A New Framework for State Aid Review of Tax Rulings* 14 EStAL 371 (2015).

Pierpaolo Rossi-Maccanico, *AG Kokott Tries to Bring Clarity to the Selectivity Test for Individual Tax Rulings* 32 EC Tax Rev. 183 (2023).

H. Onno Ruding, *Fiscal Sovereignty in the Internal Market* 19 Intertax 249 (1991).

Tim Maxian Rusche, *Artikel 108 AEUV,* in Immenga & Joachim Mestmäcker (eds), Wettbewerbsrecht (5th edn 2016, vol. 3).

Marek Rzotkiewicz, *The General Principles of EU Law and Their Role in the Review of State Aid Put into Effect by Member States* 12 EStAL 464 (2013).

Cla´udia Saavedra Pinto, *The Narrow Meaning of the Legitimate Expectation Principle in State Aid Law Versus the Foreign Investor's Legitimate Expectations* 15 EStAL 270 (2016).

Franz Jürgen Säcker, *Introduction,* in Säcker & Montag (eds), European State Aid Law (2016).

Miguel Sampol Pucurull, *Economic Penalties and Recovery of State Aid: Some Lessons from the Spanish Experience* 16 EStAL 431 (2017).

Michael Sa´nchez Rydelski, *Distinction Between State Aid and General Measures* 19 EC Tax Rev. 149 (2010).

Alberto Santa Maria, *Introduction,* in Santa Maria (ed.), Competition and State Aid: An Analysis of EU Practice 1 (2nd edn 2015).

Wolf Sauter, *Proportionality in EU Law: A Balancing Act?* 15 Camb. Yearb. Eur. Leg. Stud. 439 (2013).

Jean Schaffner & Sophie Balliet, *BEPS, EU State Aid Investigations and LuxLeaks: And What about Luxembourg?* 23 ITPJ 279 (2016).

Moritz Scherleitner & Tomi Viitala, *EU State Aid Rules as a Means of Promoting Equity Within International Taxation* 8 Nordic Tax Journal 20 (2021).

Katharina Schlücke, *Der Referenzrahmen selbst unterliegt nur einer eingeschränkten beihilferechtlichen Kontrolle* 9 ISR 439 (2020).

Arne Schnitger, *Der Einfluss des Beihilferechts auf die direkten Steuern in Deutschland* 26 IStR 421 (2017).

Wolfgang Schön, *Taxation and State Aid Law in the European Union* 36 CMLR 911 (1999).

Wolfgang Schön, *Special Charges: A Gap in European Competition Law* 5 EStAL 494 (2006).

Wolfgang Schön, *Tax Legislation and the Notion of Fiscal Aid*, in Richelle et al. (eds), State Aid Law and Business Taxation 3 (2016).

Wolfgang Schön, *State Aid in the Area of Taxation*, in Hancher et al. (eds), EU State Aids, 393 (5th edn 2016).

Jens Schönfeld & Benedikt Ellenrieder, *Vertrauensschutz bei steuerlichen Beihilfen* 27 IStR 444 (2018).

Adam Scott, *Co-operation and Good Faith: State Aid Rules and National Courts – Procedural and Interpretive Consequences* 16 EStAL 354 (2017).

Roman Seer, *Insolvenz, Sanierung und Ertragsteuern: verfassungs- und europarechtliche Überlegungen* 96 FR 721 (2014).

Maria J. Segura Catalán et al., *Third Party Rights and the State Aid Procedures Revisited by the European Courts: An Ever-Sounder State Aid Control* 10 JECLAP 212 (2019).

Eleanor Sharpston, *Legitimate Expectations and Economic Reality* 15 European L. Rev. 103 (1990).

Eleanor Sharpston, *European Community Law and the Doctrine of Legitimate Expectations: How Legitimate, and for Whom?* 11 Northwestern Journal of International Law and Business 87 (1990).

Bruce Sewell, *In Need of an Economic Reality Check: The Commission's State Aid Decision Regarding Ireland and Apple* 7 JECLAP 649 (2016).

Daniel Shaviro, *The U.S. Response to OECD-BEPS and the EU State Aid Cases* Law & Economics Research Paper Series, Working Paper Nos 16-27 (2016).

Chu Shi, *IP Boxes in Light of the BEPS Project and EU Law: Part II* 56 European Taxation 371 (2016).

Henry C. Simons, *Personal Income Taxation* (1938).

Julia Sinnig, *Turnover Taxes under State Aid Spotlight* 59 European Taxation 106 (2019).

Mario Siragusa, *The Millenium Approaches: Rethinking Article 85 and the Problems and Challenges in the Design and Enforcement of the EC Competition Rules* 21 Fordham Int. Law J. 650 (1998).

Grith Skovgaard Olykke, *The Passing-on Defence Catapulted Out of State Aid Law*, 16 EStAL 93 (2017).

Daniël S. Smit, *International Juridical Double Non-taxation and State Aid* 25 EC Tax Rev. 109 (2016).

Daniël S. Smit, *International Income Allocation under EU Tax Law: Tinker, Tailor, Soldier, Sailor* 26 EC Tax Rev. 67 (2017).

Daniël S. Smit, *State Aid and Domestic Anti-tax Avoidance Rules: Who Is in Charge? – A Preliminary Analysis*, in De Pietro (ed.), New Perspectives on Fiscal State Aid 87 (2019).

Ulrich Soltész, *Nach der Reform ist vor der Reform: Herausforderungen für die künftige europäische Beihilfekontrolle* 26 EuZW 277 (2015).

Ulrich Soltész, *EU State Aid Law and Taxation: Where Do We Stand Today* 41 ECLR 18 (2020).

Mélanie Staes, *The Combined Application of the Fundamental Freedoms and the EU State Aid Rules: In Search of a Way Out of the Maze* 42 Intertax 106 (2014).

Peter Staviczky, *De Facto Selectivity in the Light of the Recent Case Law of the General Court* 14 EStAL 332 (2015).

Oana Stefan, *General Principles in EU State Aid Law*, in Ziegler et al. (eds), Research Handbook on General Principles in EU Law 441 (2022).

Dario Stevanato, *Are Turnover-Based Taxes a Suitable Way to Target Business Profits* 59 European Taxation Issue 538 (2019).

Stanley S. Surrey, *Pathways to Tax Reform* (1973).

Joep Swinkels, *State Aid and VAT* 14 Int. VAT Monitor 311 (2005).

Rita Szudoczky, *The Sources of EU Law and Their Relationships: Lessons for the Field of Taxation* (2014).

Rita Szudoczky, *Convergence of the Analysis of National Tax Measures under the EU State Aid Rules and the Fundamental Freedoms* 15 EStAL 357 (2016).

Rita Szudoczky, *Double Taxation Relief, Transfer Pricing Adjustments and State Aid Law: Comments*, in Richelle et al. (eds), State Aid Law and Business Taxation 163 (2016).

Rita Szudoczky, *The Future of Fiscal State Aid*, in Piernas López et al. (eds), The Future of EU State Aid Law: Consolidation and Expansion 273 (2023).

Rita Szudoczky & Balázs Károlyi, *The Troubled Story of the Hungarian Advertisement Tax: How (Not) to Design a Progressive Turnover Tax* 48 Intertax 46 (2020).

Rita Szudoczky & Balázs Károlyi, *The CJEU's Approach to the Objectives of Progressive Turnover-Based Taxes: Respect for the Member States' Fiscal Sovereignty or Authorization for Circumventing EU Law?* 50 Intertax 82 (2022).

Marek Szydło, *Differential Tax Burdens of Undertakings and Internal Market Law: The Way Forward after ANGED* 56 CMLR 1093 (2019).

Anja Taferner & Jurjan Wouda Kuipers, *Tax Rulings: In Line with OECD Transfer Pricing Guidelines, but Contrary to EU State Aid Rules?* 56 European Taxation 134 (2016).

Romero J.S. Tavares et al., *The Intersection of EU State Aid and U.S. Tax Deferral: A Spectacle of Fireworks, Smoke, and Mirrors* 19 Florida Tax Review 121 (2016).

John Temple Lang, *Legal Certainty and Legitimate Expectations as General Principles of Law*, in Bernitz & Nergelius (eds), General Principles of European Community Law 163 (2000).

John Temple Lang, *The Gibraltar State Aid and Taxation Judgment: A Methodological Revolution* 11 EStAL 805 (2012).

John Temple Lang, *EU State Aid Rules – The Need for Substantive Reform* 13 EStAL 440 (2014).

John Temple Lang, *Autogrill Espana and Banco Santander: The Concept of 'General' Tax Measures Clarified for State Aid* 40 European L. Rev. 763 (2015).

B. H. ter Kuile, *Legal Aspects of Fiscal Sovereignty Within the Internal Market* 19 Intertax 503 (1991).

Ben Terra, *Value Added Tax and State Aid Law in the EU* 40 Intertax 101 (2012).

Jesko Thiede, *Das Beihilfeverfahren und die Rechte und Pflichten der Beteiligten* 26 IStR 51 (2017).

Victor Thuronyi, *Tax Expenditures: A Reassessment* 37 Duke Law Journal 1155 (1988).

Fausta Todhe, *The Rise of an (Autonomous) Arm's Length Principle in EU State Aid Rules* 18 EStAL 249 (2019).

Edoardo Traversa, *State Aid and Taxation: Can an Anti-avoidance Provision Be Selective* 13 EStAL 518 (2014).

Edoardo Traversa, *Tax Incentives and Territoriality Within the European Union: Balancing the Internal Market with the Tax Sovereignty of Member States* 6 WTJ 315 (2014).

Edoardo Traversa & Alessandra Flamini, *Fighting Harmful Tax Competition Through EU State Aid Law: Will the Hardening of Soft Law Suffice?* 14 EStAL 323 (2015).

Edoardo Traversa & Pierre M. Sabbadini, *Anti-avoidance Measures and State Aid in a Post-BEPS Context: An Attempt at Reconciliation*, in Richelle et al. (eds), State Aid Law and Business Taxation 85 (2016).

Edoardo Traversa & Pierre M. Sabbadini, *State-Aid Policy and the Fight Against Harmful Tax Competition in the Internal Market: Tax Policy in Disguise?*, in Haslehner et al. (eds), EU Tax Law and Policy in the 21st Century 107 (2017).

Stefan Trencsik & Jesko Thiede, *Beihilferecht und Entscheidungsspielräume der Verwaltung bei Gesetzesauslegung und Ermessensausübung – Am Beispiel des Steuererlasses für internationale Kunst- und Sportveranstaltungen* 95 StuW 170 (2018).

Takis Tridimas, *The General Principles of EU Law* (2nd edn 2006).

Henk van Arendonk, *The European Cooperation Project, Tax & Sovereignty* 25 EC Tax Rev. 242 (2016).

Pieter Van Cleynenbreugel, *Recovering Unlawful Advantages in the Context of EU State Aid Tax Ruling Investigations* 1 Market and Competition L. Rev. 15 (2017).

Anne Van de Vijver, *National Courts as 'Guardians' of Commission Recovery Decisions*, in De Pietro (ed.), New Perspectives on Fiscal State Aid 131 (2019).

Tim Van Helfteren, *A Restriction on the Commission's State Aid Enforcement in Fiscal Aid Cases: Fiat and Ireland V Commission* 14 JECLAP 168 (2023).

Frans Vanistendael, *Fiscal Support Measures and Harmful Tax Competition* 9 EC Tax Rev. 153 (2000).

Frans Vanistendael, *The ECJ at the Crossroads: Balancing Tax Sovereignty Against the Imperatives of the Single Market* 46 European Taxation 413 (2006).

Frans Vanistendael, *Denkavit Internationaal: The Balance Between Fiscal Sovereignty and the Fundamental Freedoms?* 47 European Taxation 210 (2007).

Jérémie van Meerbeeck, *The Principle of Legal Certainty in the Case law of the European Court of Justice: From Certainty to Trust* 41 European L. Rev. 275 (2016).

Apurva Vats, *Tax Rulings and EU State Aid: Lessons to Be Learnt from the Apple-Ireland Case* 42 ECLR 80 (2021).

Hans Verhagen, *State Aid and Tax Rulings: An Assessment of the Selectivity Criterion of Article 107(1) of the TFEU in Relation to Recent Commission Transfer Pricing Decisions* 57 European Taxation 279 (2017).

Vincent Verouden & Philipp Werner, *Introduction: The Law and Economics of EU State Aid Control*, in Werner & Verouden (eds), EU State Aid Control: Law and Economics 7 (2017).

Marta Villar Ezcurra, *State Aids and Energy Taxes: Towards a Coherent Reference Framework* 41 Intertax 340 (2013).

Peter J. Wattel, *Some Fringe Areas of EU State Aid Law in Direct Tax Matters*, in Weber (ed.), EU Income Tax Law: Issues for the Years Ahead 139 (2013).

Peter J. Wattel, *Forum: Interaction of State Aid, Free Movement, Policy Competition and Abuse Control in Direct Tax Matters* 5 WTJ 128 (2013).

Peter J. Wattel, *Stateless Income, State Aid and the (Which?) Arm's Length Principle* 44 Intertax 791 (2016).

Peter J. Wattel, *Comparing Criteria: State Aid, Free Movement, Harmful Tax Competition and Market Distorting Disparities*, in Richelle et al. (eds), State Aid Law and Business Taxation 59 (2016).

Dennis Weber, *In Search of a (New) Equilibrium Between Tax Sovereignty and the Freedom of Movement Within the EC* 34 Intertax 585 (2006).

André Wehner, *Der Sanierungserlass des BMF vom 27.3.2003: Ein Verstoß gegen EU-Beihilferecht?* 15 Neue Zeitschrift für Insolvenz- und Sanierungsrecht 537 (2012).

Wolfgang Weiß & Markus Haberkamm, *Legitimate Expectations in State Aid and the CFI* 9 EStAL 531 (2010).

Stephan Wernicke, *Vertrauensverluste – Deutschland versus Europäische Kommission?* 26 EuZW 649 (2015).

Table of Legislative Materials and Cases

[a] Legislation and Council Resolutions

[b] Commission Notices and Publications

[c] Judgments and Orders of the General Court

[d] Judgments of the Court of Justice of the European Union

[e] Opinions of the Advocate Generals

[f] Decisions of the German Constitutional Court (*Bundesverfassungsgericht*)

[g] Decisions of the German Federal Financial Court (*Bundesfinanzhof*)

[h] Commission Decisions

Index

SERIES ON INTERNATIONAL TAXATION

1. Alberto Xavier, *The Taxation of Foreign Investment in Brazil,* 1980 (ISBN 90-200-0582-0).
2. Hugh J. Ault & Albert J. Rädler, *The German Corporation Tax Law with 1980 Amendments,* 1981 (ISBN 90-200-0642-8).
3. Paul R. McDaniel & Hugh J. Ault, *Introduction to United States International Taxation,* 1981 (ISBN 90-6544-004-6).
4. Albert J. Rädler, *German Transfer Pricing/Prix de Transfer en Allemagne,* 1984 (ISBN 90-6544-143-3).
5. Paul R. McDaniel & Stanley S. Surrey, *International Aspects of Tax Expenditures: A Comparative Study,* 1985 (ISBN 90-654-4163-8).
6. Kees van Raad, *Nondiscrimination in International Tax Law,* 1986 (ISBN 90-6544-266-9).
7. Sijbren Cnossen (ed.), *Tax Coordination in the European Community,* 1987 (ISBN 90-6544-272-3).
8. Ben Terra, *Sales Taxation. The Case of Value Added Tax in the European Community,* 1989 (ISBN 90-6544-381-9).
9. Rutsel S.J. Martha, *The Jurisdiction to Tax in International Law: Theory and Practice of Legislative Fiscal Jurisdiction,* 1989 (ISBN 90-654-4416-5).
10. Paul R. McDaniel & Hugh J. Ault, *Introduction to United States International Taxation* (3rd revised edition), 1989 (ISBN 90-6544-423-8).
11. Manuel Pires, *International Juridicial Double Taxation of Income,* 1989 (ISBN 90-6544-426-2).
12. A.H.M. Daniels, *Issues in International Partnership Taxation,* 1991 (ISBN 90-654-4577-3).
13. Arvid A. Skaar, *Permanent Establishment: Erosion of a Tax Treaty Principle,* 1992 (ISBN 90-6544-594-3).
14. Cyrille David & Geerten M.M. Michielse (eds), *Tax Treatment of Financial Instruments,* 1996 (ISBN 90-654-4666-4).
15. Herbert H. Alpert & Kees van Raad (eds), *Essays on International Taxation,* 1993 (ISBN 90-654-4781-4).
16. Wolfgang Gassner, Michael Lang & Eduard Lechner (eds), *Tax Treaties and EC Law,* 1997 (ISBN 90-411-0680-4).
17. Glória Teixeira, *Taxing Corporate Profits in the EU,* 1997 (ISBN 90-411-0703-7).
18. Michael Lang et al. (eds), *Multilateral Tax Treaties,* 1998 (ISBN 90-411-0704-5).
19. Stef van Weeghel, *The Improper Use of Tax Treaties,* 1998 (ISBN 90-411-0737-1).

20. Klaus Vogel (ed.), *Interpretation of Tax Law and Treaties and Transfer Pricing in Japan and Germany*, 1998 (ISBN 90-411-9655-2).
21. Bertil Wiman (ed.), *International Studies in Taxation: Law and Economics; Liber Amicorum Leif Mutén*, 1999 (ISBN 90-411-9692-7).
22. Alfonso J. Martín Jiménez, *Towards Corporate Tax Harmonization in the European Community*, 1999 (ISBN 90-411-9690-0).
23. Ramon J. Jeffery, *The Impact of State Sovereignty on Global Trade and International Taxation*, 1999 (ISBN 90-411-9703-6).
24. A.J. Easson, *Taxation of Foreign Direct Investment*, 1999 (ISBN 90-411-9741-9).
25. Marjaana Helminen, *The Dividend Concept in International Tax Law: Dividend Payments Between Corporate Entities*, 1999 (ISBN 90-411-9765-6).
26. Paul Kirchhof, Moris Lehner, Kees van Raad, Arndt Raupach & Michael-Rodi (eds), *International and Comparative Taxation: Essays in Honour of Klaus Vogel*, 2002 (ISBN 90-411-9841-5).
27. Krister Andersson, Peter Melz & Christer Silfverberg (eds), *Liber Amicorum Sven-Olof Lodin*, 2001 (ISBN 90-411-9850-4).
28. Juan Martín Jovanovich, *Customs Valuation and Transfer Pricing: Is It Possible to Harmonize Customs and Tax Rules?*, Second Edition, 2018 (ISBN 978-90-411-6134-5).
29. Stefano Simontacchi, *Taxation of Capital Gains under the OECD Model Convention: With Special Regard to Immovable Property*, 2007 (ISBN 978-90-411-2549-1).
30. Michael Lang, Josef Schuch, & Claus Staringer (eds), *Tax Treaty Law and EC Law*, 2007 (ISBN 978-90-411-2629-0).
31. Duncan Bentley, *Taxpayers' Rights: Theory Origin and Implementation*, 2007 (ISBN 978-90-411-2650-4).
32. Sergio André Rocha, *Interpretation of Double Taxation Conventions: General Theory and Brazilian Perspective*, 2008 (ISBN 978-90-411-2822-5).
33. Robert F. van Brederode, *Systems of General Sales Taxation: Theory, Policy and Practice*, 2009 (ISBN 978-90-411-2832-4).
34. John G. Head & Richard Krever (eds), *Tax Reform in the 21st Century: A Volume in Memory of Richard Musgrave*, 2009 (ISBN 978-90-411-2829-4).
35. Jens Wittendorff, *Transfer Pricing and the Arm's Length Principle in International Tax Law*, 2010 (ISBN 978-90-411-3270-3).
36. Marjaana Helminen, *The International Tax Law Concept of Dividend*, Second Edition, 2017 (ISBN 978-90-411-8394-1).
37. Robert F. van Brederode (ed.), *Immovable Property under VAT: A Comparative Global Analysis*, 2011 (ISBN 978-90-411-3126-3).
38. Dennis Weber & Stef van Weeghel, *The 2010 OECD Updates: Model Tax Convention & Transfer Pricing Guidelines - A Critical Review*, 2011 (ISBN 978-90-411-3812-5).
39. Yariv Brauner & Martin James McMahon, Jr. (eds), *The Proper Tax Base: Structural Fairness from an International and Comparative Perspective— Essays in Honour of Paul McDaniel*, 2012 (ISBN 978-90-411-3286-4).
40. Robert F. van Brederode (ed.), *Science, Technology and Taxation*, 2012 (ISBN 978-90-411-3125-6).

41. Oskar Henkow, *The VAT/GST Treatment of Public Bodies*, 2013 (ISBN 978-90-411-4663-2).
42. Jean Schaffner, *How Fixed Is a Permanent Establishment?*, 2013 (ISBN 978-90-411-4662-5).
43. Miguel Correia, *Taxation of Corporate Groups*, 2013 (ISBN 978-90-411-4841-4).
44. Veronika Daurer, *Tax Treaties and Developing Countries*, 2014 (ISBN 978-90-411-4982-4).
45. Claire Micheau, *State Aid, Subsidy and Tax Incentives under EU and WTO Law*, 2014 (ISBN 978-90-411-4555-0).
46. Robert F. van Brederode & Richard Krever (eds), *Legal Interpretation of Tax Law*, 2014 (ISBN 978-90-411-4945-9).
47. Radhakishan Rawal, *Taxation of Cross-border Services*, 2014 (ISBN 978-90-411-4947-3).
48. João Dácio Rolim, *Proportionality and Fair Taxation*, 2014 (ISBN 978-90-411-5838-3).
49. Paulo Rosenblatt, *General Anti-avoidance Rules for Major Developing Countries*, 2015 (ISBN 978-90-411-5839-0).
50. Gaspar Lopes Dias V.S., *Tax Arbitrage through Cross-Border Financial Engineering*, 2015 (ISBN 978-90-411-5875-8).
51. Geerten M.M. Michielse & Victor Thuronyi (eds), *Tax Design Issues Worldwide*, 2015 (ISBN 978-90-411-5610-5).
52. Oktavia Weidmann, *Taxation of Derivatives and Cryptoassets*, Second Edition, 2024 (ISBN 978-94-035-2383-5).
53. Chris Evans, Richard Krever & Peter Mellor (eds), *Tax Simplification*, 2015 (ISBN 978-90-411-5976-2).
54. Reuven Avi-Yonah & Joel Slemrod (eds), *Taxation and Migration*, 2015 (ISBN 978-90-411-6136-9).
55. Alexander Bosman, *Other Income under Tax Treaties: An Analysis of Article 21 of the OECD Model Convention*, 2015 (ISBN 978-90-411-6610-4).
56. John Abrahamson, *International Taxation of Manufacturing and Distribution*, 2016 (ISBN 978-90-411-6664-7).
57. Frederik Boulogne, *Shortcomings in the EU Merger Directive*, 2016 (ISBN 978-90-411-6713-2).
58. Angelika Meindl-Ringler, *Beneficial Ownership in International Tax Law*, 2016 (ISBN 978-90-411-6833-7).
59. Andreas Waltrich, *Cross-Border Taxation of Permanent Establishments: An International Comparison*, 2016 (ISBN 978-90-411-6832-0).
60. Sergio André Rocha & Allison Christians (eds), *Tax Sovereignty in the BEPS Era*, 2017 (ISBN 978-90-411-6707-1).
61. Peter Antony Wilson, *BRICS and International Tax Law*, 2018 (ISBN 978-90-411-9435-0).
62. Louise Otis, Brigitte Alepin & Blanca Moreno-Dodson (eds), *Winning the Tax Wars: Tax Competition and Cooperation*, 2018 (ISBN 978-90-411-9460-2).

63. Marta Castelon, *International Taxation of Income from Services under Double Taxation Conventions: Development, Practice and Policy*, 2018 (ISBN 978-90-411-9594-4).
64. D.M. Broekhuijsen, *A Multilateral Tax Treaty: Designing an Instrument to Modernise International Tax Law*, 2018 (ISBN 978-90-411-9872-3).
65. John Abrahamson, *International Taxation of Energy Production and Distribution*, 2018 (ISBN 978-90-411-9101-4).
66. Leopoldo Parada, *Double Non-taxation and the Use of Hybrid Entities*, Second Edition, 2024 (ISBN 978-94-035-4666-7).
67. Richard Snoeij, *International Tax Aspects of Sovereign Wealth Investors: A Source State Perspective*, 2018 (ISBN 978-90-411-9431-2).
68. Aleksandra Bal, *Taxation, Virtual Currency and Blockchain*, 2019 (ISBN 978-94-035-0103-1).
69. Werner Haslehner, Georg Kofler, Katerina Pantazatou & Alexander Rust (eds), *Tax and the Digital Economy: Challenges and Proposals for Reform*, 2019 (ISBN 978-94-035-0361-5).
70. Eva Escribano, *Jurisdiction to Tax Corporate Income Pursuant to the Presumptive Benefit Principle: A Critical Analysis of Structural Paradigms Underlying Corporate Income Taxation and Proposals for Reform*, 2019 (ISBN 978-94-035-0640-1).
71. Jérôme Monsenego & Jan Bjuvberg (eds), *International Taxation in a Changing Landscape: Liber Amicorum in Honour of Bertil Wiman*, 2019 (ISBN 978-90-411-9234-9).
72. Kasper Dziurdź, *Non-discrimination in Tax Treaty Law and World Trade Law: The Impact of Formal, Substantive and Subjective Approaches*, 2019 (ISBN 978-94-035-0904-4).
73. Félix Daniel Martínez Laguna, *Hybrid Financial Instruments, Double Nontaxation and Linking Rules*, 2019 (ISBN 978-94-035-1074-3).
74. Jan Gooijer, *Tax Treaty Residence of Entities*, 2019 (ISBN 978-94-035-1301-0).
75. John Abrahamson, *International Taxation of Banking*, 2020 (ISBN 978-94-035-1094-1).
76. Richard Krever & François Vaillancourt (eds), *The Allocation of Multinational Business Income: Reassessing the Formulary Apportionment Option*, 2020 (ISBN 978-94-035-0614-2).
77. Ajit Kumar Singh, *Exploring the Nexus Doctrine in International Tax Law*, 2021 (ISBN 978-94-035-3363-6).
78. Galya Savir, *Regulation and Tax in Space*, 2021 (ISBN 978-94-035-3393-3).
79. Rita Julien, *Credit Method Compatibility and Constraints under EU Law: An Analysis of the Case Law of the CJEU*, 2022 (ISBN 978-94-035-2363-7).
80. Sergio André Rocha & Allison Christians (eds), *A Multilateral Convention for Tax: From Theory to Implementation*, 2022 (ISBN 978-90-411-9428-2).
81. Brigitte Alepin, Lyne Latulippe & Louise Otis (eds), *Coordination and Cooperation: Tax Policy in the 21st Century*, 2022 (ISBN 978-94-035-3740-5).
82. Chunyang Zhang, *The Role of Tax Law in Mergers and Acquisitions: A Chinese Perspective*, 2022 (ISBN 978-94-035-3741-2).

83. Florian Navisotschnigg, *Substance in International Tax Law: DEMPE Approach, Substantial Activity Requirement and Beneficial Ownership*, 2022 (ISBN 978-94-035-4895-1).
84. Mees Vergouwen, *The Effect of Directives Within the Area of Direct Taxation on the Interpretation and Application of Tax Treaties*, 2023 (ISBN 978-94-035-0907-5).
85. Rachna Matabudul, *Tax Treaty Dispute Resolution: Lessons from the Law of the Sea*, 2023 (ISBN 978-94-035-3407-7).
86. David Orzechowski-Zölzer, *The Taxation of Fees for Technical Services on the Basis of Article 12A UN Model Convention*, 2024 (ISBN 978-94-035-4297-3).
87. David Rüll, *The Resolution of International Tax Disputes: From the Established Mechanisms Towards an Institutionalised International Instrument*, 2024 (ISBN 978-94-035-2088-9).
88. Savvas Kostikidis, *Residence and Economic Substance of Subsidiary Corporations in International and European Tax Law*, 2024 (ISBN 978-94-035-3858-7).
89. Céline Braumann, *Customary International Law and Tax Jurisdiction*, 2025 (ISBN 9789-40-353-888-4).
90. Sophia Piotrowski, *Fiscal State Aid Schemes: Selectivity and Limits to Enforcement*, 2025 (ISBN 978-94-035-0389-9).

www.ingramcontent.com/pod-product-compliance
Lightning Source LLC
LaVergne TN
LVHW020643300926
849161LV00004B/786